FREEDOM OF INFORMATION LAW IN IRELAND

UNITED KINGDOM
Sweet & Maxwell
London

AUSTRALIA
LBC Information Services
Sydney

CANADA and the USA
Carswell
Toronto

NEW ZEALAND
Brooker's
Auckland

SINGAPORE and MALAYSIA
Thomson Information (S.E. Asia)
Singapore

FREEDOM OF INFORMATION LAW IN IRELAND

Maeve McDonagh
B.A., LL.B., Dip. Sys. An. (N.U.I.),
LL.M. (Monash), Solicitor

DUBLIN
ROUND HALL SWEET & MAXWELL
1998

Published in 1998 by
Round Hall Sweet & Maxwell
Brehon House
4 Upper Ormond Quay
Dublin 7

Typeset by Gough Typesetting Services, Dublin.
Printed by Redwood Books Ltd.

ISBN 1-899738-79-7

To Seámus, Macdara, Cormac, and Sorcha.

ACKNOWLEDGMENTS

Many people, both in Ireland and further afield, assisted me in the writing of this book. Special thanks are due to Gerry Kearney and Aine Stapleton, formerly of the Tánaiste's Office and now of the FOI Central Policy Unit, Department of Finance, who responded to my many queries with unfailing efficiency and good humour, and to former Minister of State Eithne Fitzgerald, who introduced the legislation, for her assistance. All my colleagues at the Law Department, University College Cork, have been very supportive. In particular I wish to thank Professor David Gwynn Morgan, Aine Ryall, John Healy and Darius Whelan, all of whom read and commented upon various draft chapters. Thanks are also due to Professor Dermot Keogh of the History Department, U.C.C., for his advice and encouragement. I also wish to acknowledge the assistance of LL.M. student, Elizabeth Skally, who provided research assistance, and of the U.C.C. law librarian, Valerie King, and the staff of the official publications and the Inter-library loans office. Others who offered advice and assistance include Dr David Craig, Director of the National Archives, and Marie Kennedy of the Office of the Houses of the Oireachtas. Much of the research for this book was undertaken in the course of a research visit to Australia in the autumn of 1996. I wish to acknowledge the assistance of the President's Research Fund, U.C.C., in funding that trip. I also wish to thank Professor Martin Chanock of the Department of Law and Legal Studies, La Trobe University, Melbourne, for providing me with all of the facilities necessary to base myself at the university during my visit, thereby facilitating the renewal of friendships with my former colleagues. Special thanks are owing to Rick Snell, Director of the FOI Research Unit, Law School, University of Tasmania, who hosted my visit to the Unit, and whose advice, assistance in sourcing research materials, and warm hospitality were much appreciated. Thanks also to Jane McMeekin of the Law School, University of Tasmania, for research assistance. Madeline Campbell of the Australian Attorney-General's Office gave generously of her time and expertise to discuss various issues. I wish to thank also the former Australian Privacy Commissioner, Kevin O'Connor, the Deputy Ombudsman for Queensland, Mr Greg Sorenson, and the Western Australian Information Commissioner, Ms Bronwyn Keighely-Gerardy, for their advice and assistance and for sending me various materials. Thanks also to Mr Jason Young of the Office of the Information and Privacy Commissioner, British Colombia, Mr Robert Gellman, Washington, D.C., Dr Ian Walden, Queen Mary and Westfield College, University of London, and Professor Yves Poullet, Faculty of Law, University of Namur, Belgium. I relied to a great extent on electronic sources of legal information in writing this book. I am grateful to those who have endeavoured to make primary legal materials available on the Internet, such as AUSTLII in Australia and ACJNet in Canada, as well as those Information Commissioners who have made their decisions available on the Internet. Those most directly involved in the production of this book were Ms Thérèse Carrick and Ms Selga Medenieks of Round Hall Sweet and Maxwell. Thérèse Carrick commissioned the book and was patient in awaiting its final delivery. Special thanks are due to the editor, Selga Medenieks, who approached the task of editing this book with great enthusiasm and maintained her good humour and patience throughout. His Honour Mr Justice McCracken has greatly honoured this work by writing the foreword. Finally, I am grateful to my husband, Seámus Gilroy, for his encouragement and support.

Maeve McDonagh
July 31, 1998

FOREWORD

Over the years Irish officialdom has acquired a reputation for secrecy and for decisions made behind closed doors. Unfortunately, as those of us who work within the legal system know well, this reputation is frequently justified. Actions brought against State agencies, or Government departments, or indeed local authorities, are bedeviled with difficulties in obtaining relevant documents and information. Disputes regarding discovery of documents are frequent as claims for privilege are made based on what is called "the public interest".

Over the last 20 years or so the courts have attempted to push open the closed doors, but of necessity only on a case-by-case basis. Even then there were some glaring anomalies, such as the decision of the Supreme Court in *Attorney General v. Hamilton.*[1] While the decision was based on an interpretation of the Constitution, objectively it seems quite illogical that a body such as the Beef Tribunal, specifically set up by the Oireachtas, was refused access to documents and information generated at Cabinet meetings, although every member of the Cabinet other than the Attorney General was a member of the Oireachtas and presumably all voted in favour of setting up the Tribunal in the first place.

The first sentence of this book states that "the passing of the Freedom of Information Act 1997 in many ways marks a milestone in the history of Irish democracy". While this may seem a very extreme statement, there is much truth in it. The words "openness in Government" have become somewhat of a cult phrase, and many people were very sceptical of it. There is no doubt that the Freedom of Information Act is a sign that that phrase has some meaning.

A foreword to a book such as this is not a book review: that is something best left to others. However, it must give some indication of the nature of the work. Although written by a university lecturer, this is not a student's textbook to be put away as soon as the examinations are over and the degree obtained. It is a serious work which is obviously the culmination of a great deal of research on an international level. The idea of legislation for freedom of information is a novel idea in this country, but it is one which has been developed widely elsewhere, both within the European Union and within Commonwealth countries where the legal systems are, like ours, based on the common law. The

---

[1] [1993] 2 I.R. 250.

interpretation of a statute which introduces a new concept will always cause difficulty, and the strength of this book is the manner in which it details how the courts in other jurisdictions have interpreted similar legislation. While obviously such decisions are not binding on our courts, nevertheless they are more and more frequently quoted and have considerable persuasive influence. The detailed inclusion of such authorities is of enormous assistance in understanding this somewhat complex legislation, with all its exceptions and exclusions.

The other aspect of this book which should be emphasised is that it is a great deal more than a mere recital of the provisions of the Act. In the course of explaining the Act, it delves into difficult areas of law which arise in the context of freedom of information. It examines in some depth the necessity at times for confidentiality on a governmental, commercial, and personal level. It recognises that at times there may be a need for secrecy in the public interest, which probably everybody would acknowledge, but goes further and examines that very difficult subject of the nature of the public interest. Finally, it ends with a very useful analysis of the relationship between the Freedom of Information Act and other legislation.

It has been said that a good lawyer does not have to know the law, but he must know where to find the law. To put this in a wider context, what is important is not knowing information, but knowing where to find it. This book will be an invaluable guide to all those who seek information for whatever reason.

Mr Justice Brian McCracken
The High Court
August, 1998

PREFACE

The genesis of this book can be traced back to 1985 when I was appointed lecturer in law at La Trobe University, Victoria, Australia. Freedom of Information had been introduced both in the State of Victoria and at federal level in Australia three years previously. An examination of the operation of that legislation comprised one of the topics of a course I taught at La Trobe. This gave me the opportunity to observe, at first hand, the teething problems associated with the implementation of FOI legislation in a country operating under a similar system of government to our own. Despite shortcomings in the legislation itself and some active obstruction of its aims by legislators in Victoria in particular, the value of its contribution to a more open environment in public administration became clear. I was pleased to find on my return to Ireland in the early 1990s that proposals for the introduction of FOI legislation were being actively considered here. Certain events which unfolded at that time had thrown the need for greater openness in government into sharp relief. Nonetheless, it would be a mistake to view the potential contribution of FOI legislation purely in terms of whether it results in the disclosure of information concerning high-profile individuals and events. Its focus is broader in that it seeks to address in a far-reaching and lasting way the information deficit in Irish public administration. It is somewhat ironic, given the aims of FOI legislation, that the Act is expressed in terms which, although one might demur from their description in the Seanad by former Senator Professor Joe Lee as "reaching the outer limits of obscurity", are certainly not immediately accessible. The need for such complexity can be defended on the grounds that the task of balancing the right of access to information against other competing interests is necessarily a complex one. The aim of this book is to explain the content of the Act whilst putting flesh on its bones by outlining the interpretation of similar provisions overseas. Given the influence of the Australian and, to a lesser extent, the Canadian legislation on the framing of the Irish provisions, the comparative focus is primarily on the legislation of those jurisdictions. Cases from New Zealand and the United States are also referred to where relevant. The book seeks also to anticipate the operation of the Irish FOI Act in the context of domestic legal imperatives and, in particular, the Irish Constitution.

CONTENTS

TABLE OF CASES

IRELAND

AUSTRALIA

CANADA

EUROPEAN UNION

European Court

European Court of Human Rights

NEW ZEALAND

UNITED KINGDOM

UNITED STATES OF AMERICA

TABLE OF LEGISLATION

IRELAND

Statutes

Freedom of Information Act 1997—*contd.*

Statutory Instruments

Constitution of Ireland

AUSTRALIA

Statutes

COUNCIL OF EUROPE

Conventions

EUROPEAN LEGISLATION

Belgium

Denmark

Finland

France

Greece

EUROPEAN UNION

UNITED KINGDOM

Statutes

Statutory Instrument

White Papers

UNITED NATIONS

UNITED STATES OF AMERICA

CHAPTER 1

BACKGROUND

CHAPTER 1

BACKGROUND

A.   Introduction

The passing of the Freedom of Information Act 1997 in many ways marks a milestone in the history of Irish democracy. Public administration in Ireland has since the founding of the State operated in an atmosphere of secrecy. This preoccupation with secrecy of official information is a hallmark of the Westminster style of government and it is reflected strongly in Irish law.[1] Whilst the effect of the Westminster system on shaping the Irish approach to disclosure of official information has undoubtedly been important, it would be misleading to explain the culture of official secrecy in Ireland purely in terms of the influence of its former colonial master. Secrecy of official information is a heritage which has been readily embraced in Ireland. Professor Dermot Keogh has proffered the view that the early years of Irish statehood were characterised by the continuous threat of subversion, and accordingly that "[t]he citizen's right to freedom of information was submerged in the effort to build strong foundations for Irish democracy".[2] The State has tended ever since to operate in a secretive and highly centralised manner,[3] with the result that openness and transparency have traditionally been alien concepts in Irish government administration.

Whatever its causes, lack of access to government information in Ireland has had serious social and political consequences. Deficiency in the dissemination of official information in Ireland has encouraged the development of lobbying by interest groups and has elevated clientilism[4] within Irish political

---

[1]   See, for example, the Official Secrets Act 1963 which was modelled on the U.K. Official Secrets Act 1911.

[2]   Keogh, "Ireland and Emergency Culture, Between Civil War and Normalcy, 1922–1961" (1995) 1(1) *Ireland: A Journal of History and Society* (Special edition: Irish Democracy and the Right to Freedom of Information), p. 4. The preoccupation with secrecy was at its most stark during the "Emergency". The Irish government's approach to censorship during that period has been ably chronicled by Donal Ó Drisceoil in *Censorship in Ireland, 1939-1945: Neutrality, Politics and Society* (Cork University Press, 1996).

[3]   Farrell, "'Cagey and Secretive': Collective Responsibility, Executive Confidentiality and the Public Interest" in *Modern Irish Democracy: Essays in Honour of Basil Chubb* (Hill and Marsh ed., Irish Academic Press, 1993), p. 82.

[4]   Chubb, "'Going about persecuting civil servants': The role of the Irish Parliamentary Representative" (1963) XI(3) *Political Studies* 272; Carty, "From Tradition to Modernity and Back Again" in *Modern Irish Democracy: Essays in Honour of Basil Chubb* (Irish Academic Press, 1993), p. 24.

culture. The role of politicians as purveyors of information about services to their client constituents has been entrenched by the lack of alternative means of accessing official information. A more open approach to the disclosure of official information would arguably threaten the power of interest groups and traditional political parties in Ireland.

Issues relating to access to government information have arisen in four, sometimes overlapping, domains. These are:

(1) access to information relating to government activities and policies;

(2) access to information about services;

(3) access to public sector information for commercial purposes;

(4) access for individuals to their own personal files maintained by government and to the means of rectifying any inaccuracies within these files.

Access to information on government activities and policies is sought by the media, by public interest groups, and by lobbyists. They argue that access to such information is a vital element in the democratic process in that it facilitates the monitoring of government activities by the public at large.[5] Events such as the Beef Tribunal have served to highlight the role of access to information in scrutinising government action. Difficulties with official channels of information have led to media reliance on the acquisition of information through so-called "leaks". Such practices are problematic in that those leaking the information are often working to their own agendas and can manipulate the media by arranging the extent and timing of their disclosures to suit their own ends.

The second area of concern is that of access to information about services. Such information often concern the entitlements of individuals. Access to information about social services is essential to ensure that such services are availed of by those for whom they exist. Historically there have been difficulties in obtaining access to detailed information relating to such services.[6] Many people resort to approaching public representatives for such information. Whilst public representatives often provide an excellent service in the supply of information, the channelling of this information through politicians creates an

---

[5] See Smyth and Brady, *Democracy Blindfolded: The Case for a Freedom of Information Act in Ireland* (Undercurrents Series, O'Toole ed., Cork University Press, Cork, 1994).

[6] See for example: Ryan, *Keeping us in the Dark: Censorship and freedom of information in Ireland* (Gill and Macmillan, 1995); Hyland, "The Irish Educational System and Freedom of Information" (1995) 1(1) *Ireland: A Journal of History and Society* (Special edition: Irish Democracy and the Right to Freedom of Information) 103; Ellis, "Freedom of Information: A Welfare Rights Perspective", Paper presented at the "Full Information for Full Citizenship" conference hosted by the National Social Service Board on December 9, 1994; *Annual Report of the Ombudsman 1995* (Irish Stationery Office), pp.14–17.

unhealthy impression that access to the service is in the gift of the public representative and is being provided as a favour rather than as a right.

The demand for access to public sector information for commercial purposes is growing rapidly. This issue constitutes an important aspect of the formulation of national and global policies on access to information in the context of the development of the "Information Superhighway". The formulation of a national information policy has been a priority in the U.S. since the early 1990s.[7] The development of information policy at E.U. level has been the subject of considerable attention also.[8] In Ireland, a report concerning the formulation of national policy on the development of the information society was published in 1997.[9] The publication of this report led to the establishment of the Information Society Commission, which published its first report in December 1997.[10] The issue of access to public sector information in electronic form is a major focus of such policy formulation. There is general consensus that inadequate attention has been paid to the development of national and global information policies which would facilitate the exploitation of the vast quantities of information held on government computers.[11]

The desire on the part of individuals to obtain access to their own personal files in the hands of government has become increasingly evident. Modern governments hold an ever-expanding amount of information about their citizens. Such information is used as the basis of important decisions affecting the lives of individuals. Lack of knowledge of what exactly is contained in personal files of individuals in government departments and agencies can have serious consequences for the individual in terms of access to services, relations with the security forces, employment prospects, etc. It can also lead to feelings of alienation from society and a sense on the part of the individual that he or she is being forced to surrender control of increasing amounts of personal information to monolithic government institutions.

The aim of improving access to official information in these four areas must, however, be balanced against other interests. In terms of access to information about government activities and policies, arguments can be advanced in favour of maintaining the secrecy of certain categories of state information. These include information the disclosure of which would prejudice national

---

[7] National Telecommunications and Information Administration, Department of Commerce, *The National Information Infrastructure: Agenda for Action* (1993).

[8] The High-Level Group on the Information Society, *Europe and the Global Information Society: Recommendations to the European Council* ("Bangemann Report"), May 26, 1994; Commission of the European Communities, *Europe's way to the Information Society: An Action Plan* COM (94) 347 final, July 19, 1994.

[9] Report of the Information Society Steering Committee, *Information Society Ireland: Strategy for Action* (1997).

[10] Information Society Commission, *Information Society Ireland* (1997).

[11] See, for example, Commission of the European Communities, *Publaw 3 Studies* (1995).

security or law enforcement, or information which would reveal the deliberations of Cabinet or the development of policy at departmental level. The provision of access to information about services is less controversial. In the case
of provision of access to information to commercial enterprises, however, a
number of policy issues arise. These include whether commercial organisations should pay for access to government information and whether the public
sector should be required to provide access to information in electronic form.
Another issue is whether commercial organisations should be allowed to charge
their customers for access to public sector information. The role of public
sector bodies in the market for the supply of information must also be considered and, in particular, whether they should compete with commercial enterprises in that market. This is an important question given the trend towards
privatisation or part-privatisation of government bodies. The final issue, namely
that of access to personal files, must be considered in the light of competing
interests such as those in law enforcement and the security of the state and the
personal privacy of others.

The Irish Act faces a major challenge in seeking to address the information deficit in the four areas outlined above, whilst striking the optimum balance in terms of the various public interests involved. It must also come to
terms with the culture of secrecy which forms an integral part of Irish political
tradition. In particular, the view that restricting access to official information
is necessary to ensure the survival of democracy must be addressed. Judging
from the political stability of those countries which practise open government,
the preoccupation with secrecy seems unnecessary to the maintenance of democracy and public order. Indeed, it can be argued that the opposite is true,
that openness is in fact a prerequisite to democracy. Bullinger, for example,
proposes that:

> "Open discussion in a pluralistic democratic society depends to a considerable
> extent on government and mass media making available the information of which
> they dispose."[12]

B. Freedom of Information in an International Context

1. Freedom of information at the domestic level

(a) Freedom of information in Europe

FOI legislation has been widely introduced at domestic level in Europe. The
Swedes were the first to introduce freedom of information measures. The right
of access to official documents in Sweden goes back to 1766 and the enact-

---

[12] Bullinger, "Freedom of Expression and Information: an essential element of democracy" (1985) 6 *Human Rights Law Journal* 339 at 353.

ment of the Freedom of the Press Act. Since then, Sweden has maintained a long and unbroken tradition of transparency.[13]

Finland shares this tradition with Sweden, which is not surprising given the fact that the two countries were part of one kingdom until 1908. The Finnish law on access to official information is similar to Sweden's, with the main difference being that the Finnish law is not part of the Constitution and can therefore be changed as easily as any other law.[14]

Norway waited until 1970 to introduce legislation relating to open government.[15] The law came into effect after a number of years of wrangling dating back to the early 1950s. This period included examination of the issue by a series of commissions.

The Danish open government law[16] was passed in 1970 after a series of arguments in various commissions and in parliament.[17] Further legislation was introduced in 1985 to establish a general right of access to government documents.[18]

The French have allowed for access to administrative documents since 1978.[19] Commercial exploitation of documents to which access is obtained under this legislation is prohibited.[20]

In the late 1980s and early 1990s a number of other E.U. countries introduced laws providing a general right of access to government information.[21] They were Greece (1986), Italy (1990), the Netherlands (1991), Belgium (1991), Spain (1992), and Portugal (1993).[22] Austria has a constitutional paragraph on general access as well as the "Auskunftpflichtgesetz" which establishes a minimal access framework. Germany, Luxembourg and the U.K. have not yet adopted general access laws.

(b) Freedom of information in the common law world

The common law world first saw the introduction of freedom of information legislation in 1966 when the United States enacted the Freedom of Informa-

---

[13] The current version of this Act is the Freedom of the Press Act 1994.
[14] Publicity of Official Documents Act 1951 (83/9.2.1951).
[15] Act No. 69 of June 19, 1970 concerning Public Access to Documents in the (Public) Administration.
[16] Access to Public Administration Files Act, June 10, 1970.
[17] See Michael, *The Politics of Secrecy: Confidential Government and the Public Right to Know* (Penguin, Harmondsworth, 1982).
[18] Law 571 19.12.85 and Law 572 19.12.85.
[19] Law of July 17, 1978 (Loi No. 78-753 du 17 Juillet 1978 de la liberté d'acces aux documents administratifs).
[20] Article 10.
[21] Commission of the European Communities, *Publaw 3 Studies* (1995) Country Reports.
[22] Greece: Law No. 1599/86; Italy: Act 241 of August 7, 1990; the Netherlands: Act 703 of October 31, 1991 Wet Openbaarsheid Bestuur, Staatblad 703; Belgium: Wet van April 11, 1994 betreffende de openbaarheid van bestuur M.B. 30.6.94; Spain: Law 30/26.11.1992; Portugal: Law 65/26.8.1993.

tion Act[23] as part of a legislative package aimed at opening government up to scrutiny. The U.S. legislation was followed by freedom of information legislation in Australia (1982),[24] New Zealand (1982)[25] and Canada (1983).[26] Such legislation has also been introduced at state and territory[27] level in Australia[28] and at provincial,[29] territory,[30] and local[31] levels in Canada.[32]

Although they differ significantly in detail, and in the manner of their enforcement, FOI measures in the common law world follow a common pattern based on the United States model. They consist of two main elements, namely the provision of a right of access to government documents and the imposition of obligations concerning the publication of information relating to the operations of government agencies. Applicants need not establish any specific interest in the matter in order to obtain access to documents. All of the legislation provides for a number of exemptions to the right of access. These cover infor-

---

[23] See American Civil Liberties Union Foundation, *Litigation under the Federal Open Government Laws* (20th ed., ACLU Foundation, Washington D.C., 1997); Justice Department, *Guide to the Freedom of Information Act* (U.S. Department of Justice, Washington D.C., 1997), published on the Internet at: http://www.usdoj.gov/oip/foi-act.htm.

[24] Freedom of Information Act 1982 (Cth). See generally Bayne, *Freedom of Information: An Analysis of the Freedom of Information Act (Cth.) And a Synopsis of the Freedom of Information Act 1982 (Vic.)* (The Law Book Company Limited, Sydney, 1984); Bayne, *The Laws of Australia* (The Law Book Company Limited, Melbourne, 1995), Pt 2.3, Chap. 3 "Freedom of Information"; Zifcak, *The Australian Administrative Law Service* (Butterworths, Sydney, 1979), Chap. 7 "Freedom of Information".

[25] Official Information Act 1982. See generally Eagles, Taggart, and Liddell, *Freedom of Information in New Zealand* (Oxford University Press, Auckland, 1992).

[26] Access to Information Act (Canada), R.S.C., 1985. See generally McNairn and Woodbury, *Government Information Access and Privacy* (De Boo, Ontario, 1989).

[27] Freedom of Information Act 1989 (Australian Capital Territory).

[28] Freedom of Information Act 1982 (Victoria); Freedom of Information Act 1989 (New South Wales); Freedom of Information Act 1991 (South Australia); Freedom of Information Act 1991 (Tasmania); Freedom of Information Act 1992 (Queensland); Freedom of Information Act 1992 (Western Australia).

[29] Right to Information Act (New Brunswick), S.N.B., 1978; Freedom of Information Act (Newfoundland), R.S.N., 1990; An Act respecting Access to documents held by public bodies and the protection of personal information (Quebec), S.Q., 1982; Freedom of Information and Protection of Privacy Act (Manitoba), C.C.S.M., 1998, c.F175; Freedom of Information and Protection of Privacy Act (Ontario), R.S.O., 1990; Freedom of Information and Protection of Privacy Act (Saskatchewan), S.S., 1990–1991; Freedom of Information and Protection of Privacy Act (British Columbia), R.S.B.C., 1996; Freedom of Information and Protection of Privacy Act (Nova Scotia), S.N.S., 1993; Freedom of Information and Protection of Privacy Act (Alberta), S.A., 1994.

[30] Access to Information and Protection of Privacy Act (Northwest Territories), S.N.W.T., 1994; Access to Information and Protection of Privacy Act (Yukon), S.Y., 1995.

[31] Municipal Freedom of Information and Protection of Privacy Act (Ontario), R.S.O., 1990; Local Authority Freedom of Information and Protection of Privacy Act (Saskatchewan), S.S., 1990–1991.

[32] See Hazell, "Freedom of Information: Lessons from Canada, Australia and New Zealand" (1991) 12(3) *Policy Studies* 38.

mation such as that pertaining to national security, foreign policy, law enforcement, the deliberative processes of agencies, trade secrets, commercial
interests of third parties and of the State, confidential information in the hands
of government and information concerning the personal affairs of others. The
New Zealand Act follows the U.S. open text approach in that many of the
provisions of both Acts, in particular those setting out the exemptions, are
formulated in rather terse terms, which require fleshing by the courts, or the
Information Ombudsman in the case of New Zealand. The Canadian and Australian federal Acts, on the other hand, contain much more detailed and specific provisions. The Canadian federal Act is subject to some broad exclusions.
These include records consisting of Cabinet secrets and Minister/adviser discussions on policy briefings and draft legislation. In the U.S., Australian and
New Zealand Acts, exemptions are stated in discretionary or permissive terms:
in other words the government body is not required to invoke the exemption
and is free to release exempt material if it wishes to do so. The Canadian
federal Act contains a mixture of discretionary and mandatory exemptions.
The latter refer to information obtained in confidence from foreign, provincial
or municipal governments,[33] personal information[34] and information supplied
to public bodies by outside sources.[35] In Australia[36] and New Zealand[37] a
mechanism exists for the certification of certain categories of information as
exempt. The effect of the issue of such a certificate is that records to which it
applies are deemed to be exempt. The issue of such certificates cannot be
reviewed. In the case of Australia, such certification is carried out by a government Minister, whereas in New Zealand it is a function of the Prime Minister or the Attorney General.

In terms of enforcement, the U.S. Act relies on the courts to decide appeals
under the FOI Act, while at federal level in Australia that task is given to a
quasi-judicial forum, the Administrative Appeals Tribunal.[38] In Canada, the
federal Information Commissioner makes non-binding decisions relating to
access but there is provision for subsequent review by the courts. In New
Zealand, the Information Ombudsman makes recommendations, but these become binding after 20 days have elapsed unless the responsible Minister di-
rects otherwise or decides by order in Council.[39] In all four jurisdictions the
burden of proving that material is exempt is placed upon the government body
which has claimed the exemption.

---

[33] Access to Information Act (Canada), R.S.C., 1985, s.13.
[34] *ibid.*, s.19.
[35] *ibid.*, s.20.
[36] Freedom of Information Act 1982 (Cth), ss.33, 33A, 34, 35 and 36.
[37] Official Information Act 1982, s.31.
[38] s. 55. Recourse may alternatively be had to the Ombudsman who can make non-binding
recommendations in relation to access: s.57.
[39] Official Information Act 1982, s.32.

(c) Freedom of information in the U.K.[40]

While there is no FOI Act in place in the U.K., some progress has been made in establishing a right of access to certain categories of public records. In the area of personal records, the Data Protection Act 1984 provides a right of access to personal information held in computerised form. In addition, private members' Bills have led to the introduction of legislation such as the Access to Personal Files Act 1987, the Access to Medical Reports Act 1988 and the Access to Health Records Act 1990. This legislation grants limited access to certain personal files, in particular to individual files held by schools, by local authority social services and housing departments, and to medical records. Rights of access to general government information are less developed. In terms of enforceable provisions, the Local Government (Access to Information) Act 1985 provides a right of access to the meetings and meeting places of local authorities, and the Environmental Information Regulations 1992[41] give a right of access to environmental information pursuant to the E.U. Directive on Freedom of Access to Information on the Environment.[42]

Although there is no general FOI legislation in place in the U.K., the issue of freedom of information has, nonetheless, been the subject of considerable debate in that jurisdiction. Controversies such as the arms to Iraq affair and the Westland helicopters saga have focused attention on openness in government and there have been regular calls for the introduction of FOI legislation.[43] A number of private members' Bills have been introduced over the years,[44] most recently the Right to Know Bill sponsored by Mark Fisher M.P. in 1993.[45] Also in 1993, a White paper on Open Government was published.[46] The White Paper proposed the introduction of a Code of Practice on Access to Government Information.[47] The (non-binding) Code came into force in April 1994. It requires government departments to respond to requests for information and includes a role for the Parliamentary Commissioner for Administration (the Ombudsman) in investigating complaints that departments have not complied with the Code. Complaints to the Commissioner of breaches of the code are few[48] and this has been attributed to the failure to publicise its exist-

---

[40] See generally Birkinshaw, *Freedom of Information: The Law, the Practice and the Ideal* (2nd ed., Butterworths, London, 1996).

[41] S.I. No. 3240 of 1992.

[42] Directive 90/313 on Freedom of Access to Information on the Environment [1990] O.J. L158/56.

[43] The most active proponent of the introduction of FOI legislation in the U.K. is the Campaign for Freedom of Information (Director: Maurice Frankel), which was founded in 1984.

[44] Private Members' Bills have been introduced by M.P.s Clement Freud (1978), Frank Hooley (1981), David Steel (1984), and Archie Kirkwood (1992).

[45] For a detailed discussion of the Bill see Birkinshaw, *op. cit.* above, n. 40, pp. 336–348.

[46] *Open Government* Cm. 2290 (1993).

[47] *ibid.*, p. 32.

[48] From April 1994, when the Code came into force, and December 1996, 119 complaints

ence.[49] The White Paper also proposed the introduction of two new statutory rights of access to information: a right for people to see personal information relating to them held by a range of public sector authorities; and a right of access to health and safety information, except in cases where disclosure would betray "necessary confidentiality".[50] At the time of writing, neither of these proposals has been acted upon.

In December 1997 a White Paper setting out proposals for the introduction of a FOI Bill was published.[51] The scope of the proposed Bill is wide. It is proposed that the legislation will cover government departments, N.H.S. bodies, private bodies working on contracted-out functions, and privatised utilities. Bodies which will be excluded from the scope of the legislation include the Security Service, the Secret Intelligence Service, the Government Communications Headquarters and the Special Forces (S.A.S. and S.B.S.). The right of access will apply to both records and information and the exercise of access rights conferred by the Act will not be limited in terms of its retrospective effect. Exemptions will be limited to the following seven areas: national security; defence and international relations; law enforcement; personal privacy; commercial confidentiality; the safety of the individual, the public or the environment; information supplied in confidence; and the integrity of the decision-making and policy advice processes in government. Most exemptions will be subject to a harm test under which information can only be withheld in circumstances where its disclosure is capable of causing substantial harm. Decisions made under the FOI Act will be subject to a public interest test. The White Paper rejected the adoption of a ministerial certificate mechanism. The Act will be enforced by an Information Commissioner with the power to issue legally enforceable decisions. The Act will also impose obligations on public authorities to publish information concerning their activities. This will include the provision of reasons for administrative decisions to those affected by such decisions. A further proposal concerns the incorporation in the new Act of rights of access to historical records currently contained in the Public Records Acts 1958–1967. The imposition of obligations on public authorities to develop standards relating to records management is also proposed.

---

about access to information were received. Of these 66 were not suitable for investigation, mostly owing to lack of evidence. In the 26 investigations completed up to January 30, 1997, the complaint was upheld or partly upheld in 17 cases and found not to be justified in nine cases. Source: Parliamentary Commissioner for Administration, *Annual Report for 1996.*

[49] Frankel, "State's Open Secrets: How effective has the new code been in making government more transparent", *The Guardian*, January 24, 1995.

[50] *Open Government, op. cit.* above, n. 46, p. 46.

[51] *Your Right to Know: The Government's Proposals for a Freedom of Information Act* Cm. 3818 (1997). See: Sheridan and Snell, "FoI developments in the United Kingdom: White Paper – 'Your Right to Know'" (1998) 73 *FoI Review* 2; Birkinshaw, "An 'all singin' and all dancin'" affair: The new Labour government's proposals for freedom of information" [1998] *Public Law* 176.

The White Paper contains a promise on the part of the Government to publish an FOI Bill in 1998.

2. Freedom of information at the international level

There are two discernible forces underlying the development of freedom of information norms at the international level. The first, and more established, of these is the view that freedom of information is a human right. Despite some early promise, progress in establishing freedom of information as an international human right has been slow. The second, and more pragmatic, motivation underlying the introduction of standards guaranteeing access to information, one which is most clearly discernible in the context of the European Union, is the view that the right of access to public sector information is essential to the development of the European information market. E.U. policy in the area of freedom of information is directed, therefore, not only at contributing to citizens' participation in the democratic process, but also at stimulating the development of the E.U. information market. The provision of access to the commercial sector of public sector information is aimed at enabling European companies to compete on a favourable basis with their counterparts in other parts of the globe. Although developments in this area are at an early stage,[52] this impetus to the introduction of freedom of information norms is likely to have significant impact in the long term.

(a) Freedom of information as a human right

The right to freedom of information has been addressed, albeit rather indirectly, in the principal international human rights instruments. In the U.N. International Covenant on Civil and Political Rights (I.C.C.P.R.) and the European Convention on Human Rights (E.C.H.R.), the two rights which provide most support to the establishment of a right to freedom of information are the rights to freedom of expression and to private life. Whilst the former would appear to offer greater support to the establishment of a general right of access to government documents, the latter has proved useful in terms of providing a right of access to an individual's own file(s) in the hands of government.

(i) The right to freedom of expression

The right to freedom of expression is contained in Article 19 of the I.C.C.P.R. Paragraph 2 provides that:

> "Everyone shall have the right to freedom of expression: this right shall include freedom to seek, receive and impart information and ideas of all kinds, regardless of frontiers, either orally, in writing or in print, in the form of art or through any other media of his choice."

---

[52] See below, pp. 22–25.

Article 10 of the E.C.H.R. protects the right to freedom of expression:

"1. Everyone has the right to freedom of expression. This right shall include freedom to hold opinions and to receive and impart information and ideas without interference by public authority and regardless of frontiers. This article shall not prevent States from requiring the licensing of broadcasting, television or cinema enterprises.

2. The exercise of these freedoms, since it carries with it duties and responsibilities, may be subject to such formalities, conditions, restrictions or penalties as are prescribed by law and are necessary in a democratic society, in the interests of national security, territorial integrity or public safety, for the prevention of disorder or crime, for the protection of health or morals, for the protection of the reputation or rights of others, for preventing the disclosure of information received in confidence, or for maintaining the authority and impartiality of the judiciary."

The inclusion in the terms of Article 19 of the I.C.C.P.R. of "freedom to seek, receive and impart information" means that this right is framed in wider terms than is its counterpart in the E.C.H.R., the relevant part of which is limited to freedom "to receive and impart information". One author suggests that freedom to seek information was deliberately left out of the text of Article 10 of the E.C.H.R. because of fears on the part of Member States of the imposition of a corresponding far-reaching duty on their part to provide information which might include classified information.[53]

It is interesting to note that in the late 1970s a draft additional protocol to the E.C.H.R. was mooted which provided that the right to freedom of expression in Article 10 was to include the freedom to seek information. However, this was not proceeded with. One reason for the reluctance to adopt the protocol was that to do so would provide grounds for a restrictive interpretation of Article 10 by those countries which did not accept the amendment. It was argued that it was best to leave well enough alone on the basis that Article 10 could, in its original form, be interpreted to include a right to seek information.[54]

The Council of Europe subsequently produced other instruments which placed greater emphasis on the right to seek and receive information. The Declaration on Mass Communication Media and Human Rights was produced in 1970. This declaration states that the right to freedom of expression:

---

[53] Osterdahl, *Freedom of Information in Question: Freedom of Information in international law and the calls for a New World Information and Communication Order (NWICO)* (Iustus Forlag, Uppsala, 1992), p. 57.

[54] Malinverni, "Freedom of Information in the European Convention on Human Rights and the International Covenant on Civil and Political Rights" (1983) 4 *Human Rights Law Journal* 443.

"shall include freedom to seek, receive, impart, publish and distribute information and ideas. There shall be a corresponding duty for the public authorities to make available information on matters of public interest within reasonable limits. . . ".[55]

In 1981 the Committee of Ministers of the Council of Europe adopted a Recommendation to Member States on access to information held by public authorities stating, *inter alia*, that everyone shall have the right to obtain, on request, information held by public authorities other than legislative bodies and judicial authorities.[56] This right is, however, subject to a number of restrictions.

In 1982, the Committee of Ministers adopted a Declaration on the Freedom of Expression and Information confirming, amongst other things, the right to seek information.[57]

Despite these statements recognising the right to seek and receive information, the right to freedom of expression in the E.C.H.R. has been interpreted in a rather restrictive manner. It appeared from some of the earlier decisions of the supervisory bodies that the right to freedom of expression would be interpreted broadly. In *X v. FRG*[58] the European Commission on Human Rights stated that:

"it follows from the context in which the right to receive information is mentioned . . . that it envisages first of all access to general sources of information . . . the right to receive information may under certain circumstances include a right of access by the interested person to documents which although not generally accessible are of particular importance."[59]

The Court of Human Rights, in *Sunday Times v. U.K,*[60] a case which concerned a challenge to the granting of an injunction by the British courts against the publication of an article about the thalidomide scandal, referred to "the right of the public to be properly informed".[61]

However, subsequent decisions have tended to interpret narrowly the scope of the right to freedom of expression as it applies to those who seek information. In *Leander v. Sweden*[62] the applicant sought access to confidential information in government files, on the basis of which he believed he had been denied a job. He sought access to the information in order that he might challenge it. The Court held that:

---

[55] Council of Europe Consultative Assembly, 21st ordinary session, resolution 428 of January 23, 1970.
[56] Recommendation No. R (81)19 on Access to Information held by Public Authorities.
[57] Adopted by the Committee of Ministers on April 29, 1982.
[58] 8383/78 decision of 3.10.79 DR17, 227.
[59] *ibid.* at 228–229.
[60] (1979–80) 2 E.H.R.R. 245.
[61] *ibid.* at 281.
[62] (1987) 9 E.H.R.R. 433.

> "Article 10 does not . . . confer on an individual a right of access to a register containing information on his personal position, nor does it embody an obligation on the Government to impart such information to the individual".[63]

The Court treated the right to receive information as being merely negative in effect saying:

> "the right to freedom to receive information basically prohibits a Government from restricting a person from receiving information that others wish or may be willing to impart to him".[64]

In *Gaskin v. United Kingdom*,[65] where the information sought by the applicant was contained in records held by a public authority relating to a time when the applicant had been in public foster care, the Court stated that Article 10 did not embody an obligation on the State concerned to impart the information in question to the individual.

In *Guerra v. Italy*[66] the Court again refused to apply Article 10 in support of a right of access to official information. This case concerned a complaint by residents of a town in Italy in which a chemical factory was situated. Their complaint was to the effect that the authorities' failure to inform local inhabitants about the hazards of the industrial activity undertaken at the factory and about the procedures to be followed in the event of a major accident as required under domestic law infringed their right to freedom of information as guaranteed by Article 10. The Court reiterated its view, first expressed in *Leander* over 10 years previously, that the right to freedom to receive information basically prohibits a government from restricting a person from receiving information that others wish or may be willing to impart to him. The decision in *Guerra* not only confirmed the Court's reluctance to allow Article 10 to ground the establishment of a right of access to official information, but also reiterated its opposition to the use of Article 10 to impose positive information dissemination obligations on the State. The Court held that the freedom to receive information referred to in paragraph 2 of Article 10 of the Convention:

> "cannot be construed as imposing on a State, in circumstances such as those of the present case, positive obligations to collect and disseminate information of its own motion".[67]

The judges decided by 18 votes to two that Article 10 was inapplicable in the circumstances of the case. Of that 18, however, six were of the view that under different circumstances to those arising in the instant case:

---

[63] (1987) 9 E.H.R.R. 433 at 456.
[64] *ibid.*
[65] (1990) 12 E.H.R.R. 36.
[66] *Guerra v. Italy*, unreported, European Court of Human Rights, February 19, 1998.
[67] *ibid.,* para. 53 of the transcript.

> "the State may have a positive obligation to make available information to the public and to disseminate such information which by its nature could not otherwise come to the knowledge of the public."[68]

These decisions appear to offer little opportunity for the use of Article 10 to found a general right of access to government information. On the other hand, it can be argued that the first two of these cases were decided in the context of an application for access to information relating to the applicant(s) and that, therefore, the issue involved was one of personal access, rather than public access.[69]

(ii) The right to private life

The right to private life is contained in Article 17 of the I.C.C.P.R. which provides:

> "No one shall be subjected to arbitrary or unlawful interference with his privacy"

and goes on to provide that everyone has the right to protection of the law against such interference or attacks.

The article of the E.C.H.R. which protects the right to private life is Article 8:

> "1. Everyone has the right to respect for his private and family life, his home and his correspondence.
> 2. There shall be no interference by a public authority with the exercise of this right except such as in accordance with the law and is necessary in a democratic society in the interests of national security, public safety or the economic well-being of the country, for the prevention of disorder or crime, for the protection of health or morals, or for the protection of the rights and freedoms of others."

In *Gaskin v. United Kingdom*[70] the right to respect for private life in Article 8 of the E.C.H.R. was successfully invoked by a person seeking access to his own records. These records, which related to a period during his childhood when he was in foster care, included contributions from a number of professionals, some of whom objected to the provision of access to the records. The Court of Human Rights found that the refusal to allow the applicant access to the records violated his right to private life. It held that the U.K. Government had breached the Convention by failing to provide for an independent author-

---

[68] *ibid.* Concurring opinion of Mrs Palm joined by Mr R. Bernhardt, Mr Russo, Mr MacDonald, Mr Makarczyk, and Mr Van Dijk.

[69] See Beers, "Public Access to Government Information towards the 21st Century" in *Information Law: Towards the 21st Century* (Korthals, Altes, Dommering, Hugenholtz, and Kabel eds, Kluwer, 1992).

[70] Above, n. 65.

ity with the power to decide whether access should be granted in circumstances where a contributor to a record failed to give his or her consent to its disclosure, or withheld such consent. In doing so, the Court recognised that there are positive obligations flowing from Article 8 of the Convention. However, it refused to express an opinion on whether general rights of access to personal data and information may be derived from Article 8.

The applicant in *Gaskin* was seeking access to his own records. The potential for the establishment of a right of access to official information under Article 8 of the Convention might have been expected to be limited to similar situations involving applications for access to an individual's personal record. The scope of Article 8 was, however, extended by the decision in *Guerra v. Italy*. Here the applicants argued that the authorities' failure to comply with domestic law requiring that the applicants be informed about the hazards arising out of the operation of a chemical factory in their town, and about the procedures to be followed in the event of a major accident had infringed their right to respect for private life. The complaint was upheld by the Court, which reiterated its earlier finding that there may be positive obligations inherent in effective respect for private or family life.[71] It confirmed the decision in *Lopez Ostra v. Spain*[72] to the effect that severe environmental pollution may affect individuals' well-being and prevent them from enjoying their homes in such a way as to affect their private and family life adversely and found that the State had failed to fulfil its obligations by delaying the provision of information to the applicants that would have enabled them to assess the risks they and their families might run if they continued to live in their home town. This decision established that in circumstances where public bodies are subject to positive obligations to disclose information, failure to meet those obligations can amount to an infringement of Article 8. It would appear to leave open the possibility of the development of a right of access to government information in circumstances where the applicant can show that his or her right to respect for private life, family, home or correspondence would be adversely affected by a refusal of access to the information sought. The recognition of such a right would, however, fall short of the establishment of a general right to freedom of information under the Convention in that it would be dependent on linking the need for access to information to the exercise of another Convention right and on the existence of positive obligations with respect to disclosure of information.

(b) Freedom of information and the European Union

E.U. developments concerning access to information have taken place at three levels. These are:

---

[71] *Airey v. Ireland* (1979–80) 2 E.H.R.R. 305.
[72] (1995) 20 E.H.R.R. 277.

(i)   the introduction of measures concerning access to documents relating to the operations of E.U. institutions;

(ii) the introduction of measures imposing obligations on Member States addressing access to information in specific sectors, namely the environment; and

(iii) the development of general policies concerning access to official information in the context of the establishment of the European information market.

(i) Access to documents of E.U. institutions[73]

The policy of introducing greater transparency to the institutional framework of the European Union first gained official recognition in the Declaration on the right of access to information contained in the Maastricht Final Act, which stated:

> "The Conference considers that transparency of the decision-making process strengthens the democratic nature of the institutions and the public's confidence in the administration. The Conference accordingly recommends that the Commission submit to the Council no later than 1993 a report on measures to improve the public access to the information available to the institutions."[74]

A commitment to openness was included in a declaration entitled "A Community close to its citizens" issued at the close of the European Council held in Birmingham on October 16, 1992, and was reaffirmed by the European Council at Edinburgh in December 1992 when the Commission was invited to continue to work on improving access to the information available to Community institutions. These requests led to the adoption by the Commission of two Communications on access to institution documents. The first, *Public Access to the Institutions Documents,*[75] contained a survey on public access to documents in the Member States, while the second, *Openness in the Community,*[76] set out basic principles governing access to documents. Developments in the area took on a more concrete character on December 6, 1993 with the approval by the Council and Commission of a Code of Conduct concerning public access to Council and Commission documents.[77] On the same day, the

---

[73] See Curtin and Meijers, "The Principle of Open Government in Schengen and the European Union: Democratic Retrogression" (1995) 32 *Common Market Law Review* 391; Piris, "After Maastricht, Are the Community Institutions More Efficacious, More Democratic and More Transparent?" (1994) 19(5) *European Law Review* 449.

[74] Declaration No. 17 annexed to the Final Act of the Treaty of the European Union, signed at Maastricht on February 7, 1992.

[75] COM (93) 191 final, May 5, 1993; [1993] O.J. C156/5.

[76] COM (93) 258 final, June 2, 1993; [1993] O.J. C166/4.

[77] 93/730/EC, [1993] O.J. L340/41.

Council adopted new rules of procedure for Council meetings[78] which deal *inter alia* with public access to the workings of Council, including official documents. On December 20, 1993 the Council adopted Decision 93/731 on public access to Council documents,[79] the aim of which was to implement the principles established by the Code of Conduct. On February 8, 1994 the Commission, in turn, adopted Decision 94/90 on public access, under Article 1 of which the Code of Conduct was formally adopted. Both the Code of Conduct and the Council Decision establish a general right of access subject to a number of exceptions. The exceptions are similar in both documents. There are two distinct types. The first consists of a mandatory exception covering a range of interests competing with freedom of information, while the second is a discretionary exception aimed at protecting the confidentiality of the Council or Commission proceedings. The mandatory exception provides that access to a document *shall* not be granted where its disclosure could undermine:

(1) the protection of the public interest (public security, international relations, monetary stability, court proceedings, inspections and investigations);

(2) the protection of the individual and of privacy;

(3) the protection of commercial and industrial secrecy;

(4) the protection of the Community's financial interests; or

(5) the protection of confidentiality as requested by the natural or legal person who supplied any of the information contained in the document or as required by the legislation of the Member State which supplied any of that information.

The discretionary exception provides that access to a Council or Commission document, as the case may be, *may* be refused in order to protect the confidentiality of the Council's/Commission's proceedings.

Decisions have been handed down by the Court of First Instance in the first two cases concerning interpretation of the Code of Conduct and the Council decision.[80] The first case[81] was brought by John Carvel, the European Affairs Editor of the *Guardian* newspaper, with the support of the Danish and Dutch governments and the European Parliament.[82] Carvel had sought access to pre-

---

[78] 93/662/EC, [1993] O.J. L304/1.

[79] 93/731/EC, [1993] O.J. L340/43.

[80] In a third case a challenge by the Netherlands government to the legal basis of the Code of Conduct and Council decision on access was rejected by the Court of Justice: Case C–58/94 *The Netherlands v. E.C. Council* [1996] 2 C.M.L.R. 996; [1996] E.C.R. I-2169.

[81] Case T–194/94 *Carvel and Guardian Newspapers Limited v. E.U. Council* [1995] 3 C.M.L.R. 359; [1995] E.C.R. II-2765; [1996] All E.R. (EC) 53.

[82] See Michael, "Freedom of Information comes to the European Union" [1996] *Public Law* 31; Campbell, "Access to European Community Official Information" (1997) 46 I.C.L.Q. 174.

paratory reports, minutes, and attendance and voting records of Council of Ministers' meetings relating to Social Affairs, Justice and Agriculture. The Social Affairs documents were sent out, although later the Council claimed this had been done in error and that they ought to have been refused. The requests relating to the Agriculture and Justice meetings were refused, the latter a month after the time limit for reply had expired. The applicant sought an annulment of the decisions to refuse access and he put forward a number of arguments in support of his claim. The only argument to be considered by the Court was that the refusals amounted to an infringement of Article 4(2) of the Council decision, which provides that "Access to a Council document may be refused in order to protect the confidentiality of the Council's proceedings". The applicant argued that the Council had expressed a blanket refusal to allow access to certain types of documents and that this amounted to an infringement of Article 4(2) because of its discretionary nature, which is evidenced by the use of the word *may*. The Court held that while the Council is obliged under Article 4(1) to refuse access to documents where certain circumstances exist, in the case of Article 4(2), the Council enjoys a discretion as to whether to refuse a request for access to documents relating to its proceedings. The Court went on to state that:

> "It is clear both from the terms of Article 4 of Decision 93/731 and from the objective pursued by that decision, namely to allow the public wide access to Council documents, that the Council must, when exercising its discretion under Article 4(2) genuinely balance the interest of citizens in gaining access to its documents against any interest of its own in maintaining the confidentiality of its deliberations."[83]

On the evidence before it, which included statements of the Danish and the Netherlands Governments relating to the conduct of the Council meeting at which the decision to refuse access was taken, the Court found that the Council did not comply with the obligation of balancing the interests involved. The decision to refuse access was annulled and Carvel obtained access to the documents.

The second case[84] concerned an application by the World Wide Fund for Nature for access to Commission documents relating to a controversial E.U.-funded visitors' centre to be located in a scenic area in the west of Ireland. The Commission had undertaken an investigation into allegations that the construction of the centre would infringe community law. The World Wide Fund for Nature was supported in the proceedings by the Swedish Government, while the Commission was supported by the French and British Governments. Two exceptions were relied upon by the Commission in denying access to the

---

[83] *Carvel and Guardian Newspapers Limited v. E.U. Council*, above, n. 81, at 2789.
[84] Case T–105/95 *WWF UK (World Wide Fund for Nature) v. E.C. Commission* [1997] 2 C.M.L.R. 55; [1997] All E.R. (EC) 300.

documents. One was the mandatory exception for documents the disclosure of which could undermine the protection of the public interest (public security, international relations, monetary stability, court proceedings and investigations) ("the public interest exception"). The other exception relied upon was the discretionary exception allowing the Commission to refuse access in order to protect the institutions' interest in the confidentiality of its proceedings (the "confidentiality exception").

The Court made an important statement on the issue of interpretation of the relevant provisions in holding that "grounds for refusing a request for access to Commission documents, set out in the Code of Conduct as exceptions, should be construed in a manner which will not render it impossible to attain the objective of transparency".[85] The Court found that the Commission was entitled to rely on the public interest exception in refusing access to documents relating to investigations which may lead to an infringement procedure, even where a period of time has elapsed since the closure of the investigation.

The Court went on to say that when such an exception is invoked by the Commission it is obliged to indicate:

> "at the very least by reference to categories of documents, the reasons for which it considers that the documents detailed in the request which it received are related to the possible opening of an infringement procedure. It should indicate to which subject matter the documents relate and particularly whether they involve inspections or investigations relating to a possible proceedings for infringement of community law".[86]

The Commission was found to have failed to have met this requirement.

With respect to the confidentiality exception, the approach adopted in *Carvel* was followed and it was held that the Commission must exercise its discretion by striking a genuine balance between, on the one hand, the interest of the citizen in obtaining access to those documents and, on the other, its own interest in protecting the confidentiality of its deliberations. The Court found there was no evidence that the Commission had fulfilled its obligations in this regard. The decision to refuse access was annulled.

The Code of Conduct and Council decision are concerned with public access to Council and Commission documents only. Developments have also taken place with respect to the provision of access to documents of other E.U. institutions. In December 1996 the European Parliament asked the Commission to present a general regulation on minimum conditions and fundamental principles of public access to European Union documents.[87] In the same month, following his inquiry into public access to documents held by the Community

---

[85] *ibid.* at 72.
[86] *ibid.* at 73.
[87] Resolution on the implementation of the legislative programme for 1996 and the Commission's programme of work for 1997 adopted on December 11, 1996.

institutions and bodies other than the Council and Commission,[88] the European Ombudsman issued a decision to the effect that:

> "failure to adopt and make easily available to the public rules governing public access to documents constitutes an issue of maladministration."[89]

The decision was accompanied by draft recommendations to the effect that:

(1) the institutions and bodies should adopt rules concerning public access to documents within three months;

(2) the rules should apply to all documents that are not already covered by existing legal provisions allowing access or requiring confidentiality; and

(3) the rules should be made easily available to the public.[90]

The consequence of the issuing of such a decision and draft recommendations by the European Ombudsman is that the bodies to whom they are addressed must send a detailed opinion relating to them to the Ombudsman within three months.[91] The Ombudsman issued a Special Report concerning the opinions in December 1997, in which he noted that 13 of the 14 bodies to which the draft recommendations were addressed had adopted rules governing public access to their documents. The exception was the Court of Justice which stated that a study of all questions concerning access to its documents was continuing. The Ombudsman did not make any formal recommendation concerning the substance of the rules adopted, but noted that, when compared with the provisions applying domestically in some jurisdictions, the rules on public access to documents held by Community institutions and bodies are generally quite limited.

The right of access to documents of the E.U. institutions has been elevated to a new status by the insertion in the Treaty of Amsterdam of a right of access to documents of the European Parliament, the Council, and the Commission. Article 191A provides as follows:

---

[88] The inquiry concerned the following Community bodies and institutions: The European Parliament, The Court of Justice, The Court of Auditors, The European Investment Bank, The Economic and Social Committee, The Committee of the Regions, The European Monetary Institute, The Office for Harmonization of the Internal Market, The European Training Foundation, The European Centre for the Development of Vocational Training (Cedefop), The European Foundation for the Improvement of Living and Working Conditions, The European Environment Agency, The Translation Centre for Bodies of the European Union, The European Monitoring Centre for Drugs and Drug Addiction, and The European Agency for the Evaluation of Medicinal Products.

[89] Decision of the European Ombudsman in the own initiative inquiry into public access to documents (616/PUBAC/F/IJH), p. 7.

[90] *ibid.* It was made clear that in the case of the Court of Justice, the European Parliament, and the European Monetary Institute, these recommendations would apply only to administrative documents.

[91] Statute of the Ombudsman, Article 3(6).

"1. Any citizen of the Union, and any natural or legal person residing or having its registered office in a Member State, shall have a right of access to European Parliament, Council and Commission documents, subject to the principles and conditions to be defined in accordance with paragraphs 2 and 3.
2. General principles and limits on grounds of public or private interest governing this right of access to documents shall be determined by the Council, acting in accordance with the procedure referred to in Article 189b within two years of the entry into force of the Treaty.
3. Each institution referred to above shall elaborate in its own rules of procedure specific provisions regarding access to its documents."

The effect of this provision is that the Council will be obliged to introduce a Regulation concerning access to documents of the three named institutions within two years of entry into force of the Treaty.

(ii) Legal measures governing access to environmental information

The E.U. has also been instrumental in setting standards with respect to access to records held by the Member States, although its activities in this regard have so far been confined to one area, namely that of the environment. The aim is to establish a common standard for accessing information on the environment across the Member States. The Directive on Freedom of Access to Information on the Environment was adopted in 1990 and entered into force at the end of 1992.[92] The Directive requires public authorities to make available information relating to the environment to any natural or legal person, at his or her request, and without his or her having to prove an interest.[93] Requests for information must be responded to as soon as possible, within two months at the latest.[94] "Information relating to the environment" is defined as:

"any available information in written, visual, aural or data-base form on the state of water, air, soil, fauna, flora, land and natural sites, and on activities (including those which give rise to nuisance such as noise) or measures adversely affecting, or likely so to affect these, and on activities or measures designed to protect these, including administrative measures and environmental management programmes".[95]

"Public authority" is defined somewhat narrowly as:

"any public administration at national, regional or local level with responsibilities, and possessing information, relating to the environment with the exception of bodies acting in a judicial or legislative capacity".[96]

---

[92] Above, n. 42.
[93] Article 3(1).
[94] Article 3(4).
[95] Article 2.
[96] Article 2.

Article 6 extends the scope of the Directive, however, by applying the access provisions to "information relating to the environment held by bodies with public responsibilities for the environment and under the control of public authorities". The access rights provided for under the Directive are subject to a large number of exceptions, all of which are expressed in discretionary terms. Member States are entitled to enact legislation which provides that a request for environmental information can be refused where it affects:[97]

(1) the confidentiality of the proceedings of public authorities, international relations and national defence;

(2) public security;

(3) matters which are, or have been, *sub judice*, or under enquiry (including disciplinary enquiries), or which are the subject of preliminary investigation proceedings;

(4) commercial and industrial confidentiality, including intellectual property;

(5) the confidentiality of personal data and/or files;

(6) materials supplied by a third party without that party being under a legal obligation to do so; or

(7) material which, if disclosed, would make it more likely that the environment to which such material related would be damaged.

A request for information may also be refused where it would involve "the supply of unfinished documents or data or internal communications, or where the request is manifestly unreasonable or formulated in too general a manner".[98] If a request is refused, reasons must be given;[99] there is also an obligation to provide a legal remedy.[100]

The Directive has been implemented in Ireland primarily by means of the Access to Information on the Environment Regulations,[101] in which the opportunity for providing for exemptions has been utilised to the fullest extent.[102]

(iii) Access to information and the development of the information market

The importance of the development of a European market in information goods and services is emphasised in a number of E.U. studies and reports.[103] The

---

[97] Article 3(2).

[98] Article 3(3).

[99] Article 3(4).

[100] Article 4.

[101] At the time of writing, the current version of the Regulations is found in S.I. No. 125 of 1998.

[102] See below, pp. 404–425.

[103] See for example: Commission of the European Communities, *White Paper on Growth,*

role of access to public sector information in the development of the information society has also been emphasised.

The European Commission, as far back as 1989, issued guidelines aimed at improving co-operation between the public and private sectors in the information market.[104] These guidelines emphasised the role of the public sector as a major producer of basic data and information, as a provider of information goods and services, and as a major consumer. The potential contribution of access to public sector information to the development of the information market was further explored in the *Publaw* studies carried out from 1991–1995.[105] These studies identified considerable divergence amongst Member States in respect of laws concerning access to public sector information. The laws of some countries posed particular obstacles to freedom of movement of information goods and services, for example laws in France,[106] Belgium,[107] and Greece,[108] which prohibit the resale of information collected under the access laws. The *Publaw 3* report emphasised the need for the development of a community legal text concerning access to public sector information. It recommended that such a legal text should be in the form of a Directive, on the basis that such an approach would make it possible to define a sufficiently flexible framework policy to allow the Member States a certain margin of manoeuvre in defining the methods of application.

The importance of public sector information in the context of the development of the information society was underlined further by developments such as the request by the European Parliament in September 1996 that new forms of electronic distribution for the dissemination of public information to all citizens at European and national level be exploited.[109] Other developments which emphasised the role of public sector information in the development of the information society include: the resolution of the Industry Council concerning new policy priorities regarding the information society, in which Member States were urged to improve access to public information through

---

Competitiveness and Employment: The Challenges and Ways Forward to the 21st Century COM (93) 700 final, December 5, 1993; The High-Level Group on the Information Society, *op. cit.* above, n. 8; Commission of the European Communities, *op. cit.* above, n. 8.

[104] Commission of the European Communities, *Guidelines for Improving the Synergy between the Public and Private sectors in the Information Market* (1989).

[105] Commission of the European Communities, *Publaw 1 Studies* (1991); Commission of the European Communities, *Publaw 2 Studies* (1993); Commission of the European Communities, *Publaw 3 Studies* (1995).

[106] Law of July 17, 1978, above, n. 19, Article 10.

[107] Wet van April 11, 1994, above, n. 22, Article 10.

[108] Law No. 1599/86, Article 16, para. 7.

[109] The request was made in the context of the Parliament's resolution on the Commission's action plan for the information society: Resolution on *Europe and the Global Information Society – Recommendations to the European Council* and on a communication from the Commission of the European Communities, *op. cit.* above, n. 8.

accelerated use of information society tools and partnerships between the public and private sector;[110] the fact that access to public sector information was one of the priority issues addressed by the ministerial declaration issued at the conference on Global Information Networks, which took place in Bonn on July 6–8, 1997;[111] and the strong arguments in favour of a freedom of information initiative in the first annual report of the Information Society Forum.[112]

Whether a Directive granting rights of access to public sector information will ultimately be developed will depend on a number of factors, not the least of which are political considerations. At a practical level, too, a number of matters will need to be addressed before such a legal text can be developed. One of the main issues faced by the Commission is the extent to which the public sector should become involved in the commercialisation of the information it produces. Originally the Commission's view, as expressed in the 1989 Guidelines, was that the role of the public sector was to produce raw data and that it should be left to the private sector to "add value" or commercialise that data.[113] However, more recent reports indicate a shift in attitude. For example, the *Publaw 3* report states that:

> "In some cases and in some sectors, public authorities are as capable as the private sector of offering information products with an added value, particularly in the field of statistical or commercial data."[114]

Some of the other issues which have been identified as posing challenges to the development of a market for public sector information are those of competition, intellectual property, and data protection. In the case of competition, unrestricted public sector participation in the information market may result in a distortion of competition. For example, the sale of information by a public sector body direct to the market places its private sector competitors at a disadvantage. Intellectual property rights can also constitute an obstacle to the dissemination of public information where public sector bodies invoke intellectual property protections in refusing to disseminate information. The issue of data protection is one which also needs to be addressed to ensure that individuals' rights to privacy are not encroached upon by the development of a market for public sector information. Other issues which will need to be dealt with include the extent to which a right of access to information in electronic form should be provided, as well as the issues of what information should be

---

[110] Council Resolution of November 21, 1996 on new policy-priorities regarding the information society (96/C 376/01), [1996] O.J. C376/1.

[111] See points 25 and 26 of the ministerial declaration on http://www2.echo.lu/bonn/final.html.

[112] First annual report to the European Commission from the Information Society Forum, June 1996.

[113] Commission of the European Communities, *op. cit.* above, n. 104.

[114] Commission of the European Communities, *Publaw 3 Studies* (1995), p. 71.

exempted from access rights, what legal recourse will be provided as a remedy, the charges to be levied for access to public sector information, and so on.

The Commission is, at the time of writing, preparing a Green Paper on public sector information in the information society which will attempt to come to terms with these various issues.

THE FREEDOM OF INFORMATION ACT 1997

THE FREEDOM OF INFORMATION ACT 1997

A. The History of the Freedom of Information Act in Ireland

The Irish Freedom of Information ("FOI") Act, in contrast to its overseas counterparts,[1] was introduced in the absence of detailed public debate on its proposed contents. Its introduction was, nonetheless, preceded by much general
discussion of the need for such legislation. Proposals for the introduction of
freedom of information legislation in Ireland can be traced back to 1985 and
the introduction by Senator Brendan Ryan of a private member's Freedom of
Information Bill in that year. Whilst that Bill was useful in placing FOI on the
Irish political agenda for the first time, it did not generate widespread publicity at the time.[2] It was really only after the commencement of the Beef Tribunal Inquiry in late 1991 that the need for greater openness in Irish government
was more generally acknowledged. Access to government information became
an important issue in the election of November 1992. The Programme for
Government of the incoming Fianna Fáil/Labour Party coalition promised,
under the heading "Broadening our democracy", to "consider" the introduction of freedom of information legislation. Further attention was focused on
the issue of access to government information by the founding, in early 1993,
of the "Let in the Light" campaign by journalists and others concerned about
issues of censorship and secrecy in Ireland. A firm commitment to the introduction of freedom of information legislation was finally set out in the Fine
Gael/Labour Party/Democratic Left programme for government of December
1994. The opening paragraphs of that document acknowledged that "the relationship between Government and the people it serves has been damaged by a
lack of openness" and, as its very first pledge, the Government promised:

> "The reform of our institutions at national and local level to provide service,
> accountability, transparency and freedom of information."[3]

---

[1] See, for example, New Zealand: Committee on Official Information, *Towards Open Government* ("Danks Report") (Government Printer, Wellington, 1980); Australia: Senate
Standing Committee on Constitutional and Legal Affairs, *Freedom of Information* (Australian Government Publishing Service, Canberra, 1979); Canada: Rankin, *Freedom of
Information in Canada: Will the Doors Stay Shut?* (Canadian Bar Association, Ottowa,
1977).

[2] This lack of interest is acknowledged by Senator Ryan in his book *Keeping us in the
Dark* (Gill and Macmillan, 1995), p. 144, where he states that coverage of the debate in
the Seanad "was about on a par with that given to the routine discussion of potholes,
school building programmes and the like".

[3] *A Government of renewal: A Policy Agreement between Fine Gael, the Labour Party and
Democratic Left* (December 1994).

A related development was the decision, announced in the Fine Gael/Labour Party/Democratic Left programme for government, to have a review of the Official Secrets Act 1963 carried out by the Dáil committee on legislation and security.[4]

The introduction of FOI legislation can, at one level, be viewed as a response to public demands for more openness and transparency in government. It also forms part of a wider programme of public service and Oireachtas reform which began in the early 1990s. These developments included the Strategic Management Initiative for the public service which led to the introduction of the Public Service Management Act 1997. Important developments in the area of Oireachtas reform included the introduction of the Ethics in Public Office Act 1995 which provides for the disclosure of interests by people holding public office, the development of a more comprehensive Oireachtas committee system, the introduction of the Committees of the Houses of the Oireachtas (Compellability, Privileges and Immunities of Witnesses) Act 1997 which gives Oireachtas committees the power to compel the attendance of witnesses before them, and the passing of the Electoral Act 1997 which provides public funding for political parties.

The Minister of State at the Department of the Tánaiste, Ms Eithne Fitzgerald T.D., was given the task of bringing forward the Bill. Ms Fitzgerald had been Minister of State at the same Department in the previous administration during which time she, and some of her senior civil servants, had undertaken a research tour of Australia and New Zealand to study the operation of freedom of information legislation in those jurisdictions. Fianna Fáil helped to maintain interest in the issue through the introduction to the Seanad by Senator Dick Roche of a Freedom of Information Bill in June 1995. This Bill reached the second stage in the Seanad but was not proceeded with.

Two years elapsed between the announcement of the promise to introduce freedom of information legislation and the publication of the Bill in December 1996. This delay is partly explained by the complexity of the legislation. Another reason for the Bill's long gestation was the extensive process of consultation undertaken with government departments, not all of whom appear to have been wholehearted in their support of the proposals.[5] The heads of the Bill were also referred to the Dáil Committee on Legislation and Security for its consideration, the first occasion on which the contents of a Bill were considered by a Dáil committee prior to drafting. Despite comprehensive consultation within the public sector, there was very little debate surrounding the

---

[4] The committee issued a report in February 1997 in which it called for the repeal of the Official Secrets Act 1963 and its replacement with criminal sanctions aimed at specific categories of information: Dáil Éireann, Select Committee on Legislation and Security, *Report on Review of the Official Secrets Act, 1963* (1997).

[5] See, for instance, Foley, "Freedom of Information plans held up by Justice Department", *Irish Times*, September 16, 1995.

detailed contents of the Bill in the wider public arena. The Bill was broadly welcomed when it was introduced in the Seanad in December 1996. The main concern of the Opposition appeared to be that it did not go far enough.[6] Some minor changes were made as the Bill progressed through the Seanad and Dáil. The Freedom of Information Act became law on April 21, 1997 and entered into force on April 21, 1998.

B. Overview of the Act

The Act is made up of four main elements. First, the Act grants a right of access to particular government records following the making of a request. This is the pivotal and probably best known aspect of freedom of information legislation. Second, the Act contains provisions requiring the publication of information relating to the operation of government departments and bodies. The third main feature of the Act are the provisions granting individuals the right to require amendment of incorrect government records containing personal information concerning them. The fourth main element of the Act consists of a statutory right to be given reasons for administrative decisions. These four elements are common to freedom of information legislation in the common law world. Each is briefly described below.

1. Right of access to records

Section 6 of the Act provides a right of access to any record held by or under the control of a public body. This right marks a departure from the traditional approach to disclosure of official documents in two main ways. First, the provision of access to official records is no longer at the discretion of the holder of those records and, second, individuals seeking access to records under the FOI Act need not show any particular interest in the records sought.

The right of access to records under the Act is not, however, absolute. The Act is restricted both in terms of its scope and by the fact that it is subject to a number of exclusions and exemptions.

(a) Scope

The scope of the Act is limited in three main respects. First, the Act applies to "records", but not to "information". Access need only be provided to information held in recorded form, but not to unrecorded verbal information or information of which someone has knowledge.

---

[6] 149 *Seanad Debates* Cols 1258–1269, *per* Senator Roche; 476 *Dáil Debates* Cols 240–245, *per* Deputy McDaid.

Second, not all bodies which hold official records are covered by the legislation. The Act applies to "public bodies", a term which encompasses all of the central government departments as well as a range of central government bodies which are listed in the First Schedule. Health Boards and local authorities will come within the scope of the Act from October 21, 1998. A number of significant State bodies are not covered by the Act. The Garda Síochána,[7] for example, are a notable exclusion, but there is provision for their inclusion by means of regulation. The Minister for Finance has the power to bring a wide range of State bodies within the purview of the Act, again by means of regulation.

The third limitation on the scope of the Act concerns the issue of retrospective effect. With two exceptions, the Act applies only to records created after its coming into operation. The exceptions arise, first, where the records sought relate to personal information of the requester and, second, where the granting of access to prior records would be necessary or expedient "in order to understand" records originating after the commencement of the Act.[8]

(b) Exclusions and exemptions

The other main restriction on the right of access to official records conferred by the Act are the exclusions and exemption provided for. Some records are excluded entirely from the application of the Act, while others may be exempted in certain circumstances. The excluded records include records which are otherwise available, records relating to courts or tribunals other than those of an administrative nature and records revealing the source of information relating to criminal law enforcement. The exemption provisions, which are contained in Part III of the Act, are aimed at balancing the right to freedom of information against other interests. The latter encompass both interests based on the common good, such as those of preserving the security of the state or maintaining law enforcement, and individual interests, such as those of privacy and confidentiality. The Act gives the body holding the records the right to claim that records which otherwise fall within the scope of the Act are exempt on certain grounds. Twelve grounds for exemption are set out in the Act. They are in respect of: meetings of the government; deliberations of public bodies; functions and negotiations of public bodies; parliamentary, court and certain other matters, law enforcement and public safety; security, defence and international relations; information obtained in confidence; commercially sensitive information; personal information; research and natural resources; financial and economic interests of the State and public bodies; and enactments relating to non-disclosure of records.

---

[7] The police force.
[8] s.6(5).

There is considerable variation in the terms in which the exemptions are expressed. One of the most important distinctions is that which can be drawn between exemptions which are subject to a public interest test and those which are not. Roughly half of the exemptions are subject to such a test, which means that even where a record falls within the terms of such an exemption provision, it can nonetheless be released where it is in the public interest so to do. Another distinction is that which exists between exemptions which are expressed in mandatory terms and those which are permissive or discretionary. Where an exemption is expressed in mandatory terms, the holder of a record which falls within the terms of the exemption is obliged to deny access to it. In the case of exemptions expressed in permissive terms, records can be released at the discretion of the head of the public body even where they fall within the scope of the exemption provision. A distinction can also be drawn between class and harm-based exemptions. While some exemptions operate by setting out the category or class of record to which the exemption applies, others are expressed in terms of the harm which could potentially be caused by disclosure. In the former case, the exemption can be invoked once it is shown that the record is one of the class referred to in the exemption. Where a harm or injury test is provided for, the exemption can only apply where proof of such harm is tendered. Another difference encountered in analysing the exemption provisions is that between exemptions which are intended to be exhaustive in scope and those which are defined in terms which are open-ended, thus allowing for the inclusion within their scope of as yet unidentified types of records. Another point of distinction between the exemption provisions arises between those which are self-contained in their terms and those which rely on the incorporation of some existing legal term of art into their definition. Finally, some exemptions can be applied autonomously by the head of the public body while the application of others requires prior consultation with third parties.

2. Publication of government information

The Act requires the publication by public bodies of two categories of information concerning their operations. Section 15 requires the publication by public bodies of a reference book setting out details of the structure, organisation and functions of the public body, and of the services it provides. It also requires publication of information on the classes of records held by the public body and of details of arrangements for obtaining access to those records and for having amendments made to personal records in its custody. Information on the body's appeals mechanisms must also be included. Section 16 requires the publication of what is often referred to as the "internal law" of the public body; in other words, the rules, guidelines, precedents and the like used by the body in making decisions or recommendations under schemes administered by that body.

3. Amendment of personal information

The Act provides a mechanism whereby public bodies who are in possession of personal information can be required to amend that information in certain circumstances. The right to amendment of incorrect personal records can be seen both as an integral part of a right to privacy in so far as it facilitates the exercise of control by individuals over personal information relating to them and as an essential aspect of maintaining the accuracy and integrity of public record systems. The Act provides for the amendment of personal information which is incomplete, incorrect or misleading. The provisions apply to all information held by a public body regardless of how access to it has been obtained. Thus it is not confined to information which has been accessed under the FOI Act. The type of amendments provided for are: the alteration of the record to make the information complete, correct or not misleading; the addition to the record of a note specifying the respects in which the public body is satisfied that the information is incomplete, incorrect or misleading; or the deletion of the information. There is also provision for the annotation of records where applications for amendment are unsuccessful. Reasonable steps must be taken to notify those to whom the affected record was given in the previous 12 months of any amendments made.

4. Right to reasons for administrative decisions

Prior to the introduction of the FOI Act, Irish administrative law had not provided a clear statement of the circumstances in which reasons for administrative decisions were required to be given. In particular, it had been suggested that the right to reasons for administrative decisions only applied in cases where the person affected by a decision indicated a serious intention to challenge it by judicial review or, where possible, appeal.[9] The FOI Act clarifies that position by providing individuals with the right to a written statement of reasons and findings of fact in respect of any act of a public body concerning that individual, provided the individual has a material interest in a matter affected by the act.[10]

C. Interpretation

The Irish FOI Act does not, in contrast to its overseas counterparts, include in its text a section setting out the purposes of the Act.[11] Such purpose clauses

---

[9] Hogan and Morgan, *Administrative Law in Ireland* (3rd ed., Round Hall Sweet & Maxwell, Dublin, 1998), p. 572.

[10] s.18.

[11] See, for example, New Zealand: Official Information Act 1982, s.4; Australia: Freedom of Information Act 1982 (Cth), s.3; Freedom of Information Act 1982 (Victoria), s.3; Freedom of Information Act 1992 (Western Australia), s.3; Freedom of Information Act

are relied upon to a significant extent in the interpretation of FOI legislation overseas. In New Zealand, for example:

> "the Ombudsmen have stressed time and time again that the Act must receive such fair large and liberal interpretation as will best attain the objects of the Act set out in sections 4 and 5."[12]

The purposes of the Irish Act are instead stated in the long title of the Act in the following terms:

> "An Act to enable members of the public to obtain access to the greatest extent possible consistent with the public interest and the right to privacy, to information in the possession of public bodies and to enable persons to have personal information relating to them in the possession of such bodies corrected and, accordingly to provide for a right of access to records held by such bodies, for necessary exceptions to that right and for assistance to persons to enable them to exercise it, to provide for the independent review both of decisions of such bodies relating to that right and of the operation of this Act generally (including the proceedings of such bodies pursuant to this Act) and for those purposes, to provide for the establishment of the office of Information Commissioner and to define its functions, to provide for the publication of such bodies of certain information about them relevant to the purposes of this Act, to amend the Official Secrets Act 1963, and to provide for related matters."

1. Status of the long title as an aid to interpretation

A statement of purpose set out in a section would appear to enjoy a superior status to one included in the long title or preamble to an Act. This was the view of the Australian federal Administrative Appeals Tribunal (A.A.T.) in *Re Babinda Co-operative Sugar Milling Association Ltd v. Australian Industrial Research and Development Board*:

> "The technique of expressing such an objective in the body of the Act, rather than in a preamble, was no doubt intended to give to its statement the authority

---

1992 (Queensland), ss.4 and 5; Freedom of Information Act 1989 (New South Wales), s.5; Freedom of Information Act 1989 (Australian Capital Territory), s.3; Freedom of Information Act 1991 (South Australia), s.3; Freedom of Information Act 1991 (Tasmania), s.3; Canada: Access to Information Act (Canada), R.S.C., 1985, s.2; Freedom of Information and Protection of Privacy Act (Manitoba), C.C.S.M., 1998, c.F175, s.2; Freedom of Information and Protection of Privacy Act (Ontario), R.S.O., 1990, s.1; Freedom of Information and Protection of Privacy Act (Nova Scotia), S.N.S., 1993, s.2; Freedom of Information and Protection of Privacy Act (British Columbia), R.S.B.C., 1996, s.2; Freedom of Information Act (Newfoundland), R.S.N., 1990, s.3; Freedom of Information and Protection of Privacy Act (Alberta), S.A., 1994, s.2.

[12] Eagles, Taggart, and Liddell, *Freedom of Information in New Zealand* (Oxford University Press, Auckland, 1992), p. 4.

or strength that, having regard to the established rules of statutory interpretation, would be lacking were it restricted to a preamble".[13]

There are two schools of thought concerning the rules of statutory interpretation as applied to long titles. On the one hand, there is the view that the long title is part of the Act and can thus be called in aid in interpreting the other provisions of a statute. The more restrictive view, on the other hand, is that the long title can only be used as an aid to interpretation in cases where the provision being examined is ambiguous. In *Minister for Industry and Commerce v. Hales*[14] Henchy J. said:

> "Counsel for the [Royal Liver Friendly] Society submits that the object of the Act may be seen more clearly by looking at its long title. I take it to be established by the modern authorities that the long title is part of the Act, but there are also modern authorities that say it is not permissible to call in aid the long title for the purpose of limiting the interpretation of a statutory provision that is clear and unambiguous [citations omitted]."[15]

This passage was quoted with approval by Griffin J. in *People (D.P.P.) v. Quilligan*,[16] who said:

> "The long title, in my view, cannot be used to modify or limit the interpretation of plain and unambiguous language, and this is, I believe, the effect of the decided cases."[17]

However, McCarthy J. in the same case appeared to be prepared to grant a superior status to the long title. He quoted with approval the statement of Lord Simon of Glaisdale in *Black-Clawson Ltd v. Papierwerke A.G.*[18] that "it [the long title] is the plainest of all guides to the general objectives of a statute" and said:

> "As in the United Kingdom, the long title is, having regard to the Standing Orders of Dáil Éireann, as much a part of the Act as any section thereof . . . It is not, in my opinion, a question of ambiguity in the construction of particular provisions; it is a question of giving a schematic interpretation where such is the plain intent of the statute."[19]

Thus, while it is clear that the objects of the Act as set out in the long title can be relied upon as an aid to interpreting the Act, the circumstances in which regard may be had to it are not entirely clear.

---

[13] (1980) 2 A.L.D. 851 at 868.
[14] [1967] I.R. 50.
[15] *ibid.* at 75.
[16] [1986] I.R. 495.
[17] *ibid.* at 519.
[18] [1975] A.C. 591.
[19] *People (D.P.P.) v. Quilligan*, above, n. 16, at 523–524.

2. Meaning of the long title

The content of the long title is itself somewhat ambiguous. While on the one hand it states that the purpose of the Act is to enable members of the public to obtain access to information in the possession of public bodies "to the greatest extent possible consistent with the public interest and the right to privacy", provision is also made in the long title for "necessary exceptions" to the right of access to records. Whilst it could be argued that the provision for the making of exceptions could be viewed as an object of the Act just as much as the creation of the access right itself, the reference in the opening lines of the long title to enabling the public to obtain access to information *to the greatest extent possible* arguably signifies the primacy of access rights over other considerations.

3. Extrinsic aids to interpretation

Apart from the text of the Act itself, the status of a number of external materials relating to the Act should be considered. These include pre-parliamentary materials, Oireachtas debates, and decisions of foreign courts. Generally speaking, the Irish courts have emphasised the primacy of the text and tend to view such external materials as worthy of consultation only as a last resort. At the pre-parliamentary stage, relevant materials might include speeches of the sponsoring Minister as well as the explanatory memorandum to the Bill. It is not clear what account would be taken of such material by a court in interpreting a statute. In the case of speeches by a Minister, the views of one Minister would be unlikely to be taken to represent the intention of the Oireachtas as a whole.[20] The explanatory memorandum, on the other hand, would be more likely to be viewed as a useful indicator of legislative intent. In *McLoughlin v. Minister for Public Service*,[21] for example, the explanatory memorandum of a Bill was examined by the Supreme Court and influenced its interpretation of the corresponding Act. In the case of parliamentary debates, the traditional approach was that they could not be used as an aid to interpretation. Costello J., in *Wavin Pipes v. Hepworth Iron Co. Ltd*,[22] signalled a departure from that approach by holding that the court could consider the parliamentary debates on the provision in question. More recent decisions have, however, tended to limit consideration of parliamentary debates to situations where provisions of a statute are ambiguous.[23] Finally, the use of decisions of overseas courts,

---

[20] As McLoughlin J. in *Minister for Industry and Commerce v. Hales*, above, n. 14, at 66 put it: "what has to be interpreted is not the intention of the Minister but the intention of the legislature as expressed in the Act".

[21] [1985] I.R. 631.

[22] [1982] F.S.R. 32.

[23] *Wadda v. Ireland* [1994] 1 I.L.R.M. 126; *Flynn and Village Crafts v. Irish Nationwide Building Society Ltd*, unreported, High Court, Lavan J., July 31, 1995.

tribunals, and Information Commissioners as an aid to interpretation must be considered. While an Irish court is not bound to follow the decisions of foreign courts, such decisions are of persuasive authority and may be followed at the option of the court. Decisions of other common law countries in particular are frequently cited and adopted by the Irish courts, especially in cases where there is no Irish authority governing the issue.[24] The foreign decisions which are likely to have most influence on the interpretation of the FOI Act are those based on legislation which bears the greatest resemblance to our own. The approach to the drafting of the Irish statute is similar to that adopted in respect of the Australian and Canadian legislation, in that it is quite detailed. This applies in particular in respect of the exemption provisions. This contrasts with the New Zealand approach, which is brief and open-textured. In substantive terms, the Irish Act, and in particular the exemption provisions, most closely resemble the provisions of the Australian federal Act and the Queensland and Western Australian State FOI Acts. Decisions of the bodies responsible for the enforcement of these Acts are therefore likely to provide a valuable source of precedent for the Information Commissioner and courts in this country.

---

[24] See Byrne and McCutcheon, *The Irish Legal System* (3rd ed., Butterworths, 1997), pp. 347–353.

CHAPTER 3

PUBLICATION OF GOVERNMENT INFORMATION, RECORDS MANAGEMENT, AND REASONS FOR ADMINISTRATIVE DECISIONS

PUBLICATION OF GOVERNMENT INFORMATION, RECORDS MANAGEMENT, AND REASONS FOR ADMINISTRATIVE DECISIONS

Amongst the features of the Freedom of Information Act which have the most potential to contribute to rendering public policy more transparent are those relating to the publication of information relating to public bodies, records management, and the giving of reasons for administrative decisions.

A. Publication of Information relating to Public Bodies

Difficulties in obtaining access to basic and often uncontroversial information in areas such as social welfare, health care, the environment, education, and security had been widely reported prior to the introduction of the Act.[1] The FOI Act seeks to address this information deficit in two ways. Section 15 places obligations on public bodies to publish information relating to their activities, while section 16 requires public bodies to disclose what is often referred to as their "internal law", *i.e.* the rules, guidelines, precedents, etc., on which their decisions are based. The obligations to publish information imposed by sections 15 and 16 apply only in respect of public bodies as defined in the Act. Those bodies which remain outside the scope of the Act will not, therefore, be obliged to publish any of the information referred to in sections 15 or 16. The obligations set out in sections 15 and 16 are not limited in terms of their retrospectivity. Public bodies must, therefore, comply with the requirements of sections 15 and 16 with respect to all of the records they hold and not just those created after the Act comes into force. The publication obligations imposed under sections 15 and 16 are limited to the extent that if any matter which is required to be published under those sections is contained in a record which is exempt, the public body need not publish the exempt matter.[2]

---

[1] See for example: Ryan, *Keeping us in the Dark: Censorship and freedom of information in Ireland* (Gill and Macmillan, 1995); Hyland, "The Irish Educational System and Freedom of Information" (1995) 1(1) *Ireland: A Journal of History and Society* (Special edition: Irish Democracy and the Right to Freedom of Information) 103; Ellis, "Freedom of Information: A Welfare Rights Perspective", paper presented at a conference hosted by the National Social Service Board entitled "Full Information for Full Citizenship" on December 9, 1994; *Annual Report of the Ombudsman 1995*, pp. 14–17.

[2] s.15(8), s.16(7).

1. Section 15

Section 15 requires the publication by public bodies of a reference book setting out a number of categories of information relating to the body. The requirements of each category are set out in section 15(1) and may be summarised as follows:

(1) a general description of the structures and organisation, functions, powers, and duties of the public body, any services it provides for the public, and the procedures by which any such services may be availed of by the public;

(2) a general description of the classes of records held by the body together with the particulars necessary to the exercise of the right of access;

(3) a general description of the material required to be published under section 16(1)(a) and (b), namely the rules procedures, practices, guidelines and interpretations used by the body, and an index of any precedents kept by the body, for the purposes of decisions, determinations or recommendations, and information relating to the manner of administration of any enactment or scheme administered by the body;

(4) the arrangements made by the body:

(a) to facilitate access to records held by the body;

(b) concerning applications for the amendment of records that relate to personal information of that individual; and

(c) to facilitate applications for reasons for decisions under section 18;

(5) the names and designations of the members of staff of the body responsible for the arrangements referred to at (4) (unless the head of the body reasonably believes that publication of that information could threaten the physical safety or well-being of the persons concerned);

(6) the address to which requests for access to records or applications for amendment of records or reasons for decisions should be directed;

(7) information relating to the right to appeal and the appeals procedure applicable both to decisions made by the body and decisions made under the FOI Act; and

(8) any additional information considered appropriate by the head of the body concerned for the purpose of facilitating the right of access.

There is provision for the extension, by regulation, of the categories of information to be provided in the reference book.[3] Public bodies are expressly

---

[3] s.15(1)(i).

required to have regard, in preparing the reference book, to the fact that the purpose of the book is to assist members of the public in ascertaining and effectively exercising their rights under the Act.[4]

The level of detail required in respect of categories (1), (2), and (3) is limited to a general description. Thus, it would appear that 15(1)(b), for example, does not require public bodies to produce comprehensive lists of all categories of records that they hold or to provide an index in respect of such records. The reference in section 15(1)(a) to functions, powers and duties of public bodies would appear to require identification of those pieces of legislation for which the body is responsible, as well as the legislation from which the body derives its powers.

Section 15(4) requires each public body to furnish a summary of its reference book to the Minister for Finance who, in turn, is obliged to publish a collation of all the summaries furnished to him or her.

2. Section 16

Section 16 requires public bodies to publish what is sometimes referred to as its "internal law", *i.e.* the rules relied upon by the body in exercising its decision-making functions. The need for such a provision was explained by the Australian Senate Standing Committee on Legal and Constitutional Affairs in the following terms:

> "Freedom of information legislation complements many principles that are an integral part of our legal system. Foremost among those principles is the rule of law, which requires that government decisions and the officials who make them should alike be answerable to the same system of law that applies to others. The chief way in which this principle has gained expression in our legal system is through the enactment of legislation that declares the rights, obligations, powers and duties of the Executive, and the correlative rights liabilities and privileges of the public. However, this objective – that government should be according to law and that all law should be published – is under challenge from the contemporary practice of enacting legislation that is couched in general terms and creates broad discretionary powers under which the Executive is permitted to adopt internal rules, policies and guidelines to supplement the Parliamentary word. If those internal supplements are hidden – inaccessible or unobtainable by the public – the rule of law is to that extent displaced."[5]

Section 16(1) requires the publication of:

> "(a) the rules, procedures, practices, guidelines and interpretations used by the

---

[4] s.15(3).
[5] Senate Standing Committee on Constitutional and Legal Affairs, *Freedom of Information: Report by the Senate Standing Committee on Constitutional and Legal Affairs on the Freedom of Information Bill 1978, and aspects of the Archives Bill 1978* (Australian Government Publishing Service, Canberra, 1979), para. 7.18.

body, and an index of any precedents kept by the body, for the purposes of decisions, determinations or recommendations, under or for the purposes of any enactment or scheme administered by the body with respect to rights, privileges, benefits, obligations, penalties or other sanctions to which members of the public are or may be entitled or subject under the enactment or scheme, and

(b) appropriate information in relation to the manner or intended manner of administration of any such enactment or scheme."

The intended effect of this provision was explained by the sponsoring Minister of State in the following terms:

"[T]he Bill provides that each public body publish all its internal rules and guidelines which it uses in decision making. In this way the public can be informed in advance of the ground rules and basis on which its application for any grant or benefit will be judged. So, for example, the guidelines used by community welfare officers in deciding on whether the amount of help with an [electricity] bill and the detailed criteria for assessing income in means tests will be publicly available."[6]

The words "rules, procedures, practices, guidelines and interpretations" are very broad and would be likely to capture any material used by public bodies for decision-making purposes. "Precedent" is defined in the *Concise Oxford Dictionary* as: "a previous case or legal decision etc. taken as a guide for subsequent cases or as a justification".

Section 16(6) requires that a precedent referred to in an index specified in section 16(1)(a) must be made available on request. No provision is made for the levying of charges for the making available of such precedents.

The consequences of not making available the information referred to in section 16(1)(a), or of supplying it in incomplete or inaccurate form, are set out in section 16(3). Note that section 16(3) does not apply in the case of non-compliance with section 16(1)(b), which requires the publication of information relating to the administration of an enactment or scheme. Where a person can show that he or she was not aware of a rule referred to in section 16(1)(a) and that, but for the non-fulfilment by a body of its obligations under section 16(1)(a), he or she would have been so aware, the public body shall "if and in so far as it is practicable to do so" ensure that the person is not to be subjected to any prejudice by reason only of the application of the rule or requirement, where the person could lawfully have avoided the prejudice, had he or she been aware of the rule or requirement. This provision shall not apply, however, in cases where the public body concerned shows that reasonable steps were taken by it to bring the rule or requirement concerned to the notice of those affected by it.[7]

---

[6] 149 *Seanad Debates* Col. 1251 (Second Stage).
[7] s.16(4).

3. Arrangements for publication of information under sections 15 and 16

Both the reference book and the material referred to in section 16 was to be published on the commencement of the Act (*i.e.* April 21, 1998[8]) and thereafter at intervals of no more than three years and "as soon as may be" after any significant alterations or additions fall to be made to the latest available reference book or publication. If a significant addition or alteration to the material is made inside the three-year period, it would appear that the reference book or the section 16 publication must be updated. The collation of summaries required to be published by the Minister for Finance under section 15(4) must be published within 15 months of the commencement of the Act, and thereafter at intervals of no more than three years or "as soon as may be" after any significant alterations or additions are made to the latest available collation of summaries. The reference book and the material referred to in section 16 must be made available for inspection free of charge at a place to be determined by the head or the Minister, as appropriate, and notice of the locations at which the books are available must be published.[9] The sponsoring Minister of State expressed the view that the reference book should be made available in public libraries and that the Minister's collation of summaries should, in addition, be made available in public offices throughout the country.[10] The Act requires that the reference book and the section 16 publication should be made available for removal free of charge or, at the discretion of the head of the public body concerned or of the Minister, for purchase. There is provision for the giving of a copy of the materials which relate to a health board or local authority to the members of such bodies.[11] This requirement was introduced by way of amendment in the Senate. Speaking in favour of the amendment, one member expressed the view that it was necessary in light of "the gulf that exists between local authority members and management".[12]

4. Sanctions for non-compliance

While no express provision is made for sanctions relating to non-compliance with sections 15 or 16 (apart from that set out in section 16(3) which is discussed above at page 42), section 36(1) gives the Commissioner the power to investigate "practices and procedures adopted by public bodies . . . for the purpose of compliance with" any of the provisions of the Act. The general

---

[8] Information relating to local authorities and health boards must be published by the date on which the Act is extended to apply to such bodies (no later than October 21, 1998), and those relating to bodies to which the scope of the Act may be extended by regulation, upon the making of such regulations (s.15(2), s.16(2)).

[9] s.15(7), s.16(5).

[10] 149 *Seanad Debates* Col. 1571 (Committee Stage).

[11] s.15(7).

[12] 149 *Seanad Debates* Col. 1570, *per* Senator Roche.

power of investigation conferred on the Information Commissioner by s.36(1) would appear to authorise the carrying out of such an investigation in relation to non-compliance with section 15 or 16. The Commissioner has the power to prepare a report of his or her findings following such an investigation[13] and it is open to the Commissioner to furnish a copy of such a report to the Minister for Finance and to the public body concerned and to append a copy of the report to his or her annual report.[14]

B.   Records Management

The importance of records management in the context of FOI was emphasised by the joint Australian Law Reform Commission/Administrative Council review of the operation of the Australian federal FOI Act:

> "Good recordkeeping and records management are . . . important to the success of the FOI Act. Without them, the right of access provided by the Act is unenforceable in practice. Agencies will be unable to locate records efficiently (if at all) and records that ought to be retained may be destroyed."[15]

Section 15(5) places an obligation on the Minister for Finance to ensure that appropriate measures are taken by public bodies with respect to the training of staff, organisational arrangements, and such other matters as the Minister considers appropriate for the purpose of facilitating compliance by the bodies with the Act. The same subsection confers on the Minister the power to introduce regulations providing for the management and maintenance of records held by public bodies. Prior to introducing such regulations, the Minister must consult with the Information Commissioner and with the Director of the National Archives. Section 15(6) provides for the preparation, by the Minister, of a report of the measures taken by public bodies pursuant to section 15(5). The report must include details of any measures taken by a public body arising from a report issued by the Commissioner pursuant to an investigation carried out under section 36(4). The Minister's report must be prepared "as soon as may be" after a three-month period beginning on the commencement of the Act and thereafter on an annual basis. The Minister must provide a copy of every such report to the joint Oireachtas Committee charged with reviewing provisions restricting the disclosure of records under section 32.

---

[13] s.36(4).
[14] s.36(5).
[15] Australian Law Reform Commission Report No. 77/Administrative Review Council, Report No. 40, *Open Government: a review of the federal Freedom of Information Act 1982* (Australian Government Publishing Service, Canberra, 1995), para. 5.8.

C. Reasons for Administrative Decisions

Prior to the introduction of the FOI Act, Irish administrative law had not provided a clear statement of the circumstances in which reasons for administrative decisions must be given. It had been suggested that apart from those cases in which there is a statutory right to reasons for decisions, a right to reasons for administrative decisions was available only in cases where the person affected by a decision indicated a serious intention to challenge it by way of judicial review or, where possible, by appeal.[16] As a result of this ambiguity in the law, the practice of giving comprehensive reasons for administrative decisions had not been uniformly embraced in Irish public administration. This problem was evident from the following observations contained in the Ombudsman's annual report for 1995:

> "Citizens are entitled to be given reasons for decisions made by public bodies. However, I find that some public bodies adopt a very minimalist approach when it comes to giving reasons for their decisions. The result is that, instead of satisfying the citizen, they only serve to undermine his or her confidence in the decision making process generally."[17]

Section 18 of the FOI Act transforms this area of administrative law by establishing a general right to reasons for administrative decisions. This right can be exercised by any person who is affected by an act of a public body and who has a material interest in a matter affected by such an act or to which the act relates. The application must be made in writing or in such other form as may be determined by the Minister for Finance. The public body has four weeks within which to provide the applicant with a statement setting out:

(1) the reasons for the act; and

(2) any findings on any material issues of fact made for the purposes of the act.

There is no requirement that people be informed on an individual basis of their rights under section 18. Section 15, which sets out the provisions regarding publication of information about public bodies, does, however, require that the reference book to be compiled pursuant to section 15 must contain information on the arrangements made by public bodies to enable a person to whom section 18(1) applies to obtain the information specified in that section.[18]

---

[16] Hogan and Morgan, *Administrative Law in Ireland* (3rd ed., Round Hall Sweet & Maxwell, Dublin, 1998), p. 572.

[17] *Annual Report of the Ombudsman 1995*, p. 18.

[18] s.15(1)(d)(iii).

1. Circumstances in which a statement of reasons must be provided

The right to a statement of reasons does not apply in respect of all administrative decisions. It is limited in the following ways:

(1) The right to a statement of reasons is available only in respect of an act of a public body

The scope of section 18 is confined to acts of the public bodies. Public bodies, for the purposes of the FOI Act, are listed in the First Schedule to the Act. There is, therefore, no right under section 18 to a statement of reasons for acts of public sector bodies which are not included in the First Schedule.

(2) The right to a statement of reasons is available only to a person who is affected by an act of the public body and who has a material interest in a matter affected by the act or to which it relates

In order to be entitled to a statement of reasons, a person must meet two requirements. The person must be affected by an act of the body and he or she must have a material interest in a matter affected by the act or to which it relates.[19] "Act" is defined in section 18 to include a decision of the body.[20] The use of the word "include" indicates that the scope of the term "act" may go beyond a decision. It could, for example, include the adoption of a course of action by a public body which did not involve the making of any decision on the part of the public body. The requirement that the person be affected by the act imposes a condition as to the standing of the person seeking the statement of reasons. In contrast to the other rights conferred by the FOI Act, it will not be open to everyone to exercise the right to a statement of reasons. The person concerned must be able to show that he or she is affected by the act. They must also establish that they have "a material interest in a matter affected by the act or to which it relates". Some assistance is provided in section 18 as to the meaning of the latter requirement. Section 18(5) provides that, for the purposes of section 18, a person has a material interest in a matter affected by an act of a public body or to which such an act relates, if "the consequences or effect of the act may be to confer on or withhold from the person a benefit without also conferring it on or withholding it from persons in general or a class of persons which is of significant size having regard to all the circumstances and of which the person is a member". It is necessary, therefore, to show that the act had a particular impact on the person concerned as compared with people who are similarly situated. "Benefit" in relation to a person is defined in section 18(6) to include:

---

[19] s.18(1).
[20] s.18(6).

(a) any advantage to the person;

(b) in respect of an act of a public body done at the request of the person, any consequence or effect thereof relating to the person; and

(c) the avoidance of a loss, liability, penalty, forfeiture, punishment or other disadvantage affecting the person.

2. The contents of the statement of reasons

Section 18(1) requires that persons to whom that section applies must be given a statement:

(a) of the reasons for the act; and

(b) of any findings on any material issues of fact made for the purposes of the act.

These requirements are very similar to the corresponding requirements of Australian and New Zealand legislation, both of which require that statements be given of the reasons for decisions and of the findings on material issues of fact.[21] The Australian Administrative Review Council (ARC) issued an explanatory memorandum which clarified the requirement to give reasons in the following way:

> "Every decision should be capable of a logical explanation. A statement of reasons should contain all the steps of reasoning linking the facts to an ultimate decision which are necessary for a person affected to understand how the decision was reached. . .
>
> The criteria relevant to the decision, the weight to be attached to each criterion, and the conclusion reached on the criteria should be stated. Clarity of explanation may make it desirable in some cases to state separately the conclusion on each criterion.
>
> The reasoning should identify any element of policy or guideline (whether in the form of a written statement or otherwise and whether emanating from the government or internal to the decision-making authority) or departmental practice which is part of the justification of the decision made.
>
> Decision-makers frequently act upon recommendations, reports, and results of investigations carried out by subordinate officers or appropriately qualified experts. Where these recommendations, et cetera, are considered in making a decision, the statement of reasons should incorporate the recommendation, et cetera, as well as the facts (and a reference to the evidence or other materials on which they are based) and the reasons leading thereto. It is insufficient merely to state that the decision-maker has relied upon the advice of a named person."[22]

---

[21] Australia: Administrative Decisions (Judicial Review) Act 1977, s.13(1); New Zealand: Official Information Act 1982, s.23(1).

[22] Administrative Review Council, *Statements of Reasons: An Explanatory Memorandum* (1979), quoted in Eagles, Taggart, and Liddell, *Freedom of Information in New Zealand* (Oxford University Press, Auckland, 1992), p. 55.

In relation to findings on material issues of fact the ARC guidelines state:

> "The matter to be included in the statement in this respect may be described as
> those matters of fact which were taken into account in making the decision. If a
> fact is relied upon, it must be set out. If a matter is considered then the findings
> of fact in relation to it must be set out. In so far as the statement of reasons does
> not set out findings of fact on a matter, it may be inferred that those facts were
> considered to be immaterial; if a court or Tribunal finds that those facts are
> material; it follows that the decision-maker has erred in law.
>
> Sometimes a material fact is established directly by the evidence or other
> material. Where, however, a material fact is inferred from other facts which are
> in turn established by evidence or other material, it may be necessary to state
> those facts and the process of inference in order to provide adequate informa-
> tion on the way in which the decision was reached.
>
> Findings of fact are distinguishable from subjective judgments or opinions.
> Where a subjective judgment or opinion is based on facts, it is desirable that
> those underlying facts should be set out as well as the judgment or opinion
> formed on the basis of them."[23]

3. Exceptions

The requirement that reasons be given for an administrative decision is subject to four exceptions. The first provides that nothing in section 18 shall be
construed as requiring the giving to a person of information contained in an
exempt record,[24] while the second states that nothing in section 18 shall be
construed as requiring the disclosure of the existence or non-existence of a
record where the non-disclosure of its existence or non-existence is required
by the Act.[25] The third exception relates to the giving of reasons for decisions
concerning public appointments. It provides that the requirement to provide a
statement of reasons does not apply to certain decisions regarding public appointments,[26] where the provision of a statement of reasons in the form required by section 18 would, in the opinion of the head of the public body
concerned, be likely to prejudice the effectiveness of the process for selecting
a person for appointment to the position or office. Where the head of a public
body decides to refuse to provide a statement of reasons on any of these grounds,
the applicant must be informed of this decision within four weeks of the re-

---

[23] *ibid.*, p. 54.
[24] s.18(2)(a).
[25] s.18(2)(b).
[26] Section 18(3) provides that the right to reasons does not apply to a decision of the Civil
Service Commissioners pursuant to subparagraph (d) or (e) of section 17(1) of the Civil
Service Commissioners Act 1956 not to accept a person as qualified for a position referred to in that section, or to a decision of the Local Appointments Commissioners
made by virtue of section 7(3) of the Local Authorities (Officers and Employees) Act
1926 not to recommend a person to a local authority for appointment to an office referred to in that section.

ceipt of the application. Finally, decisions under the FOI Act are excluded from the right to reasons for decisions set out in section 18.[27] Separate provision is made in section 8(2)(d) regarding the giving of reasons for decisions to refuse access to records under the FOI Act.[28]

4. Remedies

The FOI Act provides for the bringing of an appeal in respect of the right to reasons in relation to both the contents of a statement furnished under section 18(1) and a refusal of an application under section 18(1). This appeal can be brought, in the first instance, to the head of the public body concerned[29] (assuming the head did not make the initial decision under section 18). There is provision for appeal against the decision of the head to the Information Commissioner.[30] The Commissioner also hears appeals in cases where the head of a public body made the original decision under section 18.[31]

Failure to comply with section 18 could also result in the aggrieved person seeking an order of mandamus from the High Court to compel the decision-maker to perform its statutory duty.[32]

---

[27] s.18(6).
[28] See below, p. 79.
[29] s.14(1)(f). The internal review function can also be delegated by the head provided the person to whom it is delegated is of a higher grade than the original decision-maker: s.4(1), s.14(3).
[30] s.34(1)(a).
[31] s.34(1)(b).
[32] See Hogan and Morgan, *op. cit.* above, n. 16, p. 700.

ACCESS

CHAPTER 4

ACCESS

A. The Right of Access

Section 6(1) is the core provision of the FOI Act. It provides unambiguously for a right of access to records held by public bodies. There is no need for a person seeking to exercise that right to establish any particular interest in accessing the record concerned.[1] The introduction of this statutory right of access is not, however, intended to inhibit the utilisation of other avenues for the provision of access to records by public bodies. That is made clear by section 6(8), which provides that:

> "Nothing in this Act shall be construed as prohibiting or restricting a public body from publishing or giving access to a record (including an exempt record) otherwise than under this Act where such publication or giving of access is not prohibited by law".

B. Scope of the Act

1. Which bodies are covered?

Entities covered by the Act are known as public bodies. The Act applies only to those public bodies which are listed in its First Schedule. The First Schedule includes all the Departments of State as well as 50 agencies of central government. These include the Office of the Attorney General, the Office of the Director of Public Prosecutions, the Revenue Commissioners, the Social Welfare Appeals Office, the Office of the Ombudsman, and the Office of the Comptroller and Auditor General. The Environmental Protection Agency and An Bord Pleanála were late inclusions to the First Schedule, added at Report stage in the Dáil.[2] There is provision for the extension of the Act to health boards and local authorities no later than 18 months after the passing of the Act, which means that these bodies must be brought within the scope of the Act by October 21, 1998. The exact scheduling of the application of the Act to health boards and local authorities must be arranged with the consent of the Minister for Health and the Minister for the Environment.[3]

---

[1] s.8(4).
[2] 477 *Dáil Debates* Cols 776–778 (Report Stage).
[3] s.1(3).

Records in the possession of independent contractors employed by public bodies are covered by the Act to the extent that they relate to the service being provided to the public body.[4] For example, records of general practitioners who provide services under the General Medical Services scheme would be covered, as would records of companies carrying out services under contract to public bodies, such as cleaning companies. The application of the Act to such records extends only to those records which relate to the services being provided to the public body. A provision is deemed to be included in contracts between public bodies and independent contractors to the effect that the contractor is required, when requested by the employing public body for the purposes of the Act, to give the record to the body "for retention by it for such period as is reasonable in the particular circumstances". Failure to comply with such a request would give rise to the usual remedies provided for in respect of breach of contract.[5]

The scope of the Irish Act is relatively limited when compared with its overseas counterparts. In Australia, where the FOI Act covers all agencies apart from those expressly excluded, the scope of the Act extends to all significant public sector bodies; only about 20 agencies are expressly excluded.[6] The approach taken in the Canadian[7] and New Zealand[8] legislation is similar to that adopted in Ireland in that in those jurisdictions the legislation applies only to those bodies expressly referred to in the Act. The list of bodies covered by the Canadian and New Zealand legislation is, however, extensive. In New Zealand, for example, the Official Information Act applies to approximately 200 public bodies apart from government departments. Its scope extends to universities, schools, hospitals, the national broadcasting company, the national airline, and various semi-State bodies. In Canada the Access to Information Act covers over 100 government bodies apart from government departments and its scope extends to a number of semi-State organisations.

Unlike its overseas counterparts, the Irish Act does not cover the police force, nor does it extend to schools, universities, voluntary hospitals, or to government agencies such as Bord Fáilte, Forbairt, FÁS, the Health and Safety Executive, or to commercial State-sponsored bodies such as Aer Lingus, the ESB, Coillte, Bord Gáis, and RTÉ.

The scope of the Act can be extended to other bodies by regulation. This can only be done with the consent of the Minister responsible for the body in question. Bodies to which the application of the Act can be thus extended are listed in paragraph 1(5) of the First Schedule. They are the Garda Síochána;[9] a body, organisation or group established by or under any enactment (other than

---

[4] s.6(9). Such records are deemed to be held by the public body concerned.
[5] See Clark, *Contract Law in Ireland* (3rd ed., Sweet & Maxwell, London, 1992).
[6] Freedom of Information Act 1982 (Cth), Sched.2.
[7] Access to Information Act (Canada), R.S.C., 1985, Sched.1.
[8] Official Information Act 1982, First Sched.
[9] The police force: First Sched., para. 1(5)(a).

under the Companies Acts 1963–1990);[10] a body, organisation or group established by or under any scheme administered by a Minister;[11] a body, organisation or group established under the Companies Acts 1963–1990 in pursuance of powers conferred by or under another enactment and financed from the public purse;[12] any other body, organisation or group financed in a similar manner;[13] a company, a majority of the shares of which are held by or on behalf of a Minister;[14] any body, organisation or group appointed by the Government or a Minister;[15] any body, organisation, or group on which functions have been conferred in respect of the general public or a class of the general public by any enactment;[16] and a subsidiary of any of the aforementioned bodies.[17] The second last category was added by amendment at Committee Stage in the Seanad to allow for the extension of the Act to bodies on which statutory powers and functions have been conferred, such as the Law Society, the Bar Council, and the various medical registration boards.[18]

The application of the Act to any of the bodies listed in paragraph 1(5) of the First Schedule can be limited to specified functions of the body.[19] In the case of a semi-State organisation, for example, the application of the FOI Act might be limited to matters other than those relating to the organisation's competitive commercial activities.

Section 3(1)(c) of the Act provides that where difficulties arise during the first three years of the extension of the application of the Act to a health board, a local authority, or to any of the bodies to which it may be extended by regulation, the Minister for Finance may introduce regulations to facilitate the bringing into operation of the Act in so far as it applies to such a body. Such regulations may "do anything which appears to be necessary or expedient for bringing this Act into operation" and, to that end, may "modify a provision of this Act if the modification is in conformity with the purposes, principles and spirit of this Act".

---

[10] First Sched., para. 1(5)(b)(i).

[11] First Sched., para. 1(5)(b)(i).

[12] First Sched., para. 1(5)(b)(ii). More precisely, such a body must have been financed "wholly or partly, whether directly or indirectly, by means of moneys provided, or loans made or guarantees, by a Minister of the Government or the issue of shares held by or on behalf of a Minister of the Government".

[13] First Sched., para. 1(5)(c).

[14] First Sched., para. 1(5)(d).

[15] First Sched., para. 1(5)(e).

[16] First Sched., para. 1(5)(f). Paragraph 2 of the First Schedule provides that such bodies shall be public bodies only as respects functions that have been conferred on them in relation to the general public or a class of the general public. In other words, they shall not be subject to the requirements of the FOI Act in respect of any other functions they may carry out.

[17] First Sched., para. 1(5)(g).

[18] 149 *Seanad Debates* Cols 1414–1415 (Committee Stage).

[19] s.3(5).

The succeeding provision, section 3(1)(d), contains a similar, but more general, power to introduce regulations to facilitate the bringing into operation of the Act. Again, this provision applies in respect of any difficulty arising in the first three years after the commencement of the Act. It confers on the Minister the power to make regulations modifying a provision of the Act, again subject to the requirement that such a modification be "in conformity with the purposes, principles and spirit of the Act". The constitutionality of any regulations introduced under these provisions must be considered. Article 15.2.1° of the Constitution vests in the Oireachtas the sole and exclusive power of making laws for the State. The courts have considered, on a number of occasions, the constitutionality of legislative provisions which provide for the delegation of the legislative power.[20] Morgan's survey of the case law relating to Article 15.2.1° leads him to suggest that it may be violated in two sets of circumstances. The first is where the parent section permits the delegate to make novel legislation, *i.e.* legislation containing principles not to be found in an Act of the Oireachtas. The classic statement of this rule is found in the following statement of Finlay C.J. in the Supreme Court in *Cityview Press Limited v. An Chomhairle Oiliúna ("AnCo")*:

> "In the view of this Court, the test is whether that which is challenged as an unauthorised delegation of parliamentary power is more than a mere giving effect to of principles and policies which are contained in the statute itself. If it be, then it is not authorised; for such would constitute a purported exercise of legislative power by an authority which is not permitted to do so under the Constitution. On the other hand, if it be within the permitted limits – if the law is laid down in the statute and details only are filled in or completed by the designated Minister or subordinate body – there is no authorised delegation of legislative power."

The other way in which Article 15.2.1° may be violated is by means of what is referred to in the U.K. as a Henry VIII clause, namely a statutory provision which makes a grant of authority to make delegated legislation which may amend the parent Act. Morgan argues that a Henry VIII clause can fall foul of Article 15.2.1° where it allows for the introduction of delegated legislation which amends some statutory provision, even without introducing a novel principle.[21] This could happen, for example, where a Minister exercises "a power of regulation granted to him by the [parent legislation] so as to negative the expressed intention of the legislature".[22]

---

[20] *Pigs and Bacon Marketing Board v. Donnelly* [1939] I.R. 413; *Cityview Press v. An Chomhairle Oiliúna* [1980] I.R. 381; *The State (Gallagher, Shatter & Co.) v. de Valera* [1986] I.L.R.M. 3; *Cooke v. Walsh* [1984] I.R. 715; *Harvey v. Minister for Social Welfare* [1990] 2 I.R. 232; *McDaid v. Judge Sheehy* [1991] I.R. 1; *Meagher v. Minister for Agriculture* [1994] 1 I.L.R.M. 1. See Morgan, *The Separation of Powers in the Irish Constitution* (Round Hall Sweet & Maxwell, Dublin, 1997), pp. 235–250.

[21] *ibid.*, p. 246.

[22] *Harvey v. Minister for Social Welfare* [1990] 2 I.R. 232 at 245.

In allowing only for the making of modifications which are "in conformity with the purposes, principles and spirit" of the Act, sections 3(1)(c) and (d) have been drafted in a manner which is aimed at ensuring that they do not fall foul of Article 15.2.1°. They were referred to in the Seanad as "standard sections, which are included for a limited period . . . to deal with technical misprints that tend to creep into even the best proof read legislation".[23] It is submitted that only a very minor change to a parent statute could be construed as being in conformity with the purpose, principles or spirit of the statute and that, in any case, regulations allowing for the amendment of the FOI Act in a way which introduces some novel principle which is not found in the parent Act or which does not conform to the aims of that Act would be unconstitutional. The limited scope of the provisions was acknowledged by Minister of State Fitzgerald when she assured the Seanad that:

> "It is not possible under that kind of technical section to do something that would be so contrary to the purpose of the Bill as set out in the Long Title, which is to open up information."[24]

Where the Minister proposes to make regulations under either section 3(1)(c) or (d), a draft of the regulations must be laid before each House of the Oireachtas and a resolution approving that draft must be passed by both Houses. This procedure renders the introduction of such regulations more cumbersome than the introduction of other regulations provided for under the Act. In the case of a proposal to introduce regulations under section 3(1)(c), the Minister must also consult with such other Ministers as he or she deems appropriate. Clearly consultation with the Minister who has (or Ministers who have) responsibility for the public body concerned is what is envisaged here.

2. Who can use the Act?

The rights conferred by the Act are stated to be exercisable by every person. Section 6(1) provides that "every person has a right to . . . be offered access to any record held by a public body". "Person" as defined in the Interpretation Act 1937 includes a body corporate and an unincorporated body of persons as well as an individual and on that basis it can be argued that the exercise of access rights is not confined to individuals.[25] On the other hand, the long title to the FOI Act refers to the provision of access rights to "members of the public", which would seem to suggest that the right is exercisable only by an individual. Given the uncertain status of the long title as an aid to interpretation,[26] the better view is that the exercise of access rights is not limited to individuals but extends also to companies, partnerships, sole traders, and

---

[23] 149 *Seanad Debates* Cols 1410–1411 (Committee Stage).
[24] 149 *Seanad Debates* Col. 1411 (Committee Stage).
[25] Interpretation Act 1937, s.11.
[26] See above, pp. 33–34.

unincorporated associations. In any case, even if exercise of the access rights were confined to individuals, there is nothing in the Act to prevent an individual exercising such rights on behalf of a company.

There is no requirement that a person using the Act be an Irish citizen. The right of access could, for example, be invoked by a refugee wishing to elicit information about his or her application for refugee status.[27] There is no requirement that an application be submitted from within the jurisdiction.

3. What records are covered?

(a) Records held by a public body

Section 6 confers a right of access to records "held by a public body". While the long title refers to records "in the possession of public bodies", it is clear that the scope of the Act extends beyond those records which are in the physical possession of the public body. Section 2(5)(a) provides that a reference to a record "held by a public body" includes a reference to a record under the control of the public body. A record which is not in the possession of a public body could, nonetheless, be under its control. This could occur, for example, where an employee of a public body has taken a record home to work on it. The scope of the Act extends to records held by a public body outside the State. Thus, the Act applies to records held by embassy officials abroad. There is provision for the application of the Act to records in the possession of independent contractors of public bodies where the records relate to the service being carried out by the contractor for the public body. In such a situation, the record is deemed to be held by the public body.[28]

(b) Records excluded from the scope of the Act

Certain records are excluded from the scope of the Act. These can be broken into seven main categories: records held by courts or tribunals; records concerning certain public office holders; non-official records of Oireachtas members; records relating to official documents of either House of the Oireachtas; records relating to activities of the Information Commissioner, the Ombudsman or the Comptroller and Auditor General; records relating to confidential information concerning criminal law enforcement; and records otherwise available.

(i) Records held by courts or tribunals

The first category of records excluded from the scope of the Act are those held

---

[27] Minister of State Fitzgerald made explicit reference to the use of the Act by non-citizens in the context of their dealings with the Department of Justice under the Aliens Act 1935 and the Aliens Orders 1946–1975: 149 *Seanad Debates* Col. 1296 (Committee Stage).
[28] s.6(9). See above, p. 52.

by the courts, tribunals to which the Tribunals of Inquiry (Evidence) Act 1921 is applied, and defence service tribunals where such records relate to the courts or such tribunals or to their proceedings. This exclusion is subject to two exceptions. The exceptions are in respect of: first, records which, although they relate to court or tribunal proceedings, were not created by the court or tribunal and their disclosure to the general public is not prohibited by the court or tribunal and, second, records relating to the general administration of the court or tribunal or their offices.[29] Records relating to general administration of a court or tribunal or of their offices could include, for example, records relating to the management of those bodies.

(ii) Records concerning certain public office holders

Records which are excluded because they concern public officeholders are those held or created by the Attorney General or the Office of Attorney General,[30] the Director of Public Prosecutions or the Office of the Director of Public Prosecutions,[31] and records relating to the President.[32] There is a savings provision in respect of records concerning the general administration of the Office of the Attorney General and the Office of the Director of Public Prosecutions. Documents relating to the President, on the other hand, are entirely excluded.

(iii) Non-official records of Oireachtas members

The third category of record excluded from the Act can be referred to as non-official records of Oireachtas members. Such records are excluded from the scope of the Act by section 46(1)(e) which excludes a record relating to any of the private papers (within the meaning of Article 15.10 of the Constitution) of a member of either House of the Oireachtas. Article 15.10 provides as follows:

> "Each House shall make its own rules and standing orders, with power to attach penalties for their infringement, and shall have power to ensure freedom of debate, to protect its official documents and the private papers of its members, and to protect itself and its members against any person or persons interfering with, molesting or attempting to corrupt its members in the exercise of their duties".

This provision does not define the private papers of Oireachtas members; it does not prohibit the disclosure of such papers. Nor are there any references to the private papers of Oireachtas members in the Standing Orders of the Dáil

---

[29] s.46(1)(a).
[30] s.46(1)(b).
[31] s.46(1)(b).
[32] s.46(1)(d).

or Seanad.[33] The motivation for excluding such papers from the scope of the Act was to ensure the compatibility of the Act with the separation of powers doctrine as set out in the Constitution. In particular, it was felt that the Executive could not introduce provisions which might interfere with the right of the Houses of the Oireachtas to make their own rules in relation to the private papers of Oireachtas members.[34]

This exclusion may be considered in conjunction with the definition of "exempt record" in section 2, which is stated to include records created for or held by an office holder and which relate to the functions and activities of: (i) the office holder as a member of the Oireachtas or a political party; or (ii) a political party. Officer holders are defined as a Minister of the Government or a Minister of State or a member of the Oireachtas who holds the Office of Attorney General.[35] While such records are, strictly speaking, exempt records for the purposes of the Act, they can be more conveniently dealt with here.

Taken together, the two provisions provide a high level of protection against disclosure of records of members of the Oireachtas. In the case of Ministers and the Attorney General, the protection afforded extends to their private papers as well as to records created for or held by them, and which relate to the functions and activities of political parties or to their own functions and activities as members of the Oireachtas or political parties.

The exclusion of the non-official records of Ministers from the scope of FOI legislation is common in other jurisdictions. The Australian Act, for example, applies to "official documents of a Minister", which is defined as: "documents in the possession of the Minister in his or her capacity as a Minister and being a document that relates to the affairs of an agency or Department of State".[36] Similarly, the New Zealand Act applies to information held by a Minister of the Crown "in his official capacity".[37] In one New Zealand case where the information sought had come to a Minister through membership of a caucus committee and had not been used in relation to her portfolio, the Ombudsman found the information was not held by the Minister in her official capacity as Minister of the Crown and so did not come within the scope of the Act.[38]

It may not always be easy to distinguish the private papers of Oireachtas members from their official records. Records received in a private capacity, for example complaints received from constituents, can later become official records where the complaint is followed up at an official level.

---

[33] Dáil Éireann, *Standing Orders Relative to Public Business* (1996); Seanad Éireann, *Standing Orders Relative to Public Business* (1995).
[34] 149 *Seanad Debates* Col. 1594 (Committee Stage).
[35] s.2(1).
[36] Freedom of Information Act 1982 (Cth), s.4.
[37] Official Information Act 1982, s.2.
[38] 9 CCNO 87 (G.F. Robertson).

(iv) Records relating to official documents of either House of the Oireachtas

The next excluded category of records is that of official documents of either or both of the Houses of the Oireachtas which are required by the rules or standing orders of either or both Houses to be treated as confidential. The current Standing Orders of the Dáil[39] and Seanad[40] do not require that any official documents be treated as confidential.

(v) Records relating to activities of the Information Commissioner, the Ombudsman, or the Comptroller and Auditor General

The fifth category of excluded documents covers records relating to certain activities of three specified holders of public offices. Excluded from the scope of the Act are records relating to a review or investigation carried out by the Information Commissioner under the FOI Act;[41] records relating to an investigation or examination carried out by the Ombudsman under the Ombudsman Act 1980;[42] and records relating to certain audits, inspections or examinations carried out by the Comptroller and Auditor General.[43] The exclusion from the scope of the Act of records relating to the activities of these office-holders does not apply where the record being sought was created before the commencement of the review, investigation audit, inspection, or examination.[44] Nor does it apply in respect of records relating to the general administration of the Office of the Information Commissioner, the Ombudsman, or the Comptroller and Auditor General.[45]

(vi) Records concerning confidential criminal law enforcement information

Records concerning confidential criminal law enforcement information are excluded from the scope of the Act. This exclusion covers information the disclosure of which could reasonably be expected to reveal or lead to the revelation of the identity of a person who has provided information in confidence in relation to the enforcement of the criminal law, or the source of such law enforcement information provided in confidence to a public body.[46] This exclusion complements the exemption from the scope of the Act of records con-

---

[39] Above, n. 33.
[40] Above, n. 33.
[41] s.46(1)(c)(i).
[42] s.46(1)(c)(iii).
[43] The audits, inspections, and examinations in respect of which records are excluded are those carried out by the Comptroller and Auditor General under the Comptroller and Auditor General Acts 1923 and 1993, the Exchequer and Audit Department Acts 1866 and 1921 and any other enactment: s.46(1)(c)(ii).
[44] s.46(1)(c)(iii)(I).
[45] s.46(1)(c)(iii)(II).
[46] s.46(1)(f).

cerning confidential civil law enforcement:[47] both are discussed in the section
of the book which deals with that exemption.[48] Suffice it to say at this point
that the exclusion from the scope of the Act of records of this type, as opposed
to their exemption, is a feature of FOI legislation which is peculiar to Ireland.

(vii) Records otherwise available

The exclusion from the scope of the Act of records otherwise available[49] refers specifically to records which by virtue of an enactment or otherwise are
available for inspection free of charge or upon payment, or copies of records
which again by virtue of an enactment or otherwise are available for purchase
or for removal free of charge. This exclusion precludes the use of the FOI Act
to obtain copies of records in circumstances where such records are available
for inspection. Thus an applicant can be denied a copy of a record where a
right of inspection exists under another enactment or has been provided voluntarily.

Records will not be excluded from the scope of the Act on the basis that
they are otherwise available merely because they contain information which
constitutes personal data to which the Data Protection Act 1988 applies.[50] It
will not, therefore, be open to a body to refuse access to a record solely on the
ground that it is a record to which the access provisions in the Data Protection
Act apply. It is less clear whether this exclusion would apply to information to
which the Access to Information on the Environment Regulations applies.[51] It
would appear that such information is not "available" since access to it depends on the submission of an application. This matter is discussed further
below at pp. 406–408.

4. Retrospection

The extent to which the Act provides a right of access to records created prior
to its commencement will be important in determining the impact of the Act,
particularly in the early years of its existence. Section 6 provides that, with
two exceptions, the Act only applies to records which originate after its commencement on April 21, 1998.[52] The first exception provides for the retrospective application of the Act where the granting of access to prior records is
necessary or expedient in order to understand records created after the com-

---

[47] s.23(1)(b).
[48] See below, pp. 187–202.
[49] s.46(2).
[50] s.46(3).
[51] See below, pp. 373–394 for a discussion of the relationship between the access rights in
the FOI Act 1997 and Data Protection Act 1988.
[52] An amendment aimed at extending the application of the Act to records created two
years before its commencement was moved by Deputy O'Donnell but was withdrawn at
Report Stage in the Dáil: 477 *Dáil Debates* Cols 757–759.

mencement of the Act.[53] The other exception arises in the case of records relating to personal information of that person.[54]

The Canadian and New Zealand Acts provide for full retrospective effect. The approach taken in Australia is closer to, if less restrictive than, that adopted in Ireland. There the Act applies to all records created up to five years prior to its introduction. Where records were created before that time, the Act applies fully retrospectively in the case of personal information or information relating to a person's business, commercial, or financial affairs[55] and in the case of records "access to which is reasonably necessary to enable a proper understanding" of records to which access has already been obtained.[56] The manner of interpretation of the phrase "is necessary or expedient in order to understand records created after such commencement" in section 6(5)(a) is a crucial factor in determining the scope for retrospective effect of the Act. A literal approach could limit its application to situations where, for example, the record created prior to the commencement of the Act explains a system of coding or notation, a knowledge of which is necessary to the understanding of a record created after the commencement of the Act. On the other hand, a broad approach could allow for the granting of access to records created prior to the commencement of the Act which are more broadly relevant to matters of current interest. For example, where a record created after the commencement of the Act raises questions about the past behaviour of an official or politician, an argument could be made that access to prior records concerning the activities of that person would be necessary to the understanding of the current record. The scope of the corresponding, although not identical, phrase "reasonably necessary to enable a proper understanding of a document" in section 12(2)(b) of the Australian Act was considered in *Re Waterford and Department of the Treasury*.[57] The majority (Hall D.P. and Mr B.E. Fleming) said:

> "As a matter of ordinary English, we think that to 'understand' a document means to comprehend what is written in the document or, in other words, to comprehend what it says. In that respect, we would agree with [counsel for the respondent] that 'understanding' connotes 'intelligibility'. However the expression 'proper understanding' conveys more, in our view than just intelligibility. It adds a qualitative element the sense of which is best conveyed as 'appropriate to the circumstances' (see *The Shorter English Dictionary*, vol 2 at 1687, col 3 – meaning III(i)). These circumstances include the subject matter with which the primary document deals, the nature and extent of the information that it seeks to convey and the extent to which it conveys, by its own terms, that intended information. To use one of [counsel's] examples (. . .), a memorandum which says 'I confirm the arrangements in my earlier memorandum' is, in our

---

[53] s.6(5)(a).
[54] s.6(5)(b). See below, pp. 269–280 for a discussion of the definition of personal information.
[55] s.12(2)(a).
[56] s.12(2)(b).
[57] (1983) 5 A.L.D. 193.

view, quite intelligible as it stands. A person of normal intelligence and literacy can understand what the document says. However, to have a 'proper understanding' or an understanding that is 'appropriate' to the circumstances, which is what s 12(2)(b) is concerned to ensure, one must know the contents of the earlier memorandum that it refers to. The information that is intended to be conveyed is incomplete without that reference.

. . .

The question posed by s 12(2)(b) is not whether the information conveyed by a document is as extensive as a person with an inquiring mind might like. We agree with [counsel] that there is a valid distinction between a proper understanding of what is written in a document and a proper understanding of the subject matter with which it deals.

Finally, and most importantly, it must be noted that the question posed by s 12(2)(b) is not, as was implicit in [the applicant's] submissions, whether access to other documents is reasonably necessary to enable him to have a proper understanding of the primary documents. The question, in our view, is an objective one to be evaluated against standards of normal intelligence and literacy. It cannot depend on the subjective requirements or standards of the person seeking access."[58]

The exceptions to the rule that the Act only applies to records created after its commencement do not apply in the case of requests by members of the staff of a public body for personnel records created more than three years prior to the commencement of the Act, provided these records are not being used or are not proposed to be used in a manner which will adversely affect the interests of the individual.[59] The aim of this proviso is to ensure that access to public servants' personnel files will generally only extend back three years "but if there is anything on the file which has obstructed his or her promotion, he or she can see the full file".[60] The Act also expressly provides that the granting of access to prior records should not be construed as applying the right of access to exempt records.[61]

Provision is made for the extension by regulation of the scope of the Act to records which came into being prior to its enactment.[62] Such regulations extending the application of the Act to prior records may only be introduced following consultation with the other members of the Government. Regulations extending the retrospective effect of the Act can take one of three forms. They can simply extend the application of the Act to cover a period not previously coming within the scope of the Act.[63] Regulations could, for example,

---

[58] Above, n. 57, at 201.
[59] s.6(6).
[60] 150 *Seanad Debates* Col. 92 (Report Stage), *per* Minister of State Fitzgerald.
[61] s.6(7).
[62] s.6(4).
[63] s.6(4)(a).

be introduced to extend the scope of the Act to records created 10 years before its commencement. Alternatively, regulations can be introduced to extend the application of the Act to cover records created prior to the commencement of the Act which relate to particular matters.[64] Regulations might, for example, be introduced to apply the Act to records of the Blood Transfusion Service Board whenever created. Finally the regulations can combine the two foregoing approaches by extending the scope of the Act by reference to both the period of application of the Act and the particular matters dealt with in the records.[65] So, for example, the scope of the Act could be extended to cover records of the Department of Education created up to 15 years prior to the commencement of the Act. It is clear from the Oireachtas debates that it was intended that the provisions allowing for the extension of the retrospective effect of the Act would be put into effect without delay. The sponsoring Minister of State said:

> "After the Act has been in operation for a while, the Minister for Finance will prescribe a rolling back so one can see records created perhaps four or five years before commencement. Then a further rolling back will reveal records created ten years before and so on until files come under the aegis of the Archives Act."[66]

5. Definition of record

The rights conferred by the Act apply with respect to "records". The Act contains a wide definition of "record", going far beyond the traditional concept of a record. This definition is clearly aimed at catching all possible manifestations of information with particular regard to those involving the newer technologies. "Record" is defined to include:

> "any memorandum, book, plan, map, drawing, diagram, pictorial or graphic work or other document, any photograph, film or recording (whether of sound or images or both), any form in which data (within the meaning of the Data Protection Act 1988) are held, any other form (including machine-readable form) or thing in which information is held or stored manually, mechanically or electronically, and anything that is a part or a copy, in any form, of any of the foregoing or is a combination of two or more of the foregoing".

The definition, broad as it is, does not extend to information *per se*. The meaning of "information" was given judicial consideration in *Cullen v. Wicklow County Manager*[67] in the context of the exercise of a right of access to information provided for under the County Management Act 1940. McCracken J. approved a passage from a New Zealand decision, *Commissioner of Police v.*

---

[64] s.6(4)(b).
[65] s.6(4)(c).
[66] 149 *Seanad Debates* Col. 1424 (Committee Stage), *per* Minister of State Fitzgerald.
[67] [1997] 1 I.L.R.M. 41.

Ombudsman, in which Jeffries J., dealing with the use of the word "information" in the New Zealand Official Information Act, said:

> "The most outstanding feature of the definition is that the word 'information' is used which dramatically broadens the scope of the whole Act. The stuff of which is held by departments, ministers, or organisations is not confined to the written word but embraces any knowledge, however gained or held, by the named bodies in their official capacities. The omission, undoubtedly deliberate, not to define the word 'information' serves to emphasise the intention of the legislature to place few limits on relevant knowledge."

McCracken J. went on to hold that the applicant was entitled, on request, to see all information in written form, as well as to be verbally informed in regard to any act, matter or thing appertaining to or concerning any business or transaction of the respondent council. It is clear that the scope of the FOI Act falls short of the range of the definition of information adopted by McCracken J. in *Cullen* since the former applies to "records" and not "information". In particular, the FOI Act does not apply to information in verbal form which has not been recorded or information of which someone has knowledge.

The definition of a record in the FOI Act extends to drafts of records as well as informal notes. It also covers copies of and parts of records. It applies to records in electronic form as well as to records in paper form. In particular, it would appear to cover information stored in electronic databases since it covers "any form in which data (within the meaning of the Data Protection Act 1988) are held". Data is defined in the Data Protection Act as "information in a form in which it can be processed". Electronic mail could come within the scope of the part of the definition of record which refers to "any other form (including machine readable form) or thing in which information is held or stored . . . electronically". The inclusion in the definition of record of anything that "is a combination of two or more of the [other forms of record referred to in the definition]" means that it applies to multimedia materials.

This definition is aimed at ensuring that the Act will not become obsolete as a result of developments in technology. As a relative latecomer to FOI legislation, the drafters of the Irish Act had the opportunity to embrace from the beginning an inclusive definition of record which clearly applies to records in electronic form. The issue of the application of FOI legislation to electronic records has given rise to litigation in other jurisdictions, in particular in the U.S., where the FOIA predated widespread use of computers for the storage of government information.[68] Amending legislation was introduced in the U.S.

---

[68] See, for example, *SDC Development Corp. v. Mathews*, 542 F.2d 1116 (9th Cir. 1976); *Long v. Internal Revenue Service*, 596 F.2d 362 (9th Cir. 1979); *Yeager v. Drug Enforcement Administration*, 678 F.2d 315 (D.C. Cir. 1982); *Dismukes v. Department of the Interior*, 603 F.Supp 760 (D.D.C. 1984). See generally: Bunker and Splichal *et al.*, "Access to Government-Held Information in the Computer Age: Applying Legal Doctrine to Emerging Technology" 20 *Fla. St. U. L. Rev.* 543 (1993); Grodsky, "The Freedom of

in 1996 to bring the FOIA up to date.[69] It amends the definition of record to ensure that all electronic records will be subject to disclosure.[70]

C. Making an Application

A request for access to records must be in writing, or such other form as may be determined by the Minister for Finance.[71] The Minister could, for example, allow for the submission of requests via e-mail.[72] The request must be expressed to be made under the Act. This requirement was justified on the grounds that it would help to clarify the status of the request *vis-à-vis* eligibility for the appeals procedure.[73] The request must contain sufficient particulars to enable the record to be identified by the taking of reasonable steps.[74] Failure to do so will justify a refusal of access.[75] Access cannot be refused on this ground unless the public body concerned has assisted or offered to assist the requester in meeting the requirement in relation to the provision of the particulars needed to identify the record.[76] Where the applicant requires that access to a record be provided in a particular form, for example, a copy of a document or a computer disk, the form or manner of access required must be specified.[77]

Public bodies are placed under a general duty to give reasonable assistance to a person making a request for access to a record under the Act.[78] There is also an express duty to give reasonable assistance to a person with a disability who is seeking a record under the Act so as to facilitate the exercise by that person of their rights under the Act.[79] The Act allows the Minister for Finance

---

Information Act in the Electronic Age: The Statute is Not User Friendly" 31 *Jurimetrics J.* 17 (1990); Sorokin, "The Computerization of Government Information: Does It Circumvent Public Access Under the Freedom of Information Act and the Depository Library Program?" (1991) 24 *Colum. J.L. & Soc. Probs.* 267.

[69] Electronic Freedom of Information Act Amendments Pub. L. No. 104-231, 110 Stat. 3048, 1-2 (1996). See MacDonald, "The Electronic Freedom of Information Act Amendments: A Minor Upgrade to Public Access Law" (1997) 23 *Rutgers Computer and Technology Law Journal* 357.

[70] s.552(f)(2).

[71] s.7(1).

[72] 149 *Seanad Debates* Col. 1429 (Committee Stage).

[73] 149 *Seanad Debates* Col. 1553 (Committee Stage).

[74] s.7(1)(b).

[75] s.10(1)(b).

[76] s.10(2).

[77] s.7(1)(c).

[78] s.6(2)(a). This duty was described by Minister of State Fitzgerald as "a statutory duty to help a person find their way through the maze": 149 *Seanad Debates* Col. 1295 (Committee Stage).

[79] s.6(2)(b).

to issue guidelines in relation to the exercise by people with disabilities of their rights under the Act. The Minister must consult with other Ministers as appropriate in drawing up such guidelines and public bodies will be obliged to have regard to them.[80]

The Act imposes a duty on public bodies to assist people who request information or access to a record from the public body otherwise than under the FOI Act. Where it is not possible to provide the information other than under the FOI Act, the public body must advise the person of their right of access under the FOI Act and must assist them in making the FOI request.[81] This requirement was introduced in response to concerns expressed by various senators with respect to the effect of the requirement that requests be expressed to be requests made under the Act.[82]

Requests made under the Act must be acknowledged as soon as may be but in any case no later than two weeks after their receipt by the public body. The notification of receipt of a request must include a summary of section 41, the effect of which is that failure on the part of a public body to give a decision in relation to an access request within the statutory period will be deemed to amount to a refusal. Such a deemed refusal would then open up the relevant avenues of appeal to the requester. Particulars of the rights of review under the Act, the procedure governing the exercise of those rights, and relevant time limits must also be included with the notification.[83]

The Act provides for transfer of requests in certain cases. Section 7(3) applies in cases where the record sought is not held by the public body to which the request is directed, but is, to the knowledge of the head of that public body, held by another public body or bodies. In such a situation, the request must be given to the head of the public body whose functions are, in the opinion of the head of the public body, most closely related to the subject matter of the record, or to the body that, in the opinion of the head, is otherwise most appropriate. Such a transfer must be effected not more than two weeks after receipt of the original request.[84]

Where an application is transferred to another body, the applicant must be so informed. The body to which an application is transferred will be treated as receiving the application on the date on which it received the transferred request and the body to whom the request was originally directed will be deemed not to have received the request.[85]

Section 7(4) provides for cases in which some, but not all, of the records sought are held by the public body to which the request is originally directed.

---

[80] s.6(3).
[81] s.7(7).
[82] 149 *Seanad Debates* Col. 1430 (Committee Stage).
[83] s.7(2).
[84] s.7(3).
[85] s.7(3).

The public body to whom the request is directed must inform the applicant the name of any other public body that, to his knowledge, holds any of the records.[86]

The head of the public body to which the request is originally directed will be deemed to have the knowledge referred to in sections 7(3) and 7(4) if, by taking reasonable steps, he or she could obtain that knowledge.[87] The aim of this provision, as explained by Minister of State Fitzgerald, is "to ensure that reasonable steps are taken by public bodies to obtain knowledge about on whose desk a request should lie".[88] This means that the public body will be required to take reasonable steps on receiving an access request to determine what other body holds the records requested. The Minister for Finance is obliged to issue guidelines in relation to the transfer of applications for access to records under section 7(3) and (4).[89]

D. Decisions on Access

1. Who makes the decision?

Section 8 provides for the making of decisions on requests for access to records by the head of the public body to whom the request has been directed. However, section 4 allows the head of a public body to delegate any of his or her functions under the Act to a member of the staff of the public body concerned. Therefore, the decision whether to grant access to a record may be taken by a member of the staff of the public body to which the request is directed rather than by the head of that public body.

2. Time limits for making access decisions

Decisions on requests for access to records must, in general, be given as soon as may be and, in any case, no later than four weeks after the day on which the request is received.[90] The requester must also be notified of the decision within the four-week time limit. Where the decision is in favour of granting access, the form and manner of such access must be determined and the applicant must be given notice of the determination regarding form and manner of access within that time period also. There is provision for extension of time limits for the consideration of access requests for a period not exceeding four weeks where meeting the original time limit is not reasonably possible in view of the large quantity of records requested, or in view of the number of prior requests relating to the requested records in respect of which decisions have

---

[86] s.7(4).
[87] s.7(6).
[88] 150 *Seanad Debates* Col. 96 (Report Stage).
[89] s.7(5).
[90] s.8(1).

not yet been made.[91] Where the time limit for making a decision has been extended, the applicant must be informed of the period of the extension and the reasons for it.[92] A decision to extend the time for consideration of a request can be appealed to the Information Commissioner.[93] The four-week time limit for the making of a decision in relation to a request can also be extended where payment of a deposit (in respect of a charge for access) has been requested. In such a case, the time limit will be extended by the length of time between the making of a request for payment of the deposit to the date of its receipt.[94] Provision is also made for the extension of the time limit in cases where the charging of a deposit is annulled on appeal[95] and where an amendment is made to a request which results in the elimination of a deposit.[96]

3. Nature of decisions

Decisions can be refused, deferred, or granted. In deciding whether to grant or refuse a request for access to a record, the head of a public body is required to disregard any reason the requester gives for the request as well as any belief or opinion of the head as to the requester's reasons for making the request.[97] This provision embodies one of the main principles of FOI legislation, namely that there should be a right of access to official records independent of the need to establish an interest in such a record.

(a) Refusal of access

The main substantive ground for refusing access to a record is that the record is exempt. An exempt record is defined in section 2(1) to include records exempt under the provisions of Part III of the Act[98] as well as those records excluded from the scope of the Act by virtue of section 46.[99] Also included in the definition of exempt records are records created for or held by an office holder and which relate to the functions and activities of the office holder as a member of the Oireachtas or of a political party or which relate to the functions and activities of a political party.[100]

A number of administrative reasons for refusing access to records are provided for in section 10 of the Act. This provision allows for refusal of access

---

[91] s.9(1)(b).
[92] s.9(2).
[93] s.34(1)(d). There is no provision for internal review of such decisions.
[94] s.47(12)(a).
[95] s.47(12)(b).
[96] s.47(12)(c).
[97] s.8(4).
[98] See Chaps 6–17.
[99] See above, pp. 56–60.
[100] See above, p. 58.

requests in six sets of circumstances. The first is in the case of the non-existence of the record, or failure to locate it after all reasonable steps have been
taken to ascertain its whereabouts. Failure to locate a record may lead to questions concerning the adequacy of the search undertaken for it. The issue of
adequacy of searches has been the subject of appeals under corresponding
overseas provisions. In the Australian federal case of *Re Anti-Fluoridation
Association of Victoria and Secretary, Department of Health* the Administrative Appeals Tribunal held that:

> "the adequacy of the search effort made to locate the document should be judged
> by having regard to what was reasonable in the circumstances. . . All that can be
> required of [the agency] is that it make adequate efforts to locate the document
> within its filing system or the filing system of any body, . . . for the administra-
> tion of which it is responsible."[101]

The issue of searching for records by electronic means is not directly referred
to in the Act. This is an issue which is addressed by the U.S. Electronic FOI
Act.[102] Section 552(a)(3) of that Act requires agencies in responding to access requests to make reasonable efforts to search for the records in electronic
form or format unless such efforts would "significantly interfere with the operation of the agency's automated information systems". "Search" in the context of an FOI request is defined in the Electronic FOI Act to mean:

> "to review, manually or by automated means, agency records for the purpose of
> locating those records which are responsive to a request."[103]

This provision places an obligation on public bodies to use electronic means
to retrieve the requested record even where this may require some form of
programming.

The second administrative ground for refusal of access provided for under
section 10 arises where the record is not sought with due particularity as required under section 7(1)(b).[104] As previously noted, this ground for refusal
cannot be availed of unless the public body concerned has assisted or offered
to assist the requester in meeting the requirements of that provision.[105] Section 10 also allows for a request for access to a record to be refused where the
head of the public body is of the opinion that the request is frivolous or vexatious.[106] The issue of the compatibility of that provision with section 8(4),
which provides that in deciding whether to grant or refuse a request the requester's reasons for making the request should be disregarded, was raised in

---

[101] (1985) 8 A.L.D. 163 at 167.
[102] Above, n. 69.
[103] s.552(a)(3).
[104] s.10(1)(b).
[105] s.10(2).
[106] s.10(1)(e).

the Dáil.[107] Requests can also be refused under section 10 where publication of the record is required by law and is intended to be effected not later than 12 weeks after the receipt of the request by the head[108] and where a fee or deposit payable under the Act has not been paid.[109] Since a fee would only become due subsequent to the making of a decision on access, this reference to unpaid fees clearly relates to any amounts outstanding in respect of previous requests.[110]

Section 10 also allows for refusal of a request in cases where a large volume of records have been requested. It provides that the request may be refused where, in the opinion of the head of a public body, granting the request would, by reason of the number or nature of the records concerned or the nature of the information concerned, require the retrieval and examination of such number of records or an examination of such kind of the records concerned as to cause a substantial and unreasonable interference with or disruption of the other work of the public body concerned.[111] Before refusing a request on this ground, public bodies are required to first assist or offer to assist the applicant to amend the request so that it does not offend in the manner described.[112] This provision is based on a similar one in the Australian federal FOI Act.[113] In its joint review of the operation of that Act, the Australian Law Reform Commission and Administrative Review Council stated that agencies should not be able to use this provision just because their information management systems are poorly organised and documents take an unusually long time to identify and retrieve.[114] Exercise of the power conferred on the Minister for Finance by section 15(5) to introduce regulations concerning the management and maintenance of records held by public bodies will help to ensure that section 10(1)(c) will not be abused. The level of disruption required in order to activate section 10(1)(c) is "substantial and unreasonable interference with or disruption of the other work of the public body concerned". In the Australian federal case of *Re SRB and SRC v. Department of Health, Housing, Local Government and Community Services*, the Administrative Appeals Tribunal held that, in a large department, the disruption to be taken into account was that caused to the relevant line area, not to the resources of the entire agency.[115]

---

[107] 476 *Dáil Debates* Col. 1071 (Second Stage), *per* Deputy O'Dea.
[108] s.10(1)(d).
[109] s.10(1)(f).
[110] s.10(1)(f).
[111] s.10(1)(c).
[112] s.10(2).
[113] Freedom of Information Act (Cth), s.24(1)(b).
[114] Australian Law Reform Commission, Report No. 77/Administrative Review Council, Report No. 40, *Open Government: a review of the federal Freedom of Information Act 1982* (Australian Government Publishing Service, Canberra, 1995), para. 7.14.
[115] (1993) 33 A.L.D. 171.

An appeal can be brought against a refusal of access to a record on any of the administrative grounds set out in section 10.[116]

In certain cases, the head of a public body is required to respond to requests by refusing to grant access to the requested record, while at the same time neither confirming nor denying its existence. The justification for providing for this type of response is that, in certain circumstances, revelation of the fact that a record exists may in itself amount to a disclosure of information which would be damaging. This reasoning was supported by Walsh J. in *Murphy v. Corporation of Dublin*[117] when, discussing disclosure of documents relating to the security of the State, he said:

> "in certain circumstances the very disclosure of the existence of a document, apart altogether from the question of its production, could in itself be a danger to the security of the State".[118]

The "neither confirm nor deny" response is provided for in four circumstances. Two of these circumstances arise in the context of class type exemptions: meetings of the government (section 19); and legal professional privilege (section 22(1)(a)). Where a request relates to a record to which either of these exemptions applies, and the head of the pubic body concerned is satisfied that disclosure of the existence or non-existence of the record would be contrary to the public interest, he or she shall refuse to grant the request and shall not disclose to the requester concerned whether the record exists. Assistance as to the meaning of "public interest" in this context may be obtained by referring to the general discussion of the public interest at pp. 93–115.

The other two cases in which the "neither confirm nor deny" response is to be given arise in the context of the harm-based exemptions: law enforcement and public safety (section 23); and security, defence and international relations (section 24). The head of the public body must be satisfied that disclosure of the existence or non-existence of the record would result in the occurrence of the harm which the exemption seeks to guard against. On being so satisfied, the head of the public body concerned is obliged to refuse to grant the request and to refrain from disclosing whether the record exists.

Similar provisions are to be found in overseas FOI Acts[119] with the provision in the Irish Act most closely resembling its New Zealand counterpart. The scope for using the New Zealand provision is, however, broader. It can, for example, be used in the context of prejudice to trade secrets, unreasonable prejudice to the information supplier's or subject's commercial position. It

---

[116] Internal review is provided for in s.14(1)(a), while review by the Information Commissioner is provided for in s.34(1)(a) and (b).

[117] [1972] I.R. 215.

[118] *ibid.* at 234.

[119] Australia: Freedom of Information Act 1982 (Cth), s.25; Canada: Access to Information Act (Canada), R.S.C., 1985, s.10(2); New Zealand: Official Information Act 1982, s.10.

was nonetheless suggested by the Danks Committee that it should be used rarely outside areas such as plans to deal with terrorists, police sources, and certain highly delicate international negotiations.[120]

(b) Deferral of access

The Act allows for the deferral of access to records in three situations: first, where the record concerned was prepared solely for the information of the Houses of the Oireachtas or of a committee of either House, and copies of the record are intended to be laid before either or both Houses or to be given to the committee, or to be otherwise published to the members of the Oireachtas or the committee within a reasonable period after receipt of the request;[121] and second, where the granting of access before a particular day to certain records excluded from the scope of the exemption relating to deliberations of public bodies would be contrary to the public interest.[122] The records in question are those containing factual or statistical information or analysis, efficiency reports concerning public bodies and technical or scientific reports.[123] Guidance as to the meaning of the "public interest" in this context may be gleaned from the discussion of the role of the public interest in the FOI Act at pp. 93–115. Finally, access can be deferred where the record is held by a Department of State and the responsible Minister considers that the record or its content is of such interest to the public generally that he or she intends to inform the Oireachtas of its contents or to otherwise publish it, not later than a week after the date on which it should have been made available in response to the access request.[124]

   The reason for deferral of access to a record and the period of time within which the record will be made available must be communicated to the applicant.[125] An appeal can be made brought against a deferral. Internal review is available only in the case of a deferral arising under section 11(1)(a), *i.e.* where the record was prepared for the Houses of the Oireachtas.[126] The Information Commissioner can review deferrals based on all the grounds provided for in section 11.[127]

---

[120] Committee on Official Information, *Towards Open Government* ("Danks Report"), Vol. 2 (Government Printer, Wellington, 1980), p. 68.

[121] s.11(1)(a).

[122] s.11(1)(b).

[123] These records are excluded from the scope of s.20 (deliberations of public bodies) by paragraphs (b), (d), and (e) respectively of s.20(2).

[124] s.11(1)(c).

[125] s.8(2)(e).

[126] s.14(1)(b).

[127] s.34(1).

(c) Granting of access

(i) *Time limits for provision of access*

Where a decision is made in favour of granting access, the record must be made available forthwith in cases in which no payment is due in respect of access.[128] The record must be kept available for a further four weeks. Where a charge is payable, the record must be made available no more than one week after receipt of the fee by the public body and it must be kept available for four weeks from the date of receipt of the fee or for eight weeks from the receipt of the notice of the decision under section 8(1), whichever is the earlier.[129] The effect of this provision is that a requester will have a total of eight weeks in which to pay a fee and once that period has expired the body will no longer be obliged to provide access to the record. So if the payment is made seven weeks after the issuing of a decision under section 8(1), the record need only be kept available for one further week.

(ii) *Forms of access*

Section 12(1) of the Act provides for the granting of access to records in a number of different forms. They consist of the provision of:

(a) a copy of the record;

(b) a transcript of the information concerned;

(c) a computer disk or other electronic device containing the information;

(d) a reasonable opportunity to inspect the record;

(e) in case the record is of sound or visual images, a reasonable opportunity to hear or view the record;

(f) in case the information is in shorthand or other code, the information in decodified form and in written form or such other form as may be determined;

(g) the information in such other form as may be determined; or

(h) the information in a combination of any two or more of the foregoing.

Section 12(1)(b) originally referred to the provision of "a statement in writing of the information concerned", but this was amended through the substitution of the word "transcript" for "statement in writing" on the grounds that:

> "if it were open to the public body to give access to the statement in writing there is a possibility that it may condense and edit the information".[130]

---

[128] s.8(3)(a).

[129] s.8(3)(b).

[130] 150 *Seanad Debates* Col. 97 (Report Stage), *per* Senator Dardis.

If the applicant requires access to be given in a particular form, that form must be specified at the time the request is made.[131] Requests for access to a record in a particular form must be complied with subject to a wide range of exceptions. The exceptions are as follows:

(1) where the head of the body to whom the request is directed is satisfied that it would be significantly more efficient to give the record in another form;

(2) where the giving of access in the form requested would be physically detrimental to the record;

(3) where the giving of access in the form requested would involve an infringement of copyright (other than copyright owned by the State, the Government or the public body concerned);

(4) where the giving of access in the form requested would conflict with a legal duty or obligation of a public body; and

(5) where the giving of access in the form requested would prejudice the interests protected in Part III (the exemption provisions) or section 46 (the records excluded from the scope of the Act).[132]

There is provision for the review of a decision to grant access in a form other than that specified in a request.[133]

Difficulties may arise with respect to records in electronic form. While section 12 clearly envisages the provision of access in electronic form, in so far as it provides for the provision to the requester of a computer disk or other electronic device containing the information,[134] this does not dispose of the issue. In particular, it does not provide for the granting of on-line or Internet access to records. Nor does it deal with the problem that some records may only be accessible through the use of software and so the provision of a disk containing the record may not be sufficient to enable the requester to access it. Where the public body owns the copyright in the software, it might be required to give the requester a copy of such software to enable him or her to access the information or it might be required to deal with the issue by providing access to a computer on its premises through which access to the record can be gained. If, however, the software required to access the information is proprietary software, the issue is not so clear. A public body might refuse to provide a copy of the software to the requester on the grounds that to do so would involve an infringement of the software developer's copyright. The issue of creation of electronic records in order to meet a FOI request is not

---

[131] s.7(1)(c).
[132] s.12(2).
[133] Internal review: s.14(1)(c); review by Information Commissioner: s.34(1)(a) and (b).
[134] s.12(1)(c).

addressed either. Nor is that of the obligations imposed on public bodies when access to a record would necessitate the carrying out of programming by the public body concerned. A related issue concerns the extent to which a public body is obliged to maintain information in a form which is accessible where the software originally used to access it has been superseded.

The U.S. Electronic Freedom of Information Act Amendments[135] attempts to come to terms with some of these issues. It establishes under section 552(a)(3) an obligation on the part of agencies to provide records in the form or format requested, but only to the extent that "the record is readily reproducible by the agency in that form or format". It also establishes a preference for dissemination of information on-line or via the Internet by requiring that agencies make records created after November 1, 1996 available within one year of creation by "computer telecommunications or, if computer telecommunications means have not been established by the agency, by other electronic means".[136] Critics of the Act argue that it does not go far enough. They point to the fact that agencies may decline requests for records in particular formats if they deem it is not technically feasible to comply and that, while agencies are encouraged to provide access on-line, where they have not implemented such access, they are permitted alternative means of electronic dissemination. As one writer has put it:

> "Congress seeks to nudge agencies in the general direction of electronic access, but it is leaving open the choice of roads, and to some degree, the rate of speed at which agencies must travel."[137]

The issues of the creation of electronic records or the carrying out of programming to meet a FOI request are not addressed in the Electronic FOI Act Amendments. Nonetheless, the U.S. amendments go some way towards addressing the need to update FOI legislation to take account of technological change. The Irish Act treats information in electronic form as directly equivalent to information in paper form and does not take account of changes in the handling of information which have resulted from developments in information technology.

(iii) Access to part of a record

The granting of access to part of a record is provided for in section 13. Section 13 applies where an applicant applies for access to a record which contains exempt information and the request would on that basis be subject to refusal. Where it is practicable to give access to a copy of the record from which the exempt information has been deleted, and the copy is not misleading, the public body is obliged to provide access accordingly. In such circumstances, the

---

[135] Above, n. 69.
[136] s.552(a)(2).
[137] MacDonald, *op. cit.* above, n. 69, p. 380.

requester must be informed that the record is such a copy and must also be informed of the nature of the exempt matter contained in the record. The foregoing information need not be supplied, however, where the provisions requiring non-disclosure of the existence or non-existence of the record apply.[138] Decisions granting access to part of a record under section 13 are subject to review.[139] The granting of access to part of a record is also provided for under section 6(10). This provision applies to records in the possession of a government contractor. Where access is requested to such a record and it contains matter unrelated to the service being provided by the contractor, the head of the public body concerned is obliged, if it is practicable so to do, to prepare a copy of so much of the record as does not consist of the unrelated matter and to provide access to that copy.

(iv) Access charges

The imposition of charges for accessing records is a common feature of FOI legislation. The magnitude of FOI charges is probably the most important factor in determining the level of usage of the legislation. As the joint report of the Australian Law Reform Commission and Administrative Review Council observed:

> "It is counterproductive for the Act to encourage involvement in government but effectively disqualify citizens from participating by imposing prohibitive charges."[140]

The Act allows for charges to be levied in respect of two of the activities associated with the provision of access to records by public bodies. The two activities in respect of which a charge may be imposed are the cost of search and retrieval of records and the cost of reproducing records. Public bodies do not, therefore, have the right to impose charges in respect of other activities associated with responding to FOI requests, such as the amount of time spent by officials in deciding whether any of the exemptions apply to the requested record or the cost of consulting with third parties where that is required. The search and retrieval charges are based on an hourly rate prescribed by regulation: the hourly rate was set at £16.50 by the Freedom of Information Act 1997 (Section 47(3)) Regulations 1998 (the "Fees Regulations").[141] The number of hours in respect of which the search and retrieval charge will be levied will be based on the time that was spent or ought to have been spent in carrying out the search and retrieval efficiently.[142] Provision is also made for the prescription of the cost of reproducing records. The cost of reproduction was pre-

---

[138] s.19(5); s.22(2); s.23(2); s.24(3).
[139] Internal review: s.14(1)(d); review by Information Commissioner: s.34(1)(a) and (b).
[140] *op. cit.* above, n. 114, para. 14.2.
[141] S.I. No. 139 of 1998.
[142] s.47(3)(a).

scribed by the Fees Regulations at 3p per sheet in relation to a photocopy, 40p in relation to computer diskettes, and £8 in relation to a CD-ROM. There is provision for the setting of a maximum fee by regulation in respect of the cost of reproducing records but not in respect of search and retrieval charges.[143]

Special arrangements apply to requests for access to records containing personal information. No charge may be levied for search and retrieval of records containing personal information unless the request relates to "a significant number of records".[144] There is provision for the waiver of reproduction charges in the case of records containing personal information where it would not be reasonable, having regard to the means of the requester and the nature of the record concerned, to include such costs in the calculation of fees.[145]

Further provision for waiver or reduction of fees of both kinds is provided for where, in the opinion of the head of the public body concerned, the information contained in the record would be of particular importance to the understanding of an issue of national importance.[146] No fee will be charged where the cost of collecting it, as well as other administrative costs incurred in relation thereto, would exceed the amount of the fee.[147]

Differential treatment of applicants in respect of charging is common in FOI legislation in other jurisdictions.[148] In particular, the waiver or reduction in charges for applicants for personal information on hardship grounds is a common feature of charging regimes overseas. Such treatment is arguably justifiable on grounds of fairness. It does, however, suggest that the motive of the applicant is a relevant consideration in the making of decisions concerning access to official information. This is at odds with the underlying philosophy of freedom of information, which is to provide people with access to official information without requiring that they show any interest or standing in order to obtain access to it. Differential treatment of applicants based on their standing is provided for under section 47(4)(b) which allows for the waiver of copying charges in respect of personal information where it would not be reasonable to levy such charges "having regard to the means of the requester and the nature of the record concerned". Not only does this provision seek to take the income of the applicant into account, but it also views as relevant the nature of the record concerned.

The Act makes provision for the payment of deposits in respect of charges for access to records.[149] Deposits are payable in cases where the cost of search

---

[143] s.47(3)(b).
[144] s.47(4)(a).
[145] s.47(4)(b).
[146] s.47(5).
[147] s.47(6).
[148] See, for example, Australia: Freedom of Information Act 1982 (Cth), ss.29(4), 30A; Canada: Access to Information Act (Canada), R.S.C., 1985, s.11(6).
[149] s.47(7).

and retrieval is likely to exceed £40 or such other amount as may stand determined by the Minister for Finance. The deposit, which will be deducted from the final fee, will be set at a minimum of 20 per cent of the estimated cost of search and retrieval. No maximum percentage is provided for in the Act, so in theory a deposit could be charged equal to the full estimated cost of search and retrieval. The Act provides that the process of search and retrieval will not commence until the deposit has been paid. Where a deposit is payable, it shall be requested within two weeks of receipt of the application for access. A request for a deposit must be accompanied by an estimate of the length of time that the process of searching and retrieving the record will occupy. The requester can require the head of the body to whom the request is directed to identify amendments to the request, if any, which would reduce or eliminate the deposit payable.[150] The head is obliged to implement such amendments as are determined by the requester. The four-week time limit for the making of a decision on access will be extended by the time between the making of a request for a deposit and its payment by applicant.[151] The making of an amendment to a request will similarly extend the time limit for the making of decisions on requests. In such circumstances, the four-week time limit will begin to run from the date the request is amended.[152] The deposit will be repaid where the request is refused or granted in part.

Appeals can be made against the imposition of fees or deposits.[153]

(v) Limitations on use of records accessed under the FOI Act

The FOI Act places certain limitations on the use to which records obtained under FOI may be put. In particular, section 45(5) provides that the grant of a request shall not be taken as constituting an authorisation or approval of acts which are defamatory, in breach of confidence, in breach of copyright, or in breach of the Performers' Protection Act 1968.[154]

4. Notification of decisions

Section 8 of the Act requires that the requester be notified of the decision taken with respect to a request for access to records. The notice of decision must set out the decision which has been arrived at. It must specify the day on which the decision was made[155] and must identify the person in the public

---

[150] s.47(8).

[151] s.47(12)(a).

[152] s.47(12)(c).

[153] Internal review: s.14(1)(g); review by the Information Commissioner (provided the fee or deposit exceeds £10 or such other prescribed amount): s.34(1)(c).

[154] The Performers' Protection Act 1968 (No. 19) gives performers the right to prevent fixation or broadcasting of their live performances.

[155] s.8(2)(a).

body concerned who is dealing with the request, unless the head of the public body reasonably believes that disclosure of such information could prejudice the safety or well-being of the person concerned.[156]

Where the decision is in favour of granting the request or of granting it in part, the notice must specify the day on which and the form and manner in which access will be offered, as well as the period during which the record will be kept available for access.[157] The fee for access, if any, must also be specified.[158]

In the case of a refusal of access, the Act requires that the reasons for the decision be given to the requester. Section 8(2)(d)(i) requires that where a request for access to a record is refused, the notice must set out the reasons for refusal. Section 8(2)(d)(ii) provides that, aside from certain exceptions, the notice must also state the provision of the Act pursuant to which the request is refused and must reveal the following:

(1) findings on material issues relevant to the decision; and

(2) particulars of matters relating to the public interest which have been taken into account for the purposes of the decision.

The exceptions arise in respect of refusals of access based on the fact that disclosure of the existence or non-existence of a record would be contrary to the public interest or would damage particular interests. Such refusals are provided for in respect of records concerning meetings of the government,[159] legal professional privilege,[160] law enforcement and public safety,[161] and defence, security and international relations.[162] The basis for these exceptions is that if public bodies were required to disclose the reasons underlying decisions refusing access based on the damage which would result from the disclosure of the existence or non-existence of the record concerned, this would defeat the purpose of the provisions regarding non-disclosure of the existence or non-existence of records.

Guidance as to the requirements relating to the giving of reasons can be obtained from the Explanatory Guidelines of the Australian Administrative Review Council (ARC). These guidelines, which were developed in the context of the establishment of a statutory right to reasons for administrative decisions, explain the requirement to give reasons in the following way:

"Every decision should be capable of a logical explanation. A statement of rea-

---

[156] s.8(2)(b).
[157] s.8(2)(c)(i).
[158] s.8(2)(c)(ii).
[159] s.19.
[160] s.22(1)(a).
[161] s.23.
[162] s.24.

sons should contain all the steps of reasoning linking the facts to an ultimate decision which are necessary for a person affected to understand how the decision was reached. . .

The criteria relevant to the decision, the weight to be attached to each criterion, and the conclusion reached on the criteria should be stated. Clarity of explanation may make it desirable in some cases to state separately the conclusion on each criterion.

The reasoning should identify any element of policy or guideline (whether in the form of a written statement or otherwise and whether emanating from the government or internal to the decision-making authority) or departmental practice which is part of the justification of the decision made.

Decision-makers frequently act upon recommendations, reports, and results of investigations carried out by subordinate officers or appropriately qualified experts. Where these recommendations, et cetera, are considered in making a decision, the statement of reasons should incorporate the recommendation, et cetera, as well as the facts (and a reference to the evidence or other materials on which they are based) and the reasons leading thereto. It is insufficient merely to state that the decision-maker has relied upon the advice of a named person."[163]

Similarly the ARC's explanation of the meaning of "findings on material issues" is useful in determining the extent of the obligations imposed by section 8(2)(d)(ii). It states:

"The matter to be included in the statement in this respect may be described as those matters of fact which were taken into account in making the decision. If a fact is relied upon, it must be set out. If a matter is considered then the findings of fact in relation to it must be set out. In so far as the statement of reasons does not set out findings of fact on a matter, it may be inferred that those facts were considered to be immaterial; if a court or Tribunal finds that those facts are material; it follows that the decision-maker has erred in law.

Sometimes a material fact is established directly by the evidence or other material. Where, however, a material fact is inferred from other facts which are in turn established by evidence or other material, it may be necessary to state those facts and the process of inference in order to provide adequate information on the way in which the decision was reached.

Findings of fact are distinguishable from subjective judgments or opinions. Where a subjective judgment or opinion is based on facts, it is desirable that those underlying facts should be set out as well as the judgment or opinion formed on the basis of them."[164]

The notice of reasons must also contain particulars of matters relating to the public interest which have been taken into account for the purposes of the decision. Public interest tests are an important element in a number of the

---

[163] Administrative Review Council, *Statements of Reasons: An Explanatory Memorandum* (1979), quoted in Eagles, Taggart, and Liddell, *Freedom of Information in New Zealand* (Oxford University Press, Auckland, 1992), p. 55.
[164] *ibid.*, p. 54.

exemption provisions.[165] The notice must set out clearly each of the issues relating to public interest which were taken into account by the decision-maker in arriving at his or her decision.

The obligation to provide a notice of reasons is subject to the requirement that a notice of decision is not required to contain any matter that is of such a nature that its inclusion in a record of a public body would cause that record to be an exempt record.[166] The aim of this provision is to ensure that a public body refusing access to a record will not be required to provide information which might reveal the contents of the record.

The requirement that a notice of reasons be given under section 8(2)(d) applies only in respect of a refusal of a request for access. Separate provision is, however, made for the giving of reasons in the case of a deferral of access to a record[167] and in the case of an extension of the period for consideration of access requests.[168] In the case of other decisions made at first instance under the FOI Act, it would appear that the giving of reasons is not necessary. In particular, there would appear to be no statutory right to a statement of reasons for decisions made at first instance relating to:

(1) a grant of access in a form other than that requested;

(2) a refusal to amend a record containing personal information;

(3) a decision to grant access notwithstanding third party objections under the section 29 consultation mechanism; or

(4) a decision refusing to reduce or waive, in whole or in part, a fee or deposit under section 47(5).

Whilst none of these situations involve a refusal of access to records, they are nonetheless significant decisions in the context of the exercise of the access rights conferred by the FOI Act. Given the emphasis placed by the Act on the giving of reasons for administrative decisions, it is surprising to find that reasons need not be given for the making of these particular decisions.

---

[165] See below, pp. 93–115.
[166] s.8(5).
[167] s.8(2)(e).
[168] s.9(2).

CHAPTER 5

THE EXEMPTIONS: GENERAL ISSUES

THE EXEMPTIONS: GENERAL ISSUES

The exemptions constitute the core provisions of the Freedom of Information (FOI) Act. They allow for the making of exemptions to the right of access to records guaranteed under section 6 of the Act. This chapter explores a number of issues relating to their application. The matters addressed are: classification of the exemption provisions; the burden of proof in establishing that a record is exempt; the public interest tests relied upon in the exemption provisions; and the ministerial certificate mechanism.

A. Classification

Twelve grounds of exemption are provided for in Part III of the Act. They are in respect of:

(1) meetings of the government (section 19);
(2) deliberations of public bodies (section 20);
(3) functions and negotiations of public bodies (section 21);
(4) parliamentary, court and certain other matters (section 22);
(5) law enforcement and public safety (section 23);
(6) security, defence, and international relations (section 24);
(7) information obtained in confidence (section 26);
(8) commercially sensitive information (section 27);
(9) personal information (section 28);
(10) research and natural resources (section 30);
(11) financial and economic interests of the State and public bodies (section 31);
(12) enactments relating to non-disclosure of records (section 32).

Each of the exemptions limits the scope of the Act in order to protect other interests which are treated, in certain circumstances, as superior to the interest in freedom of information. There is, however, a considerable degree of variation in the manner in which the exemptions are expressed. These differences can be classified under the following headings:

1. Mandatory versus permissive exemptions

A number of the exemptions are mandatory. This means that the head of a public body who receives a request for records falling into one of those categories *must* refuse access to them. Mandatory exemptions are provided for in respect of the following: parliamentary, court, and certain other matters (section 22); information obtained in confidence (section 26); commercially sensitive information (section 27); personal information (section 28); and enactments relating to non-disclosure of records (section 32). Section 19, which concerns meetings of the government, contains a mixture of mandatory and discretionary provisions. The application of the other exemptions is not mandatory, which means that it remains open to the head of a public body to exercise his or her discretion in favour of disclosure, even though the record sought falls into one of the exempt categories.

The FOI Act provides immunity from legal proceedings in respect of the granting of access to records under its terms.[1] One question which arises is whether such immunity extends to discretionary disclosures. It would appear that such disclosures enjoy the same immunity from legal proceedings as is available in respect of any other grants of access to records under the FOI Act. This is because the section which provides immunity from legal proceedings (section 45(1)) applies where the provision of access is "required or authorised" by the Act. The exercise by a head of a public body of his or her discretion to grant access to a record would clearly be "authorised" by the Act. Disclosures under the FOI Act are protected against prosecution under the Official Secrets Act by section 48(1) of the FOI Act. Again, the disclosure of a record through the exercise of discretion would appear to qualify for this protection. This is because section 48(1) applies to a person who is or who reasonably believes that he or she is authorised by the FOI Act to communicate official information to another person. A person who discloses information in pursuance of a discretion conferred by the FOI Act would clearly be justified in believing that he or she is "authorised" to do so.

2. Class based exemptions versus exemptions which are subject to a harm test

Some exemptions are expressed in terms of exempting records by virtue of the class or category of records to which they belong, while others provide for the exemption of records only where their disclosure would be likely to harm a particular interest. An example of a class type exemption can be found in section 27, the commercially sensitive information exemption. Section 27 exempts from disclosure "trade secrets of a person other than the requester".[2] Once a record is shown to contain information which falls into this category, it becomes subject to the exemption provision. Other class type exemptions are

---

[1] See below, pp. 368–370.
[2] s.27(1)(a).

those concerning records relating to meetings of the government (section 19); parliamentary, court, and certain other matters (section 22); personal information (section 28); and enactments relating to non-disclosure of records (section 32). Harm-based exemptions, on the other hand, are those under which a record may only be exempted if its disclosure would result in the occurrence of a specified type of harm. For example, the exemption relating to natural resources (section 30(1)(b)) applies to records, the disclosure of which "could reasonably be expected to prejudice the well-being of a cultural, heritage or natural resource or a species or the habitat of a species, of flora or fauna".

While the majority of the exemption provisions include some form of harm test, the nature of injury required varies between the exemptions. Some exemptions refer to the harm in terms of prejudice, while in others the injury is phrased in terms of the occurrence of adverse effects, or impairment, or exposure to serious disadvantage. There are, in addition, variations in the proof of injury provided for. For example, references to "prejudice" range from "could reasonably be expected to prejudice", through "would be likely to prejudice", to plain "could prejudice". There are also variations in the degree of injury provided for. The phrase "adversely effect" appears in various states of intensity ranging from mere "adversely affect", through "serious adverse effects", to "significant adverse effects". There exists a hierarchy of exemptions in that some exemptions incorporate forms of harm test which are relatively easy to satisfy, while others are more difficult to fulfil. For example, a record will be exempt if its disclosure could reasonably be expected to "affect adversely" defence, security and international relations,[3] while records concerning functions and negotiations of public bodies will only be exempt where disclosure of the records applied for could reasonably be expected to "have a significant adverse effect" on the management functions of a public body.[4]

3. Exemptions which are conclusive versus exemptions which are subject to public interest

In some cases, the application of an exemption provision to a particular record establishes conclusively that the record is exempt from access under the Act. Roughly half of the exemptions, however, incorporate a public interest test. This means that even if the requested record falls within the scope of the exemption, the head of the public body concerned may nonetheless release it where it is in the public interest so to do.

Two main forms of public interest test are used in the Act. The first is found in section 20 and concerns deliberations of public bodies. Section 20 prescribes that a record is exempt where:

---

[3] s.24(1).
[4] s.21(1)(b).

(a) it would disclose material relating to the deliberative processes of a public body; and

(b) its disclosure would, in opinion of the head of the public body, be contrary to the public interest.

These requirements are cumulative.

The second form of public interest test, and the most common, consists of a separate subsection which follows on after the outlining of circumstances in which a record will be exempt. It provides that the exemption shall not apply where:

> "in the opinion of the head [of the public body] concerned, the public interest would, on balance, be better served by granting than by refusing to grant the request".

The following exemptions are subject to such a test: functions and negotiations of public bodies (section 21); information obtained in confidence (section 26); commercially sensitive information (section 27); research and natural resources (section 30); and financial and economic interests of the State and public bodies (section 31). A public interest test of this type partially restricts the operation of the exemption concerning law enforcement and public safety (section 23(3)), that is to say, while the withholding of the bulk of records relating to law enforcement and public safety is not subject to a public interest test, certain types of law enforcement and public safety records are subject to the operation of such a test.[5]

The personal information exemption (section 28) contains a public interest test which amounts to a variation on the second form of test described. It provides that section 28 shall not apply where the public interest that the request should be granted "outweighs" the public interest that the right to privacy of the individual to whom the information relates should be upheld.[6] This test acknowledges the existence of a public interest in the maintenance of the individual's rights to privacy, while at the same time indicating that circumstances may arise where that right will be outweighed by the public interest in disclosure. The operation of public interest tests in the FOI Act is discussed in greater detail at pp. 93–115 below.

4. Exemptions which impose consultation obligations versus exemptions which can be applied without consultation

Four of the exemption provisions oblige the head of a public body in certain circumstances to consult with third parties before deciding whether to disclose records. Two forms of consultation mechanism are provided for. Section

---

[5] s.23(3).
[6] s.28(5)(a).

29 aims to give individuals and businesses an input into the decision-making process relating to the disclosure of records which relate to them or which were supplied by them to public bodies. It applies in respect of requests concerning material obtained in confidence (section 26); commercially sensitive information (section 27); and personal information (section 28). A separate consultation procedure is provided for in respect of records relating to matters before government (section 19). It is aimed at ensuring that previous governments have an input into decisions concerning disclosure of records relating to their period in office. Neither form of consultation gives the person or body being consulted a power of veto over disclosure of information.

(a) The section 29 consultation mechanism

Section 29 comes into play where a record falls within the scope of one of three specified exemptions (information obtained in confidence, commercially sensitive information and personal information) but the head of a public body is, nonetheless, of the opinion that the public interest would, on balance, be better served by granting than by refusing to grant the request for access. In the case of personal information, the consultation requirement also applies in a second situation, namely where a decision is taken to grant access to an exempt record on the basis that the grant of the request would benefit the individual to whom the information relates.[7]

The consultation procedures set out in section 29 require the head of the public body, within two weeks of receiving a request for access to a record to which section 29 applies, to notify certain persons that the request falls to be granted in the public interest.[8] The persons who must be notified are: in the case of requests to which section 27(3) and section 28(5) apply, the person to whom the information relates; and, in the case of requests to which section 26(3) applies, the person who gave the information to the public body and, if the head of the public body considers it appropriate, the person to whom the information relates. The notification must be in writing or in such other form as may be determined by the Minister for Finance.[9] The person who is so notified then has three weeks within which to make submissions in relation to the request.[10] The time limit for the making of a decision under section 29 and for the notification of that decision is not later than two weeks after the expiration of the three-week time limit for the making of submissions or the receipt of submissions, whichever is earlier. This means that the outcome of the consultation process must be decided within two weeks of the receipt of submissions. If no submissions are received, the decision can be made within two

---

[7] s.28(5)(b).
[8] s.29(2).
[9] s.29(2).
[10] s.29(3).

weeks of the expiry of the three-week deadline for the making of submissions. The head is obliged to consider such submissions before deciding whether to grant the request.[11]

If the head cannot comply with the consultation requirements, despite having taken all reasonable steps to do so, he or she can go ahead with the decision to grant or refuse the request, provided that the Information Commissioner consents to the non-compliance.[12] Where the Commissioner does not consent to such non-compliance, he or she must direct the head as to what steps should be taken for the purpose of complying with the consultation obligation. If, having taken those steps, the head is still unable to comply with the consultation requirement, he or she must go ahead and make the decision whether to grant or refuse the request.[13] Where the head of the public body decides to go ahead with disclosure, the third party must be informed of the right to appeal that decision.[14] The section 29 consultation mechanism is discussed in greater detail below at pp. 241–243.

(b) Consultation under section 19

Section 19 includes a provision to the effect that certain categories of records relating to matters before government[15] shall not be released until the head of the public body has, in so far as it is practicable to do so, consulted with the leader of each political party to which a member of the government belonged (and with any member of that government who was not a member of a political party) that made any decision to which the record relates.[16] This is an unusual provision which does not have any overseas equivalents. The section 19 consultation mechanism is discussed in greater detail below at pp. 138–139.

5.   Exemptions which are expressed in exhaustive terms versus exemptions which are open-ended

A number of exemptions contain detailed and exhaustive descriptions of the records to which they relate. Section 22, which concerns parliamentary, court and certain other matters, for example, provides that the exemption applies to the following list of records:

(1) records which would be exempt from production in a court on the grounds of legal professional privilege;

---

[11] s.29(3)(a).
[12] s.29(5).
[13] s.29(6).
[14] s.29(3)(c).
[15] The consultation requirement applies only in respect of records referred to in s.19(1)(a) and (b). It does not apply in respect of the records referred to in s.19(1)(c).
[16] s.19(4).

(2) records the disclosure of which would constitute contempt of court;

(3) records consisting of the private papers of representatives in the European Parliament or a member of a local authority or a health board; and

(4) opinions, advice, recommendations, or the results of consultations considered by the Houses of the Oireachtas or committees of the Houses of the Oireachtas.

This is an exhaustive list of the categories of records which are covered by the exemption and the scope of section 22 is therefore limited to information which falls within these specified categories. Section 31, on the other hand, which is concerned with the protection of the financial and economic interests of the state and of public bodies, adopts an inclusive and open-ended approach to determining the scope of the exemption. It provides a long list of categories of information which are covered by the exemption, but states that the application of the exemption to those categories of records is "without prejudice to the generality otherwise"[17] of the exemption provision. Thus, there is scope for the application of this exemption to categories of information not expressly referred to in section 31.

6. Exemptions which are self-contained versus exemptions which incorporate existing legal concepts

Most of the exemptions stand alone, that is, their application does not rely on the interpretation of existing legal concepts. There are, however, exceptions to this general rule. For example, section 22, which deals with parliamentary, court and certain matters, incorporates in its terms such existing legal concepts as legal professional privilege and contempt of court, while section 26 exempts disclosures which would constitute a breach of a duty of confidence. The existing legal concept of trade secret is incorporated in the text of section 27 (commercially sensitive information) and section 31 (financial and economic interests of the State and public bodies). Such legal concepts are commonly incorporated in the exemption provisions of overseas FOI legislation. One problem associated with the incorporation of existing legal concepts in the exemption provisions is the possibility that reliance on such concepts could stand in the way of the development of a pro-disclosure jurisprudence under the Act. This concern is based on the fact that such concepts have developed in an environment which is not attuned to the objects of FOI legislation. The incorporation of existing legal concepts into the exemptions can also introduce uncertainty. This can occur where the concept referred to is ill-defined in Irish law. For example, the concept of trade secret, which is relied upon in sections 27 and 31, is not well-established in this jurisdiction.

---

[17] s.31(1).

B. Burden of Proof

Applicants for access to records may not be fully aware of the exact contents of the records they seek. As a result, they may find it difficult to establish that the records sought do not fall into the exempt categories. It is, therefore, not surprising that the Act places the burden of proof on the body or person opposing disclosure, in the context of a review by the Information Commissioner. Specifically, section 34(12) provides that a decision to refuse to grant a request shall be presumed not to have been justified, unless the head of the public body concerned shows to the satisfaction of the Information Commissioner that the decision was justified. Where the review concerns an objection against disclosure by a third party, the decision to grant access will be presumed to have been justified, unless the third party shows to the satisfaction of the Commissioner that it was not so justified.[18] This is in keeping with the approach of Walsh J. in *Murphy v. Corporation of Dublin*,[19] a case concerning executive privilege, where it was held that:

> "the burden of satisfying the court that a particular document ought not to be produced lies upon the party, or person, who makes such a claim".[20]

Different standards of proof are found in the harm tests encountered in the various exemption provisions and, indeed, different standards can be found to apply in respect of different limbs of the same exemption. The standards range from a requirement that disclosure of the record "would be likely" to result in the injury described in the exemption, through "could reasonably be expected", to "could". The "could reasonably be expected to" standard is the most commonly used. It is found in section 21 (functions and negotiations of public bodies), section 23 (law enforcement and public safety), section 24 (security, defence and international relations), section 27(1)(b) (commercially sensitive information), section 30(1)(b) (natural resources), and section 31 (financial and economic interests of the State and public bodies). The "would be likely to" standard appears in section 26(1)(a) (information obtained in confidence) and section 30(1)(a) (research), while the "could [prejudice]" standard makes its sole appearance in section 27(1)(c) (commercially sensitive information).

Similarly, varied standards are found in the Australian and Canadian legislation and in each of these jurisdictions the meaning of "could reasonably be expected to" has been subjected to judicial scrutiny. In the Canadian case of *Canada Packers v. Minister of Agriculture*[21] the Federal Court of Appeal rejected the trial judge's direct causation test, which required evidence of harm to "be detailed, convincing and describe a direct causation between disclosure

---

[18] s.34(12)(a).
[19] [1972] I.R. 215.
[20] *ibid.* at 235.
[21] (1988) 53 D.L.R. (4th) 246; 26 C.P.R. (3d) 407.

and harm". The test was rejected on the grounds that it would tend to limit the scope of the exemption in that it would preclude consideration of any indirect harm which might result from disclosure, for example, harm caused by media reporting of the information disclosed. The appeal judge also refused to equate the phrase "could reasonably be expected to" with the test of reasonable foresight in the law of negligence, on the grounds that if the decision in *Wagon Mound (No. 2)*[22] was to be interpreted as opening the door to liability for the mere possibility of foreseeable damage, that set a standard too low to apply to the Canadian Access to Information Act. Eventually, the appeal court came down in favour of a "reasonable expectation of probable harm" test.[23] That interpretation has been confirmed in subsequent Canadian decisions.[24] In Australia, the phrase "could reasonably be expected to" has also come under scrutiny. In *Re Cockcroft and Attorney General's Department*,[25] the majority of the full Federal Court (Beaumont J. and Bowen J.) expressly overturned the Administrative Appeals Tribunal's (A.A.T.'s) interpretation of the phrase, which was that an assessment of what was more probable than not was what was called for. The majority said that it was undesirable to consider the operation of the "could reasonably be expected to" standard in terms of probabilities or possibilities or the like and added:

> "To construe s.43(1)(c)(ii) as depending in its application upon the occurrence of certain events in terms of any specific degree of likelihood or probability is... to place an unwarranted gloss upon the relatively plain words of the Act. It is preferable to confine the inquiry to whether the expectation claimed was reasonably based."[26]

Their Honours held that the words were intended to receive their ordinary meaning and to require a judgment to be made "as to whether it is reasonable as distinct from something that is irrational, absurd or ridiculous"[27] to expect the harm referred to in the provision to occur.

However, Sheppard J., who delivered the minority judgment, appeared to adopt a higher standard of proof when he held that a person will not be justified in claiming exemption unless:

> "at the time the decision is made, he has real and substantial grounds for thinking that the production of the document could prejudice that supply. But, stringent though that test may be, it does not go so far as to require the decision-maker

---

[22] [1967] 1 A.C. 617; [1966] 2 All E.R. 709.

[23] *Canada Packers v. Minister of Agriculture*, above, n. 21, at 255.

[24] *Saint John Shipbuilding v. Canada (Minister of Supply and Services)* (1990) 67 D.L.R. (4th) 315 (F.C.A.) *aff'g* (1989) 24 F.T.R. 32; *Canada (Information Commissioner) v. Canada (Prime Minister)* (1993) 57 F.T.R. 180; 49 C.P.R. (3d) 79.

[25] (1986) 64 A.L.R. 97.

[26] *ibid.* at 106.

[27] *ibid.*

to be satisfied upon a balance of probabilities that the production of the document will in fact prejudice the future supply of information."[28]

In *Searle Australia Pty Ltd v. Public Interest Advocacy Centre & Anor*[29] the
Federal Court of Australia rejected a suggestion that a difference of approach
was evident in the decisions in *Cockcroft* of Bowen and Beaumont JJ. on the
one hand and Sheppard J. on the other. In particular, the court rejected counsel's submission that the majority in *Cockcroft* had suggested that it was sufficient that there be a possibility not irrational, absurd or ridiculous that the
specified consequence would occur. The court found instead that "their Honours had specifically rejected that approach, saying that the words 'could reasonably be expected' meant what they said".[30] The court went on to say that
"the practical application of their Honours' view will not necessarily lead to a
result different from that proposed by Sheppard J.".[31]

The Queensland Information Commissioner has provided the following
useful summary of the position at federal level in Australia:

> "The words call for the decision-maker... to discriminate between unreason-
> able expectation and reasonable expectations, between what is merely possible
> (e.g. merely speculative/conjectural expectations) and expectations which are
> reasonably based, ie, expectations for the occurrence of which real and substan-
> tial grounds exist."[32]

Thus, in both Canada and Australia it appears that a possibility of the specified harm occurring will not suffice, but neither is it necessary to show evidence of direct causation between disclosure and harm. Nor does it appear
necessary in either jurisdiction to show that the occurrence of the harm is
more probable than not. In both jurisdictions, the emphasis is on the reasonableness of the expectation of harm arising out of the disclosure.

Another standard of proof utilised in the harm tests is that of "would be
likely to" prejudice. This sets a standard higher than that of "could reasonably
be expected to" prejudice in that it appears to require evidence that the occurrence of the harm be more probable than not. In New Zealand, however, the
interpretation of the "would be likely to prejudice" standard to mean "more
likely than not" was rejected in favour of the lower threshold of "a distinct or
significant possibility".[33] It appears that on the basis of that decision, the "would
be likely to" prejudice test might be satisfied where there is a significant possibility of the harm occurring.

Finally, the "could prejudice" standard must be considered. This sets a

---

[28] *Re Cockcroft and Attorney General's Department*, above, n. 25, at 112.
[29] (1992) 108 A.L.R. 163.
[30] *ibid.* at 176.
[31] *ibid.*
[32] *Re B. and Brisbane North Regional Health Authority* (1994) 1 Q.A.R. 279 at 340–341.
[33] *Commissioner of Police v. Ombudsman* [1988] 1 N.Z.L.R. 385 at 404.

lower standard of proof than that required under the "could reasonably be expected to" prejudice test. In the Australian case of *News Corporation Ltd v. National Companies and Securities Commission*, Woodward J. drew a distinction between the two phrases "would or could reasonably be expected to prejudice" and "would or might prejudice" in the following terms:

> "I think that the words 'would or could reasonably be expected to... prejudice' mean more than 'would or might prejudice'. A reasonable expectation of an event requires more than a possible risk or chance of the event occurring." [34]

It is submitted that the "might prejudice" referred to by Woodward J. is similar to the "could prejudice" standard set out in section 27(1)(c) in that a mere possible risk of the harm occurring should suffice.

Issues relating to the burden of proof in the context of public interest tests are discussed in the next section.

C. The Public Interest

As previously explained,[35] two main forms of public interest test are to be found in the Act. The first, which is found in section 20, prescribes that a record is exempt where:

(a) it would disclose material relating to the deliberative processes of a public body; *and*

(b) its disclosure would, in opinion of the head of the public body, be contrary to the public interest.

The second, which is to be found in sections 21, 23, 26, 27, 28, 30, and 31 is in the form of a separate subsection which follows the outlining of circumstances in which a record will be exempt. It provides that the exemption shall not apply where "in the opinion of the head of the public body concerned, the public interest would, on balance, be better served by granting than by refusing to grant the request".[36]

1. The two tests compared

In order to satisfy the first test, which is found only in section 20 (the exemption relating to deliberations of public bodies), the head of a public body con-

---

[34] (1984) 57 A.L.R. 550 at 561.

[35] See above, pp. 85–86.

[36] The public interest test found in s.28 comprises a variation on this. It provides that s.28 shall not apply where the public interest that the request should be granted "outweighs" the public interest that the right to privacy of the individual to whom the information relates should be upheld.

cerned must be of the opinion that disclosure of the record sought would be contrary to the public interest. This requirement is essentially a negative one, in that the head must conclude that disclosure would be *against* the public interest before he or she may treat the record as exempt. It arguably entails a presumption in favour of disclosure.

The corresponding Australian federal exemption (section 36) is subject to a similar public interest test. The federal A.A.T. has held that this test requires a public body to show quite independently of the matters referred to in the first part of the exemption (section 36(1)(a)) that disclosure would be contrary to the public interest. The Tribunal said:

> "[I]n other words, the respondent is not entitled merely to rely on the matters enumerated in s.36(1)(a) in support of a claim that disclosure would be contrary to the public interest – other grounds must be shown."[37]

If a similar analysis were to be adopted here, it would mean that a public body could not simply rely on the fact that a record contained matter relating to the deliberative processes of the public body in order to ground a decision that disclosure would be contrary to the public interest. Other public interest considerations would have to be relied upon, such as, for example, the fact that disclosure of the record concerned would result in an unwarranted benefit to an individual to the detriment of the State.

The second form of public interest test is expressed in terms of a positive requirement that the head of a public body be of the opinion that disclosure would serve the public interest. This test is harder to satisfy than the negatively expressed public interest test found in section 20, for it is easier to show that disclosure will not harm the public interest than it is to show that the public interest will be positively served by disclosure.

One question which arises is what role, if any, the applicant should assume in establishing that the public interest would, on balance, be better served by granting than by refusing to grant the request? Given that the Act places the burden of proof on those opposing disclosure,[38] should it be up to the public body to prove that disclosure is contrary to the public interest? Some guidance can be gleaned from the Australian federal A.A.T.'s analysis of the same form of public interest in the Australian Act. It must be borne in mind, however, that in the Australian Act this form of public interest test is only found in harm based exemptions, whereas in the Irish Act the test is found in both harm and class based exemptions. The A.A.T.'s approach was that satisfaction of the harm test would render the disclosure *prima facie* contrary to the public interest and that the effect of the public interest test would be to allow this *prima facie* conclusion to be displaced. The Tribunal stated that, while not overlook-

---

[37] *Re Mann and Australian Taxation Office* (1985) 7 A.L.D. 698 at 710.
[38] s.34(12).

ing the fact that the Act places the onus of proving that a record is exempt on respondent public bodies, the terms in which the public interest tests are couched:

> "will require an applicant in some circumstances to raise matters, which being relevant to the public interest, weigh in favour of disclosure. It may not be enough for the applicant to rely upon the general right of access . . . and the object of the Act. . . If the applicant does raise such matters, the agency is required either to show that the matters raised by the applicant are insufficient to outweigh the public interest... or to show that there are other public interest considerations which, when added to the statutorily inherent aspects of public interest, outweigh the public interest considerations raised by the applicant".[39]

It is submitted that the same approach would be appropriate to the application of the second form of public interest test in the Irish FOI Act.

2. Determining where the public interest lies

The only explicit guidance to determining where the public interest lies appears in the exemption relating to deliberations of public bodies (section 20). Section 20(1) provides that the head of a public body in determining whether to grant or refuse a request shall consider whether the disclosure of the record "would be contrary to the public interest by reason of the fact that the requester concerned would thereby become aware of a significant decision that the body proposes to make". No other criteria for determining where the public interest lies are expressed in the public interest tests set out in the Act. This is not unusual in the context of overseas FOI legislation. The desirability of leaving the public interest undefined in the context of FOI legislation was acknowledged by the Australian Senate Standing Committee on Legal and Constitutional Affairs:

> "The Committee recognises the difficulties inherent in determining where the balance of public interest lies. At the very least, this involves a careful balancing of the public interest in citizens being informed of the processes of the government against the public interest in the proper functioning of government. This is not an easy process, and it is not susceptible to clear rules or simple formulae. Rather, each document must be carefully scrutinised and a decision made upon the merits of each individual case."[40]

Some guidance may be obtained from the text of the Act and its supporting material, and, in particular, from the long title and the parliamentary debates

---

[39] Above, n. 37, at 711.
[40] Senate Standing Committee on Legal and Constitutional Affairs, *Report on the Operation and Administration of the Freedom of Information Legislation* (Australian Government Publishing Service, Canberra, 1987), para. 9.44.

on the introduction of the Bill.[41] The purpose of the Act as stated in the long title is to:

> "enable members of the public to obtain access, *to the greatest extent possible* consistent with the public interest and the right to privacy, to information in the possession of public bodies" [emphasis added].

This strongly worded statement of purpose establishes the importance of the access rights provided under the Act whilst, at the same time, acknowledging the need to balance that right against other considerations. In her second reading speech, Ms Eithne Fitzgerald, the Minister of State responsible for the introduction of the FOI Bill, adopted language which was radical in terms of the history of access to official information in Ireland when she said:

> "Our purpose is to ensure that we adopt the most effective mechanism for ensuring that the culture and practices of secrecy in public bodies are set aside for good . . . Freedom of Information overturns the presumption of official secrecy set out in the Official Secrets Act 1963, and replaces it with the legal presumption that the public has a right to know."[42]

More specific reference to the public interest was made by the Minister when she made the following statement to the Dáil at the second stage of the passage of the Bill through that House:

> "I reassure the Deputy that political embarrassment is not a test which would satisfy the public interest test under this Bill."[43]

These are powerful statements of the strength of the public interest in the provision of access to official information. They justify the attribution to the Irish FOI Act of the same central role for the public interest as was attributed to its Queensland counterpart by the Queensland Information Commissioner when he commented that:

> "notions of the public interest constitute the basic rationale for the enactment of, as well as the unifying thread running through the provisions of, the FOI Act."[44]

Leaving aside the text of the Act and its supporting material, assistance in determining where the public interest lies may be obtained from existing case law concerning access to official information in Ireland, particularly in the areas of executive privilege and the law of confidence. The role of constitutional rights in limiting or advancing the right of access to official information must also be considered.

---

[41] See above, pp. 32–36 for a discussion of the status of these aids to the interpretation of the Act.
[42] 149 *Seanad Debates* Cols 1249–1250 (Second Stage).
[43] 476 *Dáil Debates* Col. 1068 (Second Stage).
[44] *Re Eccleston and Department of Family Services and Aboriginal and Islander Affairs* (1993) 1 Q.A.R. 60 at 74.

(a) Executive privilege

The Irish courts have had considerable practice in adjudicating on questions of the public interest in the context of claims of executive privilege in judicial proceedings. The approach of the courts to executive privilege has undergone considerable change this century. Prior to independence, deference to the Crown left it very much up to the Crown to determine what constituted the public interest and what and when official information should be made publicly available.

Interestingly, the situation did not change in the first half century of independence. As one commentator noted, "the newly independent State, having shaken off the yolk of the Crown, embraced with enthusiasm many of its privileges".[45] The view that the public interest would automatically coincide with the interests of the executive continued right up to the landmark decision of *Murphy v. Corporation of Dublin*[46] in 1972. *Murphy* concerned a claim of executive privilege made to prevent disclosure of a report of a planning inspector of the proceedings at a public inquiry. The decision in *Murphy* constituted a significant departure from the previous approach to executive privilege. The operation of the doctrine of executive privilege was treated in *Murphy* as a separation of powers issue and the role of the public interest was emphasised. These considerations were evident when, in dealing with the Minister's claim that the report was privileged, Walsh J. declared that:

> "Under the Constitution the administration of justice is committed solely to the judiciary in the exercise of their powers in the courts set up under the Constitution. Power to compel the attendance of witnesses and the production of evidence is an inherent part of the judicial power of government of the State and is the ultimate safeguard of justice in the State. The proper exercise of the functions of the three powers of government set up under the Constitution, namely, the legislative, the executive and the judicial, is in the public interest. There may be occasions when the different aspects of the public interest 'pull in contrary directions' – to use the words of Lord Morris of Borth-y-Gest in *Conway v. Rimmer* [[1968] A.C. 910, 955]. If the conflict arises during the exercise of the judicial power then, in my view, it is the judicial power which will decide which public interest shall prevail. This does not mean that the court will always decide that the interest of the litigant shall prevail. It is for the court to decide which is the superior interest in the circumstances of the particular case and to determine the matter accordingly. As the legislative, executive, and judicial powers of government are all exercised under and on behalf of the State, the interest of the State, as such, is always involved. The division of powers does not give paramountcy in all circumstances to any one of the organs exercising the powers of government over the other."[47]

---

[45] Russell, "A Privilege of the State" (1967) 2 Ir. Jur. (N.S.) 88.
[46] Above, n. 19.
[47] *ibid.* at 233–234.

The Supreme Court held that documents could not be withheld on the grounds that they belong to a particular class and that it was for the courts to decide whether it would or should look at any of the documents in issue. Guidance was also given as to the circumstances in which a claim of executive privilege would be upheld. Walsh J. said:

> "It is clear that, when the vital interests of the State (such as the security of the State) may be adversely affected by disclosure or production of document, greater harm may be caused by ordering rather than by refusing disclosure or production of the document."[48]

It was also acknowledged that executive privilege could be upheld in respect of matters other than those concerning the safety or security of the State. Walsh J. commented:

> "That is not to say that in the ordinary day-to-day administration of the executive branch of government matters may not arise whose disclosure would be contrary to the public interest. Where documents come into existence in the course of the carrying out of the executive powers of the State, their production may be adverse to the public interest in one sphere of government in particular circumstances."[49]

It was decided also in *Murphy* that it was for the courts to choose the evidence upon which it might act in any particular case, although in the case of the safety of the State it was said that:

> "[I]t might well be that the court would be satisfied to accept the opinion of the appropriate member of the executive or of the head of the Government as sufficient evidence of the fact upon a claim being made... on that ground."[50]

However, the view of Lord Reid in *Conway v. Rimmer*[51] that

> "cases would be very rare in which it could be proper to question the view of the responsible Minister that it would be contrary to the public interest to make public the contents of a particular document"[52]

was expressly rejected and it was held that the onus of satisfying the court that a particular document ought not to be produced lies upon the party making such a claim.

The decision in *Murphy* was affirmed by the Supreme Court in *Ambiorix Ltd v. Minister for the Environment (No. 1)*.[53] *Ambiorix* concerned documents relating to a decision by the Minister for the Environment to declare a site as a "designated area" for the purposes of the Urban Renewal Act 1986. The plaintiff

---

[48] *ibid.* at 234.
[49] *ibid.* at 234–235.
[50] *ibid.* at 234.
[51] [1968] A.C. 910; [1968] 1 All E.R. 874.
[52] *ibid.* at 943.
[53] [1992] 1 I.R. 277.

sought to challenge that decision on the grounds that it was *ultra vires* and, in so doing, sought access to documents and memoranda which had come into existence for the purpose of reaching the impugned decision. In the High Court, Lardner J. ordered discovery of the documents. The State appealed on the grounds that the trial judge misdirected himself in ordering the discovery and inspection of documents which were memoranda for Government and other Cabinet documents, the discovery of which, it was claimed, is contrary to the necessary requirements of confidentiality of Cabinet, Government and ministerial communications and discussions which could prejudice the confidentiality and collective responsibility of the government. The State argued that the court should reconsider its decision in *Murphy* on the basis that the principles laid down in that case were, at least in part, erroneous. It was further argued that there was absolute immunity from production for a *class* of documents, namely documents emanating at the level of not below Assistant Secretary in the public service, provided that these were documents for the ultimate consideration of Ministers of the Government, or of the Government itself, which related to the formulation of policy or proposals for legislation. The Supreme Court refused to resile from its earlier decision in *Murphy*. Finlay C.J. summarised the principles laid down in *Murphy* as follows:

"1. Under the Constitution the administration of justice is committed solely to the judiciary by the exercise of their powers in the courts set up under the Constitution.
2. Power to compel the production of evidence (which, of course, includes a power to compel the production of documents) is an inherent part of the judicial power and is part of the ultimate safeguard of justice in the State.
3. Where a conflict arises during the exercise of the judicial power between the aspect of public interest involved in the production of evidence and the aspect of public interest involved in the confidentiality or exemption from production of documents pertaining to the exercise of the executive powers of the State, it is the judicial power which will decide which public interest shall prevail.
4. The duty of the judicial power to make that decision does not mean that there is any priority or preference for the production of evidence over other public interests, such as the security of the State or the efficient discharge of the functions of the executive organ of the Government.
5. It is for the judicial power to choose the evidence upon which it might act in any individual case in order to reach that decision.

These principles lead to certain practical conclusions which are applicable to a claim of privilege by the Executive of the nature which arises in this case, and they are as follows:–

(a) The Executive cannot prevent the judicial power from examining documents which are relevant to an issue in a civil trial for the purpose of deciding whether they must be produced.
(b) There is no obligation on the judicial power to examine any particular document before deciding that it is exempt from production, and it can and will

in many instances uphold a claim of privilege in respect of a document merely on the basis of a description of its nature and contents which it (the judicial power) accepts.

(c) There cannot, accordingly, be a generally applicable class or category of documents exempted from production by reason of the rank in the public service of the person creating them, or of the position of the individual or body intended to use them."[54]

Finlay C.J. also pointed out that if a privilege of the nature and in the manner contended for on behalf of the appellants was accepted as a general proposition by the courts, one of the consequences of so doing would be that a challenge could never be mounted to a decision made by the Government or by a Minister, on the basis that it was made without material which supported it, or having regard to the consideration of material which was wholly irrelevant to it. Finlay C.J. expressly rejected a contention that documents consisting of representations made to government departments by third parties seeking to have their properties included within the designated area were privileged, saying:

> "There is not any public interest, in my view, in keeping immune from production communications between citizens and departments of the government seeking a particular decision which would favour their interest."[55]

Following these decisions, claims of executive privilege were examined in a number of cases involving communications between civil servants and Ministers. In *Geraghty v. Minister for Local Government*,[56] privilege was claimed in respect of confidential memoranda passing between a Minister and his department. Kenny J. in the High Court ordered that most of the documents in respect of which the privilege was claimed should be disclosed, but, in so doing, supported the principle that documents prepared in confidence by one civil servant for the benefit of another were entitled to privilege. The Supreme Court upheld this decision and held further that since the Minister had not been functioning under the executive power of the State, he was not entitled to claim privilege in respect of the documents.

It appears that special protection will, however, be given to correspondence between Ministers. In *Incorporated Law Society of Ireland v. Minister for Justice*[57] Murphy J. said:

> "[T]he documentation for which privilege is claimed includes correspondence passing between individual Ministers of Government. It seems to me to be right to pay particular attention to these letters to see whether their production might

---

[54] *ibid.* at 283–284.
[55] *ibid.* at 286.
[56] [1975] I.R. 300.
[57] [1987] I.L.R.M. 42.

involve any particular risk of damage to the public service as clearly Ministers will necessarily have responsibility for the access to information of a most sensitive and important nature."[58]

Such documents will not enjoy absolute immunity. Murphy J., in ordering disclosure of the letters passing between the Ministers concerned, went on to say that:

"[E]ven bearing that consideration in mind I am satisfied that there is nothing in the documentation for which this particular claim of privilege is made which has any special potential for damage in the proper administration of the public service."[59]

The protection of communications between public servants has arisen in a number of cases. In *Folens and Co. Ltd v. Minister for Education*[60] Costello J. held that while confidential communications between public servants should be protected:

"not all communications which arise in the course of administration of the Public Services are confidential. But some communications may be confidential. The court will examine the documents to see whether a claim to confidentiality can properly exist and if it does it must decide whether the public interest in maintaining confidentiality should not prevail because to do so could result in a denial of justice."[61]

The public interest in obtaining access to inter-governmental records was the subject of *W. v. Ireland (No. 1)*[62] which concerned an application for discovery of documents relating to the processing of a request for the extradition of Fr Brendan Smyth from the Republic of Ireland to Northern Ireland. Geoghegan J. referred with approval to a decision of English Court of Appeal, *Buttes Gas and Oil Company v. Hammer*[63] which had rejected the attachment of absolute public interest privilege to confidential communications between states and had reiterated the general principle that confidentiality *per se* is not a ground of objection to disclosure and he concluded:

"The question is, is there a public interest in maintaining that confidentiality, and, if so, does that particular public interest outweigh the public interest in the court having access to the full truth for the purposes of administering justice?"[64]

The role of constitutional considerations in limiting the privilege applicable to communications between states was expressed in the following terms:

---

[58] *ibid.* at 44.
[59] *ibid.*
[60] [1981] I.L.R.M. 21.
[61] *ibid.* at 22.
[62] [1997] 2 I.R. 132.
[63] [1982] A.C. 888.
[64] *W. v. Ireland (No. 1)*, above, n. 62, at 139.

"With regard to the provisions of the Irish Constitution, there is an even stronger case in this jurisdiction . . . for not countenancing any form of absolute privilege in relation to communications passing between sovereign states. The principles enunciated in *Murphy v. Corporation of Dublin* and *Ambiorix Ltd. v. Minister for the Environment (No. 1)* should be applied in considering whether an objection to production of such documents should be sustained, in the same manner as in the case of any other form of document."[65]

In applying those principles to the circumstances of the case, Geoghegan J. came down in favour of disclosure and based his decision (*inter alia*) on the following factors:

"1. The criminal proceeding to which the action relates has long been disposed of.
2. The onus of establishing that there is a greater public interest in non-disclosure is on the State, but that onus does not appear to me to have been discharged. The mere assertion that confidentiality would normally be expected is not sufficient.
3. There is no evidence before this court, either direct or even of a hearsay nature, that there is a concrete present objection by the office of the Attorney General of Northern Ireland to the production of these documents in this action.
4. While it would be understandable that both this State and the United Kingdom would want as a matter of principle to maintain a rule of confidentiality in relation to such documentation, it is difficult to see any particular reason why the United Kingdom government would be concerned about the production of the particular documents now sought to be produced in this case."[66]

The issue of executive privilege has also been examined by the courts in the context of the investigations being carried out by public bodies. In *Director of Consumer Affairs and Fair Trade v. Sugar Distributors Ltd*[67] the High Court held that privilege attached to documents concerning a complaint made to the Director of Consumer Affairs and Fair Trade that the defendant had breached the restrictive practices legislation. The court held that there is a public interest in withholding documents from disclosure in two distinct situations. The first, which was said to relate to affairs of the State and to have derived from the decision in *Murphy*, is based on the fact that the public has an interest in the proper functioning of the public service and that the proper functioning of the public service may in certain circumstances require that relevant documents be withheld from disclosure. The second situation in which it was said that the withholding of documents might be in the public interest was in the realm of the prevention and detection of crime. Costello J. stated that it had

---

[65] *ibid.* Citations omitted.
[66] *ibid.* at 139–140.
[67] [1991] 1 I.R. 225.

long been established that the non-disclosure of the identity of police inform-
ers is justified on the grounds that to do otherwise might result in the information which enables the police to deter and detect crime not being forthcoming.
He took the view that considerations of a similar nature applied to complaints
made the Director of Consumer Affairs and Fair Trade, saying:

> "[T]he Oireachtas has conferred on the Director important law enforcement func-
> tions. I am satisfied that it is in the public interest that the court should protect
> the effective functioning by the Director of his statutory powers. I am further
> satisfied that to enable him to exercise his powers effectively he must be able to
> assure complainants that information given to him (and, indeed, in certain cir-
> cumstances the names of complainants) will be treated in confidence and not
> disclosed as otherwise complaints may not be forthcoming and breaches of min-
> isterial orders are likely to go undetected. The requisite protection should em-
> brace all documents forwarded by a complainant with a complaint."[68]

However, it was acknowledged that the immunity granted cannot be an absolute one:

> "When a claim is made, as it has been in this case, that it is not in the public
> interest that relevant documents in the Director's possession should not be in-
> spected, the court should examine the documents. If satisfied that they form part
> of a complaint made to the Director by a member of the public that a breach of
> the restrictive practices legislation or orders made thereunder has occurred in-
> spection should not be allowed unless the court concludes that the documents
> might tend to show that the defendant has not committed the wrongful acts
> alleged against him."[69]

The issue of disclosure of information relating to investigations was also considered in *Private Motorists' Provident Society Limited (In Liquidation) v.
P.M.P.A. Insurance plc (Under Administration).*[70] The High Court held that
the disclosure of documents and correspondence passing between the Registrar of Friendly Societies and a government department in the course of an
investigation into a group of companies could not be opposed on the basis that
its disclosure would result in civil servants and members of the public being
less likely to speak freely with the Registrar. In the same case, an argument
that the public interest would be damaged because disclosure would undermine the Registrar's ability to carry out his functions in the future was rejected
on the basis that the objection to disclosure was based not on the contents of
the documents, but on the functions of the Registrar.

In *Skeffington v. Rooney*[71] the issue of access to documents relating to
complaints again arose. Here the plaintiff sought discovery of documents re-

---

[68] *ibid.* at 228–229.
[69] *ibid.* at 229.
[70] [1990] 1 I.R. 284.
[71] [1997] 1 I.R. 22.

lating to a complaint made by him to the Garda Complaints Board. The Supreme Court stated that:

> "the courts must balance the public interest in the production of documents which are relevant to the issues to be determined in the particular case against some other public interest which is invoked to justify their being withheld. Of the categories which have been recognised by the courts in Ireland as in other common law jurisdictions as in general protected against disclosure because of such a countervailing public interest, perhaps the most conspicuous is that embraced by legal professional privilege. . . But as Lord Hailsham of St. Marylebone pointed out in *D. v. N.S.P.C.C.* [1978] A.C. 171 at p. 230:
>
>> 'The categories of public interest are not closed and must alter from time to time whether by restriction or extension as social conditions and social legislation develop'".[72]

Ordering the release of the documents, Keane J. said:

> "In the present case, there must be weighed against the public interest in the disclosure of the documents relating to the complaint to the [Garda Síochána Complaints] Board, the public interest in ensuring that the statutory functions of the Board are not frustrated. There may be cases – of which this is not one – in which documents relating to a complaint to a Board are sought by a party to litigation other than the complainant. In such a case, depending entirely on the particular circumstances, the court might be justified in declining to allow the inspection of documents forwarded in confidence by a complainant to the Chief Executive or even the identity of a complainant."[73]

Taken together, these cases display a willingness on the part of the courts to interpret the public interest in a way which favours openness of official information. One case, decided in the 1990s, which appears to go against the general trend towards greater openness of official information is that of *Attorney General v. Hamilton.*[74] Here the Attorney General obtained a ruling from the Supreme Court that the Beef Tribunal[75] was not entitled to have disclosed to it details of Cabinet discussions. The Chief Justice based his decision on the provisions of Articles 28.4.1° and 28.4.2° of the Constitution. He concluded from the obligation placed upon the government to meet and act collectively that they must be collectively responsible and that this necessarily entailed making a single decision, whether arrived at unanimously or by a majority, and further, that it entailed as a necessity the non-disclosure of different or dissenting views held by members of the government prior to the making of decisions. The tribunal was characterised as:

---

[72] *ibid.* at 32.
[73] *ibid.* at 35–36.
[74] [1993] 2 I.R. 250.
[75] Tribunal of Inquiry into the Beef Industry.

> "an exercise of the legislative power originated by the Executive as members of the Legislature and implemented, or put into effect, by an order of the Executive pursuant to the resolution of both Houses of Parliament".[76]

The Chief Justice went on to say that the principles applicable to the question of confidentiality in this particular case were to be found in the sections of the Constitution dealing with the Executive and with the Legislature and the relationship between those two organs of State and did not fall to be dealt with under the provisions of the Constitution dealing with the fundamental rights of citizens or under the provisions of the Constitution dealing with the administration of justice and the exercise of judicial power.

The decisions in *Murphy* and *Ambiorix* were distinguished on the basis that they were "uniquely" concerned with the exercise by the judiciary of the judicial power; the Chief Justice stated that whilst some of the principles laid down in those cases with regard to the exercise of judicial power would appear to embrace discussions between members of government, at meetings of the Government, the fact that no specific claim of a special confidentiality concerning those arose in either case may mean that the issue still remains to be decided in a case in which it occurs in relation to the exercise of the judicial power.

Thus, whilst this decision appears to go against the trend of greater openness of official information, it rested on a particular constitutional provision relating to the role of the Cabinet and, in particular, on the fact that the tribunal was not engaged in the exercise of judicial power.

To sum up, developments in the law relating to executive privilege indicate that the courts are willing to look behind a claim of privilege. Access has been granted, in the public interest, to a number of different categories of records such as: memoranda for government and other Cabinet documents;[77] communications between civil servants;[78] communications between Ministers;[79] inter-State communications;[80] and documents concerning investigations being carried out by public bodies.[81]

While these cases may be useful in sketching the parameters of the public interest in accessing official information, it must be borne in mind that executive privilege cannot be equated with FOI legislation. There are important differences between them which may affect the applicability of the executive privilege case law to FOI cases. These differences result from the fact that claims of executive privilege arise in the context of judicial proceedings and

---

[76] *Attorney General v. Hamilton,* above, n. 74, at 270–271.
[77] *Ambiorix Ltd v. Minister for the Environment (No. 1),* above, n. 53.
[78] *Folens & Co. Ltd v. Minister for Education,* above, n. 60.
[79] *Incorporated Law Society of Ireland v. Minister for Justice,* above, n. 57.
[80] *W. v. Ireland (No. 1),* above, n. 62.
[81] *Private Motorists' Provident Society Limited (In Liquidation) v. P.M.P.A. Insurance plc (Under Administration),* above, n. 70; *Skeffington v. Rooney,* above, n. 71.

many of the principles enunciated in the case law are predicated on that fact.

The main difference between the public interest in executive privilege cases and FOI cases is that, in the case of the former, the public interest in withholding documents is balanced against the interest in the proper administration of justice. No such interest in the administration of justice will generally exist in the context of a FOI request. However, that is not to say that the public interest in disclosure of records under FOI will consequently be weaker than the public interest in discovery of documents in court proceedings. On the contrary, the purposes of the FOI Act, which may be taken into account in determining where the public interest lies, provide a strong statement of the need for greater openness of official information. In particular, the Act's purpose of ensuring that "we adopt the most effective mechanism for ensuring that the culture and practices of secrecy in public bodies are set aside for good"[82] is strongly supportive of the public interest in disclosure of official information.

Another difference between executive privilege and FOI is that the needs and status of the access seeker are relevant in executive privilege cases, but not in FOI cases. This is because the motive of a requestor in seeking access to records under FOI may not be taken into account.[83]

Finally, the use of documents obtained through disclosure is limited to the purposes of the court action. As Finlay J. observed in *Ambiorix*:

> "As a matter of general principle, of course, a party obtaining the production of documents by discovery in an action is prohibited by law from making any use of any description of such documents or the information contained in them otherwise than for the purpose of the action. To go outside that prohibition is to commit contempt of court."[84]

In the case of records disclosed under FOI, no such limitations on their further use may be imposed.[85]

Thus, while the approach of the courts to determining questions of public interest in executive privilege cases may be of general assistance in establishing the parameters of that concept in the context of FOI, the distinctions between the two situations in which issues of public interest are considered must be borne in mind.

(b) The law of confidence

Another area of law in which determination of questions of public interest has arisen is that of the law of confidence. While the law of confidence developed

---

[82] 149 *Seanad Debates* Cols. 1249–1250 (Second Stage).
[83] s.8(4).
[84] *Ambiorix Ltd v. Minister for the Environment (No. 1)*, above, n. 53, at 286; see also *Gormley v. Ireland* [1993] 2 I.R. 75.
[85] Provided, of course, that other laws, such as those relating to defamation, the law of confidence, and copyright, are not breached: see s.45(5).

originally to provide protection against disclosure of trade secrets and confidences, it has, in relatively recent times, been extended to cover government secrets.[86] The existence of a public interest defence to the action for breach of confidence has long been recognised. It is settled that the defence will apply to disclosures of crime or fraud,[87] misdeeds,[88] damage to the public,[89] and in other exceptional circumstances.[90] The courts have adopted a special approach to the issue of public interest in the context of government secrets. Mason J. in the Australian case of *Commonwealth of Australia v. John Fairfax & Sons Ltd* explained the basis of the distinction in the following way:

> "The equitable principle has been fashioned to protect the personal, private and proprietary rights of the citizen, not to protect the very different interests of the executive government. It acts, or is supposed to act, not according to standards of private interest but in the public interest. This is not to say that equity will not protect information in the hands of government, but it is to say that when equity protects government information, it will look at the matter through different spectacles. It may be a sufficient detriment to the citizen that disclosure of information relating to his affairs will expose his actions to public discussion and criticism. But it can scarcely be a relevant detriment to the government that publication of material concerning its actions will merely expose it to public discussion and criticism. It is unacceptable in our democratic society that there should be a restraint on the publication of information relating to government when the only vice of that information is that it enables the public to discuss, review and criticise government action."[91]

This passage was accepted by Carroll J. as correctly stating the law in Ireland in *Attorney General for England and Wales v. Brandon Book Publishers Ltd*,[92] a case taken to prevent publication in Ireland of the memoirs of a deceased former member of the British security services. Because the plaintiff was a representative of a foreign government, it was held that there was no question of the public interest in Ireland being affected. In the course of her judgment, Carroll J. stated that one of the considerations to be taken into account in deciding whether the plaintiff had a cause of action was the fact that "there is no absolute confidentiality where the parties are a government and a private individual".[93] This case is significant in that it establishes in Ireland, as in

---

[86] *Attorney General v. Jonathan Cape* (1973) 3 All E.R. 484; (1976) Q.B. 752; *Commonwealth of Australia v. John Fairfax & Sons Ltd* (1980) 147 C.L.R. 39; *Attorney General v. The Guardian and the Observer* [1988] 3 All E.R. 545, [1988] 2 W.L.R. 805; *Attorney General for England and Wales v. Brandon Book Publishers Ltd* [1986] I.R. 597.
[87] *Gartside v. Outram* (1857) 26 L.J. Ch. (N.S.) 113.
[88] *Initial Services Limited v. Putterill* [1968] 1 Q.B. 396.
[89] *Hubbard v. Vosper* [1972] 2 Q.B. 84.
[90] *Lion Laboratories Ltd v. Evans* [1985] 1 Q.B. 526.
[91] *Commonwealth of Australia v. John Fairfax & Sons Ltd*, above, n. 86, at 51.
[92] Above, n. 86, at 601.
[93] *ibid.* at 602.

Australia, the principle that the interests of government are not always synonymous with the public interest. In particular, it establishes that the confidentiality of government information may be overridden in the public interest.

The confidentiality of information supplied to the State by a third party arose in *Desmond v. Glackin (No. 2).*[94] Glackin, who had been appointed by the Minister for Industry and Commerce to enquire into issues surrounding the controversial acquisition of a site by Telecom Éireann, was given access to information supplied by the plaintiff company to the Central Bank under a statutory compulsion. The plaintiff sought an injunction to restrain Glackin from making any use of the information obtained from the Central Bank and a mandatory injunction directing him to return all of the information to the Central Bank, on the grounds (*inter alia*) that disclosure of the information amounted to a breach of the right to privacy and confidentiality at common law and under the Constitution. O'Hanlon J. in the High Court surveyed the protection afforded to the right of privacy under the Constitution and noted that it is not an unqualified right, but rather that it is "subject to the constitutional rights of others and to the requirements of public order, public morality and the common good". He concluded that:

> "while the Irish Constitution may have a significant bearing on the problem in situations such as arose for determination in *McGee v. Attorney General* [1974] I.R. 284 and *Kennedy v. Ireland* [1987] I.R. 587, we are here concerned with a situation where the protections afforded by the common law and by the Constitution are probably co-extensive".[95]

In deciding that the making available to the inspector of the information did not involve a breach of the duty of confidentiality, O'Hanlon J. said:

> "In the present case what is involved is the communication of information obtained in the course of performance of his public functions by a public body (the Minister for Finance), and the communication of that information by him to another public body (the Minister for Industry and Commerce) for use by an inspector appointed by him under the Act of 1990 in carrying out other public functions arising under the provisions of that Act.
>
> I do not share Browne-Wilkinson V-C's stated apprehension about the consequences of sharing information lawfully obtained across a wide spectrum of state agencies and consider that it may be helpful for good government and the welfare of the community. The Vice-Chancellor considered, at p. 1130, that '[t]he dossier of private information is the badge of the totalitarian state'. I would think that the protection of a free society must rest on surer grounds than the operation of the affairs of state in water-tight compartments.
>
> There appears to me to be a clear public interest in having all the information needed by the inspector for the purposes of his investigation made avail-

---

[94] [1993] 3 I.R. 67.
[95] *ibid.* at 101.

able. I do not detect the existence of any significant public interest of equal or near-equal weight in denying access by the inspector to this source of information."[96]

This decision was upheld on appeal. McCarthy J. in the Supreme Court said:

> "I am satisfied that there is no principle of law, nor indeed is there any principle of common sense, which would prohibit a Minister of State who properly has obtained from an agent carrying out on his behalf a statutory power vested in him, information which may be of assistance to another Minister of State in carrying out a statutory duty imposed on him... I would affirm with approval the statement contained in the judgment of O'Hanlon J., in respect of this particular issue, that the foundation of freedom in our society must surely have a sounder base than the possible concept of government activity carried out, of necessity, in watertight compartments."[97]

This is an important decision in that it established that the confidentiality of government information relating to third parties, in this case a private company, can be overridden in the public interest. The decision was, however, arrived at in the context of the provision of access to that information to an organ of the State (the inspector appointed by the Minister for Industry and Commerce) rather than to a third party, such as an FOI applicant. Again, there is a need for caution in applying the law relating to the public interest defence to the action for breach of confidence in the FOI context. Given that the basis of FOI legislation is the provision of access to government information, it is arguable that the public interest in disclosure should be judged in terms of the attainment of that objective, rather than in terms of whether it would ground a public interest defence to an action for breach of confidence.

(c) The public interest and constitutional rights

The application of rights recognised under the Constitution could be relevant to the determination of questions relating to the operation of public interest tests in the FOI Act.[98] In particular, the right to freedom of expression and unenumerated rights, such as the right to communicate and the right to privacy, might be invoked in supporting or opposing the use of the public interest to override the exemption provisions.

(i) Freedom of expression

The right to freedom of expression is set out in Article 40.6.1°. It provides as follows:

---

[96] *ibid.* at 102.
[97] [1993] 3 I.R. 106 at 132.
[98] See Hogan and Whyte, *Kelly: The Irish Constitution* (3rd ed., Butterworths, 1994); Casey, *Constitutional Law in Ireland* (2nd ed., Sweet & Maxwell, London, 1992).

"The State guarantees liberty for the exercise of the following rights, subject to public order and morality:—

i. The right of the citizens to express freely their convictions and opinions.

The education of public opinion being, however, a matter of such grave import to the common good, the State shall endeavour to ensure that organs of public opinion, such as the radio, the press, the cinema, while preserving their rightful liberty of expression, including criticism of Government policy, shall not be used to undermine public order or morality or the authority of the State.

The publication or utterance of blasphemous, seditious, or indecent matter is an offence which shall be punishable in accordance with law."

Two main issues arise in attempting to use this right to ground an argument that disclosure of government information is in the public interest. The first, in respect of which there is judicial uncertainty, concerns the question of whether protection afforded by the right to freedom of expression extends to information which is factual in nature. The High Court has held on two occasions – in *Attorney General v. Paperlink Ltd*[99] and *Kearney v. Minister for Justice*[100] – that the right to freedom of expression is restricted to expressions of conviction and opinion and does not apply to the dissemination of factual information. In *Paperlink*, Costello J. stated:

"It seems to me that as the act of communication is the exercise of such a basic human faculty that a right to communicate must inhere in the citizen by virtue of his human personality and must be guaranteed by the Constitution. But in what Article? The exercise of the right to communicate can take many forms and the right to express freely convictions and opinions is expressly provided for in Article 40.6.1°(i). But the activity which the defendants say is inhibited in this case is that of communication by letter and as this act may involve the communication of information and not merely the expression of convictions and opinions I do not think that the constitutional provision dealing with the right to express convictions and opinions is the source of the citizen's right to communicate."[101]

The decision in *Paperlink* was subsequently followed by Keane J. in *Oblique Financial Services Ltd v. Promise Production Co. Ltd.*[102] However, Carroll J. in *Attorney General for England and Wales v. Brandon Book Publishers Ltd*[103] took a different approach. She held, without drawing a distinction between facts and opinions, that there is a constitutional right under Article 40.6.1°(i) to publish information which does not involve any breach of copyright. The approach of Costello J. in *Paperlink* has been criticised on the grounds that

---

[99] [1984] I.L.R.M. 373.
[100] [1986] I.R. 116.
[101] *Attorney General v. Paperlink Ltd*, above, n. 99, at 381.
[102] [1994] 1 I.L.R.M. 74.
[103] Above, n. 86.

the third paragraph of the right to freedom of expression which obliges the State to make it an offence to publish "blasphemous, seditious or indecent matter" would not appear to be restricted to matters of opinion and must apply also to factual material. Since that paragraph appears to be qualified by the opening words of the Article, it has been argued that it does not make sense to restrict the introductory words to convictions and opinions.[104]

The other difficulty posed to the employment of the constitutional right to freedom of expression in arguing for the disclosure of information is that Article 40.6 has never been held to include a right to receive information to which the holder of the information does not wish to provide access. The European Court of Human Rights has held that the right to freedom of expression in the European Convention on Human Rights is merely negative in effect and does not confer a right of access to information.[105] It remains to be seen whether the Irish courts would adopt the same view.

(ii) The right to communicate

While the right to freedom of expression was of no avail to the plaintiffs in the *Paperlink* case, Costello J. went on to recognise a right to communicate information deriving from the unspecified personal rights protected by Article 40.3.1°. That right, however, was held not to be absolute. Whether the right to communicate includes a corresponding right to receive information is a moot point, although this issue was addressed in part in *Kearney v. Minister for Justice*[106] when it was held that the non-delivery of mail to the plaintiff, a prison inmate, as a result of unauthorised action taken by prison officers did amount to a breach of his right to communicate. However, since the information to which access was sought by the plaintiff were letters addressed to him, this decision is not strong authority for the proposition that there is a general right to receive communications of information.

(iii) The right to privacy

The right to privacy might be to resorted to in an attempt to restrict access to information. It could, for example, be invoked in support of an argument that the public interest tests found in the exemptions relating to information supplied to public bodies by third parties (those relating to information obtained in confidence (section 26); commercially sensitive information (section 27); or personal information (section 28)) should be applied in a manner which

---

[104] Fennelly, "The Irish Constitution and Freedom of Expression" in *Constitutional Adjudication in European Community and National Law* (Curtin and O'Keeffe ed., Butterworths, 1992), p. 183.

[105] *Leander v. Sweden* (1987) 9 E.H.R.R. 433; *Guerra v. Italy,* unreported, European Court of Human Rights, February 19, 1998. See above, pp. 12–14.

[106] Above, n. 100.

does not interfere with the right to privacy of the individual as recognised by the Constitution.

The right to privacy in the Irish Constitution is an unenunciated right. Its provenance can be traced back to 1974 when, in *McGee v. Attorney-General*,[107] a right of marital privacy was recognised by the Supreme Court. The plaintiff was a married woman with four children who had been advised against having another pregnancy. She challenged the constitutionality of the legislative provisions preventing her from obtaining access to contraceptives. The Supreme Court held in her favour by a 4-1 majority. The court held that Article 40.3.1° guaranteed a right to privacy in marital relations, including a right to decide to use contraceptives. In *Norris v. Attorney General*[108] the plaintiff attempted to have struck down statutory provisions penalising homosexual acts between consenting male adults in private by relying on the right to privacy established in *McGee*. The basis of his case, as O'Higgins C.J. put it, was:

> "that the State has no business in the field of private morality and has no right to legislate in relation to the private sexual conduct of consenting adults [and that for the State] to attempt to do so is to exceed the limits of permissible interference and to shatter that area of privacy which the dignity and liberty of human persons require to be kept apart as a haven for each citizen."[109]

Although the plaintiff failed in his action by a 3-2 majority, three of the judges appeared to accept that a right of individual privacy existed. In the 1987 case of *Kennedy v. Ireland*[110] a general right to privacy was recognised by the High Court. The plaintiffs had complained that their right to privacy had been infringed by the tapping of their telephones by the State. Hamilton P. (as he then was) upheld their claim, saying:

> "Though not specifically guaranteed by the Constitution, the right of privacy is one of the fundamental personal rights of the citizen which flow from the Christian and democratic nature of the State. It is not an unqualified right. Its exercise may be restricted by the constitutional rights of others, by the requirements of the common good and is subject to the requirements of public order and morality. . .
>
> The nature of the right to privacy must be such as to ensure the dignity and freedom of an individual in the type of society envisaged by the Constitution, namely, a sovereign, independent and democratic society. The dignity and freedom of an individual in a democratic society cannot be ensured if his communications of a private nature, be they written or telephonic, are deliberately, consciously and unjustifiably intruded upon and interfered with. I emphasise the words 'deliberately, consciously and unjustifiably' because an individual

---

[107] [1974] I.R. 284.
[108] [1984] I.R. 36.
[109] *ibid.* at 59.
[110] [1987] I.R. 587.

must accept the risk of accidental interference with his communications and the fact that in certain circumstances the exigencies of the common good may require and justify such intrusion and interference. No such circumstances exist in this case."[111]

The right to privacy was again invoked in *Desmond v. Glackin (No. 2)*.[112] The issue was the making available to a public body of information supplied to another public body by a company under statutory compulsion. The information in question was made available for use by an inspector appointed by a Government Minister to conduct an enquiry into the circumstances surrounding the controversial acquisition of property by Telecom Éireann. The plaintiff sought an injunction restraining the use by the inspector of the information. O'Hanlon J. in the High Court found that the right to privacy was co-extensive with the common law of confidentiality, but he concluded that, in the instant case, the public interest justified the provision of the information to the inspector. The Supreme Court dismissed an appeal against this decision.

Thus, while the right to privacy is recognised as a right protected by the Irish Constitution, it is clearly not an absolute right. In particular, it was explicitly recognised in *Kennedy*[113] that its protection is subject to the constitutional rights of others as well as to common good and public order and morality. In *Desmond v. Glackin (No. 2)*[114] the "public interest" was sufficient to defeat the claim for privacy. O'Hanlon J. stated that:

> "There appears to me to be a clear public interest in having all the information needed by the inspector for the purposes of his investigation made available. I do not detect the existence of any significant public interest of equal or near-equal weight in denying access by the inspector to this source of information."[115]

To summarise the position with respect to the use of constitutional rights to support or oppose the disclosure of information, it appears that, as yet, there is not any judicial authority for the use of the right to freedom of expression to ground a general right of access to information. Nor has the right to communicate been expressed to include a general right to receive information, although it can be argued that, on the basis of the decision in *Kearney v. Minister for Justice*,[116] the right to communicate encompasses a right of access to information relating to oneself. On the other hand, while a right of privacy is clearly recognised under the Constitution, that right has been found not to be absolute and its potential for restricting the right of access to government information relating to third parties must not, therefore, be overestimated.

---

[111] Above, n. 110, at 592–593.
[112] Above, n. 94.
[113] Above, n. 110.
[114] Above, n. 94.
[115] *ibid.* at 102.
[116] Above, n. 100.

(d) The public interest and FOI overseas

Some guidance as to the parameters of the public interest in FOI cases may be gleaned from overseas decisions. In *D.P.P. v. Smith*[117] the Supreme Court of the Australian state of Victoria discussed the meaning of the public interest as follows:

> "There are many areas of national and community activities which may be the subject of the public interest. The statute does not contain any definition of the public interest. Nevertheless, used in the context of this statute, it does not mean that which gratifies curiosity or merely provides information or amusement; cf *R. v. Inhabitants of the County of Bedfordshire* (1855) 24 LJBQ 81 at 84 *per* Lord Campbell LJ. Similarly it is necessary to distinguish between 'what is in the public interest and what is of interest to know': *Lion Laboratories Ltd v. Evans* [1985] 1 QB 526 at 553 *per* Griffiths LJ. . . The public interest is a term embracing matters, among others, of standards of human conduct and of the functioning of government and government instrumentalities tacitly accepted and acknowledged to be for the good order of society and for the well-being of its members. The interest is therefore the interest of the public as distinct from the interest of an individual or individuals: *Sinclair v. Mining Warden of Maryborough* (1975) 32 CLR 473 at 480 *per* Barwick CJ. There are . . . several and different features and facets of interest which form the public interest. On the other hand, in the daily affairs of the community events occur which attract public attention. Such events of interest to the public may or may not be ones which are for the benefit of the public; it follows that such form of interest per se is not a facet of the public interest."[118]

The principle that a distinction can be drawn between the public interest and that which the public is interested in was also accepted in the Australian federal FOI decision *Re Angel and Department of the Arts, Heritage and the Environment.*[119] In another Australian federal FOI case, *Re Public Advocacy Centre and Department of Community Services and Health [No. 2],*[120] the Administrative Appeals Tribunal held that "it must be shown objectively that there is a public interest in the subject matter to which the documents relate".[121]

However, that is not to say that the interests of individual members of society will be overlooked in determining the public interest. In a decision which provides an excellent overview of the concept of public interest in FOI legislation, the Queensland State Information Commissioner said:

> "While in general terms, a matter of public interest must be a matter that concerns the interests of the community generally, the courts have recognised that:

---

[117] [1991] 1 V.R. 63.
[118] *ibid.* at 75.
[119] (1985) 9 A.L.D. 113.
[120] (1991) 14 A.A.R. 180.
[121] *ibid.* at 187.

'the public interest necessarily comprehends an element of justice to the individual': *Attorney-General (N.S.W.) v. Quin* (1990) 64 ALJR 327 per Mason CJ. Thus, there is a public interest in individuals receiving fair treatment in accordance with the law in their dealings with government, as this is an interest common to all members of the community. Similarly, the fact that individuals and corporations have, and are entitled to pursue, legitimate private rights and interests can be given recognition as a public interest consideration worthy or protection, depending on the circumstance of any particular case." [122]

Overall, determination of where the public interest lies in Irish FOI cases must take place against the backdrop of the rights guaranteed under the Constitution. It must be influenced primarily by the purposes of the Act as stated in the long title. Decisions of the Irish courts in executive privilege and breach of confidence cases may be of some assistance in determining where the public interest lies, although caution must be exercised in the use of these decisions given the important differences between the purpose of those legal concepts and the philosophy underlying the FOI Act.

D.   Ministerial Certificates

1. The ministerial certificate mechanism generally

While all records which come within the scope of FOI Act exemptions can be characterised as being sensitive, at least to some degree, some are clearly viewed as being more sensitive than others. Accordingly, provision is generally made in FOI legislation for the fettering of access rights in certain situations. Such restrictions are generally of three kinds. First, a ministerial or conclusive certificate mechanism may be provided for. Such a mechanism gives a Minister the power to issue a certificate to the effect that a document to which access is sought is exempt under a particular provision of the Act. Provision is made for the issue of such certificates in the Australian and New Zealand Acts.[123] Another restriction on the provision of access to "sensitive" information consists of the limitation on powers of review in the case of certain kinds of records. Such limitations can be found in the Canadian[124] and Australian Acts.[125] Fi-

---

[122] *Re Eccleston and Department of Family Services and Aboriginal and Islander Affairs*, above, n. 44, at 80–81.

[123] There is provision in Australia for the issue of ministerial certificates in respect of Cabinet (s.34), Executive Council (s.35), and deliberative process documents (s.36), as well as documents affecting Commonwealth/State relationships (s.33A) and security, defence and international relations (s.33). In New Zealand, certificates can be issued under s.31 in respect of information relating to security, defence or international relations and law enforcement.

[124] Access to Information Act (Canada), R.S.C., 1985, s.50.

[125] Freedom of Information Act 1982 (Cth), s.58.

nally, some Acts contain a power to veto the disclosure of information where such disclosure has been recommended or ordered by a body charged with making decisions on FOI requests. Such powers of veto are found in the New Zealand[126] and Australian Acts.[127]

The approach in the Irish Act has been to provide for the issuing of ministerial certificates in certain cases and to preclude any review of the issuing of such certificates by the Information Commissioner. The issue of such certificates is, however, subject to review by the High Court in certain circumstances. There is no veto on a High Court order for disclosure of records. Features of the Irish Act which distinguish it from many of its overseas counterparts include the formal system of review with respect to the issuing of such certificates and the system for reporting on the operation of the ministerial certificates mechanism. The provisions relating to the operation of the ministerial certificates mechanism are to be found in section 25 of the Act.

2. Section 25

Section 25 allows a Minister to declare that a record is exempt by virtue of section 23 (law enforcement or public safety) or section 24 (security, defence and international relations) by issuing a certificate to that effect.[128] The effect of the issuance of such a certificate is to establish, conclusively, that the record is exempt.[129] The issuing of certificates cannot, therefore, be subject to internal review or to review by the Information Commissioner. There is, however, provision for appeal against the issue of a certificate to the High Court on a point of law.[130] Certificates remain in force for two years, but they can be renewed, subject to some restrictions.[131]

There are two main prerequisites to the issuing of ministerial certificates. First, such certificates are issued only where a request for access to a record has been refused on the grounds that the record is exempt under section 23 or section 24.[132] Thus, the record must be one which falls within the scope of one or other of these exemption provisions. Second, the Minister must be satisfied that the record is of "sufficient sensitivity or seriousness" to justify the issue of the certificate.[133] Minister for State Fitzgerald refuted the sugges-

---

[126] Official Information Act 1982, s.32.
[127] Freedom of Information Act 1982 (Cth), s.58.
[128] s.25(1)(a).
[129] s.25(3).
[130] s.42(2).
[131] Section 25(13) provides that certificates can be renewed unless the record has been held not to be an exempt record by virtue of a decision either on internal review or of the Information Commissioner which has not been reversed, or pursuant to a decision by the High Court on appeal.
[132] s.25(1)(a).
[133] s.25(1)(a).

tion made in the Dáil that the operation of this mechanism would result in the imposition of gagging writs by Ministers, saying:

> "The certificates procedure is tightly drawn and circumscribed and would only apply in the most limited and extreme circumstances . . . it is not a blank cheque for Ministers".[134]

The timing of the issuing of certificates is a matter which has given rise to controversy overseas. A public body might be tempted to issue a certificate following receipt of notice of appeal against its decision to refuse access, even though no certificate was issued at the time of the original access application. The Australian Law Reform Commission/Administrative Review Council's joint review of the operation of the Australian federal Freedom of Information Act drew attention to the problem in the following terms:

> "The Review understands that it is not uncommon for agencies to issue a conclusive certificate after an applicant has lodged an appeal with the AAT. The Review considers this practice to be an abuse of the certificate provisions. If a document truly warrants a conclusive certificate, a certificate should be issued at the time the decision is made to refuse access."[135]

The Act goes some way towards dealing with such concerns through the inclusion of section 25(2), which provides that where an application is made to a head of a public body for internal review of a decision to refuse to grant a request, a certificate cannot be issued in respect of the record concerned more than three weeks after the date of the receipt of the application. This protection only applies at the stage of internal review. The need for similar protection in the context of review by the Information Commissioner has not been met.

The certificate must set out the request in respect of which it has been issued and the provisions of sections 23 or 24 under which the record is declared to be exempt.[136] This would seem to require that the specific provisions be identified rather than allowing a reference to be made to the whole sections.

Once a certificate is issued, a copy must be furnished to the requester.[137] A copy of the certificate must also be furnished to the Taoiseach and to other Ministers of the Government as may be prescribed, together with a statement, in writing, of the reasons why the record is exempt, and of the matter by reference to which the Minister is satisfied that the record is of sufficient seriousness to justify the issue of a certificate.[138]

---

[134] 476 *Dáil Debates* Col. 1070 (Second Stage).
[135] Australian Law Reform Commission, Report No. 77/Administrative Review Council, Report No. 40, *Open Government: A Review of the Freedom of Information Act 1982* (Australian Government Publishing Service, Canberra, 1995), para. 8.20.
[136] s.25(5).
[137] s.25(6)(a).
[138] s.25(6)(b).

3. Safeguards

Two main safeguards apply with respect to the issuing of ministerial certificates. These consist of the review mechanism and reporting procedures.

(a) Review mechanism

Two forms of review are provided for: periodic review and review by the Taoiseach.

(i) Periodic review

Provision is made for periodic review of the issue of certificates by the Taoiseach jointly with such other Ministers, if any, as have been prescribed.[139] Such reviews must take place "as soon as may be" after the expiration of each period of six months beginning with the period of six months from the date of commencement of the Act. There is provision for extension, by regulation, of the six-month period to a period not exceeding 12 months. A Minister who has issued a certificate which comes within the scope of the review will be precluded from participating in the review in so far as it relates to the certificate issued by him or her.[140] Such a Minister will, however, be allowed to make submissions to the other Ministers participating in the review.

Those who carry out a review will have the right to examine all relevant records held by, or on behalf of, or under the control of, another head for the purposes of such a review.[141] This means that access must be given, for the purposes of the review, not only to those records which are held by public bodies, but also to records held by anyone in the public or private sector on behalf of the head of a public body, as well as to any records held under the control of the head of a public body, regardless of who holds those records.

Following the conduct of the review, if the review group is not satisfied, first, that the record to which the certificate relates is an exempt record or, second, that any of the information contained in the record is of sufficient sensitivity or seriousness to justify the continuance in force of the certificate, then they are required to request the Minister who issued the certificate to revoke it.[142]

(ii) Review by the Taoiseach

The Taoiseach may, at any time, review the operations of the mechanism in so far as it relates to any other Minister of the Government or to the issue of a

---

[139] s.25(7)(a).
[140] s.27(5)(b).
[141] s.27(7)(d).
[142] s.27(7)(c).

particular certificate by another Minister.[143] The Taoiseach, in carrying out such a review, will have the same rights to examine relevant records as are provided for in respect of those carrying out periodic review. He or she is subject to a similar obligation to request revocation of a certificate where he is not satisfied, first, that the record to which the certificate relates is an exempt record or, second, that any of the information contained in the record is of sufficient sensitivity or seriousness to justify the continuance in force of the certificate.

(iii) Revocation of certificates

A Minister who, as the result of the operation of either form of review, is requested to revoke a certificate, is obliged to accede to that request.[144] Once a certificate has been revoked, or where it has expired without being renewed or has been annulled by a decision of the High Court, the requester has 28 days within which to lodge an application of review of the original decision to refuse access.[145]

(b) Reporting procedures

Each Minister is obliged to furnish a report to the Information Commissioner on an annual basis, setting out the number of certificates issued by him or her in preceding year.[146] The report must also specify the provisions of section 23 or section 24 by virtue of which access to the record was refused. The report must be appended to the Annual Report of the Information Commissioner, which must be laid before the Houses of the Oireachtas.[147]

---

[143] s.27(8).
[144] s.27(9).
[145] s.25(12).
[146] s.25(11).
[147] s.40(1)(b).

CHAPTER 6

MEETINGS OF THE GOVERNMENT

CHAPTER 6

MEETINGS OF THE GOVERNMENT

A. Introduction

This exemption is concerned with protecting Cabinet papers from disclosure under the FOI Act. It is a long-established principle of Westminster-style government that the confidentiality of Cabinet papers should be maintained.[1] Arguments concerning the alleged incompatibility of FOI legislation with Westminster-style government have centred around the danger to the system of government posed by the possibility of disclosure of Cabinet papers. In particular, it is argued that if Cabinet papers were made available to the public, the notion of collective ministerial responsibility for Cabinet decisions (which is explicitly protected under the Irish Constitution[2]) would be greatly undermined. The Australian Senate Standing Committee on Constitutional Affairs in its 1979 report on the Australian FOI Bill explained the issue thus:

> "[I]t would undoubtedly be felt that if the traditional solidarity of Cabinet were to be undermined, the stability of Cabinet government as such would be weakened. Similarly, it might be felt that if the secrecy of Cabinet discussions were breached then frank discussion would no longer be possible, especially if particular points of view were to be identifiable with particular ministers who might be in a minority, and as a result the operations of the Cabinet would be impaired."[3]

Whether strict adherence to the principles of Westminster-style government is, or was ever, observed in Ireland or elsewhere, is questionable.[4] The preoccupation with Cabinet secrecy has, in any case, been reflected in the world-

---

[1] See Birkinshaw, *Freedom of Information: The Law, the Practice and the Ideal* (2nd ed., Butterworths, 1996), pp. 153–155; Farrell, "'Cagey and Secretive': Collective Responsibility, Executive Confidentiality and the Public Interest" in *Modern Irish Democracy: Essays in Honour of Basil Chubb* (Hill and Marsh ed., Cork University Press, 1993), pp. 93–95.

[2] Bunreacht na hÉireann, Article 28.4.2°.

[3] Senate Standing Committee on Constitutional and Legal Affairs, *Report by the Senate Standing Committee on Constitutional and Legal Affairs on the Freedom of Information Bill 1978, and aspects of the Archives Bill 1978* (Australian Government Publishing Service, Canberra, 1979), para. 4.15.

[4] See for example: Morgan, *Constitutional Law of Ireland* (2nd ed., Round Hall Press, 1990), p. 73; Austin, "Freedom of Information: The Constitutional Impact" in *The Changing Constitution* (Jowell and Oliver ed., 3rd ed., Clarendon, 1994), pp. 394–396; Brazier, *Constitutional Practice* (2nd ed., Clarendon, 1994), p. 142.

wide exemption of Cabinet papers from FOI legislation.[5] Whilst the acceptance of the exemption of Cabinet papers from the scope of FOI legislation is
universal, there is some variation between jurisdictions in terms of the definition of Cabinet papers used for the purposes of the exemption. The most important issue to be addressed in analysing the scope of section 19 of the Irish
FOI Act, therefore, is what constitutes Cabinet papers or, more precisely, records
concerning "meetings of the Government".

A brief description of the Cabinet process and of the records it generates
will assist in the identification of records to which this exemption may apply.[6]
Not all Cabinet meetings involve a formal gathering of all the members of the
Government. For example, "incorporeal" meetings of the Government can
take place where Ministers are consulted by telephone in circumstances where
a decision is required before the next scheduled meeting of Cabinet.[7] Therefore, while there is usually a written agenda for meetings of the Government,
this is not always the case. Records which are brought to meetings of the
Government include memoranda for Government and *aides memoire*. The
former consist of formal submissions or proposals submitted to Cabinet by
individual Ministers in respect of a particular proposal. The memorandum
will often be supplemented by appendices containing documents supporting
the proposal, such as analyses prepared by civil servants, reports of government bodies or of external consultants, draft legislation, or statistical material.
An *aide memoire* for Government records matters in respect of which no formal Government decision is required, but of which a Minister wishes to advise Government. It could, for example, consist of notice to Government that
a department intends releasing a report it has commissioned.

---

[5] See for example Australia: Freedom of Information Act 1982 (Cth), s.34; Freedom of
Information Act 1982 (Victoria), s.28; Freedom of Information Act 1989 (New South
Wales), Sched.1, cl.1; Freedom of Information Act 1991 (South Australia), Sched.1,
cl.1; Freedom of Information Act 1991 (Tasmania), s.24; Freedom of Information Act
1992 (Western Australia), Sched.1, cl.1; Freedom of Information Act 1992 (Queens-
land), s.36.
Canada: Access to Information Act (Canada), R.S.C., 1985, s.69; Right to Information
Act (New Brunswick), S.N.B., 1978, s.6(a), (g), and (h); An Act respecting Access to
documents held by public bodies and the Protection of personal information (Quebec),
S.Q., 1982, s.33; Freedom of Information and Protection of Privacy Act (Manitoba),
C.C.S.M., 1998, c.F175, s.19; Freedom of Information Act (Newfoundland), R.S.N.,
1990, s.9(1)(b)–(f) and (2); Freedom of Information and Protection of Privacy Act (Saskatchewan), S.S., 1990–1991, s.16(1); Freedom of Information and Protection of Privacy Act (Ontario), R.S.O, 1990, s.12; Freedom of Information and Protection of Privacy Act (British Columbia), R.S.B.C., 1996, s.12; Freedom of Information and Protection of Privacy Act (Nova Scotia), S.N.S., 1993, s.13; Freedom of Information and Protection of Privacy Act (Alberta), S.A., 1994, s.21.
New Zealand: Official Information Act 1982, s.9(2)(f) and (g).
[6] See Dooney and O'Toole, *Irish Government Today* (Gill and Macmillan, 1992), pp. 5–7
for a description of the conduct of meetings of the Government.
[7] *ibid.*, p. 7. See also Farrell, *op. cit.* above, n. 1, p. 93.

Minutes of Government meetings are not kept as such. Documents which record the outcome of meetings of the Government consist instead, of records of matters agreed at Government meetings, Cabinet "pinks" and published Government decisions.

Records of matters agreed at Government meetings are generally uninformative, disclosing only the details of the date, time, attendance and location of the meeting along with a record of the decisions taken at the meeting and a note of any *aide memoire* which has been dealt with by the meeting. The earlier practice of recording individual ministerial dissents from government decisions appears to have ended in the early 1920s.[8] In particular, no record is kept of discussions which take place at meetings of the Government.

Cabinet "pinks" consist of notes recording the decision arrived at by the Government members which are kept by the Secretary General to the Government.[9] These notes sometimes record more than just the decision arrived at and could possibly reveal the views of individual Ministers with respect to the decision.

Decisions of the Cabinet may be published to the general public, or they may simply be recorded in the notes of the relevant Government meeting, but not published. In the former case, a record setting out the decision will be prepared.

The foregoing discussion has concentrated on the records which are generated by the Cabinet process itself. It is possible, of course, for records relating to meetings of the Government to be generated outside of that process. For example, a record could be created within a government department which refers to a decision taken at a meeting of the Government.

Before embarking on a detailed analysis of section 19, it is worth reflecting on the background to its introduction. Section 19 was developed in the shadow of a 1992 Supreme Court decision concerning Cabinet confidentiality. The case of *Attorney General v. Hamilton*[10] arose out of the Beef Tribunal, an inquiry into allegations of illegal activities in the beef industry. During the course of the tribunal's proceedings, a former Minister was asked a question relating to discussions at a particular Cabinet meeting. The Attorney General objected to the question on the basis that matters discussed at Cabinet meetings were entitled to absolute confidentiality. The Chairman and sole member of the tribunal, Mr Justice Hamilton, declared himself entitled to receive the evidence and the Attorney General sought judicial review of that decision. O'Hanlon J. in the High Court found in favour of the Chairman of the tribunal, saying:

"In my opinion, the concession of the absolute ban on disclosure at all times and

---

[8] *ibid.*
[9] These notes are kept on pink notepaper.
[10] [1993] 2 I.R. 250.

under all circumstances of what has transpired at meetings of the Government, such as is claimed by the Attorney General in these proceedings, would not have due regard to the public interest and to the rights of the individual as guaranteed by the Constitution. If it were intended that such absolute blanket of confidentiality should take effect, in contradistinction to the legal situation prevailing in so many other democratic communities, then I would expect it to have been spelt out in clear terms in the Constitution".[11]

This view was rejected by a 3-2 majority of the Supreme Court. The Chief Justice based his decision primarily on the provisions of Articles 28.4.1° and 28.4.2° of the Constitution. Finlay C.J. held that the obligations placed upon the Government to meet and act collectively, to be collectively responsible for all the departments of State and to have a responsibility to Dáil Éireann necessarily entailed some consequential duties, which he described as follows:

"The first of th[e]se relevant to the issues arising in this appeal is the necessity for full, free and frank discussion between members of the Government prior to the making of decisions, something which would appear to be an inevitable adjunct to the obligation to meet collectively and to act collectively. The obligation to act collectively must, of necessity, involve the making of a single decision on any issue, whether it is arrived at unanimously or by a majority. The obligation to accept collective responsibility for decisions and, presumably, for acts of government as well, involves, as a necessity, the non-disclosure of different or dissenting views held by members of the Government prior to the making of decisions."[12]

In conclusion, Finlay C.J. stated:

"[T]he claim for confidentiality of the contents and details of discussions at meetings of the Government, made by the Attorney General in relation to the inquiry of this Tribunal is a valid claim. It extends to discussions and to their contents, but it does not, of course, extend to the decisions made and the documentary evidence of them, whether they are classified as formal or informal decisions."[13]

Following the decision in *Attorney General v. Hamilton*, the Government indicated its willingness to introduce a Bill to amend the Constitution in order to allow for the relaxation, in certain circumstances, of what was seen as the absolute rule in favour of Cabinet confidentiality. The Seventeenth Amendment of the Constitution (No. 2) Bill, which was introduced after the passing of the FOI Act, proposed the insertion of the following subsection in Article 28 of the Constitution:

---

[11] *ibid.* at 258.

[12] *ibid.* at 266. For comprehensive criticism of this decision see Hogan, "The Cabinet Confidentiality Case of 1992" (1993) *Irish Political Studies* 131. See also Hogan and Whyte, *Kelly: The Irish Constitution* (3rd ed., Butterworths, 1994), pp. 250–257.

[13] *Attorney General v. Hamilton*, above, n. 10, at 272.

"3° The confidentiality of discussions at meetings of the Government shall be respected in all circumstances save only where the High Court determines that disclosure should be made in respect of a particular matter—
   i. in the interests of the administration of justice by a Court, or
   ii. by virtue of an overriding public interest, pursuant to an application in that behalf by a tribunal appointed by the Government or a Minister of the Government on the authority of the Houses of the Oireachtas to inquire into a matter stated by them to be of public importance."

The amendment was carried in the ensuing referendum,[14] despite opposition from a number of eminent commentators who were of the view that its effect would be counterproductive in that, by providing for express constitutional recognition of Cabinet confidentiality, it would copperfasten such confidentiality in an unacceptably narrow form.[15]

While the constitutional amendment allows for the relaxation of the rule concerning confidentiality of Cabinet discussions in certain circumstances, these do not encompass the exercise of a person's right of access to records under the FOI Act.

The *Hamilton* decision strongly influenced the wording of the Government meetings exemption in the FOI Act. In particular, the wording of the exemption sought to prevent the disclosure under the FOI Act of records revealing Cabinet deliberations. In order to ensure that such records would not be disclosed, the part of section 19 which was aimed at exempting records relating to Cabinet discussions was, in contrast to the other elements of section 19, framed in mandatory rather than discretionary terms.

Regardless of the outcome of *Hamilton*, there was little likelihood that the FOI Act would have afforded a right of access to details of Cabinet discussions. There are two grounds on which this assertion can be made. The first is that FOI legislation in jurisdictions operating under a Westminster-style of government invariably contains exemptions in respect of records relating to Cabinet discussions[16] and there is no reason to believe that the approach adopted here would have been any different. Therefore, while the *Hamilton* decision had the effect of ensuring that the FOI Act would be framed in a manner which would prevent the provision of access to records revealing the contents of Cabinet discussions, it did not result in a more restrictive approach to the disclosure of Cabinet papers in Ireland than is found in overseas FOI regimes. A more practical reason why, regardless of the decision in *Hamilton,* the FOI Act would have been unlikely to have facilitated access to details of Cabinet-level discussions is that the Act grants a right of access to "records"

---

[14] The referendum was held on October 30, 1997.
[15] These included former Taoiseach Garrett FitzGerald, Des O'Malley, a politician with many years of Cabinet experience, and former T.D. and Senior Counsel Michael McDowell.
[16] Above, n. 5.

rather than to information. Details of Cabinet discussions are not officially minuted and they are unlikely to be otherwise recorded. They would, therefore, be unlikely to come within the scope of the access rights conferred by the Act.

B.   The Substance of the Exemption

The exemption provides as follows:

"19.—(1) A head may refuse to grant a request under section 7 if the record concerned—
  (a) has been, or is proposed to be, submitted to the Government for their consideration by a Minister of the Government or the Attorney General and was created for that purpose,
  (b) is a record of the Government other than a record by which a decision of the Government is published to the general public by or on behalf of the Government, or
  (c) contains information (including advice) for a member of the Government, the Attorney General, a Minister of State, the Secretary to the Government or the Assistant Secretary to the Government for use by him or her solely for the purpose of the transaction of any business of the Government at a meeting of the Government.

(2) A head shall refuse to grant a request under section 7 if the record concerned—
  (a) contains the whole or part of a statement made at a meeting of the Government or information that reveals, or from which may be inferred, the substance of the whole or part of such a statement, and
  (b) is not a record—
    (i) referred to in paragraph (a) or (c) of subsection (1), or
    (ii) by which a decision of the Government is published to the general public by or on behalf of the Government.

(3) Subject to the provisions of this Act, subsection (1) does not apply to a record referred to in that subsection—
  (a) if and in so far as it contains factual information relating to a decision of the Government that has been published to the general public, or
  (b) if the record relates to a decision of the Government that was made more than 5 years before the receipt by the head concerned of the request under section 7 concerned.

(4) A decision to grant a request under section 7 in respect of a record to which paragraph (a) or (b) of subsection (1) applies shall not be made unless, in so far as it is practicable to do so, the head concerned has, prior to the making of the decision, consulted in relation to the request with—
  (a) the leader of each political party to which belonged a member of the Government that made any decision to which the record relates, and
  (b) any member of the Government aforesaid who was not a member of a political party.

(5) Where a request under section 7 relates to a record to which subsection (1) applies, or would, if the record existed, apply, and the head concerned is satisfied that the disclosure of the existence or non-existence of the record would be contrary to the public interest, he or she shall refuse to grant the request and shall not disclose to the requester concerned whether or not the record exists.

(6) In this section—

'decision of the Government' includes the noting or approving by the Government of a record submitted to them;

'record' includes a preliminary or other draft of the whole or part of the material contained in the record;

'Government' includes a committee of the Government, that is to say, a committee appointed by the Government whose membership consists of—

(a) members of the Government, or

(b) one or more members of the Government together with either or both of the following:

(i) one or more Ministers of State,

(ii) the Attorney General."

The exemption is class based, in that it sets out a list of four categories of record which are exempt. Public bodies need not, therefore, consider what harm, if any, is expected to flow from disclosure of the particular record sought. Each of the four categories of Cabinet paper protected by the exemption can be characterised as relating to particular stages in the cabinet process. The first two categories relate to what can be referred to as the pre-deliberative stage, that is, that part of the Cabinet process leading up to the making of a Cabinet decision. The third category of exempted record is concerned with the deliberative stage of the Cabinet process, while the fourth category of exempted record concerns the post-deliberative stage.

The pre-deliberative exemptions are found in section 19(1)(a) and (c). These elements of the exemption are discretionary. They allow respectively for the exemption of records submitted to Government, and for the exemption of briefing records used for the purpose of transacting business at meetings of the Government. The broad aim of these elements of the exemption is to ensure that records which form the basis of Cabinet decisions cannot be made public under the FOI Act. The operation of these elements of the exemption is, however, subject to two exceptions. In the first place, pre-deliberative records containing factual information relating to Government decisions which have been published will not be exempt, nor will such records be exempt where they relate to decisions made more than five years before the application for access was received.

The third category of record covered by section 19 is relevant to the discussion stage of the Cabinet process. This limb of the exemption is found in section 19(2). It is concerned with protecting statements made at meetings of the Government. Its use is mandatory and it is not subject to any exceptions.

Finally, section 19(1)(b) exempts records relating to the post-decisional stage of the Cabinet process. This element of the exemption is expressed in discretionary terms and exempts from the scope of the Act records of the Government, other than a record by which a decision of the Government has been published to the general public. Its application is subject to the operation of both exceptions. Such records will not be exempt, therefore, where they contain purely factual material, provided that the decision to which the record relates has been made public. Nor will this limb of the exemption apply where more than five years have elapsed since the relevant Government decision was made.

The exemption is not subject to the operation of a public interest test and so, once it has been shown that a record falls within its scope, disclosure of the record in question can be denied without any reference to the public interest. The head of the public body concerned is permitted to refuse to disclose the existence or non-existence of information where such disclosure would be contrary to the public interest. Unlike some of its overseas counterparts,[17] the Irish FOI Act does not include Cabinet records amongst the categories of records in respect of which a ministerial certificate[18] can be issued.

1. Scope of the exemption: the "Government"

The arrangement of sections as well as the marginal note concerning this exemption refer to it as concerning "meetings of the Government". The Government is an entity which is given express recognition in the Constitution, being charged with the exercise of the executive power of the State[19] and is commonly referred to as the Cabinet. The Constitution stipulates that the Government shall consist of not less than seven and not more than 15 members.[20] The scope of the exemption, however, extends beyond the Government itself. It includes records submitted to the Government for their consideration by the Attorney General. It also embraces briefing materials for the Secretary or Assistant Secretary to the Government for use for the purpose of transacting business at Government meetings. The definition of Government includes a committee appointed by the Government whose membership consists of members of the Government or one or more members of the Government with one or more Ministers of State and/or the Attorney General.[21]

---

[17] See, for example, Australia: Freedom of Information Act 1982 (Cth), s.34(2), (3), (4), and (5); Freedom of Information Act 1982 (Victoria), s.28(4); Freedom of Information Act 1989 (New South Wales), s.59; Freedom of Information Act 1991 (South Australia), s.46; Freedom of Information Act 1991 (Tasmania), s.24(3); Freedom of Information Act 1992 (Western Australia), s.36; Freedom of Information Act 1992 (Queensland), s.36(3).

[18] See above, pp. 115–119.

[19] Article 28.2.

[20] Article 28.1.

[21] s.19(6).

2. Exempt categories

Each of the four limbs of the exemption will be considered in turn.

(a) Records submitted to Government – section 19(1)(a)

Records submitted to Government are exempted in the following terms:

> "19.—(1) A head may refuse to grant a request under section 7 if the record concerned—
>
> (a) has been, or is proposed to be, submitted to the Government for their consideration by a Minister of the Government or the Attorney General and was created for that purpose".

The main concern underlying the exemption from the scope of the Act of records submitted to Government is that the release of the material upon which Cabinet decisions are based could divulge a lack of unanimity in the Cabinet. The disclosure of a memorandum for Government, for example, could divulge a lack of unanimity in the Cabinet in circumstances where the memorandum advocates a certain position and the decision emanating from the Government diverges from that approach.

The wording of this element of the exemption gives rise to three main requirements:

(1) the record must have been created for the purpose of submission to the Government;

(2) the record must have been or be proposed to be submitted to the Government; and

(3) the record must have been or be proposed to be submitted for the consideration of the Government.

The first requirement means that a document is not exempt merely because it has been or is proposed to be submitted to Cabinet. As the Queensland Information Commissioner stated in referring to the similarly worded Queensland provision:[22]

> "Inquiries must be pursued into the 'genealogy' of such a document, to establish the purpose for which it was brought into existence. The time of the creation of the document is the time at which the purpose for its creation must be ascertained. The fact that it was subsequently decided to annex to a Cabinet submission, a document that was brought into existence for the purpose other than submission to Cabinet for Cabinet consideration, will not bring the document within [the Cabinet records exemption]."[23]

---

[22] Freedom of Information Act 1992 (Queensland), s.36(1)(a).
[23] *Hudson (on behalf of Fencray Pty Limited) and Department of the Premier, Economic and Trade Development* (1993) 1 Q.A.R. 123 at 134.

The rationale behind the requirement that records submitted to the Government for its consideration will only be subject to the exemption where they have been created for the purpose of such submission is explained, in the following terms, in the *Report of the Legal and Constitutional Committee of the Parliament of Victoria on Freedom of Information in Victoria*:

> "The primary focus (of the exemption) I would have thought is not so much about protecting Cabinet documents or institutions, as about protecting the processes that together form the method of Cabinet decision making. That is important, because the moment people talk about protecting and defining Cabinet documents as such, inevitably they come up with definitions that have the capacity to extend well beyond the Cabinet room and beyond the Cabinet process into the routine filing Cabinets of the bureaucracy...
>
> Ultimately I come down in favour of the kind of exemptions contained in the Victorian and Commonwealth Acts that try to focus upon protection only of deliberations and of the submissions which have always had Cabinet as their predestined recipient."[24]

The Committee went on to identify a second, and more pragmatic, reason for limiting the scope of the exemption to records created for the purpose of submission to Cabinet, which was that:

> "[i]f any document considered by the Cabinet was to be protected, it would constitute an open invitation to Ministers and officials to put documents beyond the reach of the Act simply by attaching to them Cabinet submissions."[25]

It is clear from the following comment of the sponsoring Minister that the need to protect against such practices influenced the wording of this provision:

> "Section 19 only applies to material specifically prepared for the Government. It would not be open to someone to run something past the Government thereby acquiring protection."[26]

The second requirement of section 19(1)(a) is that a record *has been or is proposed to be* submitted to the Government. The corresponding phrase in the Australian federal FOI Act (section 34(1)(a)) was interpreted by Hartigan J. of the Administrative Appeals Tribunal (A.A.T.) in the following terms:

> "It seems to me that the words of s.34(1)(a) make it clear that the time the document 'was brought into existence' is the relevant time at which to look at the document. However, the document must be one of which it can be said that it is proposed to be submitted to Cabinet. I consider that the subsection does not

---

[24] Legal and Constitutional Committee of the Parliament of Victoria, *Thirty Eighth Report to the Parliament: Report upon Freedom of Information in Victoria* (1989), para. 7.30: evidence to the committee of Mr John McMillan.

[25] *ibid.*, para. 7.32.

[26] 149 *Seanad Debates* Col. 1573 (Committee Stage), *per* Eithne Fitzgerald, Minister of State at the Department of the Taoiseach.

grant an exemption to documents that are not submitted to the Cabinet despite intentions to do so at the time of their creation. It seems to me that the subsection only grants exemption to documents already submitted or proposed to be submitted if they were created with that intention. The subsection clearly grants the exemption to documents that are proposed to be put before the Cabinet not to documents that were proposed to be put before Cabinet but never were. Thus a document may lose its claim for exemption when it is proposed no longer to submit the document to Cabinet."[27]

The third requirement is that the record must have been or be proposed to be submitted for the *consideration* of the Government. This requirement would not, therefore, be met where the record was submitted for a purpose other than its consideration by the Government. On that basis, a record which had been submitted merely for the information of the Government would not qualify for exemption. "Consideration", it is submitted, is the initial step in a process leading to the making of a decision. Where the Cabinet merely notes the content of a record and is not required to arrive at any decision in relation to its contents, the requirement that the record has been submitted for the consideration of the Government will not be met. Therefore, it is suggested that *aides memoire* for Government are not covered by this limb of the exemption.

(b) Briefing records – section 19(1)(c)

This limb of the exemption is aimed at protecting from disclosure materials used to brief Government members in relation to matters before Cabinet. It provides as follows:

> "19.—(1) A head may refuse to grant a request under section 7 if the record concerned. . .
>
>   (c) contains information (including advice) for a member of the Government, the Attorney General, a Minister of State, the Secretary to the Government or the Assistant Secretary to the Government for use by him or her solely for the purpose of the transaction of any business of the Government at a meeting of the Government."

Two conditions must be met in order for briefing materials to qualify for protection under section 19(1)(c):

(1) the material must consist of information or advice for a member of the Government, the Attorney General, a Minister of State, the Secretary to the Government or the Assistant Secretary to the Government; and

(2) the information must be for use solely for the purpose of the transaction of Government business at a meeting of the Government.

---

[27] *Re Aldred and Department of Foreign Affairs and Trade* (1990) 20 A.L.D. 264 at 265–266.

One issue which is not made clear is whether in order the qualify for protection under this provision, records must have been created for the purpose of their use as briefing materials. While it is clear that the information must have been furnished to the Government member for the purpose of its use in the transaction of Government business, it is not entirely clear from the text of section 19(1)(c) whether the generation of the information, in the first place, must have been for the purpose of its transmission to a member of the Government. This question has practical implications. In particular, clarification is required as to the applicability of this limb of the exemption to records prepared for other purposes which are subsequently used by Government members for the sole purpose of transacting Government business.

(c) Statements made at Government meetings – section 19(2)

This element of the exemption relates to the deliberative stage of the Cabinet process. It seeks to protect from disclosure records containing information relating to Cabinet deliberations. Such exemptions are common in overseas FOI Acts[28] and would have been likely to have been included in the Irish Act regardless of the decision in *Hamilton*. Before embarking on an analysis of this element of the exemption, it is worth noting that the potential application of the FOI Act to details of Cabinet discussions is greatly limited by the fact that such information is not officially recorded. It is, however, possible that a reference to the views of an individual Minister could be recorded by the Secretary to the Government on the Cabinet pinks. It is also possible for an account of a meeting of the Government and the discussions which took place at it to be created on an unofficial basis by someone who participated in the meeting.

The aim of this element of the exemption, as stated in the Dáil by the sponsoring Minister of State, was to formulate a provision which would be "sufficiently narrow to be consistent with [the decision in *Attorney General v. Hamilton*]".[29] In order to qualify for exemption, a record must meet two cumulative requirements. The first requirement, which is set out in section 19(2)(a), is fulfilled where the record contains either:

(1) the whole or part of a statement made at a meeting of the Government; or

(2) information that reveals, or from which may be inferred, the substance of the whole or part of such a statement.

The second requirement, which is found in section 19(2)(b), is aimed at limiting the scope of this limb of the exemption. It provides that section 19(2) will not apply to records falling within the scope of either section 19(1)(a) or sec-

---

[28] See above, n. 5.
[29] 477 *Dáil Debates* Col. 765 (Report Stage).

tion 19(1)(c), nor will it apply in the case of records of Government decisions which have been published to the general public. The effect of section 19(2)(b) is to exclude from the scope of section 19(2) records submitted to Government as defined in section 19(1)(a), briefing materials as defined in section 19(1)(c), and records by which Government decisions are published to the general public. This provision was introduced by way of Government amendment at Report Stage in the Dáil. The rationale for its inclusion was explained by the sponsoring Minister in the following terms:

> "This amendment also seeks to ensure that memoranda to the Government and briefing material may not be captured by this provision. It was clear from the Supreme Court judgment on Cabinet confidentiality that it literally only referred to talk around the table. It does not protect memoranda to Government or the decisions."[30]

An important issue to arise in the context of this limb of the exemption is whether the protection it affords is sufficient to meet the requirements of the constitutional amendment regarding Cabinet confidentiality. The Constitution requires that the confidentiality of discussions at meetings of the Government shall be respected in all circumstances, subject to two exceptions which are not relevant to the FOI context. Section 19(2) provides an exemption from the right of access to information conferred by the FOI Act in respect of a "statement made" at a meeting of the Government. It could be argued that statements made at a Government meeting can be distinguished from discussions at meetings of the Government. The making of a statement at a meeting is arguably a more formal process than the conduct of discussions. On that basis, it might be suggested that the scope of section 19(2) does not extend to cover all records of discussions at meetings of the Government and that, therefore, it is unconstitutional. On the other hand, the stated intention of the sponsoring Minister of State that the exemption would be consistent with the decision in *Hamilton* supports the application of section 19(2) to all records of Cabinet discussions.

It has been suggested in the context of the corresponding Australian federal exemption that where the content of any deliberation or decision of Cabinet has already been disclosed to third parties, the exemption can no longer apply. Such disclosure was characterised in one Australian case as an implied waiver of Cabinet confidentiality.[31] However, it would appear in the light of the decision in *Hamilton* that no such waiver is possible in the context of section 19(2). The issue of waiver was directly addressed by Finlay C.J. when he referred to the confidentiality of the contents and details of discussions at meetings of the Government as:

---

[30] 476 *Dáil Debates* Cols 765–766 (Report Stage).
[31] *Re Burchill and Department of Industrial Relations* (1991) 13 A.A.R. 217; (1991) 23 A.L.D. 97.

"a constitutional right which, in my view, goes to the fundamental machinery of government, and is, therefore, not capable of being waived by any individual member of a government…".[32]

(d) Records of the Government – section 19(1)(b)

Finally, the exemption addresses the post-deliberative stage of the Cabinet process by exempting under section 19(1)(b) a record of the Government other than a record by which a Government decision is published to the general public by or on behalf of the Government. This element of the exemption applies to records of Government decisions which are not made public. "Decision of the Government" is defined broadly to include the noting or approving by the Government of a record submitted to it. The scope of the exemption therefore extends to records consisting of the noting of the contents of *aides memoire* which have come before the Cabinet. While no formal minutes are currently kept in respect of meetings of the Government, this limb of the exemption would apply to minutes of Government meetings, were the taking of such minutes to be introduced in the future. It also protects from disclosure agendas for Government meetings and Cabinet "pinks". Expressly excluded from the scope of this limb of the exemption are records by which a decision of the Government is published to the general public, but only where such decisions are published *by or on behalf of the Government*. Thus, where a decision of the Government is leaked to the public, the record of that decision will be exempt.

The justification for the withholding of Government decisions was discussed in a report of the Ontarian Commission on Freedom of Information and Individual Privacy ("the Williams report").[33] The Commission rejected the argument that it was in the public interest that Cabinet decisions be made available immediately. It argued, by contrast, that there were many situations in which the announcement of Cabinet decisions should properly be delayed. These would include situations where arrangements have been entered into with other governments or with affected individuals to postpone announcement until a specific time or the occurrence of a particular event, or where plans have been developed for dealing with emergencies or other contingencies, the effectiveness of which would be diminished by public announcements. Further, the report argued that the proper forum for the announcement of the decisions of the Executive was Parliament. There was, in its view, no merit in reducing the importance of the legislature as the forum for such announcements.[34]

---

[32] Above, n. 10, at 272.
[33] *Public Government for Private People: The Report of the Commission on Freedom of Information and Individual Privacy* (1980), Vol. 2.
[34] *ibid.* at 286.

3. Drafts of Cabinet records

The definition of record contained in section 19 is expressed to include "a preliminary or other draft of the whole or part of the material contained in the record". A survey of legislation in Canada, Australia and New Zealand reveals that the Australian States of New South Wales and South Australia are the only jurisdictions where draft Cabinet records are exempt. The reluctance to extend the protection of the Cabinet records exemption to draft records is explained in the report of the Legal and Constitutional Committee of the Parliament of Victoria in the following terms:

> "Collective ministerial responsibility is engaged only when documents are submitted by Ministers to Cabinet for its consideration. Thus, earlier working papers on similar issues and draft Cabinet documents should not qualify for protection."[35]

4. Exceptions

There are two main limitations on the scope of this exemption. The first concerns the exclusion of factual material, while the second imposes a time constraint on the application of the exemption. These exceptions are only available in respect of records falling within the scope of section 19(1). They cannot, therefore, be used to obtain access to statements made at meetings of the Government.

(a) Factual material

Section 19(3)(a) provides that subsection (1) of the exemption shall not apply to a record referred to in section 19(1), if and in so far as the record contains factual information relating to a decision of the Government, but only where that decision has been published to the general public. The aim of this exception is to ensure that the raw material on which the Cabinet process operates will be subject to disclosure under the FOI Act. The need for such an exception was illustrated by the Australian Senate Standing Committee on Constitutional Affairs in its 1979 report on the Australian FOI Bill by reference to the following set of examples:

> "For instance, it is possible that a minister may order the compilation of a broad category of important statistics on Australian social or economic life, for consideration by Cabinet, in relation to a proposed policy. Again, Cabinet may require a major study, primarily of a factual nature, on the feasibility of a new policy or on the implications for Australia of a projected proposal. Reference can also be made to important reports prepared by such bodies as the Adminis-

---

[35] Legal and Constitutional Committee of the Parliament of Victoria, *Thirty Eighth Report to the Parliament: Report upon Freedom of Information in Victoria* (Government Printer, Melbourne, 1989), para. 5.27.

trative Review Council on new or proposed legislation, which we understand are often submitted to a Minister for consideration by the Cabinet. Of a comparable nature are the reports of consultants. Quite often, they are prepared, at a considerable cost to the public, to evaluate the efficiency of existing government programs." [36]

The report went on to argue that:

"(t)o disclose documents of the type to which we referred to in the previous paragraph is to disclose only the raw material on which the cabinet process operate; it is not necessarily to disclose anything about Cabinet process itself. Disclosure may conceivably damage the political fortunes of those who participate in the Cabinet process, but this essentially distinct from, and should not be confused with, the process itself. Only the latter should be protected by the exemption". [37]

Section 20 of the Act (the exemption concerning deliberations of public bodies), also contains an exception in respect of factual information. It provides that the exemption does not apply to a record if and in so far as it contains factual (including statistical) information and analyses thereof. [38]

The factual material referred to in section 19(3)(a) must relate to a *decision* of the Government. This means that factual information concerning matters currently under consideration will be exempt until a decision has been arrived at. In order to qualify for disclosure under this exception, the factual information must relate to a decision which has been published to the general public. In contrast to section 19(1)(b), the scope of this provision is not confined to decisions, the publication of which has been effected *by or on behalf of the Government.* Therefore, factual information concerning Government decisions which have become public by any means, authorised or unauthorised, will come within the scope of the exception. Since the exception applies "if and in so far as" a record contains such information, it would appear that where a record includes factual information as well as exempt material, the latter can be deleted and the factual information can be disclosed under section 19(3). Such severance of exempt material from non-exempt material would, in any case, be permitted under section 13, which provides for the granting of access to part of a record.

Factual material is excluded from the Cabinet records exemption found in the Australian [39] and Canadian Acts. [40] The concept of purely factual material also arises in the context of the separate deliberative processes exemption of

---

[36] Senate Standing Committee on Constitutional and Legal Affairs, *op. cit.* above, n. 3, para. 18.6.
[37] *ibid.*, para. 18.7.
[38] See below, pp. 152–154.
[39] Freedom of Information Act 1982 (Cth), s.34(1A); Freedom of Information Act 1989 (New South Wales), Sched.1, cl.1(2); Freedom of Information Act 1991 (South Australia), Sched.1, cl.1(2); Freedom of Information Act 1991 (Tasmania), s.24(5); Free-

the Australian Act.[41] The U.S. courts, in interpreting Exemption 5 of the Act which protects "inter-agency or intra-agency memorandums or letters which would not be available by law to a party other than an agency in litigation with the agency", have also drawn a distinction between purely factual material and material relating to deliberative processes.[42]

There are few decisions concerning the operation of the exception in the context of Cabinet records. In a case decided by the Australian federal A.A.T., it was held that matter might be "purely factual" even if its disclosure:

> "will give some indication of the subject matter of the document submitted to Cabinet. It will imply that the facts, as stated, were relevant to a matter considered by Cabinet".[43]

In the Queensland case of *Hudson (on behalf of Fencray Pty Limited) and Department of the Premier, Economic and Trade Development*,[44] the Information Commissioner considered the meaning of the exception to the Cabinet documents exemption for matter which is merely factual or statistical.[45] The Commissioner put forward the view that:

> "merely factual matter is generally to be distinguished from matter expressing the opinions and recommendations of individual Ministers on policy issues and policy options requiring Cabinet determination. Factual matter which merely provides the factual background, or informs Cabinet of relevant facts, so as to assist its deliberations on policy issues, will generally constitute 'merely factual matter'".[46]

(b) Time limit

Subsection (1) of the exemption does not apply in respect of records which relate to a decision of the Government that was made more than five years before the receipt of the request for access.[47] Similar provisions appear in the

---

dom of Information Act 1992 (Western Australia), Sched.1, cl.1(2); Freedom of Information Act 1992 (Queensland), s.36(2).

[40] Access to Information Act (Canada), R.S.C., 1985, s.69(3)(b); Freedom of Information and Protection of Privacy Act (Alberta), S.A., 1994, s.21(2)(c); Freedom of Information and Protection of Privacy Act (British Columbia), R.S.B.C., 1996, s.12(2)(c); Freedom of Information and Protection of Privacy Act (Nova Scotia), S.N.S., 1993, s.13(2)(c).

[41] Freedom of Information Act 1982 (Cth), s.36(5).

[42] *Environmental Protection Agency v. Mink*, 410 U.S. 73 (1973).

[43] *Re Anderson and Australian Federal Police* (1986) 11 A.L.D. 355; 4 A.A.R. 414 at 442, *per* Hall D.P.

[44] Above, n. 23.

[45] This exception was repealed when the Queensland Freedom of Information Act was amended in 1995.

[46] Above, n. 23, at 148.

[47] s.19(3)(b).

Canadian federal Act[48] and in a number of the Canadian provincial[49] and Australian State FOI Acts[50] (but not in the Australian federal statute). There is considerable variation in the time limits applied, but the shortest time limit provided for in any of the overseas legislation is 10 years, as opposed to the five provided for in section 19.[51] The effect of this exception is that Cabinet records, apart from those which are referred to in section 19(2), will be subject to disclosure when the decision to which they relate is more than five years old at the time the application for access is made.

C. Consultation with Former Administrations

A feature of the exemption not found in overseas FOI legislation is the requirement that a request for access to a record referred to in section 19(1)(a) or 19(1)(b) and which relates to a previous Government shall not be granted until the head of the public body concerned has consulted with the leaders of each party which formed part of that previous Government, or with any member of that previous Government who was not a member of a political party.[52] This is an unusual provision which resembles the United Kingdom convention which restricts the disclosure by the government of the day of the papers of a previous government without the consent of the previous Prime Minister concerned and the consent of the Queen.[53] It can come into play in two circumstances. The first is where access is to be granted to a record referred to in section 19(1)(a) or 19(1)(b) in pursuance of the exercise of the discretion available to the head of a public body to release such records. The second is where access is to be granted to a record referred to in section 19(1)(a) or 19(1)(b) through the operation of one of the exceptions provided for under section 19(3).

---

[48] Access to Information Act (Canada), R.S.C., 1985, s.69(3)(a).

[49] Freedom of Information and Protection of Privacy Act (Ontario), R.S.O., 1990, s.12(2)(a); Freedom of Information and Protection of Privacy Act (British Columbia), R.S.B.C., 1996, s.12(2)(a); Freedom of Information and Protection of Privacy Act (Nova Scotia), S.N.S., 1993, s.13(2)(a); Freedom of Information and Protection of Privacy Act (Alberta), S.A., 1994, s.21(2)(a); Freedom of Information and Protection of Privacy Act (Manitoba), C.C.S.M., 1988, c.F175, s.19(2)(b).

[50] Freedom of Information Act 1982 (Victoria), s.28(2); Freedom of Information Act 1991 (Tasmania), s.24(2); Freedom of Information Act 1989 (New South Wales), Sched.1, cl.1(2)(b); Freedom of Information Act 1992 (Western Australia), Sched.1, cl.1(4); Freedom of Information Act 1991 (South Australia), Sched.1, cl.1(2)(b).

[51] The time limits provided for range from 30 years in South Australia and Manitoba through 20 years at federal level in Canada, to 15 years in Ontario, British Columbia and Alberta, and 10 years in Nova Scotia, Tasmania, Western Australia, New South Wales, and Victoria.

[52] s.19(4).

[53] Birkinshaw, *op. cit.* above, n. 1, p. 216.

The consultation requirement applies only in respect of records covered by section 19(1)(a) and 19(1)(b), but not to those referred to in section 19(1)(c). It was apparently decided that it would be too onerous to impose a consultation requirement in respect of the range of records used for briefing members of the Government and others for the purpose of transacting Government business at Cabinet meetings.

The consultation requirement provided for under section 19(4) is not limited by its terms to records of the immediately preceding Government and would appear to be unlimited in its retrospectivity. The process of consultation must be undertaken only "in so far as it is practicable to do so". It is not clear what the intended effect of the fulfilment of the consultation obligation is; while it clearly does not grant a veto on disclosure to a previous administration,[54] it is it not clear what effect a negative outcome to the exercise of the consultation obligation was intended to have.

D. Non-disclosure of Existence or Non-existence of Records

Where a request relates to a record to which section 19(1) applies or would, if the record existed, apply, and the head of the public body concerned is satisfied that the disclosure of the existence or non-existence of the record would be contrary to the public interest, he or she must refuse to grant the request and must not disclose whether the record exists. The justification for this provision is that even if the records are not themselves released, the knowledge that they exist could prove damaging. Knowledge of the fact that a record exists which relates to a particular proposal submitted to Cabinet, for example, could in itself be damaging to the Cabinet process. Such provisions are commonly found in Cabinet records exemptions in overseas FOI legislation.[55] Provisions of this type are discussed in greater detail above at pp. 71–72. Regard must be had to the public interest in applying this provision. The meaning of public interest in the context of the FOI Act is discussed in greater detail at pp. 93–115.

---

[54] The possibility that this provision could be used to veto the disclosure of records was expressly rejected by the sponsoring Minister of State, Eithne Fitzgerald T.D., at Committee Stage in the Seanad: 149 *Seanad Debates* Col. 1574.

[55] See, for example, Freedom of Information Act 1982 (Cth), s.25; Freedom of Information Act 1982 (Victoria), s.27(2)(b); Freedom of Information Act 1992 (Western Australia), s.31; Freedom of Information Act 1991 (South Australia), s.23(3); Freedom of Information Act 1992 (Queensland), s.35; Access to Information Act (Canada), R.S.C., 1985, s.10(2); Freedom of Information and Protection of Privacy Act (Alberta), S.A., 1994, s.11(2); Freedom of Information and Protection of Privacy Act (British Columbia), R.S.B.C., 1996, s.8(2); Freedom of Information and Protection of Privacy Act (Nova Scotia), S.N.S., 1993, s.7(2)(c); Freedom of Information and Protection of Privacy Act (Ontario), R.S.O., 1990, ss.14(3), 21(5), and 29(2).

CHAPTER 7

DELIBERATIONS OF PUBLIC BODIES

CHAPTER 7

DELIBERATIONS OF PUBLIC BODIES

A. Introduction

The exemption considered in this chapter is concerned with ensuring that the right of access to official records does not prejudice the deliberations of public bodies. The operation of this exemption is of fundamental importance in the scheme of the FOI Act as a whole. An Australian commentator described the equivalent Australian provision as:

"the primary vehicle for the resolution of the tension between the objects of freedom of information legislation and the tradition of secrecy which has surrounded the way in which government makes decisions which affect the public or members of the public."[1]

The exemption is stated in the following terms:

"20.—(1) A head may refuse to grant a request under section 7—
    (a) if the record concerned contains matter relating to the deliberative processes of the public body concerned (including opinions, advice, recommendations, and the results of consultations, considered by the body, the head of the body, or a member of the body or of the staff of the body for the purpose of those processes), and
    (b) the granting of the request would, in the opinion of the head, be contrary to the public interest,

and, without prejudice to the generality of paragraph (b), the head shall, in determining whether to grant or refuse to grant the request, consider whether the grant thereof would be contrary to the public interest by reason of the fact that the requester concerned would thereby become aware of a significant decision that the body proposes to make.

(2) Subsection (1) does not apply to a record if and in so far as it contains—
    (a) matter used, or intended to be used, by a public body for the purpose of making decisions, determinations or recommendations referred to in section 16,
    (b) factual (including statistical) information and analyses thereof,
    (c) the reasons for the making of a decision by a public body,
    (d) a report of an investigation or analysis of the performance, efficiency

---

[1] Bayne, *The Laws of Australia* (The Law Book Company Limited, Melbourne, 1995), Part 2.3, Chap. 3 "Freedom of Information", para. 95.

or effectiveness of a public body in relation to the functions generally or a particular function of the body,

(e) a report, study or analysis of a scientific or technical expert relating to the subject of his or her expertise or a report containing opinions or advice of such an expert and not being a report used or commissioned for the purposes of a decision of a public body made pursuant to any enactment or scheme."

The application of this exemption is discretionary, which means that records which fall within its scope may be released at the discretion of the head of the public body concerned.

In order for a record to qualify for exemption under this provision, two conditions must be met. It must be shown:

(1) that the record contains material relating to the deliberative processes of the public body; and

(2) that the disclosure is contrary to the public interest.

Five categories of record are expressly excluded from the scope of section 20. The first is aimed at preventing the use of the exemption to restrict the operation of section 16 of the Act which requires publication by public bodies of certain information.[2] The second exclusion is designed to ensure that the exemption cannot be used to deny access to factual (including statistical) information or analyses thereof. The third exclusion prevents reliance on section 20 to justify withholding reasons for the making of a decision by a public body. The fourth exclusion removes reports relating to the performance, efficiency or effectiveness of public bodies or their functions from the ambit of the exemption. Finally, reports of scientific or technical reports are excluded from the scope of the exemption where such reports were not used or commissioned for the purposes of a decision of a public body under an enactment or scheme. The exceptions are examined in greater detail below. There is provision in the Act for deferral of access to records referred to in the second, fourth and fifth exceptions.[3] Such deferral is permitted where the giving of access to such records on or before a specified day would in the opinion of the head of the public body be contrary to the public interest, in which case the head of the public body concerned may defer access until after the specified day.

Deliberative process exemptions are common to all FOI Acts.[4] The formulation of section 20 has been influenced primarily by the corresponding

---

[2] See above, pp. 41–44.

[3] s.11(1)(b).

[4] See for example: Australia: Freedom of Information Act 1982 (Cth), s.36; Freedom of Information Act 1982 (Victoria), s.30; Freedom of Information Act 1989 (New South Wales), Sched.1, cl.9; Freedom of Information Act 1991 (South Australia), Sched.1,

exemption in the Australian FOI Act.[5] Case law relating to the interpretation of that exemption and to the very similarly worded exemption in the Queensland FOI Act will be considered in the analysis of the exemption. Reference will also be made to U.S. case law concerning the corresponding exemption in the U.S. FOI Act, Exemption 5. There are, however, important differences between the deliberative processes exemption contained in the Irish FOI Act and its U.S. counterpart. Unlike section 20, Exemption 5 is largely based upon the concepts of executive privilege and legal professional privilege. It provides that the U.S. FOI Act does not apply to "inter-agency or intra-agency memorandums or letters which would not be available by law to a party other than an agency in litigation with the agency". The differences in the legal framework of FOI law and the law relating to executive and legal professional privilege[6] must, therefore, be taken into account in applying Exemption 5 jurisprudence to the analysis of section 20.

B. Deliberative Processes – section 20(1)(a)

The first requirement for application of the exemption is that the record which is sought for disclosure contains matter relating to "the deliberative processes" of the public body concerned. Materials covered by this exemption are clearly not limited to inter-agency or intra-agency communications but could include material submitted to an agency by a third party such as an external consultant.

Section 20(1)(a) sets out the following list of examples of materials relating to the deliberative process: opinions, advice, recommendations and the results of consultations considered by the body, the head of a body, or a member of the body or of the staff of the body. The list of examples set out in

---

cl.9; Freedom of Information Act 1991 (Tasmania), s.27; Freedom of Information Act 1992 (Queensland), s.41; Freedom of Information Act 1992 (Western Australia), Sched.1, cl.6.

Canada: Access to Information Act (Canada), R.S.C., 1985, s.21; Right to Information Act (New Brunswick), S.N.B., 1978, s.6(g); An Act respecting Access to documents held by public bodies and the Protection of personal information (Quebec), S.Q., 1982, ss.35–40; Freedom of Information and Protection of Privacy Act (Manitoba), C.C.S.M., 1998, c. F175, s.23; Freedom of Information Act (Newfoundland), R.S.N., 1990, s.9(1)(b)–(f); Freedom of Information and Protection of Privacy Act (Ontario), R.S.O., 1990, s.13; Freedom of Information and Protection of Privacy Act (Saskatchewan), S.S., 1990–1991, s.17; Freedom of Information and Protection of Privacy Act (British Columbia), R.S.B.C., 1996, s.13; Freedom of Information and Protection of Privacy Act (Nova Scotia), S.N.S., 1993, s.14; Freedom of Information and Protection of Privacy Act (Alberta), S.A., 1994, s.23.

New Zealand: Official Information Act 1982, s.9(2)(f) and (g).

U.S.: Freedom of Information Act, 1966, Exemption 5.

[5] Freedom of Information Act 1982 (Cth), s.36.

[6] See above, pp. 105–106.

section 20(1)(a) is not exhaustive of the scope of the exemption. Nor is it sufficient that the record concerned consists of opinions, advice, recommendation or the results of consultations. In order for such materials to qualify for exemption, it must be shown that they were considered for the purposes of the deliberative processes of the body.[7] The meaning of some elements of the list set out in section 20(1)(a) have been considered by the Information and Privacy Commissioner of Ontario. The Commissioner has decided that "advice" in the context of the deliberative processes exemption must amount to more than mere information. The Commissioner elaborated on this finding by saying that:

> "generally speaking, advice pertains to the submission of a suggested course of action, which will ultimately be accepted or rejected by its recipient during a deliberative process."[8]

In the case of recommendations, the Commissioner in a later decision stated that the meaning of "recommendations" must be "viewed in the same vein" as his approach to advice.[9]

The meaning of "deliberative processes" is pivotal to the operation of the section 20. It is a concept borrowed from the corresponding exemption in Australian Act, the formulation of which was itself influenced by the interpretation of Exemption 5 of the U.S. Freedom of Information Act. In U.S. and Australian case law, a distinction has been drawn between pre-decisional documents which are protected and post-decisional documents which are not protected. In the U.S. case of *NLRB v. Sears, Roebuck & Co.*[10] it was held that memoranda explaining an agency's decisions not to file complaints was a final administrative decision and must be disclosed on the basis that the relevant exemption could never apply to final opinions or dispositions. In the Queensland case of *Re Eccleston and Department of Family Services and Aboriginal and Islander Affairs*, the Information Commissioner said that "once a deliberative process is over and a final decision has been made . . . exemption cannot be claimed in respect of the record".[11] However, the distinction between records of final decisions and deliberative material will not always be clear cut. For example, the implementation of a final decision may well give rise to the need for the making of a policy on the manner of its implementation. That such material should not be exempt from disclosure accords with the requirement imposed on agencies by section 16 of the Act to publish internal rules affecting entitlements.

---

[7] s.20(1)(a).
[8] *Re Ministry of Transportation*, unreported, Information and Privacy Commissioner, Ontario, Order 118, November 15, 1989.
[9] *Re Ministry of Consumer and Commercial Relations*, unreported, Information and Privacy Commissioner, Ontario, Order P–411, February 15, 1993.
[10] 421 U.S. 132 (1975).
[11] (1993) 1 Q.A.R. 60 at 71–72.

Not all predecisional documents have been found to come within the scope of the U.S. and Australian exemptions. In the U.S. case of *Vaughn v. Rosen (II)*[12] it was held that in order to come within Exemption 5 a document must:

> "be a direct part of the deliberative process in that it makes recommendations or expresses opinions on legal or policy matters . . . a part of the agency give and take . . . by which the decision itself is made".[13]

In the Australian federal case of *Re Waterford and Department of the Treasury (No. 2)*[14] the distinction between deliberative processes and purely administrative or procedural processes was emphasised. The Administrative Appeals Tribunal (A.A.T.) said:

> "As a matter of ordinary English the expression 'deliberative processes' appears to us to be wide enough to include any of the processes of deliberation and consideration involved in the functions of an agency. 'Deliberation' means 'The action of deliberating; careful consideration with a view to decision': see the Shorter Oxford English Dictionary. The action of deliberating in common understanding, involves the weighing up or evaluation of the competing arguments or considerations that may have a bearing upon one's course of action. In short, the deliberative processes involved in the functions of an agency are its thinking processes – the processes of reflection, for example, upon the wisdom and expediency of a proposal, a particular decision or a course of action. Deliberations on policy matters undoubtedly come within this broad description . . . It by no means follows, therefore, that every document on a departmental file will fall into this category. . . Furthermore, however imprecise the dividing line may appear to be in some cases, documents disclosing deliberative processes must, in our view, be distinguished from documents dealing with purely procedural or administrative processes involved in the functions of an agency."

It appears that in Australia the scope of the exemption is not confined to documents concerning policy formulation. While some of the remarks of Beaumont J. in the Australian case of *Harris v. Australian Broadcasting Corporation*[15] seemed to equate "deliberative" with "policy making processes", this approach was questioned by Sheppard J. in *Kavvadias v. Commonwealth Ombudsman*[16] when he said:

> "Uninstructed by His Honour's reference to the explanatory memorandum which accompanied the Bill and the American authorities, I think that I myself would have leant towards a meaning more in accord with the Shorter Oxford Dictionary definition of 'deliberative' as understood more fully when one fully considers the meanings of 'deliberate' (both the verb and the adjective) and 'deliberation'. To me, that is the ordinary meaning of the word. I would not

---

[12] 523 F.2d 1136 at 1144 (D.C. Cir. 1975).
[13] *ibid.* at 1143–1144.
[14] (1984) 5 A.L.D. 588 at 606.
[15] (1983) 50 A.L.R. 551 at 559–564.
[16] (1984) 54 A.L.R. 285.

have imported any qualification into the meaning of it based upon the need for there to be as part of the deliberative process some aspect of policy-forming. His Honour himself seems to have regarded that view as at least open in the passage from his judgment which I have cited."[17]

The approach of Sheppard J. was adopted by Davies J. in *Re Howard and Treasurer of the Commonwealth*[18] and the position at federal level in Australia was usefully summarised by the Queensland Information Commissioner in *Re Eccleston and Department of Family Services* in the following terms:

> "The position.which has come to be accepted in the Commonwealth AAT [Administrative Appeals Tribunal] is that while the term 'deliberative processes' encompasses the policy-forming processes of an agency, it extends to cover deliberation for the purposes of any decision-making function of an agency. It does not, however, cover the purely procedural or administrative functions of an agency".[19]

It appears that the scope of section 20 was, however, intended to be limited to records relating to policy formulation. The sponsoring Minister said that the aim of the section "is to protect certain narrow elements of the policy making process until a decision has been taken".[20] The operation of the policy/administration distinction in the Irish context is explored by Hogan and Morgan in the following terms:

> "Put briefly, administration assumes that there is already in existence a principle and that all the administrator has to do is to establish the facts and circumstances and then to apply the principle . . . By contrast, policy-making is largely discretionary: the policy-maker must decide, as between two alternatives, the one which he considers best in the interest of the community."[21]

To summarise, it would appear that in order to qualify as a record relating to deliberative process for the purposes of section 20, the record would have to be concerned with the policy-making processes of public bodies.

C. Public Interest

The fact that a record contains matter relating to deliberative processes of a public body will not be enough to render it exempt. It must also be established that the granting of the request would be contrary to the public interest. This form of public interest test differs from and, indeed, is stronger than those

---

[17] Above, n. 16, at 300.
[18] (1985) 7 A.L.D. 626; 3 A.A.R. 169.
[19] Above, n. 11, at 70.
[20] 149 *Seanad Debates* Col. 1576 (Committee Stage).
[21] Hogan and Morgan, *Administrative Law in Ireland* (3rd ed., Round Hall Sweet & Maxwell, Dublin, 1998), p. 4.

found elsewhere in the Act, in that it will only justify the withholding of a record where its disclosure is contrary to the public interest.[22] There is no need to show that the disclosure of the record is positively in the public interest. The strength of the public interest component of this exemption is evidenced by the sponsoring Minister's statement in the Seanad debate that the exemption does not permit "the withholding of documents because they are or were drafts or because they might mislead; they permit withholding only where damage to the public interest is certain to arise".[23]

Some guidance is provided within the text of the exemption as to the factors to be taken into account in deciding where the public interest lies. In particular, the head of public body in determining whether to grant or refuse a request must "consider whether the grant thereof would be contrary to the public interest by reason of the fact that the requester concerned would thereby become aware of a significant decision that the body proposes to make".[24] There is no corresponding provision in overseas legislation which has tended to rely on those enforcing the legislation to determine where the public interest lies. While this paragraph clearly establishes that one of the criteria to be taken into account is whether such disclosure would result in the requester becoming aware of a significant decision the body proposes to make, it is clear on account of the inclusion of the words "without prejudice to the generality of paragraph (b)" that this is but one factor to be taken into account by the head. Therefore, even if the disclosure would result in the requester becoming aware of a significant decision the body proposes to make, that would not automatically render the disclosure contrary to the public interest: it could be outweighed by other public interest factors.

The public interest relating to the disclosure of government information has been considered in the context of executive privilege in a number of Irish cases.[25] While they may be of some assistance in determining the public interest in the context of the deliberative processes exemption, reliance upon them must be tempered by the fact that there are important differences in the two areas of law.[26]

The public interest in obtaining access to deliberative process records has been considered in the context of FOI in Australia and in the U.S. In Australia a distinction has been drawn between that which is in the public interest to disclose, and that which the public is interested in. In *Re Angel and Department of Arts, Heritage and Environment*[27] the A.A.T. stated that:

"merely because there is a section of the public that is interested in a certain

---

[22] See above, pp. 93–95 for a comparison of the two forms of public interest test found in the Act.

[23] 150 *Seanad Debates* Col. 100 (Report Stage).

[24] s.20(1).

[25] These cases are considered above at pp. 97–106.

[26] See above, pp. 105–106.

[27] (1985) 9 A.L.D. 113.

activity it does not follow that disclosure of the documents related to that activity is in the public interest." [28]

In the same case, the tribunal rejected as a valid public interest consideration "the mere fact of information being "politically sensitive".[29] This finding is echoed in Minister of State Fitzgerald's assertion to the Dáil that "political embarrassment is not a test which would satisfy the public interest test under this Bill".[30]

In the U.S. case of *Jordan v. Department of Justice*, consideration was given to the issues to be taken into account in determining where the public interest lies in cases concerning deliberative process records. In discussing the relevant exemption of the U.S. Freedom of Information Act, Wilkey J., delivering the opinion of the Court of Appeals, said:

> "The privilege attaches to inter- and intra-agency communications that are part of the deliberative process preceding the adoption and promulgation of an agency policy. There are essentially three policy bases for this privilege. First, it protects creative debate and candid consideration of alternatives within an agency, and, thereby, improves the quality of agency policy decisions. Second, it protects the public from the confusion that would result from premature exposure to discussions occurring before the policies affecting it had actually been settled upon. And third, it protects the integrity of the decision-making process itself by confirming that 'officials should be judged by what they decide not for matters they considered before making up their minds'."[31]

Each of these criteria is referred to in the Australian decision of *Re Howard and Treasurer of the Commonwealth*,[32] where a total of five factors were identified as relevant to the public interest in disclosure of documents concerning deliberative processes. They were:

(1) the higher the office of the persons between whom the communications pass and the more sensitive the issues involved in the communication, the more likely it will be that the communication should not be disclosed;

(2) disclosure of communications made in the course of the development and subsequent promulgation of policy tends not to be in the public interest;

(3) disclosure which inhibits frankness and candour in future pre-decisional communications is likely to be contrary to the public interest;

(4) disclosure which will lead to confusion and unnecessary debate resulting from disclosure of possibilities considered tends not to be in the public interest; and

---

[28] Above, n. 27, at 124.
[29] *ibid.* at 123.
[30] 476 *Dáil Debates* Col. 1068 (Second Stage).
[31] 591 F.2d 753 at 772–773 (D.C. Cir. 1978).
[32] (1985) 7 A.L.D. 626; 3 A.A.R. 169.

(5) disclosure of documents which do not fairly disclose the reasons for a decision subsequently taken may be unfair to a decision-maker and may prejudice the integrity of the decision-making process.

In subsequent Australian cases, however, the trend has been in favour of giving weight to the objects of the Act and the importance of some of these factors has been called into question.[33] The most vigorous rejection of the so-called *"Howard* principles" is to be found in *Re Eccleston and Department of Family Services and Aboriginal and Islander Affairs*,[34] a decision of the Queensland Information Commissioner. The Commissioner, after exhaustively examining all five criteria, stated that:

> "it would be unsatisfactory for Queensland government agencies and Ministers to apply uncritically the five Howard criteria to determining questions under section 41(1)(b) [the deliberative processes exemption] of the FOI Act of whether or not the disclosure of deliberative process documents would be contrary to the public interest."[35]

Commenting on the first criterion, the Commissioner stated that a class claim based on the view that disclosure of high-level documents is contrary to the public interest irrespective of their contents was plainly inconsistent with the scope of the right of access which accords unconditional access to all documents irrespective of origin. This approach is in keeping with the Supreme Court's finding in the executive privilege case, *Ambiorix Ltd v. Minister for the Environment (No. 1)* that:

> "[t]here cannot . . . be a generally applicable class or category of documents exempted from production by reason of the rank in the public service of the person creating them, or of the position of the individual or body intended to use them."[36]

In objecting to the second principle, which provides that disclosure of communications made in the course of the development and subsequent promulgation of policy tends not to be in the public interest, the Commissioner referred to a decision of the federal A.A.T., *Re Dillon and Department of the Treasury*, which concerned the interpretation of the Australian federal deliberative processes exemption (section 36 of the federal FOI Act). That provision very closely resembles its Irish counterpart in that it consists of two parts, the first of which requires that the document relate to deliberative processes and the second that

---

[33] *Re Kamminga and Australian National University* (1992) 26 A.L.D. 585; *Re Chapman and Minister for Aboriginal and Torres Strait Islander Affairs* (1996) 43 A.L.D. 139; *Re Murtagh and Federal Commissioner of Taxation* (1984) 54 A.L.R. 313; *Re Eccleston and Department of Family Services and Aboriginal and Islander Affairs*, above, n. 11.
[34] Above, n. 11.
[35] *ibid.* at 109.
[36] [1992] 1 I.R. 277 at 284.

its disclosure be contrary to the public interest. The Deputy President of the
A.A.T. in *Dillon* had made the following response to a submission from counsel for the government party to the effect that the public interest leans towards
non-disclosure where the documents were made in the course of, and subsequent promulgation of, policy:

> "While I consider that this would be a matter relevant to s.36(1)(a) [the delib-
> erative processes requirement], I am unable to see its relevance to the public
> interest. The separate, twin requirement of s.36(1)(b) clearly suggests that the
> fact of a document being of a type referred to in s.36(1)(a) is of no relevance to
> a consideration of the public interest. By creating two separate requirements in
> two separate paragraphs . . . the legislature has put the two in contradistinction
> to one another. To accept [counsel's] argument would amount to a dilution of
> the public interest requirement in s.36(1)(b)."[37]

The Queensland Information Commissioner approved this finding in *Eccleston*
and went on to say:

> "In my opinion, the second Howard criterion is plainly wrong. . . To uphold the
> second Howard criterion in the very broad terms in which it is stated would
> defeat one of the main purposes of the FOI Act which is to allow citizens access
> to documents that will permit informed participation in the development of gov-
> ernment policy proposals which are of concern to them."[38]

It is not clear whether such a conclusion would be justified in the context of
the Irish exemption. The public interest limb of section 20 incorporates a requirement that the fact that disclosure would result in a requester becoming
aware of a significant decision a body proposes to make should be taken into
account in considering the public interest. That requirement is not unlike the
second Howard criterion. Thus it might be argued that the risk of disclosure of
communications made in the course of the development of policy might be a
valid, though not a determining, factor to be taken into account in deciding
where the public interest lies for the purposes of section 20.

The third *Howard* principle was questioned on the basis that arguments
based on preservation of the frankness and candour of pre-decisional communications are inimical to the very purpose of the balancing of public interests,
since such claims do not permit an inquiry as to the effect of disclosure of the
particular contents of the documents in question.

The Queensland Information Commissioner argued in respect of the fourth
factor that claims that disclosure would lead to premature debate and unnecessary confusion in the community should be treated with caution since that
type of unfounded paternalism simply operates to prevent "the very process of

---

[37] *Re Dillon and Department of the Treasury* (1986) 4 A.A.R. 320 at 332.
[38] Above, n. 11, at 103.

community debate about government proposals [which] should be valued in a democratic society".[39]

The Commissioner was prepared to concede that the taking into account of the fifth criterion might be justified in certain circumstances. That principle provides that disclosure of documents which do not fairly disclose the reasons for a decision subsequently taken may be unfair to a decision-maker and may prejudice the integrity of the decision-making process. In particular, the Commissioner was of the view that the withholding of a record would be justified where it consisted of an interim report which was critical of a particular person and that person has not yet been given the opportunity to respond to those reports. However, the Commissioner went on to endorse the view expressed by Todd D.P. of the federal A.A.T. in *Re Rae and Department of Prime Minister and Cabinet* to the effect that there is a difference between "preliminary" documents which contain criticisms of specific individuals and "preliminary" documents which reflect a stage of thinking in the policy making process. Todd D.P. had expressed his opinion on the disclosure of the latter in the following terms:

> "If the fact of a document not accurately reflecting current government policy were a determinative public interest consideration, no policy document would ever be released, for it is always possible that some person some day might read such a document in the mistaken belief that it represents current thinking... [I]t will not be enough for a respondent to rely on the mere fact of the contents of a document being subject to change to support a claim that disclosure would be contrary to the public interest."[40]

Some of the Queensland Information Commissioners' objections to the *Howard* principles are reflected in the following list of factors suggested as being irrelevant to the determination of the public interest in a review of the operation of the Australian federal Freedom of Information Act:

(1) the seniority of the person who is involved in preparing the document or who is the subject of the document;

(2) that disclosure would cause a loss of confidence in the government; and

(3) that disclosure may cause the applicant to misinterpret or misunderstand the information contained in the document because of an omission from the document or for any other reason.

The factors which were nominated as being relevant in determining the public interest were:

(1) the general public interest in government information being accessible;

---

[39] Above, n. 11, at 119.
[40] *Re Rae and Department of Prime Minister and Cabinet* (1986) 12 A.L.D. 589 at 606, *per* Todd D.P.

(2) whether the document would disclose the reasons for a decision;

(3) whether disclosure would contribute to debate on a matter of public interest;

(4) whether disclosure would enhance scrutiny of government decision-making processes and thereby improve accountability and participation.[41]

D. The Exceptions

The five exceptions to the deliberative process exemption are almost all copies of, or slight variations from, similar provisions in Australian and Canadian FOI legislation. The only one which does not appear to have been adopted from overseas legislation is section 20(2)(d), which excludes from the scope of the deliberative processes exemption reports on the efficiency of public bodies. The exception provisions operate by excluding from the scope of section 20(1) any record to which they apply. Once it is clear that an exception applies, there will be no need to embark upon an examination as to whether the record relates to the deliberative processes of the agency, or whether its disclosure would be contrary to the public interest.

1. Matter used for the making of decisions, determinations, or recommendations referred to in section 16 – section 20(2)(a)

The aim of this exception is to prevent section 20 standing in the way of disclosure of records containing what is often referred to as the "internal law" of public bodies. This provision is needed to ensure that this part of the Act is in harmony with the provisions regarding publication of information by public bodies which are set out in section 16.[42]

2. Factual (including statistical) information and analyses thereof – section 20(2)(b)

Since this exception applies "if and in so far as" a record contains information of the kind referred to, it would appear that where a record includes factual information as well as exempt material, the latter can be deleted and the factual information can be disclosed under section 20(2)(b). Such severance of exempt from non-exempt material would, in any case, be permitted under section 13, which provides for the granting of access to part of a record. This

---

[41] Australian Law Reform Commission, Report No. 77/Administrative Review Council, Report No. 40, *Open Government: A Review of the Freedom of Information Act 1982* (Australian Government Publishing Service, Canberra, 1995), para. 8.14.

[42] See above, pp. 41–44.

exception is similar to that found in the Australian Act, although the former refers to "purely factual material" rather than "factual (including statistical) information and analyses thereof". It is submitted that the only practical difference between the two is that the Australian provision does not allow in its own terms for the severance of factual material from exempt material. Therefore the meaning of the term factual material or information is substantially the same in both exceptions. What is meant by purely factual material was examined by the Australian Federal Court in *Harris v. Australian Broadcasting Corporation.*[43] Three types of material were examined. First, summaries of factual material were held to be classifiable as "purely factual material", but not if they were "of such a character as to disclose a process of selection involving opinion, advice or recommendation for the purpose of the deliberative process".[44] The second category of material examined was "conclusions expressed as findings". Here the court said that "a statement of ultimate fact may be a statement of purely factual material notwithstanding it involves a conclusion based on primary facts".[45] However, the court went on to say that a conclusion which involved opinion, advice, or recommendation for the purpose of the deliberative process might not be purely factual. The final class of material considered was judgments founded on the expertise of a person. It was held that these might be classified as purely factual, but not if the material were in the nature of or relating to an opinion, advice or recommendation for the purposes of the agency's deliberative processes. Exemption 5 of the U.S. Act does not expressly exclude factual information from its scope but the U.S. Supreme Court, in interpreting the exemption, has recognised a distinction between "materials reflecting deliberative or policy-making processes on the one hand, and purely factual, investigative matters on the other".[46] In the U.S. the practice has been that where facts are contained in a pre-decisional document, they must be segregated and disclosed unless they are "inextricably intertwined" with exempt portions. In the U.S. it has been held that there are some exceptions to the general rule that facts in deliberative documents must be disclosed. In *Mead Data Central, Inc. v. Department of the Air Force*, for example, it was stated that:

> "In some circumstances... the disclosure of even purely factual material may so expose the deliberative process within an agency that it must be deemed exempted by [Exemption 5]."[47]

It would appear that the making of such a distinction between factual information which would expose the deliberative process and other factual informa-

---

[43] (1984) 51 A.L.R. 581.
[44] *ibid.* at 586.
[45] *ibid.*
[46] *Environmental Protection Agency v. Mink*, 410 U.S. 73 at 89 (1973).
[47] 566 F.2d 242 at 256 (D.C. Cir. 1977).

tion would not be possible in the context of the Irish FOI Act since it requires a separate assessment as to whether the record contains factual information before the role of the record in the deliberative process can be examined. On the other hand, the same practical effect could be arrived at by adherence to the principles enunciated in *Harris*, which suggest that material is not factual material if it discloses opinion, advice, or recommendation for the purpose of the deliberative process.

3.   The reasons for the making of a decision by a public body – section 20(2)(c)

The rationale for including this exception is that, while there may be a justification for protecting the processes leading up to the making of a decision, no such justification exists for protecting the reasons for arriving at the decision once it has been made. The U.S. Supreme Court in *NRLB v. Sears, Roebuck & Co.* suggested that the case for disclosing the reasons for the making of a decision is even stronger where the decision involves the adoption of a particular policy when it said:

> "The public is only marginally concerned with reasons supporting a policy which an agency has rejected. . . . In contrast, the public is vitally concerned with the reasons which did supply the basis for an agency policy actually adopted."[48]

This exception complements the statutory requirement introduced by section 18 of the Act that public bodies provide reasons for decisions.[49]

4.   Performance reports – section 20(2)(d)

The inclusion of this exception, which is not found in overseas FOI legislation, makes for a more liberal approach to disclosure of deliberative process records in Ireland. It means that reports on the performance, efficiency or effectiveness of public bodies will not be exempt under section 20, although they could be exempted under some other provision of the Act.

5.   Reports of scientific or technical experts – section 20(2)(e)

The justification for excluding scientific and technical reports from the scope of the deliberative processes exemption, even in circumstances where such reports express the opinions of such experts on scientific or technical matters, is that such reports are meant to be "value free". On that basis, disclosure of scientific or technical reports should not be harmful to the deliberative proc-

---

[48] Above, n. 10, at 152.
[49] See above, pp. 45–49.

ess. In Australia, interpretation of what constitutes a scientific or technical report has excluded from its scope the report of a lawyer on the affairs of the legal department of an agency.[50] The Federal Court said that the provision was "intended to describe experts in the mechanical arts and applied sciences generally".[51] A claim that a report prepared by an academic in respect of an essay or thesis submitted amounted to a report of a scientific or technical expert was rejected by the A.A.T. in *Re James and Australian National University*.[52]

---

[50] See *Harris v. Australian Broadcasting Corporation*, above, n. 15.
[51] *ibid.* at 563.
[52] (1984) 6 A.L.D. 687.

CHAPTER 8

FUNCTIONS AND NEGOTIATIONS OF PUBLIC BODIES

FUNCTIONS AND NEGOTIATIONS OF PUBLIC BODIES

A. Introduction

The aim of this exemption is to ensure that public bodies will not be disadvantaged in the exercise of managerial functions, or in the conduct of negotiations or tests, as a result of the existence of the Freedom of Information Act. The greater part of this exemption is substantially the same as the equivalent exemption of the Australian federal FOI Act.[1] Section 21(1)(c), however, is based on a provision of the Ontarian Freedom of Information and Protection of Privacy Act.[2] Variations on this exemption are to be found in the New Zealand Act,[3] the Australian State Acts[4] and the Canadian federal and provincial Acts.[5]

The exemption is stated in the following terms:

"21.—(1) A head may refuse to grant a request under section 7 if access to the record concerned could, in the opinion of the head, reasonably be expected to—

(a) prejudice the effectiveness of tests, examinations, investigations, inquiries or audits conducted by or on behalf of the public body concerned or the procedures or methods employed for the conduct thereof,

(b) have a significant, adverse effect on the performance by the body of

---

[1] Freedom of Information Act 1982 (Cth), s.40. The equivalent exemption of the Queensland Freedom of Information Act 1992, s.40, is expressed in similar terms.

[2] Freedom of Information and Protection of Privacy Act (Ontario), R.S.O., 1990, s.18(1)(e).

[3] Official Information Act 1982, s.9(2)(j).

[4] Freedom of Information Act 1989 (New South Wales), Sched.1, cl.16; Freedom of Information Act 1991 (South Australia), Sched.1, cl.16; Freedom of Information Act 1992 (Queensland), s.40; Freedom of Information Act 1992 (Western Australia), Sched.1, cl.11.

[5] Access to Information Act (Canada), R.S.C., 1985, s.18; Right to Information Act (New Brunswick), S.N.B., 1978, s.6(c), 6(c.1)(ii); An Act respecting Access to documents held by public bodies and the Protection of personal information (Quebec), S.Q., 1982, ss.22 and 27; Freedom of Information and Protection of Privacy Act (Manitoba), C.C.S.M., 1998, c. F175, s.28; Freedom of Information Act (Newfoundland), R.S.N., 1990, s.11; Freedom of Information and Protection of Privacy Act (Saskatchewan), S.S., 1990–1991, s.18; Freedom of Information and Protection of Privacy Act (British Columbia), R.S.B.C., 1996, s.17; Freedom of Information and Protection of Privacy Act (Nova Scotia), S.N.S., 1993, s.17; Freedom of Information and Protection of Privacy Act (Alberta), S.A., 1994, ss.24 and 25.

any of its functions relating to management (including industrial relations and management of its staff), or

(c) disclose positions taken, or to be taken, or plans, procedures, criteria or instructions used or followed, or to be used or followed, for the purpose of any negotiations carried on or being, or to be, carried on by or on behalf of the Government or a public body.

(2) Subsection (1) shall not apply in relation to a case in which in the opinion of the head concerned, the public interest would, on balance, be better served by granting than by refusing to grant the request under section 7 concerned."

The exemption, the application of which is discretionary, is harm based. It is also subject to a public interest test. The exception applies where any of three separate forms of harm "could reasonably be expected" to occur. The standard of proof required to establish that harm "could reasonably be expected" to occur is discussed in detail at pp. 90–92 above. In short, decisions in Canada and Australia have established that the possibility of the specified harm occurring will not suffice to meet the burden of proof, but neither is it necessary to show evidence of direct causation between disclosure and harm. Nor does it appear necessary, in either jurisdiction, to show that the occurrence of the harm is more probable than not. In both Canada and Australia the emphasis has been upon the reasonableness of the expectation of harm arising out of the disclosure.

B.   The Records Protected

1.   Tests, examinations, investigations, inquiries, or audits – section 21(1)(a)

The first limb of the exemption is concerned with protecting the effectiveness of tests, examinations, investigations, inquiries, or audits. Records can be declared exempt where their disclosure could reasonably be expected to prejudice the effectiveness of such tests, audits, etc., or the procedures or methods employed for their conduct. The tests must be conducted by or on behalf of the public body concerned. This means that the exemption does not apply to tests carried on for third parties by private testing companies, which happen to come into the possession of a public body. This limb of the exemption varies slightly from its Australian counterpart[6] in that the latter expressly applies to

---

[6] Section 40(1) provides that subject to a public interest test set out in s.40(2), a document is an exempt document if its disclosure would or could reasonably be expected to:
   (a) prejudice the effectiveness of procedures or methods for the conduct of tests, examinations, or audits by an agency;
   (b) prejudice the attainment of the objects of particular tests, examinations or audits conducted or to be conducted by an agency.

prejudice to tests, etc., to be conducted *in the future*, whereas the Irish provision merely refers to tests "conducted by or on behalf of the public body". It could be argued on account of this wording, that prejudice to tests to be conducted in the future could not be considered in the application of section 21(1)(a). Thus, for example, a decision of the Australian federal Administrative Appeals Tribunal (A.A.T.) that the disclosure of the applicant student's answer paper after the test has been administered might prejudice its usefulness in the future[7] might not be possible in the context of the Irish provision. Disclosure of other students' answer papers was rejected in another Australian case, in which a student who had failed an examination requested a random sample of other students' response papers. Two grounds for refusing the request were upheld by the A.A.T.: first, that it is essential to the examination system that the final view of those marking an examination, if properly and fairly arrived at, should prevail; and, second, because release of such documents might encourage plagiarism.[8] If prejudice to the future conduct of tests, etc., is found not to come within the scope of section 21(1)(a), it seems that while the first of these grounds could be relied upon in denying access to records under the section 21(1)(a), the second could not, since the encouragement of plagiarism would necessarily relate to the conduct of the examination in the future.

The meaning of the term "audit" was examined by the Western Australian Information Commissioner in the context of the application of the equivalent exemption in the Western Australian FOI Act.[9] The Commissioner accepted the definition of audit in the *Concise Oxford Dictionary* as "an official examination of accounts". However, she went on to expand upon that definition by stating that, at least within the public service, the term is commonly understood to embrace examination of matters other than accounts, such as public sector agencies' performance indicators and examinations of information technology systems. The Commissioner held that the term "audit" did not, however, extend to evaluations of advertising campaigns carried on by public bodies.[10]

The fact that some of the requested information had already been leaked has been held, by the Australian federal A.A.T. in the context of a claim based on the equivalent exemption, to "not necessarily prejudice the merits of the exemption claimed".[11]

---

[7] *Re Barrell and Australian Broadcasting Corporation* (1985) 7 A.L.N. N129.
[8] *Re Redfern and University of Canberra* (1995) 38 A.L.D. 457.
[9] Freedom of Information Act 1992, Sched.1, cl.11.
[10] *Re Hassell and Health Department of Western Australia*, unreported, Information Commissioner, Western Australia, Decision No. D02594, December 13, 1994.
[11] *Re ASCIC and Australian Federal Police* (1986) 11 A.L.N. N184.

2. Management including industrial relations and management of staff – section 21(1)(b)

The second part of the exemption allows for the withholding of records, the disclosure of which could reasonably be expected to have a significant adverse effect on the performance by a public body of any of its functions relating to management (including industrial relations and management of its staff). The harm test applicable to this limb of the exemption appears to be stronger than that which applies in respect of the first limb. It requires that disclosure of the record could reasonably be expected to have a "significant, adverse effect" on the performance by the body of the specified functions. The corresponding provisions of the Australian federal Act use a standard of "substantial adverse effect". It has been held in that jurisdiction that "substantial adverse effect" imposes a stricter standard of proof than that required to show only "prejudice".[12] In particular, it has been held that the establishment "substantial adverse effect" requires evidence of a "substantial effect", in the sense of "serious" or "significant".[13] Given the equation of "substantial" with "significant", it appears that the "significant, adverse effect" standard in section 21(1)(b) is also more demanding than the "prejudice" standard found in the preceding subsection.

(a) Performance of management functions

While the exemption is expressly applied to management functions relating to industrial relations and the management of staff, it is clear that it may extend to cover other management functions also. Just what is covered by the term "functions relating to management" is not clear. Account must be taken of the sponsoring Minister of State's explanation of this provision to the Dáil Committee on Legislation and Security. Following criticism of the breadth of the provision, Ms Fitzgerald, when asked to give examples of the type of information which the provision seeks to protect, said:

> "Industrial relations is one of the areas mentioned. If a public body set out its negotiating stance and its bottom line, it would not publish them in advance of undertaking negotiations. If it was tendering for a contract for a particular building it would not give out the bottom line in advance because that would make the tendering process meaningless. That is the kind of management function covered in section 21(1)(b)."[14]

These matters would, however, already appear to be covered by other elements of the exemption: industrial relations is mentioned specifically in sec-

---

[12] *Re James and Australian National University* (1984) 6 A.L.D. 687.
[13] *Re Heaney and Public Service Board* (1984) 6 A.L.D. 310 at 319–329; *Re James and Australian National University, ibid.* at 699–700.
[14] Select Committee, L7, No. 6, Col. 164.

tion 21(1)(b) and the latter two matters would appear to be covered under section 21(1)(c).

While the Australian federal Act does not contain an exact counterpart to the exemption relating to the disclosure of records which could have a significant adverse effect on the management functions of public bodies, it does, however, exempt the disclosure of records which could reasonably be expected to have a substantial adverse effect on "proper and efficient conduct of the operations of an agency".[15] That provision has been interpreted as being capable of being extended to "the way in which an agency discharges or performs any of its functions".[16] It is submitted that the management exemption in section 21(1)(b) is not so general in its scope. It is, arguably, confined to the internal management functions of public bodies and as such could not be held to extend to records relating to the relationship between the public body and third parties. It could, for example, be applied to records concerning the management by a public body of its financial resources.

(b) Performance of functions relating to industrial relations

Section 21(1)(b) allows for the exemption of records the disclosure of which could reasonably be expected to have a significant adverse effect on the performance of a public body's functions relating to industrial relations. The corresponding Australian federal exemption is expressed in similar terms. It exempts documents, the disclosure of which could reasonably be expected to "have a substantial adverse effect on the conduct by or on behalf of the Commonwealth or an agency of industrial relations".[17] The repeal of the industrial relations limb of the Australian exemption has been recommended in a review of the operation of the FOI Act on the basis that:

> "It is not appropriate that the effect of disclosure on industrial relations determines what information is disclosed, particularly when other exemptions will adequately protect the sort of information that may give rise to industrial concerns."[18]

Industrial relations has been interpreted by the Australian federal A.A.T. as "relationships between employers and employees".[19] It has pointed out that the Australian industrial relations exemption is concerned not with adverse effects on industrial relations but with adverse effects on the *conduct* of industrial relations.[20] The same can be said of section 20(1)(b): it is concerned with

---

[15] Freedom of Information Act 1982 (Cth), s.40(1)(d).
[16] *Re James and Australian National University*, above, n. 12, at 688.
[17] Freedom of Information Act 1982 (Cth), s.40(1)(e).
[18] Australian Law Reform Commission, Report No. 77/Administrative Review Council, Report No. 40, *Open Government: A Review of the Freedom of Information Act 1982* (Australian Government Publishing Service, Canberra, 1995), para. 9.27.
[19] *Re McCarthy and Australian Telecommunications Commission* (1987) 13 A.L.D. 1 at 7.
[20] *Re Thies and Department of Aviation* (1986) 9 A.L.D. 454 at 464.

the effect of disclosure on the performance by a public body of its industrial relations functions rather than on the body's industrial relations *per se*.

On the basis of the distinction which can be drawn between adverse effects on industrial relations and adverse effects on the *conduct* of industrial relations, the A.A.T. has stated that:

> "[T]he mere fact that industrial action resulted from the disclosure did not necessarily mean that the disclosure was having an adverse effect on the conduct of industrial relations."[21]

This approach was followed in *Re McCarthy and Australian Telecommunications Commission*,[22] when the A.A.T. rejected the suggestion that the disclosure of the disputed documents in the context of ongoing industrial disputation would have a substantial adverse effect on the conduct of industrial relations, saying:

> "It may be that the supplying of the information contained in these documents to the [applicant] will either increase the level of disputation, or decrease the ability of Telecom to reach what is for it a satisfactory result in any such disputation. However, it does not seem to us that it will do either of these things to such an extent that it could be said that disclosure of the documents 'would or could reasonably be expected to have a substantial adverse effect on the conduct by [Telecom] of industrial relations'."[23]

The fact that a dispute to which the requested documents relate is at an end was accepted by the A.A.T. in *Re Heaney and Public Service Board*[24] as a factor to be taken into account in deciding whether disclosure could reasonably be expected to have a substantial adverse effect on the conduct of industrial relations. The tribunal went on to hold that the fact that the dispute has come to an end is not, however, conclusive, observing that:

> "The conduct of industrial relations over wage claims is an ongoing matter. An issue can always be revived, whether justifiably or not, as the basis of future industrial disputation."[25]

Whether the records to which access is sought were prepared for industrial relations purposes may be a factor to be taken into account. In *McCarthy* the A.A.T. adverted to the fact that the documents at issue were "not prepared . . . in the context of and for the purposes of, the relationship between employer and employee as such".[26]

---

[21] Above, n. 20, at 464.
[22] Above, n. 19.
[23] *ibid.* at 9.
[24] (1984) 6 A.L.D. 310.
[25] *ibid.* at 322.
[26] Above, n. 19, at 8.

(c) Performance of functions relating to management of the staff of the public body

Section 21(1)(b) allows for the exemption of records which, if disclosed, could reasonably be expected to have a significant adverse effect on the performance of a public body's functions relating to management of its staff. Again, there is a corresponding Australian federal provision. Section 40(1)(c) exempts documents which, if disclosed, could reasonably be expected to have a substantial adverse effect on the management or assessment of personnel by the Commonwealth or by an agency.

This exemption has been claimed, in some Australian cases, in order to justify the removal of officers' names from documents to which access was granted.[27] In others it has been applied to exempt from disclosure documents which would reveal the name of an officer who made a decision.[28] These cases have all arisen in the context of requests for access to taxation records. A distinction was drawn, in one case, between officers of higher and lower levels. The A.A.T. said:

> "We are of the opinion that there would be very real dangers of misuse of the names of officers of an agency, at least and in particular the names of officers of the Australian Taxation Office, if disclosure were made. It would be one thing for the names of officers holding delegations from the Commissioner of taxation to be released, but at lower levels we see a distinct danger of mischievous use of officers' names, with no countervailing advantage to the public."[29]

The application of the Australian equivalent of section 21(1)(b) to prevent disclosure of the names of officials can be contrasted with the exclusion of the names of staff members of public bodies from the definition of personal information for the purposes of the personal information exemption in the Irish Act.[30] Given the obvious intention on the part of the Oireachtas that the names of government officials should be subject to disclosure under the Irish Act, it is unlikely that the Australian approach of exempting from disclosure documents which would reveal the names of officials would be followed here.

The Australian federal A.A.T. has indicated that one of the factors to be taken into account in deciding whether disclosure could reasonably be expected to have a substantial adverse effect on the management, or assessment of personnel by the Commonwealth or by an agency, is the agency's practices in disclosing documents.[31]

---

[27] *Re Murtagh and Commissioner of Taxation* (1984) 6 A.L.D. 112; *Re Z and Australian Taxation Office* (1984) 6 A.L.D. 673.

[28] *Re Mann and Australian Taxation Office* (1985) 7 A.L.D. 698; *Re Lander and Australian Taxation Office* (1985) 9 A.L.N. N25.

[29] *Re Mann and Australian Taxation Office, ibid.*, at 708.

[30] s.2(1).

[31] *Re Dyrenfurth and Department of Social Security* (1987) 12 A.L.D. 577.

3. Negotiations of the Government and public bodies – section 21(1)(c)

The third strand of the exemption is concerned with protecting public bodies in a negotiating situation. It allows the head of a public body to claim the exemption, where access to the requested record could reasonably be expected to disclose positions taken, or to be taken, or plans, etc., used or followed, or to be used or followed, for the purpose of negotiations carried on, or being, or to be, carried on by or on behalf of the Government or a public body. It is a broad-ranging exemption. It applies to all kinds of negotiations, whatever their subject. It covers negotiations currently taking place and negotiations to take place in the future, as well as those which have already taken place. There is nothing in the exemption to prevent its application to negotiations between public bodies, as well as to negotiations between public bodies and private sector organisations. There is no harm test built into this part of the exemption, which means that a record can be exempted once it is shown that its disclosure could reasonably be expected to disclose matter which the exemption seeks to protect. In particular, there is no need to show that such disclosure would, in any way, cause damage to the negotiations.

(a) Past negotiations

This part of the exemption is based on section 18(1)(e) of the Ontario Act. A similar exemption is also to be found in the New Zealand Act.[32] There is no exact equivalent of this exemption in either the Australian or federal Canadian Acts. The Ontarian provision differs from section 21 in that the former is limited to negotiations "carried on or to be carried on" while the latter refers to negotiations "carried on, or being, or to be, carried on". The Ontarian provision has been interpreted as applying only to records relating to negotiations being carried on at present, or to be carried on in the future, and not to past negotiations.[33] While there is no reference to current, future, or past negotiations in the New Zealand provision, it is subject to a harm test, on account of which it has been suggested that the exemption cannot apply to past negotiations:

> "Once negotiations have been either successfully concluded or abandoned they are no longer capable of being put at risk by disclosure."[34]

---

[32] Official Information Act 1982, s.9(2)(j).

[33] The four criteria for application of the exemption were set out in *Re Ministry of Industry, Trade and Technology*, unreported, Order P–87, August 24, 1989, in the following terms: "1. the record contains positions, plans, procedures, criteria or instructions; and 2. this record is intended to be applied to negotiations; and 3. these negotiations are being carried on or will be carried on in the future; and 4. these negotiations are being conducted by or on behalf of an institution or the Government of Ontario". See also *Re Stadium Corporation of Ontario*, unreported, Order P–141, January 23, 1990.

[34] Eagles, Taggart, and Liddell, *Freedom of Information in New Zealand* (Oxford University Press, Auckland, 1992), p. 325.

Unlike its Ontarian and New Zealand counterparts, section 20(1)(c) arguably applies in respect of past negotiations, since it includes negotiations "carried on" as well as negotiations being or to be carried on. Negotiations "to be carried on" clearly refers to future negotiations, while the reference to negotiations "being carried on" covers current negotiations. Therefore, it appears that negotiations "carried on" can only refer to past negotiations. The withholding of records relating to past negotiations is difficult to justify. There may be rare occasions on which damage to current or future negotiations might be occasioned by disclosures of information relating to past negotiations, for example, where the negotiations are between the same parties or concern the same subject matter as those recently concluded. Such records would, in any case, be exempted on the basis that their disclosure could disclose information relating to current or future negotiations.

(b) Future negotiations

The inclusion of records relating to negotiations to be carried on in the future gives rise to the question whether there should be any limit on how far into the future the negotiations are expected to take place. The Ontarian Commissioner has warned against projecting too far into the future:

> "[T]o interpret the phrase 'or to be carried on by or on behalf of an institution of the Government of Ontario' to mean any possible future negotiations including those that have not been presently commenced or even contemplated, is in my view, too wide."[35]

(c) Positions, plans, procedures, criteria or instructions

A degree of precision in the identification of records which constitute "positions, plans, procedures, criteria or instructions" has been demanded by the Information and Privacy Commissioner of Ontario. Those claiming the exemption must identify those portions of the records sought which the body considers to be positions, plans, procedures, criteria and instructions, and they must indicate which of this information will be applied to negotiations.[36] Records in respect of which the Ontarian equivalent of this exemption is claimed are examined to see whether they do in fact amount to positions, plans, etc. In one case, the Information and Privacy Commissioner of Ontario concluded, on the basis of the representations of the public body concerned, that the information contained in the records in respect of which the section 18(1)(e) exemption was claimed did not represent the position which the body intended

---

[35] *Re Ministry of Industry, Trade and Technology*, unreported, Information and Privacy Commissioner, Ontario, Order 87, August 24, 1989.

[36] *Re Ontario Nature Affairs Secretariat*, unreported, Information and Privacy Commissioner, Ontario, Order P–454, May 7, 1993.

to take in its future negotiations. The Commissioner held, on that basis, that the records were not exempt.[37]

(d) For the purpose of negotiations

Materials exempted under this provision must relate to negotiations. Positions, plans, etc., adopted in respect of mere discussions will not be covered. Nor will records prepared for the purpose of assisting in the making of a recommendation. In the Ontarian case of *Re Ministry of Education and Training*,[38] access was sought by one of the parties to a dispute to a mediation report relating to that dispute. The Ministry of Education, which held the record, sought to invoke the exemption. The Information and Privacy Commissioner rejected the claim, pointing out that by the Minister's own description the information provided by the mediator was not intended to be applied to negotiations. Rather, it was intended to assist in the making of a recommendation, as the mediator had failed to reach a negotiated settlement. In order to qualify as negotiation, therefore, it would have to be shown that there are at least two parties engaged in arm's length dealings, each of the which aims to obtain an outcome favourable to itself.

C.   Public Interest

The exemption does not apply to cases in which "the public interest would, on balance, be better served by granting than by refusing to grant the request". The equivalent Australian exemption is subject to a public interest test, but the Ontarian provision is not.

The operation of the public interest tests in the Irish exemptions generally is discussed in greater detail above at pp. 93–115. In terms of its operation in the context of the exemption relating to functions and negotiations of public bodies, the Australian federal A.A.T. has held, in a departure from the traditional philosophy of FOI, that one factor to be taken into account is the interest of the applicant in obtaining access to the documents.[39]

The A.A.T. has also taken into account, in this context, the fact that an application requires disclosure of a record in order to commence legal pro-

---

[37] *Re Stadium Corporation of Ontario Ltd*, unreported, Information and Privacy Commissioner, Ontario, Order P–581, November 22, 1993.

[38] Unreported, Information and Privacy Commissioner, Ontario, Order P–858, February 7, 1995.

[39] *Re James and Australian National University*, above, n. 12, at 700–702; *Re Thies and Department of Aviation*, above, n. 20, at 465–466; *Re B and Medical Board of the ACT* (1994) 33 A.L.D. 295 at 302–303. See also the Queensland Information Commissioner's decision in *Re Pemberton and The University of Queensland* (1994) 2 Q.A.R. 293.

ceedings. In *Re Thies and Department of Aviation*,[40] a pilot's application for access to the transcript of disputed radio communications involving himself was opposed on the basis that the disclosure could reasonably be expected to:

> "(d) have a substantial adverse effect on the proper and efficient conduct of the operations of an agency; or
> (e) have a substantial adverse effect on the conduct by or on behalf of the Commonwealth or an agency of industrial relations."

The tribunal took into account the fact that the applicant, who had been dismissed as a result of an alleged failure to obey an instruction relayed to him by radio, intended to take legal action against his employer, if the content of the message was in the terms which he believed it to have been. The tribunal said:

> "There is a further public interest in a person who has suffered an actionable wrong being able to pursue a remedy in the courts; if such persons are unable to do that, they may be tempted to 'take the law into their own hands'. We take into account the fact that, if the applicant commenced an action against his former employer, he might be able to obtain from the court a summons requiring the Department to produce the tape or a transcript of it in evidence at the trial; but he needs to know what is recorded before he commences proceedings. We have come to the conclusion in the present case that the public interest in the applicant obtaining access to the transcript of the tape is considerable."[41]

In the Queensland case of *Re Pemberton and The University of Queensland*[42] the Information Commissioner considered the operation of the public interest test in the context of a claim that disclosure of referees' reports relating to an application for promotion could reasonably be expected to have a substantial adverse effect on the management or assessment by an agency of the agency's personnel. The Commissioner concluded that greater accountability and objectivity in the decision-making process relating to the system of promotion available to academics within the University of Queensland was "a public interest consideration of substance, which must be accorded appropriate weight" and ordered the disclosure of internal assessments of the applicants' suitability for promotion.[43]

---

[40] Above, n. 20.
[41] *ibid.* at 465.
[42] Above, n. 39.
[43] *ibid.* at 367.

CHAPTER 9

PARLIAMENTARY, COURT, AND CERTAIN OTHER MATTERS

CHAPTER 9

PARLIAMENTARY, COURT, AND CERTAIN OTHER MATTERS

The exemption analysed in this chapter is made up of four separate parts. They concern respectively: legal professional privilege;[1] contempt of court;[2] private papers of elected representatives;[3] and information considered by the Houses of the Oireachtas.[4] Each will be considered separately.

A. Legal Professional Privilege

It is a fundamental principle in civil litigation that, with some exceptions, all issues in legal proceedings should be admissible. One of those exceptions is legal professional privilege. This exception is justified on the basis that a client needs to be able to consult with his or her lawyer without fear that such communications will be disclosed in evidence in court. The need to exempt communications of this type from the scope of FOI legislation is widely recognised overseas.[5]

---

[1] s.22(1)(a).
[2] s.22(1)(b).
[3] s.22(1)(c)(i).
[4] s.22(1)(c)(ii).
[5] See for example: Australia: Freedom of Information Act 1982 (Cth), s.42(1); Freedom of Information Act 1982 (Victoria), s.32(1); Freedom of Information Act 1989 (New South Wales), Sched.1, cl.10(1); Freedom of Information Act 1991 (South Australia), Sched.1, cl.10(1); Freedom of Information Act 1991 (Tasmania), s.29(1); Freedom of Information Act 1992 (Queensland), s.43(1); Freedom of Information Act 1992 (Western Australia), Sched.1, cl.7(1);
Canada: Access to Information Act 1982, s.23.; Right to Information Act (New Brunswick), S.N.B., 1978, s.6(f); An Act respecting Access to documents held by public bodies and the Protection of personal information (Quebec), S.Q., 1982, s.31; Freedom of Information Act (Manitoba), C.C.S.M., 1998, c. F175, s.27; Freedom of Information Act (Newfoundland), R.S.N., 1990, s.11(d); Freedom of Information and Protection of Privacy Act (Saskatchewan), S.S., 1990–1991, s.22; Freedom of Information and Protection of Privacy Act (Ontario), R.S.O., 1990, s.19; Freedom of Information and Protection of Privacy Act (British Columbia), R.S.B.C., 1996, s.14; Freedom of Information and Protection of Privacy Act (Nova Scotia), S.N.S., 1993, s.16; Freedom of Information and Protection of Privacy Act (Alberta), S.A., 1994, s.26.
New Zealand: Official Information Act 1982, s.9(2)(h).
U.S.: Freedom of Information Act 1966, Exemption 5.

The exemption, the application of which is mandatory, is stated in the following terms:

> "22.—(1) A head shall refuse to grant a request under section 7 if the record concerned—
>
> > (a) would be exempt from production in proceedings in a court on the ground of legal professional privilege".

It is necessary to look beyond the text in order to appreciate the scope of this exemption, for it directly incorporates into the FOI Act the common law relating to legal professional privilege. Its closest counterpart is the equivalent Australian federal exemption, which is also mandatory and which exempts a document if it "is of such a nature that it would be privileged from production in legal proceedings on the ground of legal professional privilege".[6] The equivalent Canadian federal exemption is discretionary.[7] The New Zealand legal professional privilege exemption leaves room for divergence from the common law of legal professional privilege through its incorporation of an express public interest test.[8]

In order to delineate the scope of this exemption, it is necessary to outline the main features of the law relating to legal professional privilege in Ireland.[9] The objects of common law privilege were set out by Jessel M.R. in *Anderson v. Bank of British Columbia*[10] in the following passage which was cited with approval by Finlay C.J. in the leading Irish authority, *Smurfit Paribas Bank Limited v. A.A.B. Export Finance Limited (No. 1)*:[11]

> "The object and meaning of the rule is this: that as, by reason of the complexity and difficulty of our law, litigation can only be properly conducted by professional men, it is absolutely necessary that a man, in order to prosecute his rights or to defend himself from an improper claim, should have recourse to the assistance of professional lawyers, and it being so absolutely necessary, it is equally necessary, to use a vulgar phrase, that he should be able to make a clean breast of it to the gentleman with whom he consults with a view to the prosecution of his claim, or the substantiating of his defence against the claim of others; that he should be able to place unrestricted and unbounded confidence in the professional agent and that the communications he so makes to him should be kept secret, unless with his consent (for it is his privilege, and not the privilege of the confidential agent), that he should be enabled properly to conduct his litigation. That is the meaning of the rule."[12]

---

[6] Freedom of Information Act 1982, s.42(1).
[7] Access to Information Act (Canada), R.S.C., 1985, s.23.
[8] Official Information Act 1982, s.9(2)(h).
[9] See further: Fennell, *The Law of Evidence in Ireland* (Butterworth (Ireland) Ltd, Dublin, 1992), pp. 166–178; Cahill, *Discovery in Ireland* (Round Hall Sweet & Maxwell, Dublin, 1996), pp. 48–56.
[10] (1876) 2 Ch. D. 644 at 649.
[11] [1990] 1 I.R. 469.
[12] *ibid.* at 476.

1. The subject matter of legal professional privilege

Legal professional privilege applies at common law both to communications concerning litigation and to legal advice.[13]

(a) Communications concerning litigation

In applying the privilege to communications concerning litigation, the main issue to be considered is whether, in order to qualify for privilege, a communication must have been created in the course of actual or expected litigation. The circumstances in which the communication came into existence were examined in the Australian case of *Grant v. Downs*.[14] It was held that the communication must have been brought into existence for the sole purpose of submission to legal advisers for advice, or for use in legal proceedings. However, the House of Lords in *Waugh v. British Railways Board*[15] preferred the minority view of Barwick C.J. in *Grant v. Downs* which rejected the sole purpose test in favour of a dominant purpose test. Lord Wilberforce expressed the test in the following terms:

> "It appears to me that unless the purpose of submission to the legal adviser in view of litigation is at least the dominant purpose for which the relevant document was prepared, the reasons which require privilege to be extended to it cannot apply. On the other hand to hold that the purpose, as above, must be the sole purpose, would, apart from difficulties of proof, in my opinion, be too strict a requirement, and would confine the privilege too narrowly".[16]

The dominant purpose test was adopted by the Irish High Court in *Silver Hill Duckling Limited v. Minister for Agriculture*.[17]

(b) Legal advice

In order for legal advice to be privileged, it is not necessary that it be given in contemplation of legal proceedings. The advice must, however, be given by a lawyer acting in a legal capacity. As emphasised in *Smurfit*:

> "After some difference of opinion it has been established that the privilege is not confined to the conduct of litigation, or to advice obtained for the purposes of existing or contemplated litigation. It applies to communications between client and solicitor in respect of all matters that come within the ordinary scope of professional employment."[18]

---

[13] *Greenough v. Gaskill* (1833) 1 M.Y. & K. 98; *Minter v. Priest* [1929] 1 K.B. 655; (1930) A.C. 558.
[14] (1976) 135 C.L.R. 674; 51 A.L.J.R. 198; 11 A.L.R. 577.
[15] [1980] A.C. 521; [1979] 2 All E.R. 1169; [1979] 3 W.L.R. 150.
[16] *ibid.* at 533.
[17] [1987] I.R. 289.
[18] *Smurfit Paribas Bank Limited v. A.A.B. Export Finance Limited (No. 1)*, above, n. 11, at 477, quoting Greer L.J. in *Minter v. Priest*, above, n. 13, at 683–684.

Australian case law has established that legal advice must be distinguished from policy making advice to which the privilege cannot apply.

In the Australian federal FOI case of *Waterford v. Commonwealth*[19] it was held that the privilege will not apply where the communications relate to the provision, by a lawyer who is a government employee, of advice as to the policy to be followed in the administration of an Act.[20]

Privilege cannot be claimed in respect of legal assistance. As Finlay C.J. stated in *Smurfit*:

> "There are many tasks carried out by a lawyer for his client and properly within the legal sphere, other than the giving of advice, which could not be said to contain any real relationship with the area of potential litigation. For such communications there does not appear to me to be any sufficient public interest or feature of the common good to be secured or protected which could justify an exemption from disclosure."[21]

The types of record in respect of which this exemption might be sought are communications between lawyers and client public bodies, and communications between lawyers and clients which are not public bodies, but where the communications happen to come into the possession of a public body. While the first category of document is clearly covered by the privilege, its application to the second category is not so clear. At common law, legal professional privilege may generally only be claimed by a client and is not available to a third party uninvolved in the litigation or potential litigation. However, in *Re Dwyer and Department of Finance*[22] the Australian federal Administrative Appeals Tribunal (A.A.T.) found that the legal professional privilege exemption in the Australian FOI Act could be relied upon by the agency, even though the person, who for the purposes of legal professional privilege was the client, was not the agency. The tribunal noted, in arriving at that conclusion, that under the Australian FOI Act, a document is exempt "not 'if it would be privileged' but 'if it is of such a nature that it would be privileged'".[23] On the basis of that decision, it could be argued that section 22, referring as it does to records which "would be exempt from production in proceedings in a court on the ground of legal professional privilege", does not extend to records in the possession of a public body in situations where the body is not the client.

---

[19] (1987) 163 C.L.R. 54.
[20] *ibid.* at 77, *per* Brennan J.; at 84–85, *per* Deane J.; and at 103, *per* Dawson J.
[21] *Smurfit Paribas Bank Limited v. A.A.B. Export Finance Limited (No. 1)*, above, n. 11, at 478.
[22] (1985) 8 A.L.D. 474.
[23] *ibid.* at 479–480.

2. Whose advice?

The privilege may be claimed in respect of advice given by salaried lawyers or private lawyers.[24] In *Geraghty v. Minister for Local Government*[25] it was held that it extends to communications from legal advisors employed by the public service.[26]

3. Loss of privilege

Apart from waiver, communications do not lose their privileged status. At common law the privilege can be waived by the client. It is not clear what the effect of waiver is on the exemption.

4. Public interest

There is no public interest test in the text of the exemption, but Finlay C.J. in *Smurfit* emphasised the role of the public interest in common law legal professional privilege cases as follows:

> "The existence of a privilege or exemption from disclosure for communications made between a person and his lawyer clearly constitutes a potential restriction and diminution of the full disclosure both prior to and during the course of legal proceedings which in the interests of the common good is desirable for the purpose of ascertaining the truth and rendering justice. Such privilege should, therefore, in my view, only be granted by the courts in instances which have been identified as securing an objective which in the public interest in the proper conduct of the administration of justice can be said to outweigh the disadvantage arising from the restriction of disclosure of all the facts."[27]

Privilege has been refused on grounds of public policy in cases of abuse. In *R v. Cox & Railton*[28] privilege was refused to legal communications used in furtherance of fraud. Stephen J. stated that:

> "The reason on which the rule is said to rest cannot include the case of communications criminal in themselves or intended to further any criminal purpose, for the protection of such communications cannot possibly be otherwise than injurious to the interests of justice and to those in the administration of justice."[29]

---

[24] *Alfred Crompton Amusement Machines Ltd v. Customs and Excise Commissioners (No. 2)* [1972] 2 Q.B. 102; [1972] 2 All E.R. 353; [1972] 2 W.L.R. 835 (CA).

[25] [1975] I.R. 300.

[26] *ibid.* at 312.

[27] *Smurfit Paribas Bank Limited v. A.A.B. Export Finance Limited (No. 1)*, above, n. 11, at 477.

[28] (1884) 14 Q.B.D. 153.

[29] *ibid.* at 167.

This decision was accepted by the Supreme Court in *Murphy v. Kirwan*[30] as part of Irish law and the circumstances in which a refusal of privilege would be justified were extended by Finlay C.J. when he said:

> "the essence of the matter is that professional privilege cannot and must not be applied so as to be injurious to the interests of justice and to those in the administration of justice where persons have been guilty of conduct of moral turpitude or of dishonest conduct even though it may not be fraud."[31]

Thus, it would appear that the granting of legal professional privilege is subject to public interest considerations at common law. This, in turn, can be said to import a public interest test into the FOI legal professional privilege exemption.

5. Disclosure of the existence or non-existence of a record

Where a request relates to a record to which section 22(1)(a) applies or would, if the record existed, apply, and the head of the public body concerned is satisfied that the disclosure of the existence or non-existence of the record would be contrary to the public interest, he or she must refuse to grant the request and must not disclose whether the record exists.[32] The justification for this provision is that even if the records are not themselves released, the knowledge that they exist could prove damaging. Knowledge of the fact that a record exists which relates to a communication between a public body and its legal advisors on a particular issue could, for example, be damaging to the litigation strategy being pursued by the body. Provisions of this type are discussed in greater detail above at pp. 71–72. Regard must be had to the public interest in applying this provision. The meaning of public interest in the context of the FOI Act is discussed in greater detail at pp. 93–115.

B.   Contempt of Court

This mandatory exemption provides as follows:

> "22.—(1) A head shall refuse to grant a request under section 7 if the record concerned . . .
>
> (b) is such that its disclosure would constitute contempt of court".

---

[30] [1993] 3 I.R. 501.
[31] *ibid.* at 511.
[32] s.22(2).

Similar exemptions are provided for in the Australian[33] and New Zealand[34] FOI Acts. The rationale behind the inclusion of such an exemption in the original Australian Freedom of Information Bill was explained by the Senate Standing Committee on Constitutional and Legal Affairs in the following terms:

> "Parliament and the courts have unique functions, and have traditionally had powers to regulate their own proceedings that have been regarded as a necessary incident to their functions. The Bill, which is designed to open up to public scrutiny the operations of the Executive, should not unnecessarily interfere with the other organs of the State with consequences that cannot at the outset be entirely foreseen."[35]

This is another of the exemptions which relies on the interpretation of an existing legal concept to clarify its application. For that reason, the law relating to contempt of court in Ireland must be examined. Contempt of court is generally dealt with at common law in Ireland,[36] although the right to freedom of expression in the Irish Constitution and in the European Convention on Human Rights also have a role to play.

1. Common law contempt

It is accepted that contempt falls into two categories: civil and criminal.[37]

(a) Civil contempt

Civil contempt was described by Diplock J. in *Attorney-General v. Times Newspapers Ltd*[38] as "disobedience by a party to a civil action of a specific order of the court made by him in that action".[39] Such contempt could arise in the context of disclosure of records under the FOI Act, where such disclosure would be in contravention of a specific court order.

---

[33] Freedom of Information Act 1982 (Cth), s.46(1)(a); Freedom of Information Act 1989 (New South Wales), Sched.1, cl.17; Freedom of Information Act 1991 (South Australia), Sched.1, cl.17; Freedom of Information Act 1992 (Queensland), s.50; Freedom of Information Act 1992 (Western Australia), Sched.1, cl.12.

[34] Official Information Act 1982, s.18(c)(ii).

[35] Australian Senate Standing Committee on Constitutional and Legal Affairs, *Report on the Freedom of Information Bill 1978, and aspects of the Archives Bill 1978* (Australian Government Publishing Service, Canberra, 1979), para. 23.12.

[36] There are also a number of statutes containing contempt-like powers: see McGonagle, *A Textbook on Media Law* (Gill and Macmillan, Dublin, 1996), p. 164.

[37] Lowe, *The Law of Contempt* (3rd ed., Butterworths, London, 1996).

[38] [1974] A.C. 273; [1973] 3 All E.R. 54; [1973] 3 W.L.R. 298.

[39] *ibid.* at 307.

(b) Criminal contempt

There are a number of categories of criminal contempt. Ó Dálaigh C.J. gave the following examples in *Keegan v. de Burca*[40] when he said that criminal contempt:

> "consists in behaviour calculated to prejudice the due course of justice, such as contempt *in facie curiae*, words written or spoken or acts calculated to prejudice the due course of justice or disobedience to a writ of *habeas corpus* by the person to whom it is directed — to give but some examples of this class of contempt."[41]

In addition to these three forms of contempt, the Irish courts have also recognised a form of contempt known as scandalising the court.[42]

(i) Contempt in facie curiae

Contempt *in facie curiae* was described in *State (D.P.P.) v. Walsh*[43] as "conduct which is obstructive or prejudicial to the course of justice, and which is committed during court proceedings".[44] The following examples of contempt in the face of the court were referred to in *Keegan v. de Burca*: disorderly conduct in court, intimidating the jury, or hurling insults at the judge. It has been accepted that a refusal to answer a question also amounts to contempt *in facie curiae*.[45] None of these activities is likely to result from the disclosure of records under the FOI Act.

(ii) Words or acts calculated to prejudice the due administration of justice

Lord Diplock in *Attorney-General v. Times Newspapers Ltd* identified three requirements for the attainment of the due administration of justice. He said:

> "The due administration of justice requires first that citizens should have unhindered access to the constitutionally established courts of criminal or civil jurisdiction for the determination of disputes as to their legal right and liabilities; secondly, that they should be able to rely on obtaining in the courts the arbitrament of a tribunal which is free from bias against any party and whose decision will be based on those facts only that have been proved in evidence adduced before it in accordance with the procedure adopted in courts of law; and thirdly that, once the dispute has been submitted to a court of law, they should be able to rely

---

[40] [1973] I.R. 223.
[41] *ibid.* at 227.
[42] [1981] I.R. 412; *Desmond v. Glackin (No. 1)* [1992] I.L.R.M. 490; [1993] 3 I.R. 1.
[43] *ibid.* at 412.
[44] *ibid.* at 421.
[45] *Keegan v. de Burca*, above, n. 40; *Re Kevin O'Kelly* (1974) 108 I.L.T.R. 97.

on there being no usurpation by any other person of the function of that court to decide it according to law."[46]

Diplock J. provided examples of the commission of each of the three forms of contempt against the due administration of justice. In terms of the citizen's unhindered access to the courts, it was said that:

> "to hold a party up to public obloquy for exercising his constitutional rights to have recourse to a court of law for the ascertainment of his legal rights and obligations is calculated to prejudice the first requirement for the due administration of justice: the unhindered access of all citizens to the established courts of law."[47]

Such prejudice to the administration of justice could occur as a result of the disclosure under the FOI Act of records containing threats against a litigant. This is not likely to occur often in practice.

The second form of conduct identified by Diplock J. as interfering with the due administration of justice was conduct calculated to prejudice through disregard for the citizen's right to an unbiased hearing in the courts and to expect that the court's decision should be based only on facts that have been proved in evidence. This was referred to as the commonest kind of contempt; the example given was:

> "publication, generally in a newspaper, of statements or comments about parties to pending litigation or about facts at issue in litigation".[48]

Such conduct, it was stated, raises the question whether:

> "the publication complained of involved a risk of causing someone who might be called on to serve as a juror to be prejudiced against a party or to form a preconceived view of the facts before the evidence was adduced in court, or a risk of influencing someone who might be called as a witness to alter his evidence or to decline to testify".[49]

This sort of prejudice could occur as a result of the release under FOI of details of the criminal record of an accused person, for example.

The rule that contempt is committed by conduct (usually publication) calculated to impair the administration of justice in a particular case which is pending is sometimes known as the *sub judice* rule. The rule was defined in *Attorney General for New South Wales v. John Fairfax & Sons Ltd*[50] in the following terms:

---

[46] *Attorney-General v. Times Newspapers Ltd,* above, n. 38, at 309.
[47] *ibid.* at 310.
[48] *ibid.* at 309.
[49] *ibid.*
[50] [1980] 1 N.S.W.L.R. 362.

"[C]ontempt will be established if a publication has a tendency to interfere with the due administration of justice in the particular proceedings."[51]

That definition was endorsed by O'Hanlon J. in *Desmond v. Glackin (No. 1)*.[52]

Breach of the *sub judice* rule can only arise in the context of a specific case. In addition, litigation must be proceeding or be known to be imminent.[53] Proceedings are said to be imminent from the issue of a writ in a civil case, or the laying of charges in a criminal one, although it has been suggested that, at common law, criminal proceedings are imminent from the time when a suspect is about to be arrested.[54]

The third form of conduct identified by Diplock J. as interfering with the due administration of justice was the usurpation of the function of a court to decide a dispute according to law. This form of contempt was referred to in *Attorney-General v. Times Newspapers Ltd*[55] as "trial by newspaper",[56] *i.e.* public discussion or comment on the merits of a dispute which has been submitted to a court of law or on the alleged facts of the dispute before they have been found by the court on the evidence adduced before it. Disclosure under FOI of a record which prejudges the issues that a court has to determine would result in prejudice of this kind.

While it is clear that an action may constitute a contempt of court if it interferes with the administration of justice in a particular case, it has been suggested that it can also be contempt to commit an action which interferes with the administration of justice as a continuing process.[57]

In terms of the standard of proof of interference with the due administration of justice necessary to ground a finding of contempt, it was held in *Desmond v. Glackin (No. 1)*[58] that there is a need to show a real risk as opposed to a remote possibility of prejudice. This issue was also examined in *Re Altman and Family Court of Australia*,[59] a case concerning the Australian FOI contempt exemption. The Australian federal A.A.T. held that for a contempt of this kind to arise, it is necessary to show that disclosure is likely to interfere with the administration of justice, or that there is a real tendency for it to do so. The tribunal held that it is not enough that it might make it more difficult for the court to carry out its task because it will be subject to greater public scrutiny.

---

[51] Above, n. 50, at 368.
[52] [1993] 3 I.R. 1.
[53] *Attorney-General v. Times Newspapers Ltd*, above, n. 38, *per* Diplock J.
[54] *R. v. Horsham Justices, ex parte Farquharson* [1982] 2 All E.R. 269.
[55] Above, n. 38.
[56] *ibid.* at 311.
[57] *Prothonotary v. Collins* (1985) 2 N.S.W.L.R. 549 at 554 and 565.
[58] Above, n. 52, at 18.
[59] (1992) 15 A.A.R. 236.

(iii) Disobedience to a writ of habeas corpus

Such a contempt arises where a writ of habeas corpus is disobeyed. It could not arise from disclosure of records under the Freedom of Information Act.

(iv) Scandalising the court

Scandalising the court was said in *State (D.P.P.) v. Walsh*[60] to occur:

> "where what is said or done is of such a nature as to be calculated to endanger public confidence in the court which is attacked and, thereby, to obstruct and interfere with the administration of justice."[61]

A more colourful description of this form of contempt was provided by Gavan Duffy P. in *Attorney General v. Connolly*[62] when he said that this form of contempt occurs:

> "where the defendant has held up the judges in a capital trial to the odium of the people as actors playing a sinister part in a caricature of justice."[63]

The Supreme Court in *State (D.P.P.) v. Walsh* was clearly mindful of the constitutional position when it elaborated upon its definition of contempt by scandalising the courts by saying:

> "It is not committed by mere criticism of judges as judges, or by the expression of disagreement – even emphatic disagreement – with what has been decided by a court. The right of citizens to express freely, subject to public order, convictions and opinions is wide enough to comprehend such criticism or expressed disagreement."[64]

There is no requirement that such scandalisation take place in the course of a trial.[65] A contempt of this type could conceivably arise out of the disclosure of records under the FOI Act, for example where the record imputes corruption on the part of a judge acting in his or her legal capacity. In *Re Altman and Family Court of Australia* the A.A.T. held that the disclosure of the unsettled transcript of a judgment of the Family Court would not amount to a contempt of this kind. The tribunal said:

> "The idea that the authority of a court or judicial officer or the determinations of a court or judicial officer can be detracted from by the publication of such determinations themselves, even in unsettled form, suggests erroneously that there is something defective in unsettled judgments. Were members of the pub-

---

[60] Above, n. 42.
[61] *ibid.* at 421.
[62] (1947) I.R. 213.
[63] *ibid.* at 220.
[64] Above, n. 42, at 421.
[65] *Attorney-General v. Times Newspapers Ltd*, above, n. 38, at 309, *per* Diplock J.

lic to form such views then the authority of the courts would indeed be under-mined."[66]

2. Motive of applicant

The motive or purpose of the applicant in seeking access to the record must, in keeping with the philosophy of freedom of information, be disregarded. This was confirmed in the Australian case of *Re Altman and Family Court of Australia*,[67] where it was held that the contempt exemption will only make a document an exempt document where public disclosure will be contempt of court: the fact that the document may subsequently be used in a way which is in contempt of court is not relevant.

3. Public interest

No public interest test is expressly provided for in the text of the exemption. However, it appears that the common law of contempt itself incorporates a public interest test. In *Attorney-General v. Times Newspapers Ltd*, Lord Reid said:

> "The law on this subject is and must be founded entirely on public policy. It is not there to protect the private rights of parties to a litigation or prosecution. It is there to prevent interference with the administration of justice and it should, in my judgment, be limited to what is reasonably necessary for that purpose. Public policy generally requires a balancing of interests which may conflict. Freedom of speech should not be limited to any greater extent than is necessary but it cannot be allowed where there would be a real prejudice to the administration of justice."[68]

The need to balance the public interest in the administration of justice against freedom of discussion was upheld by O'Hanlon J. in *Desmond v. Glackin (No. 1)*.[69] The first respondent was an inspector who had been appointed by the second respondent, the Minister for Industry and Commerce, to investigate the controversial purchase of land by Telecom Éireann. The applicant wished to have the inspector's appointment quashed and in order to do so he sought and obtained the leave of the High Court to challenge the appointment by way of judicial review. On the day following the High Court's decision granting leave to apply for judicial review, the second respondent gave a radio interview in the course of which it was alleged he had committed contempt of court. The applicant applied to the High Court for an order of attachment of

---

[66] Above, n. 59, at 246.
[67] *ibid.* at 247.
[68] Above, n. 38, at 294.
[69] Above, n. 52.

the second respondent for contempt of court. In dismissing the application,
O'Hanlon J. said:

> "We are here dealing with an ongoing matter of public interest which has occu-
> pied the minds of the public for many months past. In this situation, and particu-
> larly in the context of the second respondent's utterances being a response to
> serious allegations made against him by the first applicant which had already
> been well publicised, I consider the case falls well within the scope of the ex-
> ceptional situations referred to by both Lord Reid and Lord Simon of Glaisdale
> in the *Attorney-General v. Times Newspaper Ltd.* [1974] A.C. 273 where 'the
> law strikes [the balance] in favour of freedom of discussion'."[70]

In Ireland, the law of contempt must also be viewed in the light of constitutional rights, in particular the right to freedom of expression.[71] The right to
freedom of expression was referred to by O'Hanlon J. in arriving at his decision that contempt of court had not been committed in *Desmond v. Glackin
(No. 1)*.[72] The right to freedom of expression is, of course, subject to restrictions, namely those relating to public order and morality and the authority of
the State.

Article 10 of the European Convention on Human Rights also protects the
right to freedom of expression. Paragraph 2 of that right places a number of
restrictions on its operation.[73] In *Sunday Times v. U.K. (No. 1)*[74] the U.K.
Attorney-General had imposed an injunction preventing publication of a discussion of the merits of a negligence action against the makers of a drug alleged to have caused birth deformities. The granting of the injunction was
upheld by the U.K. courts on the basis that the article constituted contempt of
court. The case was taken to the European Court of Human Rights, where it
was held that the restriction that the injunction imposed on the right to freedom of expression was disproportionate and thus unnecessary in a democratic
society for the protection of the authority of the judiciary. That decision was
accepted by O'Hanlon J. as persuasive authority in the interpretation of the
right to freedom of expression in the Irish Constitution in *Desmond v. Glackin
(No. 1)*.[75]

---

[70] Above, n. 52, at 33.
[71] Article 40.6.1°.
[72] Above, n. 52, at 28.
[73] See above, pp. 11–14.
[74] (1980) 2 E.H.R.R. 245.
[75] Above, n. 52.

C.   Private Papers of Elected Representatives

The third element of section 22 is the exemption of private papers of representatives in the European Parliament, local government and members of health boards:

> "22.—(1) A head shall refuse to grant a request under section 7 if the record concerned...
>
>   (c) consists of—
>   (i) the private papers of a representative in the European Parliament or a member of a local authority or a health board".

Access to such papers will of course only become an issue where private papers of representatives are in the possession of a public body such as a local authority or health board, for example. This exemption complements the exclusion from the scope of the Act of records relating to the private papers (within the meaning of Article 15.10 of the Constitution) of a member of either House of the Oireachtas.[76] Because this exemption is mandatory, the effect of this element of the exemption is, to all intents and purposes, the same as the effect of the exclusion from the scope of the Act of records relating to the private papers of Oireachtas members. There is no definition of "private papers" in the Act. Difficulties could arise in distinguishing private papers of members of local authorities and health boards from official records of such bodies. For example, the status of letters written to members which are then forwarded to the authorities would be uncertain.

D.   Information Considered by the Houses of the Oireachtas

The fourth element of this exemption, s.22(1)(c)(ii), is concerned with exempting records containing information considered by the Houses of the Oireachtas or committees of those Houses for the purposes of the proceedings of those bodies. It covers records consisting of:

> "(ii) opinions, advice, recommendations, or the results of consultations, considered by—
>   (I)   either House of the Oireachtas or the Chairman or Deputy Chairman or any other member of either such House or a member of the staff of the Office of the Houses of the Oireachtas for the purposes of the proceedings at a sitting of either such House, or
>   (II) a committee appointed by either such House or jointly by both such Houses and consisting of members of either or both of such Houses or a member of such a committee or a member of the staff of the Office

---

[76] s.46(1)(e). See above, pp. 57–58.

of the Houses of the Oireachtas for the purposes of the proceedings at a meeting of such a committee."

In order to fall within the scope of the exemption, the record must fulfil three conditions:

(1) it must constitute opinions, advice, recommendations or results of consultations;

(2) such records must have been considered by one of the following:
    (a) either House of the Oireachtas;
    (b) the Chairman or Deputy Chairman of either House;
    (c) a member of either House or of a committee of either House;
    (d) a staff member of the Office of the Houses of the Oireachtas;
    (e) a committee of either House or a joint committee of both Houses consisting of members of either or both such houses; and

(3) such consideration must have been for the purposes of the proceedings at a sitting of either House, or at a meeting of a committee, as the case may be.

This exemption must be considered alongside the exclusion from the scope of the Act, by virtue of section 46(1)(e), of an official document of either or both Houses of the Oireachtas "that is required by the Rules or Standing Orders of either or both such Houses to be treated as confidential". The current standing orders of the Dáil[77] and Seanad[78] do not require that any documents be treated as confidential.

The main difference between the exemption and exclusion is that the former is concerned with protecting records from disclosure which constitute the raw material of the proceedings of the Houses of the Oireachtas and committees, while the latter is concerned with protecting official documents from disclosure. Official documents are not defined in the Act but could be taken to include reports or proceedings of committees of the Houses of the Oireachtas.

The justification put forward in the Oireachtas for the section 46(1)(e) exclusion was that this is an area in which, by virtue of Article 15.10 of the Constitution, the Houses of the Oireachtas make their own rules.[79] It would appear that a similar justification can be understood as the basis for section 22(1)(c)(ii).

There are roughly analogous provisions in the Australian federal Act and in the New Zealand Act. In Australia, for example, section 46 of the federal FOI Act exempts from disclosure documents which infringe the privilege of

---

[77] Dáil Éireann, *Standing Orders Relative to Public Business* (1996).
[78] Seanad Éireann, *Standing Orders Relative to Public Business* (1995).
[79] 149 *Seanad Debates* Col. 1594 (Committee Stage).

the parliament. It has been suggested that the most relevant privilege concerns the rule that it is a breach of privilege for a person to publish the evidence given to, or the report of, a parliamentary committee before the committee has reported to the parliament or House and before the committee has authorised publication of the evidence of the report.[80]

In New Zealand a request may be refused on the basis that the making available of the information would constitute contempt of parliament.[81] Such a contempt, it has been suggested, would occur where there is a breach of the Standing Order providing that the proceedings and reports of select committees are not to be published or divulged until the committee has reported to the House.[82]

The scope of the exclusion and exemption concerning information considered by the Houses of the Oireachtas in the Irish Act appears to go beyond that contemplated by the Australian and New Zealand provisions. Between them, the exclusion and exemption apply not only to reports or proceedings of parliamentary committees, but also to consultants' reports and legal opinions and advice considered by committees. Nor is there any time limit on the operation of the exclusion or exemption. There is, for example, no provision for the lapsing of the provisions on the making of its report by a committee to the House.

---

[80] Bayne, *Freedom of Information: An Analysis of the Freedom of Information Act 1982 (Cth.) And a Synopsis of the Freedom of Information Act 1982 (Vic.)* (Law Book Company, Sydney, 1984), p. 223.

[81] s.18(c)(ii).

[82] Eagles, Taggart, and Liddell, *Freedom of Information in New Zealand* (Oxford University Press, 1992), pp. 468–478.

CHAPTER 10

LAW ENFORCEMENT AND PUBLIC SAFETY

LAW ENFORCEMENT AND PUBLIC SAFETY

A. Introduction

While the need to protect law enforcement information is widely recognised overseas,[1] the protection afforded by the Irish FOI Act to information concerning law enforcement and public safety is particularly extensive. In the period leading up to publication of the Bill, it became clear that the Department of Justice was concerned about the possible impact of FOI legislation on records relating to law enforcement.[2] This concern is reflected in the strength of the provisions limiting access to such information. The main aim of this chapter will be to provide an analysis of the law enforcement and public safety exemption in the Act. Before embarking on that analysis, it is worth pointing out that there are three other factors which limit the use of the FOI Act in obtaining access to law enforcement records. First, the Act does not apply to the Garda Síochána.[3] Provision has, however, been made for extension of the Act by regulation to the gardaí.[4] The second limitation on the use of the Act to obtain access to records relating to law enforcement is the exclusion from the scope of the Act of information which could be reasonably be expected to

---

[1] Australia: Freedom of Information Act 1982 (Cth), s.37; Freedom of Information Act 1982 (Victoria), s.31; Freedom of Information Act 1989 (New South Wales), Sched.1, cl.4; Freedom of Information Act 1991 (South Australia), Sched.1, cl.4; Freedom of Information Act 1991 (Tasmania), s.28; Freedom of Information Act 1992 (Queensland), s.42; Freedom of Information Act 1992 (Western Australia), Sched.1, cl.5.
Canada: Access to Information Act (Canada), R.S.C., 1985, s.16; Right to Information Act (New Brunswick), S.N.B., 1978, s.6(e), (h.1), (h.2), and (i); An Act respecting Access to documents held by public bodies and the Protection of personal information (Quebec), S.Q., 1982, s.28; Freedom of Information Act (Manitoba), C.C.S.M., 1998, c.F175, s.25; Freedom of Information Act (Newfoundland), R.S.N., 1990, s.11(b); Freedom of Information and Protection of Privacy Act (Saskatchewan), S.S., 1990–1991, s.15(1); Freedom of Information and Protection of Privacy Act (Ontario), R.S.O., 1990, s.14; Freedom of Information and Protection of Privacy Act (British Columbia), R.S.B.C., 1996, s.15; Freedom of Information and Protection of Privacy Act (Nova Scotia), S.N.S., 1993, s.15; Freedom of Information and Protection of Privacy Act (Alberta), S.A., 1994, s.19(1).
New Zealand: Official Information Act 1982, s.6(c).
U.S.: Freedom of Information Act 1966, Exemption 7.
[2] Foley, "Freedom of information plans held up by Justice Department", *Irish Times*, September 16, 1995.
[3] The police force.
[4] First Sched., para. 1(5)(a).

disclose the identity of a confidential source of information in relation to the enforcement of any criminal law.[5] Such information is the subject of exemption, rather than exclusion, provisions in overseas FOI legislation.[6] Finally, there is provision for the issuing of ministerial certificates in respect of records concerning law enforcement. The signing by a Minister of such a certificate has the effect of establishing that the record to which it relates is exempt. A decision by a Minister to sign a ministerial certificate is not subject to review by the Ombudsman. The mechanics and effect of the issuance of ministerial certificates is discussed above at pp. 115–119.

The exemption is stated in the following terms:

"23.—(1) A head may refuse to grant a request under section 7 if access to the record concerned could, in the opinion of the head, reasonably be expected to—

(a) prejudice or impair—
    (i)   the prevention, detection or investigation of offences, the apprehension or prosecution of offenders or the effectiveness of lawful methods, systems, plans or procedures employed for the purposes of the matters aforesaid,
    (ii) the enforcement of, compliance with or administration of any law,
    (iii) lawful methods, systems, plans or procedures for ensuring the safety of the public and the safety or security of persons and property,
    (iv) the fairness of criminal proceedings in a court or of civil proceedings in a court or other tribunal,
    (v)   the security of a penal institution,
    (vi) the security of the Central Mental Hospital,
    (vii) the security of a building or other structure or a vehicle, ship, boat or aircraft,
    (viii) the security of any system of communications, whether internal or external, of the Garda Síochána, the Defence Forces, the Revenue Commissioners or a penal institution,
(b) reveal or lead to the revelation of the identity of a person who has given information to a public body in confidence in relation to the enforcement or administration of the civil law or any other source of such information given in confidence, or
(c) facilitate the commission of an offence.

(2) Where a request under section 7 relates to a record to which subsection (1) applies, or would, if the record existed, apply, and the head concerned is satisfied that the disclosure of the existence or non-existence of the record would have an effect specified in paragraph (a), (b) or (c) of that subsection, he or she

---

[5] s.46(1)(f).
[6] See for example: Australia: Freedom of Information Act 1982 (Cth), s.37(1)(b); Canada: Access to Information Act (Canada), R.S.C., 1985, s.16(1)(c)(ii).

shall refuse to grant the request and shall not disclose to the requester concerned whether or not the record exists.

(3) Subsection (1) does not apply to a record—

    (a) if it—

        (i) discloses that an investigation for the purpose of the enforcement of any law, or anything done in the course of such an investigation or for the purposes of the prevention or detection of offences or the apprehension or prosecution of offenders, is not authorised by law or contravenes any law, or

        (ii) contains information concerning—

            (I) the performance of the functions of a public body whose functions include functions relating to the enforcement of law or the ensuring of the safety of the public (including the effectiveness and efficiency of such performance), or

            (II) the merits or otherwise or the success or otherwise of any programme, scheme or policy of a public body for preventing, detecting or investigating contraventions of the law or the effectiveness or efficiency of the implementation of any such programme, scheme or policy by a public body,

    and

    (b) in the opinion of the head concerned, the public interest would, on balance, be better served by granting than by refusing to grant the request concerned.

(4) In subsection (1) 'penal institution' means—

    (a) a place to which the Prisons Acts, 1826 to 1980, apply,
    (b) a military prison or detention barrack within the meaning, in each case, of the Defence Act, 1954,
    (c) Saint Patrick's Institution, or
    (d) an institution established under the Children Act, 1908, in which young offenders are detained."

The law enforcement and public safety exemption is not a mandatory exemption. The head of a public body has the discretion to release records falling within the scope of section 23. While the main criminal law enforcement agency of the State, the Garda Síochána, remains outside the scope of the Act, there are a number of other bodies with criminal and civil law enforcement responsibilities which are subject to the Act and might seek to invoke this exemption. They include the Office of the Director of Public Prosecutions, the Attorney General's Office, and enforcement authorities on a range of issues embracing the environment, competition law, companies, taxation and social security. Section 23 contains a limited public interest provision. It is aimed at ensuring that bodies with law enforcement responsibilities cannot hide behind the law enforcement exemption in an effort to prevent the disclosure of records revealing wrongdoing or inefficiency on their part. Section 23 also allows the head of a public body to refuse to reveal the existence or non-existence of law enforcement information in certain circumstances.[7]

There are three strands to the exemption. The first, section 23(1)(a), is harm based. It exempts the disclosure of records which could reasonably be expected to prejudice or impair any of a broad range of law enforcement activities. The second part of the exemption, section 23(1)(b), exempts records which could reasonably be expected to disclose the identity of a confidential source of information. Finally, section 23(1)(c) provides for the exemption of records the disclosure of which could reasonably be expected to facilitate the commission of an offence. All three strands of the exemption adopt the same standard of proof, namely that granting the request "could reasonably be expected to" result in the consequences specified. Canadian and Australian FOI jurisprudence on the meaning of this phrase is discussed in greater detail above at pp. 90–92. To summarise, decisions in those jurisdictions have established that the mere possibility of the specified consequences ensuing will not suffice to meet the "could reasonably be expected to" standard. It will not, however, be necessary to show evidence of direct causation between disclosure and the specified consequences, nor will it be necessary to establish that the occurrence of the specified consequences is more probable than not. In both jurisdictions, the emphasis is on the reasonableness of the expectation of harm arising out of the disclosure.

B. The Exempt Categories

1. Section 23(1)(a)

This part of the exemption is directed to the harmful consequences that could result from disclosure of a record, rather than to the nature of the document itself. Section 23(1)(a) can be used to deny access to records on the basis that their disclosure could reasonably be expected to prejudice or impair any of a long list of law enforcement related activities. The list encompasses both criminal and civil matters and it is detailed and extensive by comparison with its counterparts in overseas legislation.

(a) Prejudice/Impair

The type of harm which must reasonably be expected to result from disclosure is "prejudice or impairment". The use of two different terms here is somewhat confusing. It would have been more satisfactory, for reasons of clarity, to have confined the test to one or other of these terms. Prejudice is the term used in the Australian federal and New Zealand legislation, both of which use a harm

---

[7] See below, p. 202 for a discussion of this provision.

based approach in their law enforcement exemptions.[8]

The protection of most of the interests listed is likely to be confined to particular situations. For example, prejudice or impairment to the investigation of offences under section 23(1)(a)(i) would arguably have to be shown to relate to the likelihood of such prejudice arising in the context of a particular criminal investigation rather than in respect of criminal investigations in general. Other elements of the exemption which would appear to be confined to particular cases include prejudice or impairment to: the enforcement of or compliance with or the administration of any law (section 23(1)(a)(ii)); the fairness of criminal proceedings in a court or of civil proceedings in a court or other tribunal (section 23(1)(a)(iv)); and the security of a building, structure or vehicle (section 23(1)(a)(vii)). Evidence of prejudice in a particular instance may also be required in respect of: prejudice to the prevention or detection of offences under section 23(1)(a)(i); the apprehension or prosecution of offenders (section 23(1)(a)(i)); the security of a penal institution under section 23(1)(a)(v) and of the Central Mental Hospital (section 23(1)(a)(vi)); and in the case of prejudice to radio and telecommunications information of the Garda Síochána, the Defence Forces, the Revenue Commissioners, or a penal institution (section 23(1)(a)(viii)).

On the other hand, prejudice to the effectiveness of lawful methods, systems, plans, or procedures for prevention, detection or investigation of offences (section 23(1)(a)(i)) need not be shown to arise in respect of a particular case, nor arguably would prejudice to lawful methods, systems, plans or procedures for ensuring public safety (section 23(1)(a)(iii)). It is not clear whether prejudice to lawful methods, systems, plans or procedures for ensuring the safety or security of persons and property (section 23(1)(a)(iii)) would have to be shown to exist in respect of a specific case. The reference to "lawful methods", etc., would seem to indicate that it is not necessarily related to particular cases.

The practical effect of the distinction between interests requiring evidence of prejudice in a particular case and those which do not is that in the former case, the evidence of harm must go beyond a blanket assertion on the part of the head of the public body that disclosure of the records would be prejudicial. Each application for access to such records must, instead, be considered on a case-by-case basis. The case-by-case approach was upheld in New Zealand in the context of a claim that disclosure of the requested records would be likely to prejudice the fair trial of an accused. It was held that the claim for exemption must, in all cases, relate to the information actually being sought rather

than to kinds or classes of information.[9] In the U.S. case of *NLRB v. Robbins*

---

[8] Australia: Freedom of Information Act 1982 (Cth), s.37; New Zealand: Official Information Act 1982, s.6(c); in Canada, the term used is "be injurious to": Access to Information Act (Canada), R.S.C., 1985, s.16(1)(c).

[9] *Commissioner of Police v. Ombudsman* [1985] 1 N.Z.L.R. 578; [1988] 1 N.Z.L.R. 385.

Tire & Rubber Co.[10] the Supreme Court held that the disclosure of records could reasonably be expected to "interfere with enforcement proceedings" where the government demonstrates that the information relates to a pending or prospective law enforcement proceeding. However, the Supreme Court rejected the suggestion that "interference with enforcement proceedings" must always be established on a document-by-document basis, holding that determination of the exemption's applicability may be made "generically", *i.e.* through the lodgment of affidavits which specify the distinct, generic categories of documents at issue and the harm that would result from their release, rather than requiring extensive, detailed itemisations of each document.[11]

(b) Interests protected under section 23(1)(a)

The matters coming within the scope of this part of the exemption have been divided into 15 separate components for the purpose of analysis, with some words being repeated for reasons of clarity.

(i) Section 23(1)(a)(i): Prejudice or impair the prevention of offences

This provision is aimed at protecting records from disclosure which contain information on the prevention of specific offences, rather than more general information concerning techniques and plans for the prevention of breaches or evasions of the law, since the latter is referred to separately elsewhere (see (vi) below). Its wording suggests that it is confined to the disclosure of records which could reasonably be expected to prejudice or impair the prevention of offences sometime in the future and, on that basis, it could not be used to deny access to records concerning prevention of a crime which has already taken place.

(ii) Section 23(1)(a)(i): Prejudice or impair the detection of offences

Again, this provision appears to be directed at records concerning detection of a particular crime rather than information concerning detection of criminal activity in general.

(iii) Section 23(1)(a)(i): Prejudice or impair the investigation of offences

Here again, investigation of a particular offence must be involved. The exemption cannot be availed of unless there is a prospect of proceedings. The disclosure of records concerning the prosecution may be found not to prejudice the investigation of the offence once proceedings have been commenced.

---

[10] 437 U.S. 214 (1978).
[11] *ibid.* at 236.

dice the investigation of the offence once proceedings have been commenced. This was the effect of the New Zealand Court of Appeal's decision in *Commissioner of Police v. Ombudsman*.[12]

This limb of the exemption cannot be availed of after the investigation has closed. Thus, the U.S. equivalent was interpreted as not being intended to "endlessly protect material simply because it [is] an investigatory file".[13] This approach has been confirmed in Australia.[14] Difficulty may arise, however, in ascertaining when an investigation has been determined, since decisions not to proceed with investigations are rarely publicised.

(iv) Section 23(1)(a)(i): Prejudice or impair the apprehension of offenders

Arguably, what is protected here is information which would be likely to prejudice the apprehension of a particular offender. Again it would seem that once the offender has been apprehended, the exemption should no longer apply.

(v) Section 23(1)(a)(i): Prejudice or impair the prosecution of offenders

What is at issue here is potential damage to specific pending or contemplated prosecutions. The question arises: at what stage in a prosecution should records be released? In the New Zealand case of *Commissioner of Police v. Ombudsman*,[15] the New Zealand Court of Appeal decided that once summary proceedings have commenced, the disclosure of prosecution evidence would not be likely to prejudice the investigation of offences or the right to a fair trial. Presumably the effect of that decision could be extended to cover damage to the prosecution itself.

(vi) Section 23(1)(a)(i): Prejudice or impair the effectiveness of lawful methods, systems, plans or procedures for prevention, detection or investigation of offences

In contrast to the foregoing provisions, this part of section 23 is not confined to particular cases. Instead, it provides protection to records containing general information relating to the methods, systems, plans and procedures for prevention, detection and investigation of offences. Delineating the scope of this provision in terms of the prevention of offences will be difficult, in that the prevention of offences could encompass a wide range of activities. The operation of the harm test will serve to limit its scope somewhat. For example, the term "prevention of breaches of law" could apply to all documentation concerning Neighbourhood Watch activities, but these would only be subject to the exemption, where their release could reasonably be expected to preju-

---

[12] Above, n. 9.
[13] *NLRB v. Robbins Tire & Rubber Co.*, above, n. 10, at 232.
[14] *Re Edelsten and Australian Federal Police* (1985) 4 A.A.R. 220.
[15] Above, n. 9.

dice such prevention. An example of what might fall within the scope of the provision is contingency plans for the prevention of unlawful activities. In the U.S. it has been held that in order for techniques or procedures to qualify for cover under this provision, they must not be already well known to the public. For example, such techniques as the use of post office boxes,[16] the tagging of fingerprints,[17] and pretext telephone calls[18] have been denied protection under the equivalent U.S. provision.[19]

(vii) Section 23(1)(a)(ii): Prejudice or impair the enforcement of any law

This provision is likely to be confined to enforcement in a particular case. It is not clear exactly what the boundaries of the term are. Law enforcement activities such as prevention, detection and investigation of offences have already been given separate treatment. The main difference would appear to be that this provision applies to civil as well as criminal matters.

(viii) Section 23(1)(a)(ii): Prejudice or impair compliance with any law

This element of the exemption covers compliance with both criminal and civil law. It is not clear whether "compliance with any law" is confined to the question of compliance with Irish law or whether it would extend to compliance with Ireland's obligations under international law. In an Australian case, "breach of law" was interpreted to mean breach of Australian law, but the court expressly left open the question of how the interpretation of the phrase "breach of law" might be affected by international agreements entered into by Australia.[20]

(ix) Section 23(1)(a)(ii): Prejudice or impair the administration of any law

The difference between enforcement and administration of a law may not be readily apparent, but administration is arguably the broader term. Law enforcement activities would only take place where the person the subject of them has acted or might act in breach of the law, whereas the administration of law can encompass a broader range of activities not directly connected with a breach of the law. It could include, for example, activity which involves the gathering of information in order to monitor whether a person is complying with the law. In Australia, administration of the law has been held to include the activities of a Royal Commission set up to investigate allegations of extensive criminal activities.[21] Presumably it would also apply to the activities of

---

[16] *Dunway v. Webster*, 519 F. Supp. 1059 at 1082–1083 (N.D. Cal. 1981).
[17] *Ferguson v. Kelley*, 448 F. Supp. 919 at 927 (N.D. Ill. 1977).
[18] *Rosenfeld v. United States Department of Justice*, 57 F. 3d. 803 at 825 (9th Cir. 1995).
[19] Freedom of Information Act 1966, Exemption 7(E).
[20] *Conte v. Australian Federal Police* (1985) 7 A.L.N. N71.
[21] *Re Gold and Australian Federal Police* (1994) 37 A.L.D. 168.

tribunals of inquiry in Ireland.

One issue which has arisen in the context of this exemption is the relationship between FOI and the laws relating to discovery. The issue could arise where an application is made for access to records of a public body by a person who is involved in litigation with that body. Such a request may be aimed at getting a more complete picture of the matter in dispute, obtaining an evidentiary or tactical advantage, or assessing the prospects for success. At issue is whether the rules relating to discovery should take priority over FOI, such that the latter should be suspended or deferred where litigation is underway, or whether FOI should take precedence. There has been considerable variation in the treatment of this issue as between the various jurisdictions. The Australian federal appeals bodies, for example:

> "are not overly sympathetic to the use of FOI as substitute for discovery while other proceedings are on foot, and are inclined to agree that in practice the litigant/FOI applicant should be turned back to the court process as the appropriate means by which to seek access to the relevant documents".[22]

In New Zealand and in the Australian States of Victoria, Tasmania, and Western Australia, there has been greater tolerance of the use FOI rights in the litigation context. In the New Zealand case of *Commissioner of Police v. Ombudsman*,[23] for example, it was held that a defendant in summary criminal proceedings was entitled to obtain access to police briefs setting out the evidence of witnesses. That decision was followed in the Victorian case of *Re Sobh and Victoria Police*.[24] In that case an argument that police briefs in respect of summary criminal proceedings were exempt on the basis that their disclosure would "prejudice the proper administration of law" was rejected.

(x) Section 23(1)(a)(iii): Prejudice or impair lawful methods, systems, plans or procedure for ensuring the safety of the public

The prejudice or impairment referred to in this limb of the exemption need not be shown to arise in respect of a particular case. This part of the exemption could be invoked in respect of records concerning methods for dealing with civil disasters. A wider interpretation was, however, placed on the equivalent Australian federal exemption in *Re Parisi and Australian Federal Police*.[25] The Administrative Appeals Tribunal, in deciding on an application for access to records relating to the internment of the applicant during the war, stated that in its view:

---

[22] Moe, "FOI Access in the Litigation Context", paper delivered at INFO2: 2nd National Freedom of Information Conference, Gold Coast, Australia, March 7, 1996, p. 6.

[23] Above, n. 9.

[24] *Re Sobh and Victoria Police* (1992) 5 V.A.R. 371 (Administrative Appeals Tribunal, Victoria); *Sobh v. Police Force of Victoria* (1994) 1 V.R. 41 (Supreme Court of Victoria, Appeal Division).

[25] s.37(2)(c), in *Re Parisi and Australian Federal Police* (1987) 14 A.L.D. 11.

"the words 'public safety' ought not to be confined to any particular situation. They should certainly not be confined to what might be described as civil emergencies, such as bush fires or floods, as was suggested by counsel for the applicant. They should not be confined in our view even to court cases involved in the enforcement of the lawful methods referred to in the paragraph. Obviously in time of war, considerations of public safety and lawful methods for their protection are much wider than in times of peace. To the extent that the documents in question refer to these methods and to the extent to which their disclosure could reasonably be expected to prejudice the maintenance of these methods, then we consider that the respondents are both entitled to rely upon the paragraph in question."[26]

In another Australian case, in which access was sought to the transcript of radio communications between the applicant and an aircraft control unit, it was held that "public safety" means safety from violations of the law and breaches of the peace and does not extend to air travel safety, except to the extent that that might be put at risk by such violations or breaches.[27]

(xi) Section 23(1)(a)(iii): Prejudice or impair lawful methods, systems, plans or procedures for ensuring the safety of the public and the safety or security of persons and property

The protection provided under this part of the exemption is indirect in that, rather than protecting against the disclosure of records which would be prejudicial to the security or safety of the public or the safety or security of persons and property, it is confined to records disclosing information likely to prejudice *lawful methods*, etc., for ensuring the safety of the public and the safety or security of persons and property. On that basis, it would appear to apply only to matters such as plans and procedures for protection of the public in general and for persons such as public figures, rather than to the disclosure of information which would endanger the public or such persons. Similar provisions in FOI legislation in other jurisdictions are phrased in direct, rather than indirect, terms. The U.S. version of this provision has been held to justify withholding of the names of FBI agents or other law enforcement personnel, as well as information that might lead to the revelation of their identities in circumstances where their safety would be endangered by disclosure.[28]

---

[26] Above, n. 25, at 17.
[27] *Re Thies and Department of Aviation* (1986) 9 A.L.D. 454.
[28] See *Maroscia v. Levi*, 569 F.2d 1000 (7th Cir. 1977); *Scherer v. Kelley*, 584 F.2d 170 (7th Cir. 1978); *Shaver v. Bell*, 433 F. Supp. 438 (N.O. Ga. 1977).

(xii) Section 23(1)(a)(iv): Prejudice or impair the fairness of criminal proceedings in a court or of civil proceedings in a court or other tribunal

The motivation for including this exemption is to prevent the use of the Act to obtain access to records, the disclosure of which could result in unfairness in the conduct of particular court proceedings. It could apply, for example, where such disclosure could reasonably be expected to generate prejudicial pre-trial publicity. This exemption goes beyond disclosure of records in contempt of court since there is a separate exemption for that in the Act.[29] Indeed, in a decision of the New Zealand Court of Appeal, it was held that the Ombudsman had erred in law by equating the right to a fair trial with contempt of court principles.[30] Instead, the court held that the corresponding provision in the New Zealand Act was intended to:

"ensure that a disclosure . . . could not be used to prejudice an accused's trial, whether or not a publication in contempt of Court were committed."[31]

This limb of the exemption applies not only to criminal trials but also to civil cases and determinations of tribunals.

(xiii) Section 23(1)(a)(v): Prejudice or impair the security of a penal institution

Penal institution is defined to include a place to which the Prisons Acts 1826-1980 apply, places of military detention, Saint Patrick's Institution, and institutions in which young offenders are detained.[32] This provision could protect records from disclosure which contain information on matters such as staffing of penal institutions, since the release of such information might be found to be prejudicial to the security of the institution. It could not, however, apply to the disclosure of records which would not prejudice security, such as reports concerning conditions within prisons.

(xiv) Section 23(1)(a)(vii): Prejudice or impair the security of a building or other structure or a vehicle, ship, boat, or aircraft

This provision is aimed at protecting documents such as plans of sensitive government structures, but there is nothing to prevent its application to privately owned buildings, structures or vehicles, boats, etc., in respect of which information is held by public bodies. Thus, it could potentially have very broad application, preventing access to plans of all sorts of buildings, vehicles, etc.,

---

[29] s.22(1)(b).
[30] *Commissioner of Police v. Ombudsman*, above, n. 9.
[31] *ibid.* at 391.
[32] s.23(4).

which have been lodged with public bodies, but only in cases where access could reasonably be expected to prejudice or impair the security of such buildings or vehicles.

(xv) Section 23(1)(a)(viii): Prejudice or impair the security of any system of communications, whether internal or external, of the Garda Síochána, the Defence Forces, the Revenue Commissioners, or a penal institution

This provision does not exempt communications systems of the gardaí, the Defence Forces, the Revenue Commissioners, or penal institutions from the scope of the Act *per se*, but instead exempts the disclosure of records which could reasonably be expected to prejudice or impair systems of communications of the kind referred to. It is not confined to protecting systems of communications used in connection with law enforcement but applies to communications systems used for any purpose by the bodies referred to.

2. Section 23(1)(b): Confidential sources of information

This part of the law enforcement exemption is closely related to the exclusion from the scope of the Act, under section 46(1)(f), of information which would be likely to disclose the identity of a confidential source of information in relation to the enforcement of any criminal law. These two provisions were included to prevent the Act being used in way which could discourage informants from providing the authorities with confidential information useful to the investigation of breaches of the law or generally useful in the administration of the law.

While the scope of the exclusion in section 46(1)(f) is concerned with confidential sources relating to the enforcement of the criminal law, section 23(1)(b) applies to confidential sources relating to the enforcement and administration of the civil law. The main practical difference in terms of the application of the exemption set out in section 23(1)(b) and the exclusion provided for under section 46(1)(f) is that, in the case of the former, the head of a public body has a discretion whether to invoke the exemption, whereas, in the case of records excluded from the Act under section 46(1)(f), no such discretion exists and the information is outside the scope of the Act. Otherwise, the two provisions are very similar and, for that reason, the exemption and exclusion will be considered together. In order for each to apply, the following conditions must be met:

(1) the information must have been given in confidence;

(2) the information must relate to the enforcement or administration of the civil law (section 23(1)(b)) or the enforcement of the criminal law (section 46(1)(f)), as the case may be;

(3) the granting of the request must reasonably be expected to:
  (a) reveal or lead to the revelation of the identity of the person who has given the information; or
  (b) reveal or lead to the revelation of the identity of any other source of the information.

It is clear that information provided expressly in confidence will qualify for protection. Circumstances could also arise where the exclusion or exemption would apply even though no express promise of confidentiality was given. Thus, it has been held both in the U.S. and in Australia that a promise of confidentiality can be implied.[33] However, in another U.S. case, the Supreme Court rejected the presumption that all sources supplying information to the FBI in the course of a criminal investigation are confidential sources, in favour of a "more particularized approach" under which agencies seeking to invoke the relevant exemption must prove expectations of confidentiality based upon the circumstances of each case.[34] In an Australian case, the term "confidential source" was said to be capable of including a diplomatic source, official or unofficial, as well as members of other police forces, to the extent that they may pass on information obtained from a confidential source.[35] In both the U.S. and Australia, the notion that a government agency can be a confidential source has been firmly rejected.[36] In the U.S. the exemption has been held to apply to information provided by a wide variety of individuals and institutions, such as victims of crime, citizens providing unsolicited allegations of misconduct, citizens responding to inquiries from law enforcement agencies, private employees responding to Occupational Health and Safety Act investigators about the circumstances of an industrial accident, employees providing information about their employers, prisoners, mental healthcare facilities, medical personnel, commercial or financial institutions, state and local law enforcement agencies, and foreign law enforcement agencies.[37]

The use of a balancing test to determine whether the public interest supports the existence of a confidential source has been rejected in the U.S. and Australia. In both those jurisdictions, as is the case here, the applicability of the exemption/exclusion hinges on the circumstances under which the information is provided, not on the harm resulting from disclosure, and therefore

---

[33] *Luzaich v. United States*, 435 F. Supp. 31 (1977), approved in the Australian case *Department of Health v. Jephcott* (1985) 62 A.L.R. 421.

[34] *Department of Justice v. Landano*, 113 S. Ct. 2014 at 2022 (1993).

[35] *Re Anderson and Department of Special Minister of State (No. 2)* (1986) 11 A.L.N. 239.

[36] In the U.S. in *Retail Credit Co. v. FTC* 1976-1 Trade Cas. (CCH) ¶ 60, 727 n 3 (D.D.C., May 10, 1976) and in Australia in *Re Anderson and Department of Special Minister of State (No. 2), ibid.*

[37] Justice Department, *Guide to the Freedom of Information Act* (1997), p. 301.

no balancing test is applied.[38] As the Australian Federal Court put it in *Department of Health v. Jephcott*:

> "If a source of information is properly to be regarded as a confidential source then there is in my view, no room for the concept of a 'substantial risk that the administration of the law will be impaired'. Either it is established that a source is a confidential source or it is not."[39]

In another Australian case the motive of the person supplying the information was treated as irrelevant to the possible application of the equivalent Australian provision.[40]

3. Section 23(1)(c): Facilitate the commission of an offence

This part of section 23 is aimed at preventing the FOI Act being used to gather information which could facilitate the commission of an offence. This element of the exemption has no counterpart in the Australian or New Zealand law enforcement exemptions. It appears to be based on section 16(2) of the Canadian Access to Information Act. That provision exempts records which contain information which could reasonably be expected to facilitate the commission of an offence and goes on to provide the following examples of information coming within its scope: (a) information on criminal methods or techniques; (b) technical information relating to weapons or potential weapons; and (c) information on the vulnerability of particular buildings or other structures or systems, including computer or communications systems, or methods employed to protect such buildings or other structures or systems. While category (c) is already covered by other elements of section 23, records containing information coming within categories (a) and (b) can be taken to constitute examples of the type of information designed to be protected by section 23(1)(c).

C.   Public Interest Test

The application of section 23 is subject to a limited public interest test which is designed to ensure that law enforcement agencies cannot invoke the exemption in order to refuse access to records revealing wrongdoing or inefficiency on their part. It allows for disclosure of certain law enforcement records where, in the opinion of the head of the public body concerned, the public interest would, on balance, be better served by granting than by refusing to grant the

---

[38] See U.S. cases: *Jones v. FBI*, 41 F.3d 238 (6th Cir. 1994); *McDonnell v. United States*, 4 F.3d 1227 (3rd Cir. 1993); *Nadler v. Department of Justice*, 955 F.2d 1479 (11th Cir. 1992).

[39] Above, n. 33, at 425.

[40] *Re Gold and Australian Federal Police*, above, n. 21.

request for access. Three categories of record are covered by this test. They are:

(1) records which disclose that an investigation for the purpose of the enforcement of the law, or anything done in the course of such an investigation or for the purposes of the prevention or detection of offences or the apprehension or prosecution of offenders is not authorised by or contravenes any law;

(2) records containing information concerning the performance of the functions of a public body including functions relating to the enforcement of the law or the ensuring of the safety of the public; and

(3) records containing information concerning the merits or the success or otherwise of any programme, scheme or policy of a public body for preventing, detecting or investigating contraventions of the law or the effectiveness or efficiency of the implementation of any such programme, scheme or policy by a public body.

Records falling into the first of these categories includes records which reveal the commission of crimes or civil wrongs in the course of an investigation, such as, for example, the use of breaking and entering or assault by law enforcement officers in order to obtain evidence. Given that this category extends to cover activities which are "not authorised by law", it could also extend to records revealing activities of law enforcement authorities which exceed their powers without attracting tortious or criminal liability. It might arguably be extended to investigations based on improper motives. For example, an investigation which is aimed at discrediting the person under investigation, rather than uncovering any wrongdoing would arguably not be "authorised by law". In the U.S., for example, it has been held that the corresponding exemption does not extend to cover "investigatory activities wholly unrelated to law enforcement agencies legislated functions of preventing risks to national security and violations of criminal laws and of apprehending those who do violate the laws".[41] Some investigations have both proper and improper motives and, in such cases, it would be necessary to decide in what circumstances the existence of such mixed motives would result in the investigation being not authorised by law. The second category of record could include reports on the overall performance of a law enforcement body, while the third could cover records relating to the effectiveness of campaigns aimed at preventing or detecting breaches of the law.[42]

---

[41] *Pratt v. Webster*, 673 F.2d 408 at 420–421 (D.C. Cir. 1982).

[42] The operations of public interest tests in the Act are discussed in greater detail above at pp. 93–115.

D.   Non-disclosure of Existence or Non-existence of Records

Where the head of a public body is satisfied that disclosure of the existence or
non-existence of a record would have the effect specified in paragraphs (a),
(b), or (c) of section 23(1), he or she must refuse to grant the request and must
not disclose whether the record exists. The aim of this provision is to prevent
a person obtaining access to sensitive law enforcement information through
"fishing expeditions". For example, if a person suspected that he or she was
under investigation by a law enforcement agency, he or she could request access to all records relating to himself or herself in the possession of that agency.
Even if the records themselves were not released, the very fact of their existence could provide the applicant with valuable information and could give
him or her the opportunity to rearrange his or her affairs so as to avoid detection. Similarly, if a person wanted to discover whether a particular individual
was acting as an informer, he or she could issue a request to the relevant public body for all records relating to the suspected informant. Again, confirma-
tion of the mere fact that a file relating to that person was held by the public
body concerned could suffice to reveal that he or she was, in fact, acting as an
informer. Provisions of this type are discussed in greater detail above at pp.
71–72.

DEFENCE, SECURITY, AND INTERNATIONAL RELATIONS

CHAPTER 11

DEFENCE, SECURITY, AND INTERNATIONAL RELATIONS

A. Introduction

The protection of sensitive information relating to defence, security, and international relations is a common feature of FOI legislation.[1] The processing of sensitive information relating to Northern Ireland is also a feature of Irish government activities and the need to protect such information has received express recognition in the text of the FOI Act. The justification for limiting access to such information was acknowledged by one commentator in the following terms:

> "Even the most passionate libertarian will accept that there are times when secrecy is a good thing. . . Details of negotiating positions or sensitive discussions in the Northern Ireland peace process should be protected."[2]

Government departments likely to hold information falling within the scope of this exemption include the Departments of Defence, Justice and Foreign Affairs. Defence information is, of course, also held by the Defence Forces and that body is included in the list of public bodies covered by the Act. The Garda Síochána,[3] who hold considerable amounts of security-related information, are not covered by the Act, at least for the moment.[4] As a result, much security-related information will remain outside the scope of the Act pending the introduction of regulations extending the application of the Act to that body.

The exemption provides as follows:

> "24.—(1) A head may refuse to grant a request under section 7 in relation to a record (and, in particular, but without prejudice to the generality otherwise of this subsection, to a record to which subsection (2) applies) if, in the opinion of the head, access to it could reasonably be expected to affect adversely—

---

[1] Australia: Freedom of Information Act (Cth), s.33; Canada: Access to Information Act (Canada), R.S.C., 1985, s.15; New Zealand: Official Information Act 1982, s.6(a); U.S.: Freedom of Information Act 1966, Exemption 1.

[2] O'Toole, "Something genuinely radical is about to happen", *Irish Times*, December 15, 1995.

[3] The police force.

[4] The application of the Act can be extended to An Garda Síochána by regulation: see First Sched., para. 1(5)(a).

    (a) the security of the State,

    (b) the defence of the State,

    (c) the international relations of the State, or

    (d) matters relating to Northern Ireland.

(2) This subsection applies to a record that—

    (a) contains information—

        (i) that was obtained or prepared for the purpose of intelligence in respect of the security or defence of the State, or

       (ii) that relates to—

          (I) the tactics, strategy or operations of the Defence Forces in or outside the State, or

        (II) the detection, prevention, or suppression of activities calculated or tending to undermine the public order or the authority of the State (which expression has the same meaning as in section 2 of the Offences against the State Act, 1939),

    (b) contains a communication between a Minister of the Government and a diplomatic mission or consular post in the State or a communication between the Government or a person acting on behalf of the Government and another government or a person acting on behalf of another government,

    (c) contains a communication between a Minister of the Government and a diplomatic mission or consular post of the State,

    (d) contains information communicated in confidence to any person in or outside the State from any person in or outside the State and relating to a matter referred to in subsection (1) or to the protection of human rights and expressed by the latter person to be confidential or to be communicated in confidence,

    (e) contains information communicated in confidence from, to or within an international organisation of states or a subsidiary organ of such an organisation or an institution or body of the European Union or relates to negotiations between the State and such an organisation, organ, institution or body or within or in relation to such an organisation, organ, institution or body, or

    (f) is a record of an organisation, organ, institution or body referred to in paragraph (e) containing information the disclosure of which is prohibited by the organisation, organ, institution or body.

(3) Where a request under section 7 relates to a record to which subsection (1) applies, or would, if the record, existed, apply, and the head concerned is satisfied that the disclosure of the existence or non-existence of the record would prejudice a matter referred to in that subsection, he or she shall refuse to grant the request and shall not disclose to the requester concerned whether or not the record exists."

The exemption is not mandatory, so it will be open to the head of a public body to voluntarily release records falling within its terms. It is a harm based exemption which allows the head of a public body to refuse to disclose a record where its disclosure could reasonably be expected to "adversely affect" four matters: namely, the security of the State, the defence of the State, the international relations of the State, and matters relating to Northern Ireland. Clarification of the scope of the exemption is provided in section 24(2), which lists a number of categories of information to which the exemption may apply, assuming access to the information could reasonably be expected to result in the damage specified in section 24(1). The list can be arranged into seven categories, namely:

(1) intelligence information: section 24(2)(a)(i);

(2) information relating to the tactics, strategy or operations of the Defence Forces: section 24(2)(a)(ii)(I);

(3) information relating to activities tending to undermine public order or the authority of the State: section 24(2)(a)(ii)(II);

(4) diplomatic communications: section 24(2)(b) and (c);

(5) confidential communications: section 24(2)(d) and (e);

(6) information relating to negotiations between the State and international organisations of states or E.U. bodies: section 24(2)(e); and

(7) information of international organisations the disclosure of which is prohibited: section 24(2)(f).

The head of a public body is entitled, by virtue of section 24(3), to refuse to disclose the existence or non-existence of information which would prejudice the security or defence of the State, the conduct of international relations, or the interests of the State in relation to Northern Ireland.

A further restriction on the disclosure of information concerning defence, security and international relations arises from the fact that it is one of the two categories of records in respect of which a ministerial certificate may be issued under section 25 (the other being records concerning law enforcement and public safety). The signing by a Minister of such a certificate has the effect of establishing that the record is exempt. A decision by a Minister to sign a ministerial certificate is not subject to review by the Ombudsman. The mechanics and effect of the issuance of ministerial certificates is examined above at pp. 115–119.

In terms of its structure, section 24 most closely resembles its counterpart in the federal Canadian Act.[5] Both exemptions commence with a harm test covering damage to international relations, defence and security related matters, followed by a list of categories of information to which the exemption applies. It is clear from the wording of both provisions that this list is provided for illustrative purposes and is not intended to be exhaustive. Nor does it have

---

[5] Access to Information Act (Canada), R.S.C., 1985, s.15.

an existence independent of the harm test. In other words, it will not suffice for a record to fall within one of the listed categories in order for the exemption to apply. Its disclosure must also be reasonably expected to lead to the damage outlined in the harm test. This reading of section 15 of the Canadian Access to Information Act was confirmed by the Federal Court in *Do-Ky v. Canada (Minister of Foreign Affairs and International Trade)*:[6]

> "[I]n section 15(1) the language refers to information which, if disclosed, would reasonably result in injury. The paragraphs thereafter . . . serve as examples of the general principle. . .".[7]

B.   The Harm Test

The test to be imposed in the application of section 24 is whether, in the opinion of the head of public body, access to the record "could reasonably be expected to affect adversely" the interests protected by the provision.

The standard of proof required to establish that harm "could reasonably be expected" to occur is discussed in detail above at pp. 90–92. In short, decisions in Canada and Australia have indicated that establishing the possibility of the specified harm occurring will not suffice to meet the burden of proof, but neither is it necessary to show evidence of direct causation between disclosure and harm; nor does it appear necessary in either jurisdiction to show that the occurrence of the harm is more probable than not. In both jurisdictions the emphasis is on the reasonableness of the expectation of harm arising out of the disclosure.

1. Adverse effect

The type of harm which must be established in order to invoke this exemption is "adverse effect". The degree of harm required under this provision can be contrasted with that provided for under other exemptions. For example, section 21, which deals with functions and negotiations of public bodies, requires a "significant adverse effect", while section 31, which concerns financial and economic interests of the State and public bodies, demands evidence of a "serious adverse effect". The establishment of an adverse effect will clearly be easier to achieve than a "significant" or "serious" adverse effect. It is roughly analogous to the term "damage", which is used in the Australian defence, security and international affairs exemption,[8] or "be injurious to", which is found in the equivalent Canadian provision.[9]

---

[6] (1997) 143 D.L.R. (4th) 746; 71 C.P.R. (3d) 447 (F.C.T.D.).
[7] *ibid.* at 755.
[8] Freedom of Information Act 1982 (Cth), s.33.
[9] Access to Information Act (Canada), R.S.C., 1985, s.15.

2. Interpretation of the harm test

A number of principles have emerged from interpretation of the term "damage" in the Australian context. It has been held that the damage need not be tangible, nor does it need to be quantifiable in monetary terms.[10]

Australian decisions have also established that disclosure can be damaging on the grounds of its cumulative effect. This principle is known as the jigsaw or mosaic effect. It is based on the notion that information which may be harmless when considered in isolation may, when combined with other seemingly innocuous pieces of information, result in the disclosure of information which is damaging.[11] The U.S. courts have also accepted the jigsaw argument in FOI cases relating to security information. In *Halperin v. C.I.A.*[12] Circuit Judge Wilkey said:

> "We must take into account, however, that each individual piece of intelligence information, much like a piece of a jigsaw puzzle, may aid in piecing together bits of information even when the individual piece is not of obvious importance in itself".[13]

U.S. case law, which has been approved in Australia[14] and in Canada,[15] has established that even if a fact is the subject of widespread media and public speculation, its official acknowledgement could cause damage to security. This principle was established in *Afshar v. Department of State*[16] where it was said that:

> "[E]ven if a fact . . . is the subject of widespread media and public speculation, its official acknowledgement by an authoritative source might well be new information that could cause damage to the national security. Unofficial leaks and public surmise can often be ignored by foreign governments that might perceive themselves to be harmed by disclosure of their cooperation with the CIA, but official acknowledgement may force a government to retaliate."[17]

Similarly, the release of documents by mistake has been held, in Australia, to be insufficient to defeat a claim.[18] Other principles which have emerged from Australian decisions include the finding that evidence of a reasonable expec-

---

[10] *Re Maher and Attorney-General's Department* (1985) 7 A.L.D. 731 at 742.
[11] *Re Throssell and Australian Archives (No. 2)* (1987) 14 A.L.D. 292; *Re Slater and Cox* (1988) 15 A.L.D. 20; *Re McKnight and Australian Archives* (1992) 28 A.L.D. 95.
[12] 629 F.2d 144 (1980).
[13] *ibid.* at 150.
[14] *Re Reithmuller and Australian Federal Police* (1985) 8 A.L.N. N92; *Re Slater and Cox*, above, n. 11.
[15] *Do-Ky v. Canada (Minister of Foreign Affairs and International Trade)*, above, n. 6.
[16] 702 F.2d 1125 (D.C. Cir. 1983).
[17] *ibid.* at 1130–1131.
[18] *Re Robinson and Department of Foreign Affairs* (1986) 11 A.L.N. N48.

tation of generalised damage to relationships with other States will not suffice
to ground a claim for exemption. Instead, there must be damage to relations in
the relevant respect.[19]

One important issue which has arisen in both Canada and Australia is
whether, in order for the exemption to apply, it is sufficient that damage can be
said to flow from the mere fact of disclosure of the requested record or whether
it is necessary that the contents of the record be considered. In the Australian
federal case of *Re Angel and Department of Arts, Heritage and the Environment*[20] it was held that in order to satisfy the similarly worded Commonwealth/
State relations exemption[21] it is sufficient that the mere fact of a document
being disclosed would cause, or could reasonably be expected to cause, damage to relations between the Commonwealth and a State.[22] In the Canadian
case *Do-Ky v. Canada (Minister of Foreign Affairs and International Trade)*[23]
the exemption included, in its list of illustrations of the type of information
which would be covered by its terms, information that "constitutes diplomatic
correspondence exchanged with foreign states".[24] The Federal Court held that:

> "In the case of diplomatic notes, the government may lawfully exempt them
> from release because to release them would reasonably be expected to harm
> international relations. This is true not necessarily because the information therein
> is sensitive but simply because the notes constitute confidential diplomatic com-
> munications and the international community has a reasonable expectation that
> such notes will remain confidential."[25]

However, the court stopped short of equating the exemption with a class exemption. It said that section 15 was an injury and not a class exemption and
continued as follows:

> "These notes are not exempt because they are diplomatic notes but because they
> are expected to be confidential documents irrespective of their contents."[26]

Thus, it would appear that in both those jurisdictions it is sufficient that the
damage could reasonably be expected to result from the fact of disclosure of
the records in question, regardless of their contents.

---

[19] *Re Guy and Department of Transport* (1987) 12 A.L.D. 358 at 363; *Re O'Donovan and
Attorney-General's Department* (1985) 8 A.L.D. 528 at 532.
[20] (1985) 9 A.L.D. 113.
[21] s.33A.
[22] Above, n. 20, at 120.
[23] Above, n. 6.
[24] s.15(1)(h).
[25] Above, n. 6, at 756.
[26] *ibid.* at 758.

C.   The Records Protected

1. Security of the State

Examples of the types of information which are protected under this heading can be found amongst the categories of information listed in section 24(2). The security of the State could, for example, be adversely affected by the disclosure of information "obtained or prepared for the purpose of intelligence in respect of the security . . . of the State", which is referred to in section 24(2)(a)(i). It could also be harmed by the disclosure of information that relates to "the detection, prevention or suppression of activities calculated or tending to undermine the public order or the authority of the State" referred to in section 24(2)(a)(ii)(II).

A number of cases concerning security of the State have been considered by the Australian federal Administrative Appeals Tribunal (A.A.T.). From these the following principles have emerged.

(a) Flow of information

Ensuring the continued flow of security and intelligence information is recognised as a justification for withholding records. In *Re Slater and Cox*[27] the importance of the flow of information in the context of the security of the State was expressed by the A.A.T. in the following terms:

> "Security is a particularly sensitive area and particularly dependent for its effectiveness upon an adequate flow of information".[28]

In another Australian case, *Re Throssell and Australian Archives (No. 2)*,[29] Neaves J. also referred to the danger of inhibiting the flow of information when he said:

> "The material before the Tribunal tends to support the conclusion that the disclosure to the public of the records identified in the certificate could have the result of impairing the degree of trust and confidence which foreign governments place in the Government of the Commonwealth and, in consequence, of inhibiting the flow of information relating to security which might otherwise come to Australia from the overseas governmental agencies concerned and, possibly, similar agencies in other overseas countries. If such a result ensued, damage would be caused to the security and international relations of the Commonwealth."[30]

---

[27] Above, n. 11.
[28] *ibid.* at 29.
[29] Above, n. 11.
[30] *ibid.* at 295.

(b) Preventing security organisations from obtaining information

Another principle recognised by Australian case law is that of ensuring that disclosure does not result in security organisations being prevented from obtaining information about the activities of terrorists. In *Re Slater and Cox* the danger posed to the security of the State when security organisations are prevented from obtaining information was adverted to in the following terms:

> "Disclosure of information could reasonably be expected to cause damage to security if it enables those engaged in espionage, sabotage, subversion, active measures of foreign intervention or terrorism to be better able to prevent a security organisation from obtaining information about their activities."[31]

(c) Identification of officers or agents

In *Re Throssell and Australian Archives (No. 2)*[32] it was held that disclosure of the fact that a particular person has gathered information for an intelligence organisation could reasonably be expected to damage the security of the Commonwealth.

(d) Information illegally or improperly obtained

In *Re McKnight and Australian Archives*[33] the federal A.A.T. decided that, even where information has been illegally or improperly obtained, its disclosure could be held to be damaging to the ongoing operations of the security organisation. Johnston P. expressed the view that:

> "[E]ven if the collection of any particular piece of information in dispute had travelled outside the strict boundaries of the task given to ASIO in the Prime Ministerial Directives, that does not, of itself, invalidate the claim to exemption. Even if, to put the case at its highest, the information had been illegally or improperly obtained, its disclosure could still seriously prejudice the ongoing operations of ASIO. To say that is not to sanction any possible breach of the law: it is to say that release to someone such as the applicant is not an appropriate remedy."[34]

2. The defence of the State

This limb of the exemption could apply to intelligence-related information "obtained or prepared in respect of the . . . defence of the State" which is protected under section 24(2)(a)(i). It would clearly encompass information relating to "the tactics, strategy or operations of the Defence Forces in or out-

---

[31] Above, n. 11, at 29.
[32] Above, n. 11.
[33] Above, n. 11.
[34] *ibid.* at 112–113.

side the State" which is exempted under section 24(2)(a)(ii)(I). Records relating to defence operations overseas are covered by the exemption. While the list of categories of information in subsection (2) is not exhaustive of the scope of the exemption, non-operational matters are unlikely to be covered. Records relating to administrative matters such as, for example, the planned closure of defence facilities are, on that basis, unlikely to come within the scope of this exemption. Nor is it likely that records concerning the handling of publicity relating to defence matters would fall within the terms of the exemption. An example of the type of record likely to be covered is found in the Australian federal case of *Re Hocking and Department of Defence*,[35] in which it was held that the part of an army manual relating to tactical responses and army procedures for dealing with terrorism was exempt.

3. International relations of the State

Requests may be refused where access to a record could reasonably be expected to affect adversely the international relations of the State. Illustrations of the type of information which might be held to be exempt under this heading are found in section 24(2)(b) to (f). These provisions cover diplomatic communications (section 24(2)(b) and (c)), confidential communications (section 24(2)(d) and (e)), information relating to negotiations between the State and international organisations of States or E.U. bodies (section 24(2)(e)), and the disclosure of records which is prohibited by international organisations (section 24(2)(f)).

Principles which have emerged from Australian and Canadian case law concerning damage to international relations include the following:

(a) Loss of confidence

The fact that the government of another country might lose confidence in the domestic government has been held to be a valid ground for exempting records. In the Australian federal case of *Re Maher and Attorney-General's Department*[36] Davies J. said:

> "[I]f it can reasonably be anticipated that the disclosure of the document would lessen the confidence which another country would place on the Government of Australia, that is a sufficient ground for a finding that the disclosure of the document could reasonably be expected to damage international relations. Trust and confidence are intangible aspects of international relations."[37]

---

[35] (1987) 12 A.L.D. 554.
[36] Above, n. 10.
[37] *ibid.* at 742.

Loss of confidence was also accepted as a valid ground for application of the exemption by Neaves J. in the Australian federal case *Re Throssell and Australian Archives (No. 2).*[38]

(b) Relationships between particular persons

In *Maher*, the A.A.T. held that the possibility of damage to relationships between particular persons in the context of international relations was a relevant consideration in the application of the exemption.

> "International relations have never been matters easy to define or quantify. Regard must be had, inter alia to the relationship between particular persons in one government and persons in another. Damage to personal relationships may cause considerable harm for a time at least." [39]

(c) Attitude of foreign governments

In *Re Throssell and Australian Archives (No. 1),*[40] Davies J. of the A.A.T., in arriving at a decision that disclosure of the requested record would be damaging, appeared to take into account the absence of consent to disclosure on the part of the overseas body which had communicated the information to the Australian agency to which the request was directed. He said:

> "In the present case, the disclosure of documents which were communicated in confidence from the overseas security organisation to the Australian security organisation and to the release of which the overseas security organisation has not consented is a matter which reasonably could be expected to cause damage to the relationships between the two security organisations and therefore to Australia's international relationships."[41]

It was accepted by the A.A.T. in *Re Slater and Cox* that the views of foreign governments in relation to disclosure must be afforded considerable weight.[42] In *Re State of Queensland and Australian National Parks and Wildlife Service*[43] and *Re Guy and Department of Transport*[44] the A.A.T., in the context of the similarly worded exemption relating to damage to relations between the Commonwealth and a State of Australia, also accepted that attitudes to release were relevant.

It is not clear, however, that the attitude to disclosure of the other government concerned will be conclusive in determining whether a record concerning international relations will be released. In *Re O'Donovan and Attorney-*

---

[38] Above, n. 11.
[39] *Re Maher and Attorney General's Department,* above, n. 10, at 742.
[40] (1986) 10 A.L.D. 403.
[41] *ibid.* at 406–407.
[42] Above, n. 11, at 28.
[43] (1986) 13 A.L.D. 158.
[44] Above, n. 19.

General's Department[45] Deputy President Hall of the federal A.A.T. refused to treat expressions of concern about disclosure on the part of a foreign government as conclusive, saying:

> "[A] mere allegation that disclosure could reasonably be expected to cause damage to the international relations of the Commonwealth is not enough. Neither is the mere fact that another Government has expressed concern about the disclosure of the communication. Whether disclosure of a particular document could 'reasonably' be expected to cause damage to the international relations of the Commonwealth may well involve difficult questions of judgment and degree."[46]

The issue of the attitude of foreign governments has also been explored in Canada. In *Do-Ky v. Canada (Minister of Foreign Affairs and International Trade)*[47] an objection to disclosure by a foreign government appeared to be treated as conclusive. The Federal Court said:

> "The harm is more than speculative because Country D was specifically asked about the release of the notes and answered that they did not want the notes to be made public. This alone justifies nondisclosure despite the fact that some of the information contained in one of the notes had already been accessed by the Applicant. To release these documents would be a diplomatic breach. To act contrary to a direct request from a foreign state would harm the reputation of Canada in the international community as a state which deals fairly with its counterparts. Additionally, as the entire diplomatic process relies on integrity and trust, Canada would, if it released diplomatic notes without concern for the opinions of foreign states affected, harm its own ability to function effectively on the international level."[48]

It was also made clear in *Do-Ky* that Canada will not enquire into the motives of foreign States in attempting to prevent disclosure of information. The court said:

> "[O]nce a state requests that diplomatic correspondence remain confidential there is no need for the Canadian government to assess the reasons of that country. It is sufficient if they have made the request of the Canadian government. Indeed it would be a diplomatic lapse were the Canadian government to sit in judgement of the rationale of the foreign state except in the most extreme circumstances."[49]

The Australian approach is to be preferred. While the attitude of foreign governments is clearly an important factor to be taken into account in determining whether disclosure of a record could reasonably be expected to adversely affect the international relations of the State, it is not clear that disclosure of

---

[45] Above, n. 19.
[46] *ibid.* at 534.
[47] Above, n. 6.
[48] *ibid.* at 758.
[49] *ibid.* at 760.

records in circumstances where a foreign government objects will necessarily damage Ireland's international relations in every case.

4. Matters relating to Northern Ireland

This category differs from the preceding three in that it seeks to protect against the disclosure of information which could harm matters relating to a particular geographical area, rather than to protect against the disclosure of information which could damage specific interests, namely security, defence, or international relations. It is very broadly framed in that there is no requirement that the matters relate to Northern Irish security or defence or international relations matters. It could conceivably be applied to prevent disclosure of records which could adversely affect commerce or tourism in Northern Ireland. Given the expansion of cross-border co-operation in these and other areas, it is likely that an increasing amount of information relating to such initiatives will come into the hands of public bodies. In the absence of a public interest test in section 24, it would appear that the Act affords greater protection to non-security related records concerning Northern Ireland than to similar records relating to the Irish Republic.

Examples of information likely to be exempted under this heading may be found in all of the categories set out in subsection (2). Interestingly, there is no direct reference in that list to information relating to negotiations between the Government and another government or between the Government and any political or other grouping. Information relating to negotiations is given express protection, but only where the negotiations take place between the State and an international organisation of States, a subsidiary of such an organisation, or an institution or body of the E.U.[50] However, negotiations between Government representatives and the parties to the Northern Ireland conflict would be likely to fall within the purview of section 24(2)(d), which covers information communicated in confidence to any person in or outside the State and relating to a matter referred to in subsection (1) (namely security, defence, international relations, or matters relating to Northern Ireland), provided the information was expressed by the person communicating it to be confidential or to be communicated in confidence. In any case, the categories set out in subsection (2) are not exhaustive of the scope of the exemption, so there is nothing to prevent the making of a decision to the effect that a record is exempt which is of a kind not expressly included in section 24(2).

5. Confidential communications

Unlike its Australian and Canadian counterparts, section 24 does not provide specifically for the exemption of confidential communications received from

---

[50] s.24(2)(e).

foreign governments or international organisations. While it does list such communications in section 24(2), they are only exempt where their disclosure could result in harm of the kind referred to in subsection (1). In Australia and Canada, on the other hand, information is exempt where it divulges confidential communications received from foreign governments and international organisations regardless of whether there is any likelihood of harm arising from disclosure of such information. Notwithstanding this difference in structure, it is useful to consider the operation of the confidential communications exemption in those jurisdictions because information which is communicated in confidence within the terms of section 24(2)(d) or (e) may be found to satisfy the harm test set out in section 24(1). Some guidance on the application of section 24 to confidential communications can therefore be gleaned from the Australian and Canadian authorities.

There is, however, an important distinction to be drawn between section 24(1)(d) and section 24(1)(e), the effect of which is to render most of the ensuing discussion of the Australian and Canadian decisions irrelevant in the case of paragraph (d). While both refer to information communicated in confidence, the protection afforded by section 24(1)(d) is limited to communications expressed to be confidential or to be communicated in confidence. Neither section 24(1)(e) nor the relevant Australian or Canadian provisions are confined to situations involving express requirements as to confidentiality.

The circumstances in which matter or information can be said to have been communicated in confidence were considered at length in *Re Maher*.[51] It was held that the scope of the exemption was not confined to communications which, if disclosed, would give rise to an action for breach of confidence. Instead, it was established that the exemption would apply in the case of communications the subject of an express or implied agreement as to confidentiality. It was also the view of Davies J. that, in certain circumstances, communications could be confidential as a result of a general understanding that communications of that nature would be treated in confidence. He said:

> "[C]ommunications need not be made under any express agreement or even any necessarily implied agreement as to confidentiality but pursuant to a general understanding that communications of that nature will be treated in confidence... The cases referred to in *Re Howard and the Treasurer* make it plain that there is a general understanding that communications at the highest level of government which are of a sensitive nature will be so treated. It is equally to be expected that sensitive communications between the two governments will be so regarded".[52]

The understanding that inter-governmental communications will be treated as confidential, however, appears to be confined to communications at higher

---

[51] *Re Maher and Attorney-General's Department,* above, n. 10.
[52] *ibid.* at 739–740.

levels of government. As Davies J. said in *Re Maher*:

> "Clearly the higher the office of the persons between whom the communications pass, the more likely it is that the communications may be confidential".[53]

The desire to confine the presumption of confidentiality to communications taking place at higher levels is also evident from the Australian federal A.A.T.'s decision in *Re State of Queensland and Australian National Parks and Wildlife Service*,[54] a case which concerned the related Commonwealth/State exemption. The Tribunal said:

> "The present application appears to have arisen from a view on the part of the applicant that there was a tacit understanding that all communications between the applicant and its authorities and the Commonwealth and its authorities were confidential. We do not accept this view. There are many communications between authorities of the Commonwealth and authorities of the State of Queensland which are of a purely routine nature involving no sensitivity. We do not accept that there is any general understanding that all such communications are confidential. Although a different exemption was at issue in this case it appears logical to limit implications of confidentiality of inter-governmental communications to those taking place at high levels of government rather than exempting all routine communications."[55]

The principle that a communication must be confidential at the time it was made and that confidentiality cannot be created retrospectively was established in *Re Maher*. Davies J. agreed with the applicant's contention that:

> "if a communication is not made in a confidential situation, then confidentiality cannot be claimed simply because some officer has subsequently looked at the letter and has thought that it ought to have been confidential".[56]

Even if a communication was confidential at the time it was communicated, it appears that the passage of time may result in a loss of that confidentiality. In *Re Throssell (No. 2)* it was accepted that material may lose its confidential character over a period of time.[57]

The fact that a record is viewed as confidential by a foreign government at the time of the hearing of a dispute regarding its disclosure was deemed to be irrelevant in *Re Robinson*.[58] The A.A.T. was interested only in establishing whether the information had been communicated in confidence in the first place.

---

[53] Above, n. 10, at 740.
[54] Above, n. 43.
[55] *ibid.* at 159.
[56] *Re Maher and Attorney-General's Department,* above, n. 10, at 740.
[57] *Re Throssell and Australian Archives (No. 2)*, above, n. 11.
[58] *Re Robinson and Department of Foreign Affairs*, above, n. 18.

D. Non-disclosure of Existence or Non-existence of Records

Where the head of a public body is satisfied that disclosure of the existence or non-existence of a record would prejudice the security, defence, or international relations of the State or matters relating to Northern Ireland, he or she must refuse to grant the request and must not disclose whether the record exists. The basis for this provision is that even if the records are not themselves released, the knowledge that they exist could prove damaging. Those involved in subversive activities could, for example, apply for information relating to themselves as a means of finding out whether their activities had brought them to the attention of the security forces. This provision is discussed in greater detail above at pp. 71–72.

CONFIDENTIALITY

CHAPTER 12

CONFIDENTIALITY

A. Introduction

Information is frequently supplied to public bodies in confidence. The supply of such information can be effected in different circumstances. The information may be supplied voluntarily, or it may be supplied under compulsion. It may relate to the person supplying the information, or to third parties. It may originate from outside or within public bodies. It may be supplied on the express understanding that its confidentiality be maintained or otherwise. The preservation of the confidentiality of information supplied to public bodies can be important for two reasons. First, disclosure of information obtained in confidence may interfere with the supplier's expectation that the information will be treated as confidential. This may have implications in terms of protecting privacy of individuals or maintaining trade secrets or the secrecy of government information. The second, and more pragmatic, reason for maintaining the confidentiality of information supplied to public bodies is that the maintenance of the confidentiality of such information may be necessary to ensure its continued supply. Those who voluntarily supply information to public bodies may be discouraged from continuing to do so, if the information supplied is subject to disclosure under the FOI Act.

This exemption, which is mandatory, reflects both of these concerns. It provides as follows:

"26.—(1) Subject to the provisions of this section, a head shall refuse to grant a request under section 7 if—

(a) the record concerned contains information given to the public body concerned in confidence and on the understanding that it would be treated by it as confidential (including such information as aforesaid that a person was required by law, or could have been required by the body pursuant to law, to give to the body) and, in the opinion of the head, its disclosure would be likely to prejudice the giving to the body of further similar information from the same person or other persons and it is of importance to the body that such further similar information as aforesaid should continue to be given to the body, or

(b) disclosure of the information concerned would constitute a breach of a duty of confidence provided for by a provision of an agreement or enactment (other than a provision specified in column (3) of the Third Schedule of an enactment specified in that Schedule) or otherwise by law.

(2) Subsection (1) shall not apply to a record which is prepared by a head or any other person (being a director, or member of the staff of, a public body or a person who is providing a service for a public body under a contract for services) in the course of the performance of his or her functions unless disclosure of the information concerned would constitute a breach of a duty of confidence that is provided for by an agreement or statute or otherwise by law and is owed to a person other than a public body or head or a director, or member of the staff of, a public body or a person who is providing or provided a service for a public body under a contract for services.

(3) Subject to section 29, subsection (1)(a) shall not apply in relation to a case in which, in the opinion of the head concerned, the public interest would, on balance, be better served by granting than by refusing to grant the request under section 7 concerned."

The exemption consists of two main parts, which are set out respectively in paragraphs (a) and (b) of section 26(1). Because of the use of the disjunctive term "or" between these two paragraphs, it seems clear that they constitute two separate elements of section 26, with each setting forth a distinct test for determining the application of the confidentiality exemption. This formulation is closely related to that of a number of the Australian State Freedom of Information Acts,[1] each of which has a confidentiality exemption which contains two separate limbs expressed in terms similar to those of section 26. Other jurisdictions have single tests for determining exemption on the basis of confidentiality. New Zealand's provision,[2] for example, approximates section 26(1)(a), while the Australian federal provision[3] is similar to section 26(1)(b).

In order for section 26(1)(a) to apply, three cumulative conditions must be met:

(1) the information in question must have been given to the public body concerned in confidence and on the understanding that it would be treated as confidential;

(2) disclosure must be likely to prejudice the future supply of such information; and

(3) it must be of importance to the body that such future supply should continue.

Section 26(1)(b) applies where disclosure of the information concerned would constitute a breach of a duty of confidence provided for by a provision of an agreement or enactment or otherwise by law. While section 26(1)(b) appears to incorporate the general law relating to the action for breach of confidence,

---

[1] Freedom of Information Act 1982 (Victoria), s.35; Freedom of Information Act 1989 (New South Wales), Sched.1, cl.13; Freedom of Information Act 1991 (South Australia), Sched.1, cl.13; Freedom of Information Act 1991 (Tasmania), s.33; Freedom of Information Act 1992 (Queensland), s.46; Freedom of Information Act 1992 (Western Australia), Sched.1, cl.8.

section 26(1)(a) seems to be aimed at protecting confidential communications in circumstances where they would not be afforded protection from disclosure by an action for breach of confidence. The exception provided for in section 26(2) places important limitations on the use of the section 26 to protect records prepared internally by public bodies. The use of the exemption is also subject to a public interest test, which is set out in section 26(3).

There is a possibility of overlap between the two limbs of the exemption. The scope of section 26(1)(a) would appear, in one sense, to be narrower than that of section 26(1)(b) in that the former applies only in situations where disclosure of the information would be likely to prejudice the future supply of information, whereas the latter is more general in its application. On the other hand, the opening sentence of section 26(1)(a) is broadly worded and, unlike section 26(1)(b), it does not closely resemble the essential elements of the action for breach of confidence. It seems, therefore, that section 26(1)(a) might be held to apply to situations where neither section 26(1)(b), nor indeed the action for breach of confidence, could be employed

B.   Relationship between the Exemption and the Action for Breach of Confidence

One of the most important issues to be considered when analysing this exemption is the extent to which it incorporates in its terms the substantive law relating to breach of confidence. If the exemption is found to amount to a codification of the law relating to breach of confidence, then its interpretation can be based on the body of case law which has developed since the emergence of the action for breach of confidence in the nineteenth century. If, on the other hand, the exemption is expressed in a manner which distinguishes it from the action for breach of confidence, it must be considered on its own terms. One of the consequences of a finding that the exemption does not incorporate the law relating to breach of confidence is that the defences available in respect of that action will not be available to combat the withholding of information under section 26. These defences include the equitable defences of unclean hands,[4] and delay, as well as the public interest defence.[5] The taking into account of the public interest is, however, provided for expressly in the terms of the exemption,[6] but only in respect of records to which section 26(1)(a) applies.

---

[2] Official Information Act, s.9(2)(ba).
[3] Freedom of Information Act 1982 (Cth), s.45.
[4] This can be pleaded where the plaintiff's conduct has been so improper that he or she should be refused equitable relief.
[5] See Gurry, *Breach of Confidence* (Clarendon Press, Oxford, 1984), Part 7.
[6] s.26(3).

Whilst a finding that the terms of the exemption approximates the law of breach of confidence would undoubtedly be convenient in terms of facilitating reliance on an existing body of case law, it can be argued that given the different circumstances in which the action for breach of confidence and the FOI confidentiality exemption arise, they have little in common. The action for breach of confidence typically arises where the confider, A, confides information in the confidee, B, who discloses or intends to disclose the information to a third party, C. A may then take an action against B seeking a remedy in respect of the disclosure or intended disclosure. The confidentiality exemption in FOI legislation, on the other hand, is usually invoked when the confider, A, confides information to a public body, B, and a requester, C, applies for access to such information. B may then invoke the exemption in an effort to withhold the information. In the former case, the confidentiality of the communication is being invoked by the confider, whilst in the latter, the interest in maintaining the confidentiality of the communication is often as much a concern of the confidee as it is of the confider. Further, while disclosure under FOI legislation is generally considered on the basis that it is to the world at large, disclosure of confidential information where it is allowed under the law of confidence is often on the basis that it is to a particular person. Given these differences of emphasis, the application of the principles of the law of confidence to the withholding of access to government information may not always be a smooth process.

Another, more practical, argument against incorporation of the law of confidence into the confidentiality exemption derives from the complexity and uncertainty of that area of law. In Australia, where the law of confidence has been incorporated into the confidentiality exemption, it has been argued that the complexity of the law can make the exemption difficult for public bodies to apply.[7] However, a suggestion that the exemption be redrafted to make it self-contained was rejected on the basis that it should be left to develop in line with the common law relating to the action for breach of confidence, rather than becoming a separate, potentially inconsistent regime.[8]

An examination of the question whether either limb of section 26 incorporates the substantive law relating to the action for breach of confidence requires, first, that the main components of that action be delineated.

The action for breach of confidence has been said to consist of three main elements. These were set out by Megarry J. in the leading case of *Coco v. A.N. Clark (Engineers) Limited*:[9]

---

[7] Australian Law Reform Commission, Report No. 77/Administrative Review Council, Report No. 40, *Open Government: A Review of the Freedom of Information Act 1982* (Australian Government Publishing Service, Canberra, 1995), para. 10.32.

[8] *ibid.*

[9] [1969] F.S.R. 415.

> "[T]hree elements are normally required if, apart from a contract, a case of breach of confidence is to succeed. First the information itself . . . must have 'the necessary quality of confidence about it'. Secondly, that information must have been imparted in circumstances imposing an obligation of confidence. Thirdly, there must be an unauthorised use of that information to the detriment of the party communicating it."[10]

This formulation, which has been accepted in Irish law,[11] is cumulative: in other words, each of the three requirements outlined above must be met. An expanded version of this formulation has been adopted in the context of Australian FOI cases. This test, which was first set out by Gummow J. in *Corrs, Pavey, Whiting & Byrne v. Collector of Customs*[12] and has been widely applied in Australia,[13] demands the satisfaction of five criteria:

> "The plaintiff (i) must be able to identify with specificity, and not merely in global terms, that which is said to be the information in question, and must also be able to show that (ii) the information has the necessary quality of confidentiality (and is not, for example, common or public knowledge), (iii) the information was received by the defendant in such circumstances as to import an obligation of confidence, and (iv) there is actual or threatened misuse of that information . . . It may also be necessary . . . that unauthorised use would be to the detriment of the plaintiff."[14]

1. Relationship between section 26(1)(a) and the action for breach of confidence

The essence of this limb of the exemption is that the information be "given in confidence and on the understanding that it be treated by it [the public body] as confidential".

These opening words are then qualified by two requirements, both of which must be satisfied in order for the exemption to apply: first, that in the opinion of the head of the public body disclosure of the information would prejudice the future supply of such information; and, second, that it is of importance to the public body that such information continue to be supplied. Once these elements are established, the application of the exemption is mandatory.

---

[10] Above, n. 9, at 419–420.
[11] *House of Spring Gardens v. Point Blank Limited* [1984] I.R. 611.
[12] (1987) 14 F.C.R 434; 74 A.L.R. 428; 7 A.A.R. 187; 13 A.L.D. 254.
[13] *Re Kamminga and Australian National University* (1992) 15 A.A.R. 297; *Re Toren and Department of Immigration and Ethnic Affairs*, unreported, Commonwealth Administrative Appeals Tribunal, No. Q93/578, October 10, 1994; *Re B and Brisbane North Regional Health Authority* (1994) 1 Q.A.R. 279; *Re Pemberton and The University of Queensland* (1994) 2 Q.A.R. 293; *Re Coventry and Cairns City Council* (1996) 3 Q.A.R. 191; *Re Sutherland and Brisbane North Regional Health Authority and Smith* (1995) 2 Q.A.R. 449; *Re "EDH" and Griffith University and Lewis* (1996) 3 Q.A.R. 315.
[14] Above, n. 12, at 443. Citations omitted.

Applying the criteria set out by Megarry J. in *Coco v. A.N. Clark*, this limb of the exemption does not appear to satisfy the first element of the action for breach of confidence. There is no reference in section 26(1)(a) to the nature of the information communicated and, in particular, no requirement that it have "the necessary quality of confidence about it". The second prerequisite of the action for breach of confidence, namely that the information has been imparted in circumstances imposing an obligation of confidence, is likely to be satisfied by the requirement that the information be given "in confidence and on the understanding that it be treated by it as confidential". As for the third requirement, while there is a reference in section 26(1)(a) to a detriment of a kind, *i.e.* prejudice to future supply of such information, it is a detriment which would be suffered by the confidee, whereas the action for breach of confidence requires that the detriment accrue to the person communicating the information, that is, to the confider. Therefore, it seems clear that section 26(1)(a) does not incorporate the action for breach of confidence.

2.   Relationship of section 26(1)(b) with the action for breach of confidence

This part of the exemption provides for the mandatory refusal of access where disclosure of the information concerned "would constitute a breach of a duty of confidence provided for by a provision of an agreement or enactment... or otherwise by law". There is explicit reference in the provision to only one of the three elements of the action for breach of confidence, namely the duty or obligation of confidence. On that basis it might be argued that section 26(1)(b) was not intended to incorporate the action for breach of confidence.

On the other hand, the reference to duties of confidence provided for *by law* links the exemption to the action for breach of confidence. Given the fact that the exemption makes separate provision for duties of confidence provided for by agreements and enactments, the reference to duties of confidence provided for by law can only relate to the duty of confidence arising in the context of an action for breach of confidence. Another reason for arguing that incorporation has indeed been effected is that the action for breach of confidence is subject to a public interest defence. While the Act provides expressly for a public interest test to be applied to records exempt under paragraph (a), there is no such public interest test in place in respect of paragraph (b). This is most likely because it was assumed that paragraph (b) incorporates the action for breach of confidence along with its own public interest defence.

Interestingly, the first part of section 26(1)(b) corresponds quite closely to the original formulation of the Australian confidentiality exemption, which was that "[a] document is an exempt document if its disclosure under this Act would constitute a breach of confidence".[15] When that wording was inter-

---

[15] Freedom of Information Act 1982 (Cth), s.45(1).

preted as not incorporating the common law action for breach of confidence,[16] it was amended to place the issue of incorporation beyond doubt. It now reads:

"A document is an exempt document if its disclosure under this Act *would found an action*, by a person other than the Commonwealth *for breach of confidence*".[17]

Given the strong influence of the Australian legislation on the formulation of the Irish FOI Act, it seems unfortunate that, assuming the intention was to incorporate the action for breach of confidence, this was not made more explicit.

C. Analysis of Section 26(1)(a)

Having disposed of the threshold issue of whether section 26(1)(a) incorporates the law relating to the action for breach of confidence, the focus of attention can now be shifted to the substance of section 26(1)(a) to ascertain the circumstances in which this limb of the exemption will apply. Section 26(1)(a) applies where the following conditions are fulfilled:

1. the information must have been given in confidence and on the understanding that it be treated as such; and

2. its disclosure would be likely to prejudice the giving to the body of further similar information; and

3. it is of importance to the public body that further similar information should continue to be given to the body.

Each of these requirements will be examined in turn.

1. The information must have been given in confidence and on the understanding that it be treated as such

Two issues arise here. The first concerns the nature of the information covered by this element of section 26(1)(a), and the second turns on the circumstances in which information can be said to have been given in confidence and on the understanding that it be treated as confidential.

---

[16] *Re Witheford and Department of Foreign Affairs* (1983) 3 A.L.D. 534. Here it was held that the exemption applied to a situation in which one public servant had given information to another, upon the footing that the recipient of the information was under a duty to keep the information confidential even though disclosure would not amount to an actionable breach of confidence.

[17] Emphasis added. Freedom of Information Act 1982 (Cth), s.45(1), as amended by the Freedom of Information Laws Amendment Act 1983 (Cth), s.23, and Freedom of Information Laws Amendment Act 1986 (Cth), s.14.

(a) The nature of the information

The most difficult issue to come to terms with in considering this paragraph is the nature of the information covered by it. No effort has been made to limit its scope to the type of information covered by the action for breach of confidence, namely "information which has the necessary quality of confidence about it". It would, therefore, appear to encompass any information given in confidence and on the understanding that it be treated as confidential. This could include information which is clearly not confidential in the legally accepted sense, such as, for example, information which is in the public domain.

Nor does there appear to be any restriction on the source of the information for the purposes of this paragraph. This provision applies, therefore, to information supplied by an external confider, as well as to information supplied by other public bodies (inter public body information) and even possibly to information supplied from one person to another within the same public body (intra public body information), although the application of section 26(1)(a) to this last category is uncertain since it might be argued that information already in the possession of one person in a public body could not be "given" to that same public body.

(b) Information given in confidence and on the understanding that it be treated as confidential

The application of the section 26(1)(a) appears to be dependent on the existence of a mutual understanding on the part of both confider and confidee that the information be treated as confidential. To take the opposite approach, of allowing the threshold condition for application of the paragraph to be established on a unilateral basis, would mean that an obligation to treat information as confidential for the purposes of the exemption could be thrust upon the person supplying the information or upon the public body, as the case may be. The former analysis is supported by the sponsoring Minister's statement during the Seanad debate on the meaning of "understanding" in the context of the personal information exemption to the effect that it means understanding by both parties and that "it would not be open to only one person to have an understanding that it [the information] be treated as confidential".[18]

It appears from the requirement that the information be "given in confidence" that the understanding as to confidentiality would have to arise at the time the information was supplied to the public body, and it would not be open to the confider to claim confidentiality at a later stage. This principle was approved in the Australian federal case of *Re Maher and Attorney-General*,[19] which was concerned with the operation of the exemption of confidential com-

---

[18] 150 *Seanad Debates* Cols 88–89 (Committee Stage).
[19] *Re Maher and Attorney-General's Department* (1985) 7 A.L.D. 731.

munications from foreign governments and international organisations. The Administrative Appeals Tribunal (A.A.T.) held that:

> "if a communication is not made in a confidential situation, then confidentiality cannot be claimed simply because some officer has subsequently looked at the letter and has thought that it ought to have been confidential".[20]

While no express agreement as to confidentiality is required, it is necessary to establish on an objective basis that the information was imparted in confidence. It would not be enough for the confider to stamp the material confidential in order to obtain the protection of the exemption.

The express inclusion in section 26(1)(a) of information, the supply of which is required by law, was designed to deal with uncertainty in the law relating to breach of confidence on the issue of whether information which is, or could have been, obtained by compulsion can be subject to an obligation of confidence. It makes it clear that, for the purposes of the application of section 26(1)(a), information which was supplied under compulsion will be protected by the exemption. The supply of such information must, however, have been required by law. The exemption does not cover information which someone is compelled to supply through the exercise of a public body's economic muscle or under contract. The inclusion of information the disclosure of which "*could have been required*" is designed to include situations where, although information has been supplied voluntarily, such supply could have been obtained under legal compulsion.

2. Disclosure would be likely to prejudice the giving to the body of further similar information

A record will only fall within the scope of section 26(1)(a) if, in the opinion of the head of the public body which receives the information, its disclosure would be likely to prejudice the future supply of similar information. This part of section 26(1)(a) is similar to the corresponding provisions of the Australian State FOI Acts[21] and the New Zealand Act.[22]

In order for this element of section 26(1)(a) to be satisfied, it must be shown that, in the opinion of the head of the public body concerned, future supply of similar information would be likely to be prejudiced. There is no need to show any actual harm to suppliers, but merely that they or others would

---

[20] Above, n. 19, at 740.
[21] Freedom of Information Act 1982 (Victoria), s.35(1)(b); Freedom of Information Act 1991 (South Australia), Sched.1, cl.13(b)(i); Freedom of Information Act 1991 (Tasmania), s.33(1)(b); Freedom of Information Act 1989 (New South Wales), Sched.1, cl.13(b)(ii); Freedom of Information Act 1992 (Queensland), s.46(1)(b); Freedom of Information Act 1992 (Western Australia), Sched.1, cl.8(2)(b).
[22] Official Information Act 1982, s.9(2)(ba).

be discouraged from supplying similar information in the future. In terms of the standard of proof required, the public body must show that disclosure "would be likely to prejudice" such supply. This is the same standard as that adopted in the corresponding New Zealand exemption. It seems to require that there be evidence that the occurrence of the harm be more probable than not. In New Zealand, however, the interpretation of the "would be likely to prejudice" standard to mean "more likely than not" was rejected in favour of the lower threshold of "a distinct or significant possibility".[23] The standard utilised in the Australian federal Act is the "could reasonably be expected to prejudice" standard.[24]

That there must be some genuine prejudice to the future supply of information, as opposed to a likelihood that it would be supplied in a different manner, was established in the Queensland case of *Re Sutherland and Brisbane North Regional Health Authority and Smith*.[25] In that case it was held that the fact that medical practitioners might, in the future, be more careful in framing the terms in which the necessary information is conveyed would be either a benefit or a neutral development, rather than a detrimental one.

The information sought to be withheld must be "similar" to the information, the supply of which would be prejudiced in the future. In interpreting these words in the equivalent exemption of the Victorian FOI Act in *Richards v. Law Institute of Victoria*, Dixon J. of the County Court said:

> "[T]he words 'similar information' refer to information of the class or character contained in the case under consideration, and the precise contents of the information in the particular case are not relevant."[26]

The information, the supply of which would allegedly be prejudiced, must, therefore, be described in order to establish whether it falls into the same class or is of the same character as the information which forms the subject of the access request.

Account may be taken of likely prejudice not only to the supply of similar information by a person who has supplied the information which is the subject of the access request, but also to the supply of similar information by others. The taking into account of prejudice to the future supply of information by the same person is not expressly provided for under overseas versions of this exemption. As regards the destination of the information, it is clear that the only prejudice to future supply of information which can be taken into account is that to the body to which the current request is directed. It is not open to the head of a public body to take into account the likely prejudice to future supply of information to other public bodies or to the government as a whole.

---

[23] *Commissioner of Police v. Ombudsman* [1988] 1 N.Z.L.R. 385 at 404.
[24] See above, p. 92, for a comparison of these two standards of proof.
[25] Above, n. 13.
[26] Unreported, County Court, August 13, 1984, p. 9.

Where the supply of information to a public body is compulsory, it could be argued that no danger to future supply could be established. However, the fact that the supply of information is compulsory does not guarantee compliance. It might be argued that disclosure of information could have the effect of discouraging compliance with rules requiring the compulsory supply of information.

3. It is of importance to the public body that further similar information should continue to be given to it

This provision differs significantly from its New Zealand and Australian counterparts in that while the Irish provision requires merely that future supply be of importance to the public body concerned, the Australian and New Zealand provisions apply the more stringent requirement that such future supply be in the public interest.

In terms of discharging the requirement that future supply of information be of importance to the body, it must be shown that the receipt of such information is of significance to the body in terms of being necessary to the carrying out of its functions.

D. Analysis of Section 26(1)(b)

Section 26(1)(b) applies to breaches of a duty of confidence provided for in three situations: by agreement; under an enactment; or otherwise by law.

1. Agreement

Since most commentators accept that an obligation of confidence can be founded on a contractual provision,[27] there was no need to separately refer to duties of confidence arising out of an agreement; such agreements as to confidentiality would have been covered by duties of confidence provided for "otherwise by law". The most important issue arising in the context of agreements as to confidentiality is whether they can override the FOI Act. A person may, for example, enter into an agreement to supply information to a public body. Such an agreement may contain an express confidentiality clause. Where such a clause is contained in the agreement, the question arises whether the information can be disclosed under the FOI Act. If the answer to this question is no, it could lead to the aims of the Act being circumvented through the wide-

---

[27] See Gurry, *op. cit.* above, n. 5, p. 35, and Lavery, *Commercial Secrets: The Action for Breach of Confidence in Ireland* (Round Hall Sweet & Maxwell, Dublin, 1996), p. 25.

spread insertion of express confidentiality clauses into formal agreements for the supply of routine information to public bodies.

The original text of the Freedom of Information Bill[28] protected against abuse by requiring that all confidentiality agreements entered into by public bodies be submitted to the Information Commissioner for his or her approval. This provision was removed at Report Stage in the Dáil. The reason given for its removal was that it could compromise the independence of the Information Commissioner by involving him or her in approving confidentiality agreements which he or she might be asked to overturn at a later stage. It was felt that any possible abuse of confidentiality agreements could, instead, be addressed by the Commissioner in the context of his or her power to review the operation of the FOI Act under section 36.[29] It is also open to the Commissioner to refer to such abuse in the context of the exercise of his or her powers under section 39 (which deals with the publication by the Commissioner of commentaries on the practical application of the Act), or section 40 (which concerns the publication of the Commissioner's annual report).

There are other limitations on the circumvention of the aims of the FOI Act through the use of confidentiality clauses in agreements. One important limitation is that not all promises to keep information secret will amount to "a duty of confidence provided for by a provision of an agreement" as required by section 26(1)(b). The distinction was explained by the Queensland Information Commissioner in the following terms:

> "An express contractual obligation of confidence ordinarily arises in circumstances where the parties to a disclosure of confidential information wish to define clearly their respective rights and obligations with respect to the use of the confidential information, thereby enabling the parties to anticipate their obligations with certainty. A mere promise to keep certain information secret, unsupported by consideration, is incapable of amounting to a contractual obligation of confidence, and its effectiveness as a binding obligation would depend on the application of the equitable principles . . .".[30]

It appears also that express confidentiality clauses can only apply to information which has "the necessary quality of confidence about it" as required by the action for breach of confidence. As Gurry said in the leading text on the action for breach of confidence:

> "Theoretically, it is possible to have an express contractual obligation not to use or disclose information which is common knowledge, but in practice, it is difficult to see how any meaning or effect could be given to such an obligation by the courts."[31]

---

[28] Freedom of Information Bill, 1997, s.26(3) (as passed by the Seanad).
[29] 477 *Dáil Debates* Col. 769 (Report Stage).
[30] *Re B. and Brisbane North Regional Health Authority,* above, n. 13, at 297.
[31] *op. cit.* above, n. 5, p. 65.

The use of express confidentiality clauses in agreements for the supply of information to public bodies will also be limited by the operation of the public interest test. It is likely that the use of a confidentiality clause in an agreement with the intention of deliberately placing the information beyond the reach of the Act would be deemed to be unacceptable on public interest grounds. In the Australian case of *Re Baueris and Commonwealth*,[32] when a claim was made that a confidentiality agreement was a sham in the sense that it had been entered into in order to take the information outside the scope of the FOI Act, the A.A.T. examined the agreement to see whether its terms accorded with the true position. General contractual defences such as illegality, mistake, or duress may also apply in defeating an express confidentiality clause in an agreement. In *A. v. Hayden*[33] the Australian High Court held that a court would not aid the enforcement of an express contractual obligation of confidentiality in a case where its effects would be contrary to public policy.

2. Enactment

Confidentiality provisions can be found in many enactments. Some of these are listed in the Third Schedule to the Act. The effect of section 26(1)(b) is to leave in place, for the purposes of the exemption, all statutory confidentiality provisions apart from those listed in the Third Schedule.

This provision complements the preservation of prohibitions on disclosure in other enactments under section 32. The part of section 32 which is concerned with review of such enactments is also relevant to confidentiality provisions of enactments. Section 32(2) requires a joint committee of both Houses of the Oireachtas to review the operation of any provisions of any enactment that require or authorise the non-disclosure of a record.[34] The purpose of such review would be to weed out all those non-disclosure provisions which are not in keeping with the spirit and purposes of the Act. The power of review clearly extends to confidentiality provisions of enactments.

3. Otherwise by law

This provision applies to disclosures of information which would constitute a breach of a duty of confidence provided "otherwise by law". This element of the exemption appears to be directed at situations where disclosure of information would found an action for breach of confidence in situations where there is no agreement and no statutory requirement as to confidentiality. Case law concerning the action for breach of confidence has established that the

---

[32] (1987) 75 A.L.R. 327; 13 A.L.D. 470.
[33] (1984) 156 C.L.R. 532.
[34] See below, pp. 327–328.

obligation to respect confidence is not limited to cases where the parties are in a contractual relationship.[35]

In considering the terms of the equivalent provision in the Queensland Act, the Queensland Information Commissioner said that it required:

> "the test of exemption to be evaluated by reference to a hypothetical legal action in which there is a clearly identifiable plaintiff, possessed of appropriate standing to bring a suit to enforce an obligation of confidence said to be owed to that plaintiff, in respect of information in the possession or control of that agency or Minister faced with an application for access under . . . the FOI Act to the information in issue."[36]

The application of this limb of the exemption must be examined in terms of the three elements of the action for breach of confidence.

(a) Nature of the information

Not all information will qualify for the protection of the action for breach of confidence and consequently of section 26(1)(b). The information must have the necessary quality of confidence about it. It is necessary to specifically identify the information at issue in order to establish that it is confidential. Case law concerning this element of the action for breach of confidence has established that the law of confidence does not cover information in the public domain[37] and this limitation has been accepted by the Irish courts.[38] However, it would appear that only relative secrecy is required so that information will have the necessary quality of confidence about it even if, for example, it is widely known within a particular organisation.

In terms of the inherent value of the information, it has been held that the action for breach of confidence will not extend to protect information which amounts to no more than "trivial tittle tattle".[39] There is, however, no requirement that the information have commercial value.[40] It is likely that confidentiality can be lost with the passage of time. It has been established that although a person's identity is ordinarily not information which is confidential in quality, the connection of a person's identity with the imparting of confidential information can itself be secret information capable of protection by the action for breach of confidence.[41] Examples of the types of information which,

---

[35] *Saltman Engineering Co. Ltd v. Campbell Engineering Co. Ltd* (1948) 65 R.P.C. 203 at 211.

[36] *Re B. and Brisbane North Regional Health Authority*, above, n. 13, at 296.

[37] *Saltman Engineering Co. Ltd v. Campbell Engineering Co. Ltd*, above, n. 35.

[38] *Aksjeselskapet Jotul v. Waterford Iron Foundries Ltd*, unreported, High Court, McWilliam J., November 8, 1977; *House of Spring Gardens v. Point Blank Limited*, above, n. 11.

[39] *Coco v. A.N. Clark (Engineers) Limited*, above, n. 9, at 421.

[40] *Nicrotherm Electrical Co. Ltd v. Percy* [1957] R.P.C. 207; *Moorgate Tobacco v. Philip Morris Ltd* (1983–1984) 156 C.L.R. 414.

[41] *D v. N.S.P.C.C.* [1977] 1 All E.R. 589; [1978] A.C. 171; *G v. Day* [1980] 1 N.S.W.L.R. 24.

in the context of the Australian FOI Act, have been held to meet the requirement that information be confidential in nature include: the date on which a pharmaceutical company had imported a particular drug;[42] the reason a person was refused employment;[43] referees' reports;[44] material sent in support of an application for approval of a contraceptive device;[45] information on parish finances;[46] and a letter containing adverse comments on the applicant's performance of his employment duties.[47]

(b) The obligation of confidence

The law relating to the action for breach of confidence provides that, in the absence of any express obligation of confidentiality, a duty of confidence can be said to arise in two circumstances. Such a duty can arise, firstly, in the context of particular relationships. Such relationships are said to arise between professional persons and their clients, between employees and employers, or where a relationship is based on mutual trust and understanding.[48] The second situation in which an obligation of confidence may arise is where information was supplied for a particular purpose. This limited purpose test was adopted by Mr Justice Costello in *House of Spring Gardens Limited v. Point Blank Limited* when he said:

> "if the informant himself has expended skill, time and labour on compiling the information, then he can reasonably regard it as of value and he can reasonably consider that he is conferring on its recipient a benefit. If this benefit is conferred for a specific purpose then an obligation may be imposed to use it for that purpose and for no other purpose."[49]

In the case of communications with and within public bodies, it is possible that a duty of confidence could be founded either on the relationship between the parties[50] or, as is more likely, because the information was supplied for a limited purpose.

In terms of adducing evidence as to the existence of a duty of confidence, the views of both confider and confidee must be objectively considered. Again

---

[42] *Corrs, Pavey, Whiting & Byrne v. Collector of Customs*, above, n. 12.

[43] *Re Cockcroft and Attorney General's Department* (1986) 64 A.L.R. 97.

[44] *Re Kamminga and Australian National University*, above, n. 13; *Re Pemberton and The University of Queensland*, above, n. 13.

[45] *Searle Australia Pty Ltd v. Public Interest Advocacy Centre & Anor* (1992) 108 A.L.R. 163; 36 F.C.R. 111; 16 A.A.R. 28.

[46] *Re Baueris and Commonwealth*, above, n. 32.

[47] *Re Coventry and Cairns City Council*, above, n. 13.

[48] See Gurry, *op. cit.* above, n. 5, Part 4, and Lavery, *op. cit.* above, n. 27, Chap. 4.

[49] Above, n. 11, at 663.

[50] In the Australian case of *Re Marzol and Australian Federal Police and Australian Customs Service*, unreported, Commonwealth Administrative Appeals Tribunal, April 3, 1986, it was held that a duty of confidence could be founded on the nature of the relationship between a parole officer and a parolee.

the stamping of a document as confidential by either confider or confidee will not be conclusive evidence of such confidentality.

The matters to be taken into account in determining whether an obligation of confidence exists were explored in the Australian FOI case, *Smith Kline and French Laboratories (Australia) Ltd v. Department of Community Services and Health*[51] in the following terms:

> "To determine the existence of confidentiality and its scope, it may be relevant to consider whether the information was supplied gratuitously or for a consideration; whether there is any past practice of such a kind as to give rise to an understanding; how sensitive the information is; whether the confider has any interest in the purpose for which the information is to be used; whether the confider expressly warned the confidee against a particular disclosure or use of the information - and no doubt, many other matters."[52]

Another matter which has been taken into account in an Australian FOI case is whether the information was solicited or unsolicited, with an obligation of confidence being more likely to be attached to solicited information.[53]

(c) Unauthorised use to the detriment of the confider

This requirement can be broken into two parts: firstly, whether the disclosure would constitute an unauthorised use of the information; and, second, whether detriment is likely to be occasioned to the confider.

(i) Unauthorised use

Evidence of unauthorised use of the information must be adduced. This means that the disclosure of the information must go beyond what is permitted having regard to the scope of the obligation of confidence. Whether the use of the information is unauthorised will depend on the facts of the case. In the Australian FOI case *Joint Coal Board v. Cameron*[54] the Federal Court put forward the following test:

> "It is, in essence, a question of fact whether, in the circumstances, it was the intention of the parties at the time of communication of the information that the recipient should be at liberty, consistently with the confidence reposed, to divulge the information to a limited class of persons".[55]

In the circumstances of the case, the court held that disclosure to the applicant, who had supplied the information to the public body in the first place, was not

---

[51] (1991) 28 F.C.R. 291; (1991) 99 A.L.R. 679.
[52] *ibid.* at 302–303.
[53] *Re Toren and Department of Immigration and Ethnic Affairs*, above, n. 13.
[54] (1990) 19 A.L.D. 329; (1990) A.L.R. 208.
[55] *ibid.* at 339.

an unauthorised use of the confidential information, thus establishing that disclosure to a particular applicant may not amount to unauthorised use.

It would appear that where a supplier of information to a public body is made aware at the time of supplying the information that it is subject to disclosure under the FOI Act, then such disclosure cannot amount to unauthorised use.

(ii) Detriment to the confider

There is a lack of consistency in reported cases on the issue of detriment. On the one hand, cases such as *Coco v. A.N. Clark (Engineers) Limited,*[56] *Seager v. Copydex,*[57] and *Commonwealth of Australia v. John Fairfax & Sons Ltd*[58] are authority for the proposition that detriment is necessary, whilst, on the other hand, cases such as *X v. Y*[59] and the Australian FOI case *Re Kamminga and Australian National University*[60] reject the need to establish detriment. It appears that in the case of government confidences, *i.e.* where the information being disclosed concerns the actions of a public body, detriment must be shown. This principle was established by Mason J. in *Fairfax* when he said:

> "It may be a sufficient detriment to the citizen that disclosure of information relating to his affairs will expose his actions to public discussion and criticism. But it can scarcely be a relevant detriment to the government that publication of material concerning its actions will merely expose it to public discussion and criticism. It is unacceptable, in our democratic society, that there should be a restraint on the publication of information relating to government when the only vice of that information is that it enables the public to discuss, review and criticise government action."[61]

This statement of the law was approved by Carroll J. in *Attorney General for England and Wales v. Brandon Book Publishers Ltd.*[62]

The following pragmatic and useful approach to the issue of detriment generally was adopted by the Queensland Information Commissioner in *Re B. and Brisbane North Regional Health Authority*:

> "[It] is probably necessary, and certainly prudent, to apply s.46(1)(a) of the FOI Act [the confidentiality exemption] on the basis that it must be established that detriment is likely to be occasioned to the original confider of the confidential information if it were to be disclosed. It appears, however, that detriment is fairly easily established. In particular, it is not necessary to establish that threat-

---

[56] Above, n. 9.
[57] [1967] 2 All E.R. 415.
[58] (1980) 147 C.L.R. 39.
[59] [1988] 2 All E.R. 648.
[60] Above, n. 13.
[61] *Commonwealth of Australia v. John Fairfax & Sons Ltd*, above, n. 58, at 51.
[62] [1986] I.R. 597.

ened disclosure will cause detriment in a pecuniary sense: 'detriment can be as ephemeral as embarrassment . . . a loss of privacy or fear . . . and indirect detriment, eg, the confidential information may gravely injure some relation or friend'. Moreover, in Attorney-General v Guardian Newspapers, Lord Keith of Kinkel (with whom Lord Jauncey agreed) said: 'I would think it a sufficient detriment to the confider that information given in confidence is to be disclosed to persons to whom he would prefer not to know of it, even though the disclosure would not be harmful to him in any positive way.' Lord Griffiths appeared to treat detriment as sufficiently established without economic loss of social amenities."[63]

What is clear is that the detriment must accrue to the confider and not to the confidee. Therefore, in circumstances where a person supplies information to a public body, and a third party makes a request for access to that information, what must be taken into account is the detriment to the person originally supplying the information, rather than the detriment to the public body.

E.   Exception of Internal Records

Section 26(2) is aimed at limiting the use of the confidentiality exemption to restrict disclosure of records emanating from within public bodies. This approach is in keeping with the manner in which the action for breach of confidence has been applied in cases where the government is the confider.[64]

The exception applies in respect of records prepared by staff members or contractors of public bodies in the course of the performance of their functions. Such records will only be subject to the confidentiality exemption where their disclosure would constitute a breach of the duty of confidence *and* that duty is owed to someone other than a head, director, staff member or contractor of a public body. The phrase "in the course of the performance of his or her functions" is used to distinguish records prepared by a staff member or contractor of a public body in his or her capacity as such a staff member or contractor from acts done in other capacities, *e.g.* in a purely private or personal capacity.[65]

---

[63] Above, n. 13, at 326–327. Citations omitted.

[64] *Commonwealth v. John Fairfax & Sons Ltd,* above, n. 58; *Attorney General for England and Wales v. Brandon Book Publishers Ltd,* above, n. 62.

[65] In the Queensland case of *Re Pemberton and The University of Queensland,* above, n. 13, it was held that reports on a staff member written by academics in their capacity as Head of Department, Dean or Pro-Vice Chancellor were covered by the exception. However, a reference from an internal academic on a staff member's application for promotion was held to have been written in a personal capacity.

F. The Public Interest

The public interest test which is set out in section 26(3) provides that section 26(1)(a) will not apply where, in the opinion of the head of the public body concerned, the public interest would, on balance, be better served by granting than by refusing to grant the request. This provision is subject to the third party consultation provision set out in section 29, the effect of which is discussed below at pp. 241–243.

There is no statutory public interest test for records coming within the scope of section 26(1)(b). It is, however, well established that the action for breach of confidence is itself subject to a public interest defence[66] and, therefore, the exemption of records from the scope of the Act on the basis of section 26(1)(b) is subject to the operation of this defence. This public interest defence to the action for breach of confidence will be considered before the scope of the public interest test provided for under section 26(3) is analysed.

1. The public interest defence to the action for breach of confidence

The parameters of the public interest defence to the action for breach of confidence continue to be in a state of development. It is settled that the defence will apply in the case of disclosure of crime or fraud,[67] misdeeds,[68] damage to the public[69] and, in exceptional cases, to other circumstances.[70] The need to balance the interest in confidentiality against the interest in disclosure has been emphasised in a number of cases.[71] It has been suggested, however, that such a balancing only comes into play where issues such as crime, fraud, misdeeds or danger to the public are present and that, therefore, the concept of balancing of interests does not constitute an extension of the defence.[72]

In *Desmond v. Glackin (No. 2)*[73] the scope of the public interest defence was interpreted broadly by O'Hanlon J. in the High Court; the learned judge's approach was later approved by the Supreme Court on appeal. The issue was the making available to a public body of information supplied by a company to another public body under statutory compulsion. The information in question was made available for use by an inspector appointed by a Government Minister to conduct an enquiry into the circumstances surrounding the contro-

---

[66] See Gurry, *op. cit.* above, n. 5, Part 7, and Lavery, *op. cit.* above, n. 27, Chap. 8.

[67] *Gartside v. Outram* (1857) 26 L.J.Ch. (NS) 113.

[68] *Initial Services Limited v. Putterill* [1968] 1 Q.B. 396.

[69] *Hubbard v. Vosper* [1972] 2 Q.B. 84.

[70] *Lion Laboratories v. Evans* [1985] 1 Q.B. 526.

[71] *Woodward v. Hutchins* [1977] All E.R. 751; *X v. Y*, above, n. 59.

[72] *Smith Kline & French Laboratories (Australia) Limited v. Department of Community Services* (1990) 95 A.L.R. 87, *per* Gummow J.

[73] [1993] 3 I.R. 67.

versial acquisition of property by Telecom Éireann. The plaintiff sought an injunction restraining the use by the inspector of the information. O'Hanlon J. stated:

> "I would think that the protection of a free society must rest on surer grounds than the operation of the affairs of state in water-tight compartments. There appears to me to be a clear public interest in having all the information needed by the inspector for the purposes of his investigation made available. I do not detect the existence of any significant public interest of equal or near-equal weight in denying access by the inspector to this source of information."[74]

This decision, which appears to favour a balancing approach to the application of the public interest defence, establishes that the action for breach of confidence and consequently of section 26(1)(b) is subject to strong public interest considerations in situations where the person seeking access to the information is a public body. It is also significant in establishing the public interest defence to the action for breach of confidence in Ireland generally.

The scope of the public interest defence in the context of government confidences was examined in the Australian federal case of *Commonwealth of Australia v. John Fairfax & Sons Ltd.*[75] Mason J. drew the following distinction between the role of the public interest defence in relation to confidential government information and other types of information:

> "The equitable principle has been fashioned to protect the personal, private and proprietary rights of the citizen, not to protect the very different interests of the executive government. It acts, or is supposed to act, not according to standards of private interest, but in the public interest. This is not to say that equity will not protect information in the hands of the government, but it is to say that when Equity protects government information it will look at the matter through different spectacles."[76]

Mason J.'s statement of the law in *Fairfax* was approved by Carroll J. in *Attorney General for England and Wales v. Brandon Books Ltd.*[77] The use of the action for breach of confidence to restrict access to internal records of public bodies is, in any case, severely limited by section 26(2).

2. The public interest test in section 26(3)

Guidance with respect to the operation of the statutory public interest test which applies to section 26(1)(a) may be gleaned from the decisions concerning the operation of the public interest test in the context of the action for breach of confidence generally. It is clear, however, that a broader approach to

---

[74] Above, n. 73, at 102.
[75] Above, n. 58.
[76] *ibid.* at 51.
[77] Above, n. 62.

the determination of the public interest is required in the context of the operation of a public interest test forming part of a FOI Act. The basis of the Irish FOI Act as declared in the long title to the Act is the provision of a right of access to government information. The public interest in disclosure or the withholding of information should, therefore, be judged in terms of attainment of that objective, rather than on the basis of whether disclosure would reveal crimes, fraud, misdeeds or danger to the public. As to the most appropriate manner for determining where the public interest lies, it is clear from the use of the phrase "on balance" that what the Oireachtas had in mind was a balancing of the public interest in disclosure against the public interest in maintaining the confidentiality of the information.

G. Consultation with Third Parties

Where the head of a public body decides to disclose information obtained in confidence on public interest grounds, there is an obligation on the head, under section 29, to carry out a process of consultation. This consultation or "reverse FOI mechanism", as it is also known, is aimed at giving people likely to be affected by FOI disclosures the opportunity to have an input into the decision of whether to release information.

Section 29 provides that before the head of a public body can decide to grant a request for access to information obtained in confidence on public interest grounds, he or she must comply with the consultation requirements set out in that section. These oblige the head of the public body concerned, within two weeks of receiving a request, to notify the person who gave the information to the public body and, if he or she considers it appropriate, the person to whom the information relates, informing him or her that the request falls to be granted in the public interest.[78] The notification must be in writing, or in such other form as may be determined by the Minister for Finance.[79] The person who is so notified then has three weeks within which to make submissions in relation to the request.[80]

The head is obliged to consider such submissions before deciding whether to grant the request.[81] The outcome of the consultation process must be decided within two weeks of receipt of submissions or, if no submissions are received, within two weeks of the expiry of the three-week deadline for the making of submissions.[82] Persons notified under section 29 must be informed

---

[78] s.29(2).
[79] s.29(2).
[80] s.29(2)(ii).
[81] s.29(3)(a).
[82] s.29(4).

in writing of the decision arrived at and of their right of appeal.[83] The requester also has the right to appeal a decision under section 29.[84]

The requester will be appealing a decision to refuse access to the information, while a person notified under section 29 will be appealing against the decision of the head to disclose the information. Appeals must be brought within two weeks of notification of the decision.[85] The Commissioner is obliged to notify the requester, any third party consulted under section 29, and the head of the public body concerned of the bringing of an appeal;[86] each of them has the right to make submissions to the Commissioner in relation to the appeal.[87] These submissions must be taken into account by the Commissioner for the purposes of the review.[88]

If the head cannot comply with the consultation requirements, despite having taken all reasonable steps to do so, he or she can go ahead with the decision to grant or refuse the request, provided that the Information Commissioner consents to the non-compliance.[89] Where the Commissioner does not consent to such non-compliance, he or she must direct the head as to what steps should be taken for the purpose of complying with the consultation obligation. If, having taken those steps, the head is still unable to comply with the consultation requirement, he or she must go ahead and make the decision whether to grant or refuse the request.[90]

Section 34(12)(a) places the burden of proof on the person objecting to the disclosure. It provides that a decision to grant a request to which section 29 applies, shall be presumed to have been justified, unless a third party consulted under section 29 shows to the satisfaction of the Commissioner that the decision was not justified.

One question which has arisen in Australia is whether the identity of the requester should be revealed to a person in respect of whom consultation obligations arise. There is nothing in the Australian or, for that matter, the Irish FOI Act to prevent a public body identifying the requester to the third party. On the one hand, it can be argued that since the applicant will not be restricted in how he or she uses the information if the request is successful, the identify of the requester is irrelevant, and to disclose it to the third party may give him or her a false expectation that the information will go no further than the requester. On the other hand, the identity of the applicant may be relevant to the third party's consideration of whether they could consider the record to be

---

[83] s.29(3).
[84] s.34(1) and 34(15).
[85] s.34(4)(a).
[86] s.34(6).
[87] s.34(8).
[88] s.34(8).
[89] s.29(5).
[90] s.29(6).

exempt. If the third party does not know who is seeking the information, he or she may object to release of the information when, if the applicant was known, he or she would not object. In some cases, the requester may have genuine grounds for opposing disclosure of his or her identity to the third party. The Australian ALRC/ARC review of the operation of the Australian federal FOI Act considered this issue but did not make any definitive recommendation on the matter, saying instead that it should be left to the discretion of the public body. However, the review did state that it will generally be desirable to give the requester the opportunity to comment before his or her identity is disclosed to the third party and that it should be made clear to the third party that the requester will not be prevented from distributing the record as he or she sees fit, should the request for access be granted.[91] Given that the basis of the Act is openness, it is submitted that the identity of the requester should, as a general rule, be disclosed. It should, as suggested, be made clear to third parties that information released under freedom of information is disclosed to the world at large.

---

[91] Australian Law Reform Commission/Administrative Review Council, *op. cit.* above, n. 7, para. 10.17.

CHAPTER 13

COMMERCIALLY SENSITIVE INFORMATION

CHAPTER 13

COMMERCIALLY SENSITIVE INFORMATION

A. Introduction

Public bodies hold large quantities of commercial information. Such information may be generated within the public body or it may be supplied to the public body by third parties. Information may be supplied voluntarily, as in the case of tender documents, or on a compulsory basis, in order to fulfil regulatory requirements, for example, in relation to taxation. Much of this information has commercial value and, in some cases, the provision of access to it could greatly benefit competitors. Section 27 of the FOI Act, in common with its overseas equivalents,[1] is designed to ensure that commercially sensitive information will not become accessible through the operation of the access rights conferred by the Act. The exemption is expressed in the following terms:

"27.—(1) Subject to subsection (2), a head shall refuse to grant a request under section 7 if the record concerned contains—

(a) trade secrets of a person other than the requester concerned,

(b) financial, commercial, scientific or technical or other information whose disclosure could reasonably be expected to result in a material financial loss or gain to the person to whom the information relates, or

---

[1] Australia: Freedom of Information Act 1982 (Cth), s.43; Freedom of Information Act 1982 (Victoria), s.34; Freedom of Information Act 1989 (New South Wales), Sched.1, cl.7; Freedom of Information Act 1991 (South Australia), Sched.1, cl.7; Freedom of Information Act 1991 (Tasmania), s.31; Freedom of Information Act 1992 (Queensland), s.45; Freedom of Information Act 1992 (Western Australia), Sched.1, cl.4.
Canada: Access to Information Act (Canada), R.S.C., 1985, s.20; Right to Information Act (New Brunswick), S.N.B., 1978, s.6(c) and s.6(c.1); Freedom of Information Act (Newfoundland), R.S.N., 1990, s.11(f); An Act respecting Access to documents held by public bodies and the Protection of personal information (Quebec), S.Q., 1982, ss.23, 24, 27; Freedom of Information and Protection of Privacy Act (Manitoba), C.C.S.M., 1998, c.F175, s.18; Freedom of Information and Protection of Privacy Act (Ontario), R.S.O., 1990, s.17(1); Freedom of Information and Protection of Privacy Act (Saskatchewan), S.S., 1990–1991, s.19(1); Freedom of Information and Protection of Privacy Act (British Columbia), R.S.B.C., 1996, s.21(1)(a) and (b); Freedom of Information and Protection of Privacy Act (Nova Scotia), S.N.S., 1993, s.21(1)(a); Freedom of Information and Protection of Privacy Act (Alberta), S.A., 1994, s.20(1).
New Zealand: Official Information Act 1982, s.8.
U.S.: Freedom of Information Act 1966, Exemption 4.

could prejudice the competitive position of that person in the conduct of his or her profession or business or otherwise in his or her occupation, or

(c) information whose disclosure could prejudice the conduct or outcome of contractual or other negotiations of the person to whom the information relates.

(2) A head shall grant a request under section 7 to which subsection (1) relates if—

(a) the person to whom the record concerned relates consents, in writing or in such other form as may be determined, to access to the record being granted to the requester concerned,

(b) information of the same kind as that contained in the record in respect of persons generally or a class of persons that is, having regard to all the circumstances, of significant size, is available to the general public,

(c) the record relates only to the requester,

(d) information contained in the record was given to the public body concerned by the person to whom it relates and the person was informed on behalf of the body, before its being so given, that the information belongs to a class of information that would or might be made available to the general public, or

(e) disclosure of the information concerned is necessary in order to avoid a serious and imminent danger to the life or health of an individual or to the environment.

(3) Subject to section 29, subsection (1) does not apply in relation to a case in which, in the opinion of the head concerned, the public interest would, on balance, be better served by granting than by refusing to grant the request under section 7 concerned."

There are three limbs to this exemption, the application of which is mandatory. The first, section 27(1)(a), which amounts to a class type exemption, protects trade secrets against disclosure. It is followed by two harm based provisions. The first of these, section 27(1)(b), covers financial, commercial, scientific, technical or other information. There are two strands to the harm test provided for under section 27(1)(b). The first exempts records, the disclosure of which could reasonably be expected to result in material financial loss or gain to the person to whom the information relates, while the second exempts records where their disclosure could prejudice the competitive position of that person in the conduct of his or her profession or business or otherwise in his or her occupation. The third limb of the exemption, section 27(1)(c), is also harm based. The disclosure of records containing information which could prejudice the conduct or outcome of contractual negotiations or other negotiations of the person to whom the information relates is exempted.

Section 27(2) sets out a number of exceptions to the exemption. It provides that the head of a public body shall disclose a record to which the exemption relates in the following circumstances:

(a) where the person to whom the record relates consents;

(b) where information of the same kind is publicly available;

(c) where the record relates only to the requester;

(d) where the person concerned has been informed prior to the supply of the information that the information constitutes part of a class of information liable to be made publicly available;

(e) where disclosure is necessary to prevent serious and imminent threat to the life or health of an individual or to the environment.

The exemption is also qualified by a public interest test which provides that section 27(1) will not apply where, in the opinion of the head of the public body concerned, the public interest would, on balance, be better served by granting than by refusing to grant the request. This operation of the public interest test is subject to the third party consultation provisions set out in section 29.

Each limb of the exemption refers to commercially sensitive information of a "person". Person is defined in the Interpretation Act 1937 "as importing a body corporate (whether a corporation aggregate or a corporation sole) and an unincorporated body or persons as well as an individual".[2] It therefore includes individuals, partnerships, companies and unincorporated associations. It is not clear whether the exemption applies in respect of commercially sensitive information relating to public bodies, or whether its scope is limited to the protection of commercially sensitive information of private sector "persons". There is nothing in the text of section 27 to limit its application to the private sector.

It is arguable that, given the existence in the Act of separate protection for financial and economic interests of the State and public bodies under section 31, and bearing in mind the purpose of the Act, as stated in the long title, to enable members of the public to obtain access to information "to the greatest extent possible", section 27 should be confined to commercially sensitive information of private individuals or bodies other than public bodies. This was the approach of the Australian Federal Court when the application of the corresponding Australian exemption (section 43) of the Australian federal Act to commercial information of public bodies arose for consideration in *Harris v. Australian Broadcasting Corporation*.[3] Although the application of section 43 was not expressly limited to commercial information of persons outside the public sector, Beaumont J. held that:

---

[2] s.11.
[3] (1983) 50 A.L.R. 551.

"[T]he benefit of the operation of section 43 is not available to a person within an agency or undertaking. Nor, in my view, is it available to the agency or undertaking itself: the section read in conjunction with section 3(1)(b) [the objects section] and the explanatory memorandum make it plain enough that it is a provision the object of which is to protect, within reasonable limits, the interests of third parties dealing with the agency or undertaking and supplying information to it in the course of that dealing . . . ".[4]

Similarly, in the U.S., where the relevant exemption refers to "information obtained from a person",[5] it has been established that where the information is generated by the government, it cannot fall within the scope of the exemption.[6]

B.   Trade Secrets: Section 27(1)(a)

The first category of commercially sensitive information protected under section 27 is that of records which contain trade secrets. The exemption provided in respect of trade secrets is a class exemption, the application of which depends on the scope of the legal concept of trade secrets.

One issue which arises is whether trade secrets amount to an independent legal concept, or whether they are merely a category of confidential information. This has some significance in practical terms in that, if the latter is true, regard must be had to the applicability of the three elements of the action for breach of confidence to information sought to be exempted on the basis that it is a trade secret. The three prerequisites of the action for breach of confidence are: first, that the information have the necessary quality of confidence about it; second, that information has been imparted in circumstances imposing an obligation of confidence; and third, that there was an unauthorised use of that information to the detriment of the party communicating it.[7] The leading authority on the law of confidence, Gurry, has written that the term "trade secret" is not generally used as a term of art by the English courts but that it may be profitably employed to describe "that class of confidential information which is associated with business or industry".[8] This approach was supported by the statement of Gowans J. in the Australian case of *Ansell Rubber Co. Pty Ltd v. Allied Rubber Industries Pty Ltd* to the effect that the concept of trade secrets was only "a particular subject matter to which the principles relating to breach of confidence have been applied".[9] The Irish courts, too, appear to be pre-

---

[4] Above, n. 3, at 565.
[5] Exemption 4.
[6] *Consumers Union v. Veterans Administration*, 301 F. Supp. 796 at 803 (S.D.N.Y. 1969); *Grumman Aircraft Engineering Corporation v. Renegotiation Board*, 425 F.2d 578 at 582 (D.C. Cir. 1970).
[7] *Coco v. A.N. Clark Engineers Limited* [1969] F.S.R. 415 at 419–420.
[8] Gurry, *Breach of Confidence* (Clarendon Press, 1984), p. 7.
[9] [1967] V.R. 37 at 46.

pared to treat trade secrets as an aspect of confidential information in general.[10]

However, it can be argued that in the context of FOI legislation, trade secrets cannot be equated with confidential information. The Irish trade secrets exemption is based largely on its Canadian and, to a lesser extent, its Australian counterparts. Each of these was, in turn, based on the trade secrets exemption in the U.S. FOI Act. In the U.S., trade secrets are recognised as an independent legal concept. They were defined in the U.S. *Restatement of Torts* as long ago as 1939.[11] Thus, it can be argued that a distinction can be drawn for the purposes of the FOI Act between confidential information and trade secrets. This approach makes sense in view of the separate provision in the Act for the exemption of information obtained in confidence.[12]

The existence of a distinction between "trade secrets" and confidential information is supported by the Queensland Information Commissioner's approach to the trade secrets exemption in the Queensland FOI Act, which has been to emphasise the first requirement of the action for breach of confidence, while downplaying the significance of the other elements of the action. In *Re Cannon and Australian Quality Egg Farms Ltd*,[13] the Commissioner said that the application of the trade secrets exemption:

> "depends primarily on the proper characterisation of the information in issue as matter that would disclose trade secrets of an agency or other person. There is no need to specifically identify a confider or confidee, nor to explore whether the circumstances of communication of the information give rise to an obligation of confidence."[14]

The acceptance of a distinction between "trade secrets" and confidential information may lead to an understanding of "trade secrets" which is narrower in scope than the type of information protected under the action for breach of confidence. Whether it does depends on the definition of trade secrets adopted for the purpose of section 27(1)(a). U.S. jurisprudence with respect to the trade secrets exemptions has resulted in the development of two opposing views of the scope of the concept. The first is based largely on the definition of trade secrets in the *Restatement of Torts*. It defined trade secret broadly as:

> "[Any] formula, pattern, device, or compilation of information which is used in one's business, and which gives him an opportunity to obtain an advantage over competitors who do not know or use it."[15]

---

[10] *House of Spring Gardens v. Point Blank Ltd* [1984] I.R. 611.
[11] Sec.757, comment b (1939).
[12] s.26.
[13] (1994) 1 Q.A.R. 491.
[14] *ibid.* at 507.
[15] Above, n. 11.

This definition has been relied upon by the U.S. Supreme Court in a non-FOI setting[16] and has also been referred to in a number of U.S. FOI cases.[17] It was, however, rejected by the District of Columbia Circuit in *Public Citizen Health Research Group v. FDA*[18] as being "inconsistent with the language of the FOIA and its underlying policies". The court held instead that for FOI purposes, the term "trade secret" should be limited in meaning to:

> "a secret, commercially valuable plan, formula, process, or device that is used for the making, preparing, compounding, or processing of trade commodities and that can be said to be the end product of either innovation or substantial effort".[19]

The difference between these two definitions is that under the *Restatement*, virtually any compilation of business information would amount to a trade secret, whereas under the *Public Citizen* test, the designation "trade secret" is limited to information relating directly to the production process.

In Canada, a narrow approach to the definition of trade secret has been adopted at federal level. In *Merck Frosst Canada Inc. v. Canada (Minister of Health and Welfare)*[20] it was accepted, *obiter,* that the term "trade secret" should be reserved for more "technical production information". And in *Société Gamma Inc. v. Canada (Department of the Secretary of State)*[21] it was stated that the term "trade secrets" must be given a reasonably narrow interpretation. A trade secret, it was held, must be something probably of a technical nature which is guarded very closely and is of such peculiar value to the owner of the trade secret that harm to him would be presumed by its mere disclosure.[22] A broader view has, however, been adopted in Ontario. The following definition of trade secrets, taken from a report of the Alberta Institute of Law Research and Law Reform,[23] was approved by the Information and Privacy Commissioner:

> "information including but not limited to a formula, pattern, compilation, programme, method, technique, or process or information contained or embodied in a product, device or mechanism which

---

[16] *Kewanee Oil Co. v. Bicron Corp.,* 416 U.S. 470 at 474–475 (1974).

[17] *Washington Research Project, Inc. v. HEW,* 504 F.2d 238 at 245 n 8 (D.C. Cir. 1974); *Union Oil Co. of California v. Federal Power Commission,* 542 F.2d 1036 at 1044 (9th Cir. 1976); *Chevron Chemical Co. v. Castle,* 443 F. Supp. 1024 at 1032 n. 4 (N.D. Cal. 1978).

[18] 704 F.2d 1280 (D.C. Cir. 1983).

[19] *ibid.* at 1288. This definition was based on a similar definition set forth in a pre-FOIA case defining the term: *Norwegian Nitrogen Products Co. v. United States Tariff Commission,* 6 F.2d 491 at 495 (D.C. Cir. 1925), *vacated as moot,* 274 U.S. 106 (1927). It has been expressly adopted by the U.S. Tenth Circuit in the FOI case: *Anderson v. Department of Health and Human Services,* 907 F.2d 936 at 944 (10th Cir. 1990).

[20] (1988) 22 C.P.R. (3d) 177 (F.C.T.D.).

[21] (1994) 56 C.P.R. (3d) 58; 79 F.T.R. 42 (F.C.T.D.).

[22] *ibid.* at 62–63.

[23] Alberta Institute of Law Research and Law Reform, *Trade Secrets* (1986).

(i)   is or may be used in a trade or business,

(ii) is not generally known in that trade or business,

(iii) has economic value from not being generally known, and

(iv) is the subject of efforts that are reasonable under the circumstances to maintain its secrecy."[24]

In Australia, the meaning of "trade secrets" has also been subjected to scrutiny in the FOI context. In *Searle Australia Pty Ltd v. Public Interest Advocacy Centre & Anor*[25] the narrower *Public Citizen* approach to the definition of trade secrets appeared to be favoured by the Federal Court when it made the following statement:

> "An aspect of the concept of 'trade secrets' . . . is that the secrets must be used in or useable in the trade. A trade secret is an asset of the trade. Past history and even current information, such as mere financial particulars, may be confidential. The law may protect disclosure of such information by a person who has obtained it in the course of a relationship which requires confidentiality, such as that of employee, solicitor or accountant. But such information may not be a trade secret."[26]

Thus, in order to qualify as a trade secret under the Australian FOI Act, the information must be more than confidential information: it must be used in or useable in the trade.

The Australian Federal Court has, however, stopped short of requiring that a trade secret be technical in nature. In *Re Organon (Australia) Pty Ltd and Department of Community Services and Health*[27] the Administrative Appeals Tribunal (A.A.T.) set out seven factors to which regard should be had in determining the existence of trade secrets for the purposes of the FOI Act. They were:

(1) whether the information is of a technical character;

(2) the extent to which the information is known outside the business of the owner of that information;

(3) the extent to which the information is known by persons engaged in the owner's business;

(4) measures taken by the owner to guard the secrecy of the information;

(5) the value of the information to the owner and to his competitors;

(6) the effort and money spent by the owner in developing the information;

---

[24] *Re Etobicoke Board of Education*, unreported, Information and Privacy Commissioner, Ontario, Order M–29, July 30, 1992.

[25] (1992) 108 A.L.R. 163.

[26] *ibid.* at 174.

[27] (1987) 13 A.L.D. 588.

(7) the ease or difficulty with which others might acquire or duplicate the secret.[28]

All but the first of these indicia had been listed by Gowans J. in *Ansell Rubber*[29] as the factors relevant to a determination of whether information constituted a trade secret. In *Searle*, the Federal Court on appeal eschewed the requirement of technicality. The court said:

> "It may be that the more technical the information is, the more likely it is that, as a matter of fact, the information will be classed as a trade secret. But technicality is not required."[30]

To summarise, it appears that the term "trade secret" in FOI legislation applies to a narrower range of information than confidential information. The requirement that the information be technical in nature appears to be inherent in the U.S. *Public Citizen* definition of "trade secret". Such a requirement is also part of the Canadian definition of "trade secret". In Australia, despite the rejection of the technicality requirement, it is clear from the decision in *Searle* that the fact that information is confidential will not automatically render it a "trade secret".

It is clear that in all jurisdictions the requirement of secrecy is of the utmost importance. For example, in the Canadian case of *Merck Frosst Canada Inc. v. Canada (Minister of Health and Welfare)*[31] the court concluded that a document which indicates the drug manufacturer's intention to change the dosage size of a product was not a trade secret, since the information had been disclosed in a product which was no longer a secret, trade or otherwise.[32]

C.   Other Commercially Sensitive Information: Section 27(1)(b)

The second limb of the exemption offers protection against disclosure to a wider category of information than is protected under the trade secrets provision, but only where the requirements of one or other of its two harm tests is met. The protection of commercially sensitive information, apart from trade secrets, is a common feature of FOI legislation.[33] Section 27(1)(b) is expressed

---

[28] Above, n. 27, at 593–594.
[29] *Ansell Rubber Co. Pty Ltd v. Allied Rubber Industries Pty Ltd*, above, n. 9.
[30] *Searle Australia Pty Ltd v. Public Interest Advocacy Centre*, above, n. 25, at 174.
[31] Above, n. 20.
[32] See also *Canada Post Corp. v. Canada (Minister of Public Works)* [1993] 3 F.C. 320 (T.D.), *aff'd* (1993), 64 F.T.R. 62 (F.C.A.); and *Matol Botanical International Inc. v. Canada (Minister of National Health and Welfare)* (1994) 84 F.T.R. 168 (F.C.T.D.) where it was held that information disclosed in a product monograph is no longer a secret.
[33] Canada: Access to Information Act (Canada), R.S.C., 1985, s.20(1)(c); New Zealand:

in terms almost identical to section 20(1)(c) of the Canadian Access to Information Act. In order to qualify for exemption under this provision it must be shown that:

1. the requested record falls within the scope of section 27(1)(b); and

2. its disclosure satisfies one of the harm tests.

1. Scope of section 27(1)(b)

This part of the exemption applies to "financial, commercial, scientific, technical or other information". It is likely that the "other information" referred to must be information of a type similar to financial, commercial, scientific or technical information. The Australian counterpart of this exemption refers to "business, commercial and financial affairs". This provision has been interpreted as being intended "to embody the totality of money-making affairs of an organisation or undertaking as distinct from its private or internal affairs".[34] While section 27(1)(b) is framed in broader terms in that it extends to the additional categories of scientific and technical information, it is clear that it, too, was not intended to cover information relating to the private or internal affairs of undertakings.

(a) Financial and commercial information

The following definition of the term "commercial information" has been adopted by the Ontarian Information and Privacy Commissioner in interpreting the equivalent provision in the Ontario Freedom of Information and Protection of Privacy Act 1990:

> "[C]ommercial information is information which relates solely to the buying, selling or exchange of merchandise or services. The term 'commercial' information can apply to both profit-making enterprises and non-profit organizations, and has equal application to both large and small enterprises." [35]

The Ontarian Commissioner also put forward a definition of financial information which provides that:

> "financial information refers to *specific data* on the use and distribution of money, such as information on pricing practices profit and loss data, overhead and operating costs."[36]

Official Information Act 1982, s.8; Australia: Freedom of Information Act 1982 (Cth), s.43(1)(b) and (c); U.S.: Freedom of Information Act 1966, Exemption 4.

[34] *Re Cockcroft and Attorney General's Department* (1985) 12 A.L.D. 462 at 467.

[35] *Re Ministry of Municipal Affairs*, unreported, Information and Privacy Commissioner, Ontario, Order P–493, July 9, 1993.

[36] *Re Ministry of Health*, unreported, Information and Privacy Commissioner, Ontario, Order 80, July 26, 1989. Emphasis included in original definition.

One form of commercial/financial information which has given rise to case law in both Canada and Australia is information relating to tenders. In the Western Australian case of *Re Maddock Lonie and Chisholm (a firm) and Department of State Services*[37] the Information Commissioner decided that disclosure of the prices offered by unsuccessful tenderers did not qualify for exemption under the relevant exemption, but that detailed descriptions of the manner in which tender prices were calculated (disclosing a company's margins, costs and approach to tendering) did qualify for exemption under that provision.[38] In the Queensland case of *Re Sexton Trading Co. Pty Ltd and South Coast Regional Health Authority*[39] access was granted to prices of individual items making up a tender for the supply of a range of goods. Access was granted on the basis that the documents in issue did not contain any indications of the component elements of the tender price for each item. The Commissioner noted that there was nothing in the documents which directly disclosed the third party's margins, or the costs at which the third party could obtain materials from its suppliers.[40] In the Ontarian case of *Ontario Northland Transportation Commission*,[41] the applicant, who was an unsuccessful tenderer, had been informed of the name of the successful tenderer and of the total amount of the successful tenderer's offer. He sought access to a range of other information relating to the tender. The Commissioner held that disclosure of the amount of time the tenderer would require to complete construction and the unit prices for different types of work to be carried out would could reasonably be expected to result in one of the types of harm specified in the exemption. He ordered that the names of the sub-contractors the tenderer intended to use be disclosed, but not the amounts to be paid to each sub-contractor.

In Ireland, the disclosure of information relating to tenders is regulated by a combination of E.U. law and domestic guidelines.[42] The E.U. provisions, which apply in respect of contracts which exceed specified thresholds, have been imported into Irish law by way of statutory instruments.[43] They require that unsuccessful tenderers be informed of the name of the successful tenderer

---

[37] Unreported, Information Commissioner, Western Australia, Decision No. D01595, June 2, 1995.
[38] *ibid.* at paras 33, 43, and 46.
[39] (1995) 3 Q.A.R. 132.
[40] *ibid.* at 140.
[41] Unreported, Information and Privacy Commissioner, Ontario, Order 166, May 4, 1990.
[42] See generally: McCourt, *Public Buyer Guide: A guide to Public Sector Procurement and E.U. Regulations* (An Bórd Trachtála/Irish Institute of Purchasing and Materials Management, Dublin, 1996); Hogan and Morgan, *Administrative Law in Ireland* (3rd ed., Round Hall Sweet & Maxwell, Dublin, 1998), pp. 124–128.
[43] European Communities (Award of Public Service Contracts) Regulations, 1993 (S.I. No. 173 of 1993); European Communities (Award of Public Works Contracts) (Amendment) Regulations, 1994 (S.I. No. 293 of 1994); European Communities (Award of Public Supply Contracts) (Amendment) Regulations, 1993 (S.I. No. 292 of 1994).

and of the reasons for rejection of his or her tender.[44] In the case of contracts
which are for amounts lower than the E.U. thresholds, the rules relating to
public procurement are to be found in the *Public Procurement Book* (1994),
also known as the "Green Book". The Green Book recommends that contracting Authorities adopt a policy of releasing general information to unsuccessful tenderers if they enquire why their tenders were unsuccessful. It suggests,
for example, that they may be told that they were unsuccessful on price grounds.
However, the Book urges that the disclosure of such information should be
done without revealing information about other tenders which could enable
the price or other details of other tenders to be identified.[45] If the approach of
the Information Commissioners in Western Australia, Queensland and Ontario to access to tender information is adopted in this jurisdiction, disclosure
of information relating to tenders could extend beyond the requirements of the
relevant E.U. Directives and the guidelines in the Green Book to include details such as the names and prices submitted by unsuccessful tenders, the prices
of individual items, and names of sub-contractors.

(b) Scientific and technical information

The Ontarian Information and Privacy Commissioner has defined scientific
information as:

> "information belonging to an organized field of knowledge in either the natural,
> biological or social sciences or mathematics. In addition, for information to be
> characterized as scientific, it must relate to the observation and testing of spe-
> cific hypothesis or conclusions and be undertaken by an expert in the field."[46]

Technical information was defined as:

> "information belonging to an organized field of knowledge which would fall
> under the general categories of applied sciences or mechanical arts. Examples
> of these fields would include architecture, engineering or electronics. While,
> admittedly, it is difficult to define technical information in a precise fashion, it
> will usually involve information prepared by a professional in the field and
> describe the construction, operation or maintenance of a structure, process, equip-
> ment or thing."[47]

In the British Columbian case *Cowichan Estuary Preservation Society and
Ministry of Environment, Lands and Parks*[48] it was held that environmental

---

[44] Council Directive 92/50/EEC, Art. 12; Council Directive 93/36/EEC, Art. 7; Council
Directive 93/37/EEC, Art. 8.

[45] *Public Procurement Book* (1994), para. 5.15.

[46] *Re Ontario Native Affairs Secretariat*, unreported, Information and Privacy Commissioner, Ontario, Order P–454, May 7, 1993.

[47] *ibid.*

[48] Unreported, Information and Privacy Commissioner, British Columbia, Order 56, October 4, 1995.

tests fall within the meaning of technical information for the purposes of the relevant exemption.

2. The harm tests in section 27(1)(b)

(a) Material loss or gain

The first harm test provided for under section 27(1)(b) exempts the disclosure of records which "could reasonably be expected to result in a material financial loss or gain to the person to whom the information relates". This provision differs from its federal Canadian counterpart[49] in that the loss or gain must accrue to the person to whom the information relates, while in Canada the loss or gain may accrue to a third party. Third party is defined in the Canadian federal Act to mean any person other than the person who made the request or a government institution. The scope of the Irish exemption is, therefore, slightly narrower than the Canadian one, since in Canada it is sufficient to demonstrate loss or gain to any person. Under the Irish provision, loss or gain to the person to whom the information relates must be established.

This difference in phrasing is also significant in terms of the application of the exemption to records, the disclosure of which could result in material *gain*. The justification for the inclusion in FOI legislation of exemptions relating to business information is that disclosure under FOI should not be damaging to businesses which have dealings with public bodies. Such damage may come about through the disclosure of business information which results in unfair advantage to the competitors of those who do business with public bodies. This latter aspect of the protection afforded to businesses is seen in the exemption of records, the disclosure of which could result in material gain. The equivalent Canadian provision applies in the case of material gain to *any person,* and will, therefore, apply to situations where disclosure is likely to result in gain to a business competitor of the person to whom the information relates. Section 27(1)(b), on the other hand, exempts the disclosure of records which could reasonably be expected to result in a material gain *to the person to whom the information relates.* It would appear that in applying this element of the harm test, the fact that a third party might gain from the disclosure of the information may not be taken into account.

An example of the type of situation to which this provision could apply would be one in which a public body has in its possession information relating to a company, which if disclosed would be beneficial to that company. This element of the exemption would prevent that company from engineering the disclosure of the information in an attempt to benefit itself, for example, by encouraging a journalist to make an application for access to the relevant records.

---

[49] Access to Information Act (Canada), R.S.C., 1985, s.20(1)(c).

In Canada, the main issue to have arisen in respect of interpretation of this provision is that of the standard of certainty required by the phrase "could reasonably be expected to". The standard of proof required to establish that harm "could reasonably be expected" to occur is discussed in detail above at pp. 90–92. In short, decisions in Canada[50] and in Australia[51] have indicated that the possibility of the specified harm occurring will not suffice to meet the burden of proof, but neither is it necessary to show evidence of a direct causation between disclosure and harm. Nor does it appear necessary, in either jurisdiction, to show that the occurrence of the harm is more probable than not. In both jurisdictions the emphasis is on the reasonableness of the expectation of harm arising out of the disclosure.

Given the reference to "material financial" loss or gain, it is clear that the loss or gain must be pecuniary in nature. In terms of the scale of harm required, in the Canadian case of *Burns Meats Ltd v. Canada (Minister of Agriculture)*[52] a company showed that previous disclosures of similar material had caused a loss of $200,000 to $300,000, which amounted to less than one per cent of the company's annual sales. The court held that the exemption did not apply since the company's sales would be affected to a relatively minor degree. In Australia, information which is aged or out of date has been held to have no financial value.[53]

(b) Competitive harm

The second harm test provided for under section 27(1)(b) exempts records, the disclosure of which could prejudice the competitive position of the person to whom the information relates in the conduct of his or her profession or business, or otherwise in his or her occupation. The standard of proof of harm required, *i.e.* "could prejudice", is lower than that required under the "could reasonably be expected to prejudice" test. In the Australian case *News Corporation Ltd v. National Companies and Securities Commission*,[54] Woodward J. drew a distinction between two analogous phrases in the following terms:

> "I think that the words 'would or could reasonably be expected to ... prejudice' mean more than 'would or might prejudice'. A reasonable expectation of an event requires more than a possibility, risk or chance of the event occurring."[55]

---

[50] *Canada Packers v. Minister of Agriculture* (1988) 53 D.L.R. (4th) 246; 26 C.P.R. (3d) 407.

[51] *Re Cockcroft and Attorney General's Department*, above, n. 34; *Searle Australia Pty Ltd v. Public Interest Advocacy Centre Anor*, above, n. 25. See also the Queensland case *Re B. and Brisbane North Regional Health Authority* (1994) 1 Q.A.R. 279.

[52] (1987) 14 F.T.R. 137 (F.C.T.D.).

[53] *Re Angel and Department of Arts, Heritage and Environment* (1985) 9 A.L.D. 113.

[54] (1984) 57 A.L.R. 550.

[55] *ibid.* at 561.

The type of prejudices of which proof of occurrence is required under the terms of this part of the exemption is prejudice to the competitive position of the person to whom the information relates in the conduct of his or her profession or business, or otherwise in his or her occupation. In the U.S. it has been held that in order to demonstrate the likelihood of competitive harm arising out of a disclosure under the FOI Act, the public body must:

(1) show that the person who has supplied the information to the public body faces actual competition;[56] and

(2) demonstrate with specific and direct evidence the likely consequences of disclosure.[57]

The requirement that the existence of actual competition be established is aimed at providing a higher degree of protection against disclosure of commercial information to companies engaged in competitive business activities, than to those operating in monopoly situations. In meeting the second of these requirements, it has been held in the U.S. that generalised allegations of competitive harm will not suffice.[58]

The competitive harm must arise in the conduct of the profession or business or occupation of the person to whom the information relates. The meaning of professional affairs in the context of the Australian commercial information exemption was considered in *Young v. Wicks*.[59] A request had been made for access to information which included information relating to Young's capacity as a pilot. In the Federal Court, Beaumont J. stated that the ordinary meaning of "professional" was associated with theology, law and medicine, but observed further that whether a particular vocation was a profession was subject to changing views within the community. However, as the applicant had failed to provide any evidence in support of his argument, his Honour was not willing to expand the traditional notion of professional affairs to include pilots' affairs.[60]

In the Queensland case of *Re Pope and Queensland Health*,[61] the Queensland Information Commissioner listed the following set of indicators as to when a vocation answers the description of a "profession" for the purposes of the relevant provision of the Queensland Act:

"(a) The vocation requires special advanced knowledge and skill with respect to

---

[56] *Worthington Compressors, Inc. v Costle*, 662 F.2d 45 (D.C. Cir. 1981); *Gulf & Western Industries Inc. v. U.S.*, 615 F.2d 527 (D.C. Cir. 1980); *National Parks and Conservation Association v. Kleppe*, 547 F.2d 673 (D.C. Cir. 1976).

[57] *ibid.*

[58] *Public Citizen Health Research Group v. FDA*, above, n. 18.

[59] (1986) 13 F.C.R. 85.

[60] *ibid.* at 90.

[61] (1994) 1 Q.A.R. 616.

some department of learning or science, which is used in its application to the affairs of others. The knowledge concerned has both a theoretical and practical aspect to it. The focus of the department of learning or science is primarily on the exercise of the intellect as opposed to performance of solely physical or manual skill. This factor would be characterised by completion of some form of tertiary study involving successful completion of assessment as a mandatory prerequisite for entry into the profession.

(b) As well as this study, requirements may exist for admission into, or by, a body or association that has control over membership of the group claiming to comprise the profession, perhaps by enforcing a recognised standard of ability as a prerequisite to entry.

(c) There be some ongoing requirement for good conduct by members of the profession, in the sense that commission of a breach of recognised standards of professional and ethical conduct will lead to disciplinary action being taken against the offender, with serious breaches resulting in loss of membership of the profession. This requirement will extend beyond satisfactory performance in the delivery of professional services, and will extend to a requirement that the person be of good character in the conduct of his or her life generally. These requirements give rise to professional codes of conduct which may either be established by the professional association itself, or by legislation. The professional code of conduct should not merely be voluntary; the obligation to comply with the code of conduct should be mandatory for all members of the profession.

(d) The aims of the professional group should include altruistic public service; members are intended to put the interests of the community before self-interest or the interests of their professional colleagues.

(e) There is widespread community acceptance and recognition of the vocation as a profession."[62]

D. Information Concerning Negotiations: Section 27(1)(c)

The final part of section 27 is aimed at exempting from disclosure information which could prejudice the conduct or outcome of contractual or other negotiations of the person to whom the information relates. The standard of proof of harm necessary appears, on the basis of Australian authority, to be satisfied by proof of possibility of the harm occurring.[63]

The meaning of the phrase "could reasonably be expected to interfere with contractual negotiations", which is used in the equivalent Canadian federal provision,[64] has been considered by the Canadian Federal Court. In *Société*

---

[62] Above, n. 61, at 635.
[63] See above, pp. 90–92 for a more detailed discussion of the standards of proof of harm required under the FOI Act.
[64] Access to Information Act (Canada), R.S.C., 1985, s.20(1)(d).

Gamma Inc. v. Canada (Department of the Secretary of State)[65] the court held it must refer to an obstruction of those negotiations and not merely the heightening of competition. Such a requirement could reasonably be attributed to section 27(1)(c) also on the grounds that the need to establish "prejudice to the conduct or outcome of negotiations" demands something more than just increased competition. In *Canada (Information Commissioner) v. Canada (Minister of External Affairs)*[66] the Federal Court held that the Canadian provision is intended to catch contractual situations not involving the day-to-day sales of a product. It was, however, conceded that the provision may have some relevance with respect to international sales.

E. Exceptions

Five exceptions to the application of section 27(1) are provided for. They arise in the following circumstances:

1. Where there is consent to disclosure

The first exception prevents the invocation of the exemption in circumstances where the person to whom the record relates has consented to its disclosure. The consent must be in writing or "in such other form as may be determined". "Determined" is defined in the definitions section[67] to mean determined by the Minister for Finance. The Minister may, for example, decide to allow for the giving of consent by electronic means.

2. Where information of the same kind is publicly available

This exception applies in two sets of circumstances. The first is where information of the same kind in respect of persons generally is available to the general public. Such information could, for example, consist of information available for inspection in public offices or information which has been published elsewhere. The second situation in which the exception applies is where information of the same kind in respect of classes of persons of significant size is publicly available.

3. Where the record relates only to the requester

The aim of this exception is to ensure that the exemption relating to commercially sensitive information cannot be used to deny access to records concerning the person making the request. It is clear from the use of the word "only"

---

[65] Above, n. 21.
[66] (1990) 72 D.L.R. (4th) 113; 28 C.P.R. (3d) 301.
[67] s.2.

that the exception is limited to records relating to the requester alone. It cannot be invoked in respect of records relating jointly to the requester and another undertaking.

4. Where the person has been informed of the possible disclosure

The fourth exception applies to information given to a public body by the person to whom the information relates in circumstances where the individual was informed prior to supplying the information that it was of a class that would or might be made available to the general public. The aim of this exception is to ensure that routine commercial information can be disclosed without the necessity of going through the consultation procedure provided for in section 29. There is no requirement that the person consent to such disclosure. The fact that the person supplying the information is informed of possible disclosure in advance gives him or her, at least in theory, the option of declining disclosure of the information to the public body concerned. The consequences of a failure to supply the information may, however, be such that there is no real choice to so decline.

5. Where disclosure is necessary to avoid danger to life, health, or the environment

This exception is the only substantive exception to the exemption. It prevents the use of section 27 to deny access to records which are necessary to avoid danger to life, health, or the environment. It could apply, for example, where the sensitive commercial information to which access is sought relates to a chemical company and includes information concerning a danger posed to public health or the environment. The use of the words "serious" and "imminent" raises two important questions in relation to the application of this exception: the first concerns the extent of the danger necessary to justify the exception and the second the imminence of that danger. There is no equivalent exception in overseas FOI legislation. The Canadian federal commercial information exemption does, however, contain a public interest test in which reference is made to the need to balance the harm likely to be caused by disclosure against the public interest in public health, public safety, or protection of the environment but this has not been subjected to judicial consideration.[68]

F.   Public Interest

The public interest test contained in section 27(3) provides that the commercially sensitive information exemption will not apply where, in the opinion of

---

[68]   Access to Information Act (Canada), R.S.C., 1985, s.20(6).

the head of the public body concerned, the public interest would, on balance,
be better served by granting than by refusing to grant the request. This provision is subject to the operation of the third party consultation provisions set
out in section 29, the effects of which are discussed above at pp. 241–243.

One issue which has arisen overseas in the context of the application of
public interest tests in commercially sensitive information exemptions is
whether a distinction should be drawn between compulsorily acquired commercial information and other commercial information. In particular, should
information which has been compulsorily acquired from private undertakings
be subject to disclosure under the FOI Act? Decision-makers in Australia and
New Zealand are slow to allow public interest considerations to justify disclosure of compulsorily acquired commercial information. In the Australian case
of *Re Actors' Equity Association of Australia and Australian Broadcasting
Tribunal [No. 2]*[69] the Administrative Appeals Tribunal drew a distinction
between "truly government documents" and documents that "consist simply
of business information supplied to government by direction with the authority of statute". The tribunal indicated that, in its view, the public interest factor
should be applied with greater force in the case of the former, on the grounds
that they are documents in which "governments dealings with business" are
involved. The reluctance to allow public interest considerations to ground disclosure of compulsorily acquired commercial information is also evident in
the approach of the New Zealand Ombudsman in the *Maui Gas Reserves*[70]
case. In refusing an application for access to information which had been supplied to a public body under statutory compulsion, the Ombudsman stated:

> "Because the information had been supplied under compulsion . . . any preju-
> dice which might arise from its disclosure would clearly be unreasonable."[71]

Such a restrictive approach to the operation of the public interest test in the
case of compulsorily acquired commercial information might not be adopted
here, since the public interest plays a more prominent role in the Irish commercial information exemption than in its Australian and New Zealand counterparts. On the one hand, it might seem logical in applying a public interest
test to give great weight to public interest considerations favouring the disclosure of "truly government information" as opposed to information compulsorily acquired, on the grounds that, in the latter case, the person or business has
no option but to supply such information to the relevant public body. On the
other hand, it could be argued that the very fact that information has been
acquired under statutory compulsion may be indicative of strong public interest in such information being disclosed under FOI.

---

[69] (1985) 7 A.L.D. 584; 3 A.A.R. 1.
[70] 9 CCNO 114 (N. Tollemarche).
[71] *ibid.* at 118.

G.   Consultation with Third Parties

Where the head of a public body decides to disclose commercially sensitive information on public interest grounds, he or she is obliged under section 29 to carry out a process of consultation. This consultation or "reverse FOI mechanism", as it is also known, is aimed at giving businesses likely to be affected by FOI disclosures the opportunity to have an input into the decision whether to release information. As previously discussed,[72] the consultation procedures set out in section 29 require the head of the public body, before disclosing a record to which the consultation requirements apply, to notify the person to whom the information relates, informing him or her that the request falls to be granted in the public interest.[73] Any person who is so notified has the right to make submissions in relation to the request[74] and the head is obliged to consider such submissions before deciding whether to grant the request.[75] Both the requester and any third party notified under section 29 have the right to appeal such a decision to the Information Commission.[76] Allowance is made in certain circumstances for non-compliance with the consultation requirements.[76]

---

[72] See above, pp. 241–243.
[73] s.29(2).
[74] s.29(3).
[75] s.29(3)(a).
[76] s.34(1) and 34(15).
[77] s.29(5) and 29(6).

CHAPTER 14

PERSONAL INFORMATION

CHAPTER 14

PERSONAL INFORMATION

A. Introduction

Government departments and agencies store vast quantities of information relating to individuals. Opening up access to government records through freedom of information legislation leaves open the possibility that private information relating to individuals will be disclosed. For this reason, FOI legislation must take account of the need to balance the right to freedom of information against the right to privacy. Section 28 is aimed at achieving the necessary balance.

This exemption must, of course, operate against the backdrop of the right to privacy as protected under the Constitution.[1] The existence of a constitutional right to privacy might be seen to favour an interpretation of section 28 that would rank the protection of privacy above the right of access to government records. The courts have, however, emphasised that the right to privacy in the Irish Constitution is not an absolute right. As Hamilton P. stated in *Kennedy v. Ireland*:[2]

> "It is not an unqualified right. Its exercise may be restricted by the constitutional rights of others, by the requirements of the common good and is subject to the requirements of public order and morality."[3]

Similarly, in *Desmond v. Glackin (No. 2)*,[4] O'Hanlon J. in the High Court concluded that the public interest justified the disclosure of information in respect of which the right to privacy was claimed. The Supreme Court dismissed an appeal against this decision.

It would appear, therefore, that there are no constitutional grounds for interpreting the personal information exemption in a way which favours privacy interests over the right of access to government records.

The exemption, which is mandatory, provides as follows:

> "28.—(1) Subject to the provisions of this section, a head shall refuse to grant a request under section 7 if, in the opinion of the head, access to the record concerned would involve the disclosure of personal information (including personal information relating to a deceased individual).

---

[1] See above, pp. 112–114.
[2] [1987] I.R. 587; [1988] I.L.R.M. 472.
[3] *ibid.* at 592.
[4] [1993] 3 I.R. 67.

(2) Subsection (1) does not apply if—

   (a) subject to subsection (3), the information concerned relates to the re-
        quester concerned,
   (b) any individual to whom the information relates consents, in writing or
        such other form as may be determined, to its disclosure to the requester,
   (c) information of the same kind as that contained in the record in respect
        of individuals generally, or a class of individuals that is, having regard
        to all the circumstances, of significant size, is available to the general
        public,
   (d) the information was given to the public body concerned by the indi-
        vidual to whom it relates and the individual was informed on behalf of
        the body, before its being so given, that the information belongs to a
        class of information that would or might be made available to the gen-
        eral public, or
   (e) disclosure of the information is necessary in order to avoid a serious
        and imminent danger to the life or health of an individual,

but, in a case falling within paragraph (a) or (b), the head concerned shall ensure
that, before the request under section 7 concerned is granted, the identity of the
requester or, as the case may be, the consent of the individual is established to
the satisfaction of the head.

(3) Where a request under section 7 relates to—

   (a) a record of a medical or psychiatric nature relating to the requester
        concerned, or
   (b) a record kept for the purposes of, or obtained in the course of the car-
        rying out of, social work in relation to the requester,

and, in the opinion of the head concerned, disclosure of the information concerned to the requester might be prejudicial to his or her physical or mental
health, well-being or emotional condition, the head may decide to refuse to
grant the request.

(4) Where, pursuant to subsection (3), a head refuses to grant a request under
section 7—

   (a) there shall be included in the notice under section 8(1) in relation to
        the matter a statement to the effect that, if the requester requests the
        head to do so, the head will offer access to the record concerned, and
        keep it available for that purpose, in accordance with section 8(3) to
        such health professional having expertise in relation to the subject-
        matter of the record as the requester may specify, and
   (b) if the requester so requests the head, he or she shall offer access to the
        record to such health professional as aforesaid, and keep it available
        for that purpose, in accordance with section 8(3).

(5) Where, as respects a request under section 7 the grant of which would, but
for this subsection, fall to be refused under subsection (1), in the opinion of the
head concerned, on balance—

(a) the public interest that the request should be granted outweighs the public interest that the right to privacy of the individual to whom the information relates should be upheld, or

(b) the grant of the request would benefit the individual aforesaid,

the head may, subject to section 29, grant the request.

(6) Notwithstanding subsection (1), the Minister may provide by regulations for the grant of a request under section 7 where—

(a) the individual to whom the record concerned relates belongs to a class specified in the regulations and the requester concerned is the parent or guardian of the individual, or

(b) the individual to whom the record concerned relates is dead and the requester concerned is a member of a class specified in the regulations.

(7) In this section 'health professional' means a medical practitioner, within the meaning of the Medical Practitioners Act, 1978, a registered dentist, within the meaning of the Dentists Act, 1985, or a member of any other class of health worker or social worker standing prescribed, after consultation with such (if any) other Ministers of the Government as the Minister considers appropriate."

The main thrust of section 28 is to exempt personal information from disclosure unless it falls within the scope of the exceptions set out in section 28(2). This formulation arguably establishes a presumption in favour of the exemption of personal information from the scope of the FOI Act. This is similar to the approach adopted in Canada and in Western Australia. In each of those jurisdictions, personal information is, subject to certain exceptions, exempt from disclosure.[5] The effect of this presumption is, however, tempered by the fact that the operation of both exemptions is subject to a public interest test.[6]

These provisions can be contrasted with the personal information exemption in the Australian federal Act, which was based on the U.S. privacy exemption. The Australian exemption provides that documents are only exempt where their disclosure would involve the *unreasonable* disclosure of personal information about any person. No exceptions are provided for.

The advantage of the Canadian, Western Australian, and Irish approach is that its scope is relatively clear. The exemption applies to all personal information not explicitly excepted and subject, of course, to the operation of the public interest test. Another advantage of this approach is that it allows for the exclusion from the scope of the exemption of certain categories of information, for example, routine information. The Australian approach, on the other hand, is arguably more favourable to disclosure. This is because, instead of

---

[5] Canada: Access to Information Act (Canada), R.S.C., 1985, s.19; Western Australia: Freedom of Information Act 1992, Sched.1, cl.3.

[6] Canada: Privacy Act (Canada), R.S.C., 1985, s.8(2)(m)(i); Western Australia: Freedom of Information Act 1992, Sched.1, cl.3(6).

establishing a presumption favouring exemption, it provides that documents will only be exempt where their disclosure would involve the unreasonable disclosure of personal information. The inclusion of the word "unreasonable" in the exemption has been interpreted as requiring the balancing of the public interest against the privacy of individuals.[7] A disadvantage of the Australian exemption is that because it is not subject to any exceptions, public bodies are obliged to assess all applications for access to personal information, including those involving information of a purely routine nature, to see whether their disclosure would involve the unreasonable disclosure of personal information. A proposal that the Australian Act be amended to include a presumption favouring the exemption of personal information, subject to appropriate exceptions, was rejected by the joint Australian Law Reform Commission/Administrative Review Council review of the operation of the Australian Act for two reasons. These were, first, that such an approach would not be in keeping with the general philosophy of the FOI Act that information should not be disclosed unless harm will result from the disclosure, and, second, because it would run the risk that personal information would be withheld merely because it did not fall within one of the exceptions prescribed in the Act.[8] Given the incorporation of a public interest test in the Irish exemption, however, it could be argued that the end result is much the same. Personal information will only be subject to disclosure where the public interest in disclosure outweighs the public interest in upholding the right to privacy.

In order to qualify for exemption under section 28, it must be shown that the information in question is "personal information" for the purposes of the Act. Personal information is defined in detail in section 2 of the Act. That definition includes a non-exhaustive list of the types of information which are covered by the term "personal information", as well as a list of categories of information which are excluded from the definition of personal information for the purposes of the Act. Again the approach is the same as that adopted in the Canadian legislation, as the latter also catalogues the types of personal information covered by the exemption. This is in contrast to the Australian and New Zealand open textured approach which utilises a somewhat terse definition of personal information, the scope of which is left to be determined by usage and decisions on appeals. The advantage of the more expansive approach to defining personal information in the Irish and Canadian Acts is that it provides guidance to both applicants and public bodies as to what constitutes personal information for the purposes of the Act. This approach has none-

---

[7] *Colakovski v. Australian Telecommunications Corp.* (1991) 100 A.L.R. 111; 29 F.C.R. 429; 113 A.A.R. 2612; 23 A.L.D. 1; *Re Chandra and Department of Immigration and Ethnic Affairs* (1984) 6 A.L.N. N257.

[8] Australian Law Reform Commission, Report No. 77/Administrative Review Council, Report No. 40, *Open Government: A Review of the Freedom of Information Act 1982* (Australian Government Publishing Service, Canberra, 1995), para. 10.6.

theless been rejected by the joint Australian Law Reform Commission/Administrative Review Council review on the grounds that it does not provide sufficient flexibility.[9]

Three categories of information are expressly excluded from the definition of personal information. They are: information relating to the performance of their functions by government employees; information relating to the performance of their functions by government contractors; and the views of individuals in relation to public bodies. The exclusion of such information was designed to prevent public bodies invoking the personal information exemption in order to refuse requests for access to information concerning the performance of their functions by government employees or contractors. This issue has been identified as giving rise to problems in Australia where there is no such express exclusion of information concerning public servants, as a result of which government agencies have attempted, on occasion, to use the personal information exemption to resist disclosure of such information.[10]

The public interest test, which is found at section 28(5), allows for the disclosure of personal information, where in the opinion of the head of the public body concerned the public interest in disclosure clearly outweighs any invasion of privacy, or where disclosure would clearly benefit the individual to whom the record relates. Disclosure under this provision cannot, however, take place until the individual to whom the record relates has been consulted in the manner set out in section 29.

There is provision in the Act for the disclosure through a third party health professional of personal information of a medical, psychiatric or social work nature.[11] Provision is also made for the introduction of regulations to deal with requests for access to personal information made by the parents or guardians of the individual concerned[12] and also for the making of regulations in relation to access to records relating to deceased persons.[13]

B.   Definition of Personal Information

The opening paragraph of the definition states that "personal information" means:

"information about an identifiable individual that—

---

[9]   Above, n. 8, para. 10.8.

[10]   Australian Law Reform Commission/Administrative Review Council, Discussion Paper No. 59, *Freedom of Information* (Australian Government Publishing Service, Canberra, 1995), para. 6.28.

[11]   s.28(3).

[12]   s.28(6)(a).

[13]   s.28(6)(b).

> (a) would, in the ordinary course of events, be known only to the individual or members of the family, or friends, of the individual, or
>
> (b) is held by a public body on the understanding that it would be treated by it as confidential".

This is followed by a statement to the effect that, without prejudice to the generality of the opening paragraph, the definition of personal information includes the following list of categories of information:

> "(i) information relating to the educational, medical, psychiatric, or psychological history of the individual,
>
> (ii) information relating to the financial affairs of the individual,
>
> (iii) information relating to the employment or employment history of the individual,
>
> (iv) information relating to the individual in a record falling within section 6(6)(a),
>
> (v) information relating to the criminal history of the individual,
>
> (vi) information relating to the religion, age, sexual orientation or marital status of the individual,
>
> (vii) a number, letter, symbol, word, mark or other thing assigned to the individual by a public body for the purpose of identification or any mark or other thing used for that purpose,
>
> (viii) information relating to the entitlements of the individual under the Social Welfare Acts as beneficiary (within the meaning of the Social Welfare (Consolidation) Act, 1983) or required for the purpose of establishing whether the individual, being a claimant (within the meaning aforesaid), is such a beneficiary,
>
> (ix) information required for the purpose of assessing the liability of the individual in respect of a tax or duty or other payment owed or payable to the State or to a local authority, a health board or other public body or for the purpose of collecting an amount due from the individual in respect of such a tax or duty or other payment,
>
> (x) the name of the individual where it appears with other personal information relating to the individual or where the disclosure of the name would, or would be likely to, establish that any personal information held by the public body concerned relates to the individual,
>
> (xi) information relating to property of the individual (including the nature of the individual's title to any property), and
>
> (xii) the views or opinions of another person about the individual".

1. The opening paragraph

The information must meet two criteria in order to be classified as personal information for the purposes of the exemption: the first is concerned with the person who is the subject of the information, while the second relates to the nature of the information. The two criteria are:

(1) the information must be information about an identifiable individual; and

(2) the information must be either:
  (a) information that would, in the ordinary course of events, be known only to the individual or members of the family, or friends, of the individual; or
  (b) information that is held by a public body on the understanding that it would be treated by it as confidential.

This definition of personal information is more detailed and specific than its Canadian or Australian counterparts. In Canada, the opening paragraph of the personal information definition simply defines personal information as "information about an identifiable individual that is recorded in any form".[14] Similarly, in Australia personal information is defined as "information or an opinion . . . about an individual whose identity is apparent or can reasonably be ascertained, from the information or opinion".[15] In order to qualify as "personal information" for the purposes of the section 28, not only must the information concerned relate to an identifiable individual, it must also meet the requirements of either paragraph (a) or paragraph (b). Because both of these conditions must be met, the Irish personal information exemption is narrower than its overseas equivalents. However, the relatively restricted nature of the Irish exemption is not likely to expose to disclosure information of any great sensitivity. Instead, its effect will be to remove routine information from the scope of the exemption. This will have beneficial effects in terms of the administration of the Act. In particular, it means that the consultation process will not have to be activated in the case of applications for routine information. This has been identified as one of the problems associated with the operation of the personal information exemption in the Australian federal Act.[16]

(a) The subject of the information

The information must be information about an identifiable individual. This means that it must be possible to identify an individual from a perusal of the record. The individual need not be named, but he or she must be identifiable. Information unrelated to any particular person will not satisfy the threshold test. The exemption will only apply in respect of personal information relating to individuals and not to legal persons or groups. The distinction between individuals and groups may not always be clear cut, however. For example, the release of information relating to employment practices by a public body, may indirectly result in disclosure of personal information concerning individual employees. Such disclosures could result in an invasion of the privacy

---

[14] Privacy Act (Canada), R.S.C., 1985, s.3.
[15] Freedom of Information Act 1982 (Cth), s.4.
[16] Australian Law Reform Commission/Administrative Review Council, *op. cit.* above, n. 8, para. 10.16.

interests of those individuals affected. It would, however, be contrary to the spirit of the legislation if public bodies were given free rein to rely on the personal information exemption to reject requests for access to records on the basis that their disclosure would involve the disclosure of personal information relating to legal persons or groups. The danger of applying the public interest exemption to groups was adverted to by Jackson J. in the Canadian case *Montana Band of Indians v. Canada (Minister of Indian and Northern Affairs)*,[17] when he said:

> "While I do not rule out the possibility that information about small groups may, in some cases, constitute personal information, the mere fact that one can divide the group's assets by the number of its members does not support such a finding. To hold otherwise would be to distort the intention of the personal information exemption."[18]

A similar approach was taken by the New Zealand Information Ombudsman in a case where disclosure of the names and addresses of organisations employing six or more temporary workers was opposed on the basis that it would infringe the privacy of those workers. The Ombudsman held that it was necessary for the Department to show precisely how individual workers could be traced and contacted by a requester armed only with their employer's identity.[19]

(b) The nature of the information

The definition covers two categories of information:

(1) information about an identifiable individual which would, in the ordinary course of events, be known only to the individual or members of the family or friends of the individual; and

(2) information about an identifiable individual that is held by a public body on the understanding that it would be treated as confidential.

The first category is concerned with information which would generally be accepted as private, in that its circulation is limited to friends or family members of the individual. The second category is less clear. It refers to information held by a public body "on the understanding that it would be treated as confidential". The understanding referred to was described by Minister of State Fitzgerald as a mutual understanding "of both parties determined either explicitly or by longstanding custom and practice".[20]

---

[17] (1988) 51 D.L.R. (4th) 306; 26 C.P.R. (3d) 68.
[18] *ibid.* at 314.
[19] 5 CCNO 87 (G.R. Laking).
[20] 149 *Seanad Debates* Col. 1416 (Committee Stage).

The effect of the inclusion of paragraph (b) in the definition is to extend the scope of the personal information exemption beyond information that is known only to the individual, or his or her immediate circle, to any information about an identifiable individual which is held by a public body on the understanding that it would be treated by it as confidential. Whilst an extension of the definition might be justified, the utilisation of the concept of confidentiality to achieve this aim might be questioned in view of its complexity and bearing in mind, in particular, the existence of a separate confidentiality exemption.[21]

2. Relationship of the opening paragraph to the list of categories of information

The opening paragraph of the definition of personal information is followed by a statement that, without prejudice to the generality of that definition, personal information includes a list of specific types of information which are set out in categories numbered (i) to (xii). The use of the phrase "without prejudice to the generality of the foregoing" suggests that information other than that listed can satisfy the definition. This was the approach adopted by La Forest J. of the Canadian Supreme Court when, in interpreting the corresponding provisions of the Access to Information Act in *Dagg v. Minister of Finance*,[22] he said:

> "In its opening paragraph, the provision states that 'personal information' means 'information about an identifiable individual that is recorded in any form including, without restricting the generality of the foregoing . . .'. On a plain reading, this definition is undeniably expansive. Notably, it expressly states that the list of specific examples that follows the general definition is not intended to limit the scope of the former . . . [I]f a government record is captured by those opening words, it does not matter that it does not fall within any of the specific examples."[23]

A different question is whether in order to amount to personal information, information must always satisfy the terms of one or other limb of the opening paragraph, even if it comes within the scope of one of categories (i) to (xii). On the one hand, it might be argued that, based on the use of the words "and ... includes", each of the categories of information listed constitutes an additional and separate limb of the definition. On that basis, it would not be necessary for the information to come within the scope of the opening paragraph in order to constitute personal information within the meaning of the Act.

On the other hand, it can be argued that the opening paragraph defines personal information for the purposes of the Act and that the list of categories

---

[21] s.26.
[22] (1997) 148 D.L.R. (4th) 385.
[23] *ibid.* at 405.

merely amounts to a set of examples to which the definition may be applicable. In that case, in order to amount to personal information, all information would have to satisfy the opening paragraph. The structure of the definition is similar to that found in the relevant Canadian provision, section 3 of the Privacy Act. In *Sutherland v. Canada (Minister of Indian and Northern Affairs)*[24] the Canadian Federal Court appeared to require satisfaction of the opening paragraph of the definition in addition to one of the categories of specific types of information when, in deciding that the requested information amounted to personal information for the purposes of the Act, it was stated that it came within:

> "the opening words of the definition of 'personal information' *and* the words 'information relating to financial transactions in which the individual has been involved' in para. (b)."[25]

This is the more satisfactory approach.

3. Interpretation of the listed categories

The list of categories of information covered by the definition is broad and is similar in many respects to that found in the Canadian Access to Information Act. A number of the corresponding categories have been the subject of judicial interpretation by the Canadian courts.

The category of financial information was considered in *Sutherland*.[26] The Canadian definition refers to "information relating to financial transactions in which the individual has been involved", which differs somewhat from "information relating to the financial affairs of the individual", the phrase used in the Irish definition.[27] In *Sutherland* it was held that the names of persons who owed money to an Indian association, or for whom the association guaranteed a loan, or whose salary was individually set out, came within the scope of the definition of personal information and the words "information relating to the financial transactions in which the individual has been involved".

Information relating to employment has also been subject to judicial consideration in Canada. The definition of personal information in the Irish Act includes both information relating to employment and information relating to employment history,[28] while the Canadian provision covers only the latter. In *Canada (Information Commissioner) v. Canada (Secretary of State for External Affairs)*[29] a distinction was drawn between personal and job-related infor-

---

[24] [1994] 3 F.C. 527 (T.D.).
[25] *ibid.* at 535. Emphasis added.
[26] Above, n. 24.
[27] s.2(1) def. of "personal information", para. (ii).
[28] s.2(1) def. of "personal information", para. (iii).
[29] (1989) 64 D.L.R. (4th) 413; 28 C.P.R. (3d) 301.

mation. This case concerned an application for disclosure of security classifications required for certain positions. The department had released the names of 25 people employed on temporary contracts, but refused to disclose their security classifications, on the basis that the classifications could be linked to the names and so amounted to personal information. It was held that the classifications were not personal information since each classification was an attribute of the position itself. Because it was information which related primarily to a job and not to the individual who held it, it fell outside the definition of personal information.

In the same case, the security classifications were held not to constitute "any identifying number or symbol or other particular assigned to the individual" on the grounds that such particulars will only fall within the definition of personal information where they relate to the individual, and not to the position held by an individual. This category of personal information is similar to "number, letter, symbol, word, mark or other thing assigned to the individual by a public body for the purpose of identification or any mark or other thing used for that purpose" referred to at paragraph (vii) of the Irish definition of personal information.

A number of cases have concerned applications for access to names of individuals. Names constitute personal information for the purposes of both the Canadian and Irish Acts in two circumstances only. The first, which is identical in both jurisdictions, is where the name appears with other personal information relating to the individual. The second situation in which a name constitutes personal information for the purposes of the Irish Act is where disclosure of the name would establish that any personal information held by the public body concerned relates to the individual. The Canadian provision is a variation on that; it applies where "disclosure of the name itself would reveal information about the individual". The Irish provision would appear to be broader. Because information will amount to personal information for the purposes of the Act, if its disclosure will reveal that any personal information held by the body relates to the individual, there is no need for the disclosure of the name to reveal any substantive information about the individual. Under the Canadian provision, on the other hand, the information will only amount to personal information if its disclosure would reveal substantive information about the individual.

The Canadian courts have had some difficulty in arriving at a consistent interpretation of this provision. In *Noël v. Great Lakes Pilotage Authority Ltd*,[30] where an application was made for access to a list of the names of ships' officers who were not subject to compulsory pilotage on the Great Lakes, it was held that the names of the officers did not amount to personal information for the purposes of the Act. Dubé J. stated that:

---

[30] (1987) 45 D.L.R. (4th) 127.

"An individual's name does not constitute personal information unless, as provided in s.3(i) of the Privacy Act, disclosure of the name itself reveal (personal) information about the individual . . . Disclosure of the names alone would not reveal any employment history, apart from the fact that the individuals in question had made at least ten passages in the Great Lakes pilotage area . . . ".[31]

A different result was arrived at in *Dagg,* a case in which an application was made for access to sign-in logs maintained in respect of a place of work. The Canadian Supreme Court held that the names in the sign-in logs constituted personal information for the purposes of the Act on the grounds that their disclosure would reveal information about the individuals. La Forest J. found that:

"In his access to information request, the appellant asked for copies of the log signed by employees on specific days. Even if the Minister disclosed only the name of the employees listed on those logs, the disclosure would reveal that certain identifiable persons attended their workplace on those days. The disclosure of the names would thus 'reveal information about the individual'".[32]

In *Mackenzie v. Canada (Minister of National Health and Welfare)*[33] an application was made for the names of medical practitioners whose prescribing privileges had been revoked or restricted. It was held that revealing the names of physicians would necessarily reveal that the individual had had his or her prescription privileges revoked, which would entail personal information within the meaning of the definition.

It is difficult to reconcile these decisions, since in *Noël* the names could be linked with other personal information, just as they could in the latter two cases. In *Noël* the names could be linked with the fact that the named persons were entitled to navigate the Great Lakes without a pilot, a privilege which was only afforded to those who had completed 10 passages through the area.

4. Exclusions from the definition of personal information

Certain types of personal information are expressly excluded from the definition of personal information for the purposes of section 28. The aim is to ensure that the personal information exemption cannot be invoked to deny access to information concerning the carrying out of work for public bodies, either by Directors or staff members of such bodies, or by independent contractors such as consultants. Nor can it be used to deny access to the views or opinions of an individual in relation to a public body, its staff or the business or performance of the functions of a public body. The excluded categories of information are:

---

[31] Above, n. 30, at 130.
[32] *Dagg v. Minister of Finance,* above, n. 22, at 410.
[33] (1994) 88 F.T.R. 52; 59 C.P.R. (3d) 63.

"(I) in a case where the individual holds or held office as a director, or occupies or occupied a position as member of the staff, of a public body, the name of the individual or information relating to the office or position or its functions or the terms upon and subject to which the individual holds or held that office or occupies or occupied that position or anything written or recorded in any form by the individual in the course of and for the purpose of the performance of the functions aforesaid,

(II) in a case where the individual is or was providing a service for a public body under a contract for services with the body, the name of the individual or information relating to the service or the terms of the contract or anything written or recorded in any form by the individual in the course of and for the purposes of the provision of the service, or

(III) the views or opinions of the individual in relation to a public body, the staff of a public body or the business or the performance or the functions of a public body."[34]

Again the approach is similar to that taken in the Canadian federal Act. The Canadian Act specifies a number of categories of information which are expressly excluded from the definition of personal information.[35]

The issue of where the onus lies of establishing whether the exclusions apply arose for consideration in *Dagg*. The Canadian Supreme Court held that since the Access to Information Act places the onus on the government to show that it is authorised to refuse to disclose a record:

"it is clear that even where it has been shown that the record is *prima facie* personal information, the government retains the burden of establishing that a record does not fall within one of the exceptions . . .".[36]

Given the fact that section 34(12)(b) of the Irish Act places the onus of justifying a refusal to grant a request for access to a record on the head of the public body concerned, a similar conclusion to that arrived at in *Dagg* as to the onus of proof applicable with respect to the exceptions can be justified in the context of the Irish Act.

(a) Exclusions (I) and (II)

The exclusion of information concerning government employees and contractors covers four main types of information. These are: the name of the individual; information relating to the position or its functions; information concerning the terms of employment or contract; and anything written or recorded by the individual in the course of and for the purposes of his or her work. One important issue arising is whether these exclusions are limited to

---

[34] s.2(1).

[35] Access to Information Act (Canada), R.S.C., 1985, s.19(2); Privacy Act (Canada), R.S.C., 1985, s.8.

[36] *Dagg v. Minister of Finance,* above, n. 22, at 412.

information of a factual nature. This was how the corresponding exclusion in the Canadian definition of personal information was interpreted. In *Canada (Information Commissioner) v. Canada (Solicitor General)*[37] it was held that only factual matters about a worker will come within the terms of the exclusions and, on that basis, qualitative job performance evaluations will be exempt from disclosure. Jerome J. stated:

> "There is no indication that qualitative evaluations of an employee's performance were ever intended to be made public. Indeed it would be most unjust if the details of an employee's job performance were considered public information just because that person is in the employ of the government."[38]

The U.S. approach, too, has generally been to exempt employee performance evaluations.[39]

While the first three of the elements of exclusions (I) and (II) clearly relate to factual information, the position of the fourth is not so clear. It covers "anything written or recorded by the individual in the course of and for the purpose of the performance of their functions". Arguably it relates not just to factual details concerning the position and its functions, but also to other information of a more speculative nature, such as the views or opinions of the individual on work-related issues. The disclosure of the job performance evaluations of individuals would not, however, come within the scope of this exclusion, because they would not be "written or recorded by the individual".

In *Canada (Information Commissioner) v. Canada (Secretary of State for External Affairs)*[40] Dubé J. held that security classifications attaching to positions fell within the terms of the corresponding exclusion from the Canadian definition of personal information on the grounds that such information relates to services performed and not to the individual.[41]

In *Dagg* the Canadian Supreme Court, in considering whether the information requested fell within the terms of the exclusion from the Canadian definition of information relating to the position, function, or responsibilities of an individual, held that such information will consist of the kind of information disclosed in a job description. More particularly:

> "It will comprise the terms and conditions associated with a particular position, including such information as qualifications, duties, responsibilities, hours of work and salary range."[42]

---

[37] [1988] 3 F.C. 551 (T.D.).

[38] *ibid.* at 558.

[39] *Campbell v. U.S. Civil Service Commission*, 539 F.2d 58 (10th Cir. 1976); *Gilbey v. Department of Interior*, No. 89–0801 (RCL), 1990 U.S. Dist. LEXIS 14021 (D.D.C. October 22, 1990).

[40] Above, n. 29.

[41] *ibid.* at 418–419.

[42] Above, n. 22, at 414.

The issue of access to salary details of a particular official arose in *Rubin v. Canada (Privy Council, Clerk)*.[43] Since the relevant Canadian exclusion covers information relating to the salary range of the individual, it was held that the specific salary details and the *per diem* remuneration of the official were not covered by the exclusion and consequently were exempt from disclosure. However, it was held in the same case that information relating to non-monetary compensation should be disclosed on the basis that if the government could provide secret non-monetary remuneration, public information about an official's salary range would become meaningless. While there is no express reference to salary in the list of exclusions from the definition of personal information in section 2, it would appear that specific salary details and details of consultancy payments, as well as non-monetary compensation, could come within the scope of "the terms on which the person holds or held that office" or, in the case of contractual arrangements, "the terms of the contract". Such information would, therefore, fall outside the scope of the personal information exemption and would be subject to disclosure.

In the case of contractors, the question arises whether the exclusion applies only to information concerning individual contractors, such as consultants, or whether it applies in respect of individuals employed by companies which have contracted to provide services to public bodies. In *Canada (Information Commissioner) v. Canada (Secretary of State for External Affairs)*,[44] the information at issue concerned 25 workers who did not have direct contracts with the government but were employed through a private personnel agency. It was held *obiter* that such information fell within the terms of the exclusion and was therefore outside the scope of the personal information exemption, on the basis that:

> "There is nothing in the scheme of the Act which would provide more privacy to the individual who is hired by the government through a personnel agency."[45]

(b) Exclusion (III)

The third exclusion covers an individual's views or opinions in relation to public bodies or the staff, business or performance of the functions of a public body. Thus, it would not be open to an agency to refuse access to the views of a person who had, for example, undertaken a review of the public body. Where, however, such information constituted personal information relating to the staff of such a body, for example information touching on the performance of individual staff members, such information could constitute personal information relating to the staff member.

---

[43] (1993) 48 C.P.R. (3d) 337.
[44] Above, n. 29.
[45] *ibid.* at 420.

C. Exceptions to the Personal Information Exemption

The personal information exemption is subject to a number of exceptions.
These are set out in section 28(2) and cover five areas:

(a) where the information concerns the requester;

(b) where there is consent to the disclosure;

(c) where the information is publicly available;

(d) where the individual has been informed of the possibility of disclosure;
and

(e) where disclosure is necessary to avert danger to life or health.

These exceptions are roughly analogous to the exceptions to the personal information exemption in the Canadian Act.[46] Some of the exceptions are in
similar terms to exceptions to the principles regarding disclosure of personal
information set out in section 8 of the Irish Data Protection Act 1988. For a
discussion of the relationship between the Freedom of Information Act and
the Data Protection Act, see below, pp. 373–394.

It is not entirely clear who is responsible for establishing whether the personal information to which access is sought falls into one of these categories.
There is provision to the effect that in cases falling within paragraphs (a) or
(b) of the subsection, the identity or consent of the requester, as the case may
be, must be established to the satisfaction of the head.[47] This would seem to
suggest that the onus is on the applicant to raise the possible application of the
exceptions. This would not, however, be in keeping with the placing of the
burden of justifying a refusal of access on the head of a public body in the
circumstances of a review by the Information Commissioner.[48] The better view
would be that the onus of proving whether the exceptions apply is on the
public body. The extent of the enquiry to be carried out by the head of the
public body in determining whether the exceptions apply was considered in
the Canadian case of *X v. Canada (Minister of National Defence).*[49] While the
difficulty of ascertaining whether the exceptions apply was acknowledged, it
was held that it would not be sufficient for the heads of government institutions to simply state that they are unaware or that they do not know if the
exceptions apply. Rather, they should be in a position to state what activities
or initiatives were undertaken in this regard.[50]

---

[46] Access to Information Act (Canada), R.S.C., 1985, s.19(2).
[47] s.28(2).
[48] s.34(12).
[49] [1992] 1 F.C. 77 (T.D.).
[50] *ibid.* at 102.

1. Where the information concerns the requester

This operation of this exception is subject to section 28(3), which makes special arrangements for the disclosure of information of a medical, psychiatric or social work nature, details of which are discussed below. That exception apart, the intention is that the personal information exemption will not be used to deny access to records relating to the person making the request. Any or all of the other exemptions can, however, be invoked in respect of a request for records concerning the requester.

It is not clear whether the exception applies in circumstances where the requester has authorised another person, such as a solicitor or social worker, to apply for access on his or her behalf. The corresponding exception in the Data Protection Act refers to a disclosure made to the data subject concerned or to a person acting on his behalf.[51]

Difficulties may arise when a person applies for documents containing information which relates not only to themselves, but also to others. The public body will have to decide on the applicability of this exemption to such a situation. The corresponding exception in Queensland provides that matter is not exempt *merely* because it relates to information concerning the personal affairs of the person by whom, or on whose behalf, an application for access is made. In *Re B. and Brisbane North Regional Health Authority*[52] the word "merely" was interpreted by the Queensland Information Commissioner to mean "nothing more than something specified" and, on that basis, it was held that if matter relates to information concerning the personal affairs of another person as well as the applicant, then the exception does not apply.[53] Section 28(1)(a) contains no qualifying words such as "merely" or "solely"; therefore, it appears that the exception will apply in respect of all records containing information relating to the requester, even if they also contain information relating to others. This means that records containing joint personal information of the requester and another person is subject to disclosure to the requester under the FOI Act.

The third party consultation procedures set out in section 29 do not apply to disclosures of joint personal information. Those consultative measures only come into effect where the request for information would fall to be refused under section 28. Since there is no refusal in a case in which an exception is applicable, there would be no requirement that the other person to whom the joint personal information relates be consulted.

---

[51] Data Protection Act 1988, s.8(g).
[52] (1994) 1 Q.A.R. 279.
[53] *ibid.* at 344.

2. Where there is consent to disclosure

The second exception prevents the use of the personal information exemption in circumstances where the individual to whom the information relates has consented to its disclosure. For example, a request by a third party for information relating to an individual in circumstances where the individual has consented to the disclosure of the information would prevent the personal information exemption being invoked by the public body to which the request was made.

The consent is required to be in writing or "such other form as may be determined". The function of making such determinations is conferred on the Minister for Finance.[54] It is not clear whether consent needs to be express or whether the individual's consent could be implied. It could be argued that it is open to the head of a public body to determine that the conduct of an individual amounts to a form of consent for the purposes of the consent exception. This might arise, for example, where the individual has failed to respond to notice of intention to disclose.

Nor is it clear whether the consent must be expressed by the individual to whom the information relates or whether it can be channelled through a representative. There is a somewhat similar exception in the Data Protection Act and there the consent may be signalled by a person acting on behalf of the data subject.[55]

3. Where the information is publicly available

The third exception arises where similar information is available to the general public. It applies in two sets of circumstances. The first is where information of the same kind in respect of individuals generally is available to the general public. The second is where information of the same kind in respect of classes of individuals of significant size is publicly available.

The Canadian federal Act also contains an exception relating to information which is publicly available. In *Canada (Information Commissioner) v. Canada (Minister of Public Works)*[56] the names of former MPs in receipt of pensions were held to be publicly available in that they could be gleaned from the Canadian Directory of Parliament in the parliamentary library, even though a person needs permission to use the library. It was also noted that the requested information could be gleaned from other sources, such as a *Who's Who of Canada*,[57] old newspapers, etc. However, the names of MPs who, due to insufficient duration of service, were not automatically entitled to a pen-

---

[54] s.2(1).
[55] Data Protection Act 1988, s.8(h).
[56] (1997) 70 C.P.R. (3d) 37.
[57] *ibid.* at 47.

sion, but instead had to purchase some years of their pension, were found not to be publicly available.[58] In another Canadian case, it was held that disclosure to the media of some of the information sought did not mean that it was publicly available. The applicant sought disclosure of information relating to an offence committed by a Canadian soldier on service in Croatia. The court held that the information was not publicly available, since disclosure to the media had occurred inadvertently and only for one document.[59]

4. Where the individual has been informed of possible disclosure

The fourth exception applies to information given to a public body by the person to whom it relates, in circumstances where the individual was informed prior to supplying the information that it was of a class that would or might be made available to the general public.

This exception allows public bodies to indicate that certain classes of personal information may be made publicly available. It has the effect of allowing public bodies to release routine information without having to go through the consultation procedure outlined in section 29. There is no requirement that the individual consent to such disclosure; however, the fact that the individual is informed of its possible disclosure *prior* to supplying it gives him or her the opportunity of deciding against its supply. The extent to which this is a realistic option will depend on the financial or other pressures surrounding supply of the information to the public body.

5. Where disclosure is necessary to avoid danger to life or health

The fifth exception concerns disclosure of information necessary in order to avoid a serious and imminent danger to the life or health of an individual. It echoes an exception to the principles against disclosure of personal information under the Data Protection Act.[60] It could be applied, for example, in the case of psychiatric records which reveal that a patient has a mental condition which makes him a danger to others, or in the case of records which reveal that a youth worker or teacher has been convicted of offences against children.

This exception differs from the previous exceptions in that it amounts to a substantive ground for disclosing personal information, while the other exceptions are more procedural in nature. The invocation of this exception could lead to a situation where the requester's reasons for seeking access to the records concerned would be taken into account. This would involve a depar-

---

[58] Above, n. 56.
[59] *Terry v. Minister of National Defence* (1994) Admin.L.R. (2d) 122; 86 F.T.R. 266 (F.C.T.D.).
[60] Data Protection Act 1988, s.8(d).

ture from the general rule set out in section 8(4) that the requester's motives
are irrelevant. It is the type of issue which would normally be considered in
the context of the application of a public interest test. There is no direct equivalent of this exception in overseas FOI legislation, but instead the issue of danger to life or health has been considered as relevant to determining whether
the public interest requires disclosure of personal information. In a U.S. case
the disclosure of the names and addresses of servicemen who had participated
in atmospheric nuclear weapons testing programmes was held to be in the
public interest because it was necessary in connection with the conduct of
scientific and medical studies relating to the adverse health effects of exposure to atomic radiation.[61]

D. Health/Social Work Access Modification Provisions

These provisions are based on similar provisions in the Australian federal
Act.[62] They allow for a person to be refused access to a record of a medical,
psychiatric or social work nature relating to themselves where, in the opinion
of the head of the public body requested, disclosure would be prejudicial to
that person's physical or mental health, wellbeing or emotional condition.
Where access is refused on this basis, the requester can require that access to
the record be offered to a health professional[63] specified by the requester who
has expertise "in relation to the subject-matter of the record".[64]

The aim of the provision is to give the individual to whom the information
relates indirect access to the information and, as it has been expressed in an
Australian report, "to ensure that people receive 'disturbing' information in a
supportive environment".[65] In Australia, caution in the exercise of such discretion has been urged. The New South Wales Privacy Committee, for example, in a submission to the ALRC/ARC review of the Australian federal FOI
Act, argued that there are very few cases where disclosure could harm a person and suggested that the provision be limited.[66]

The criteria for applying the Australian federal provision were explored in
Re K and Director General of Social Security.[67] It was held that the test for
applying the provision involves three steps: the first is whether the document

---

[61] *National Association of Atomic Veterans Inc. v. Director, Defense Nuclear Agency,* 583
F. Supp. 1483 (D.D.C. 1984).
[62] Freedom of Information Act 1982 (Cth), s.41(3).
[63] Health professional is defined to mean a medical practitioner, a dentist or a member of
any other class of health worker or social worker to be prescribed by the Minister: s.28(7).
[64] s.28(4)(a).
[65] Australian Law Reform Commission/Administrative Review Council, *op. cit.* above, n.
8, para. 10.21.
[66] *ibid.*
[67] (1984) 6 A.L.D. 354.

contains information of a medical or psychiatric nature;[68] the second is whether, if the information were to be disclosed directly to the applicant, there is a real and tangible possibility, as distinct from a fanciful, remote or far-fetched possibility, of prejudice to the physical or mental health or well-being of the applicant; and third, if there is a real and tangible possibility of such prejudice, the decision-maker, in exercising his or her discretion to direct that indirect access be given, should consider the nature and extent of any real and tangible possible prejudice and the likelihood of it occurring.

The decision concerning the extent to which the individual should be informed of the contents of the record is left in the hands of the health professional.

These provisions bear some similarity to restrictions imposed on access rights under the Data Protection Act. The relevant regulations require that access be refused where granting a request would be likely to cause serious harm to the physical, mental or emotional health of the data subject.[69] These provisions are compared below at pp. 385–388.

E. Personal Information of Deceased Persons

By virtue of section 28(1), the exemption applies to personal information relating to a deceased individual. There is provision in section 28(6) for the making of regulations providing for the grant of a request for access to a record relating to a deceased person where the requester concerned is a member of a class specified in the regulations. While it could be argued that a deceased person has no need for privacy, it is most likely that the exemption of personal information relating to deceased persons was inserted to protect the relatives and friends of deceased persons. While the weight of authorities in the U.S. is that personal privacy interests lapse upon the death of the individual, the courts have upheld claims of exemption on a theory that surviving family members may have cognisable privacy interests in government records relating to the death of a loved one. For example, x-rays and photographs from President Kennedy's autopsy were held to be exempt because public display of the records would cause extreme anguish to the Kennedy family;[70] also, NASA was permitted to withhold a tape recording of voices of astronauts aboard the final flight of the Challenger space shuttle.[71]

Draft regulations concerning access to records of deceased persons have

---

[68] The Australian provision does not refer to social work information.

[69] Data Protection (Access Modification) (Health) Regulations 1989 (S.I. No. 82 of 1989); Data Protection (Access Modification) (Social Work) Regulations 1989 (S.I. No. 83 of 1989).

[70] *Katz v. National Archives and Records Administration*, 862 F. Supp. 476 (D.D.C. 1994).

[71] *New York Times Co. v. NASA*, 728 F. Supp. 628 (D.D.C. 1991).

been prepared and are expected to be submitted for consideration by the Cabinet in October 1998. It is understood that the draft regulations restrict the disclosure of access to records of deceased persons to the following classes of person:

(1) the personal representative of the deceased acting in due course of administration of the estate of the deceased or any person acting with the consent of the personal representative so acting;

(2) a person or persons nominated, for the purpose of accessing their records, by the deceased when living, either in a proved will or in another instrument in writing which has been signed by the deceased and duly witnessed by an independent witness;

(3) a person appointed by the courts or statute; and

(4) such other person or persons as the public body deems appropriate, taking into account all of the relevant circumstances and following such enquiries and consultations as the public body deems necessary. Particular account should be taken of the relationship (if any) of the requester to the deceased.

The first of these categories appears to confer on the personal representatives of deceased persons an automatic right of access to all records relating to deceased persons. This would include records other than those directly concerned with the administration of the estate and could include sensitive records, such as those revealing that the deceased had suffered from a disease such as AIDS. The second category provides for the somewhat unlikely situation in which a deceased person had prior to death given his or her consent to disclosure to a particular person. The third category, which covers persons appointed by the courts or statute, could include cases where the estate and subsequent affairs of the deceased are taken over by a court or State agency. The final category is catch-all in nature. It allows a public body to release records relating to deceased persons where appropriate. While regard should be taken of the relationship (if any) of the requester to the deceased, the provision of access to the spouses of deceased persons is not automatically provided for. This approach was taken on the grounds that such access might be inappropriate in certain circumstances.

The operation of these regulations would be subject to the other provisions, including the exemption provisions, of the FOI Act.

F.   Requests by Parents or Guardians

Section 28(6) allows for the making of regulations to provide for the granting of requests for access to information relating to individuals who belong to a class specified in the regulations and the requester is the parent or guardian of the individual. Draft regulations have been prepared and are expected to be submitted for consideration by the Cabinet in October 1998. It is understood that they provide for the granting of access to the parents or guardians of the following classes of persons:

(1) persons over the age of majority, who have a mental condition or mental incapacity or severe continuing physical disability, as certified by a registered medical practitioner, and who by reason of which are incapable of exercising their rights under the Act, unless other arrangements have been made by a court or by statute;

(2) minors as defined in the Age of Minority Act 1985 at the date of the request, unless other arrangements have been made by court or statute.

In the case of the first category of persons, the decision as to whether a person is capable of exercising his or her rights under the Act will be taken by the public body concerned. The fact that a person might be physically as well as mentally incapable of exercising such rights is catered for. A registered medical practitioner would have to certify the existence of a mental condition or incapacity or severe continuing physical disability. The second category covers minors of all ages irrespective of whether they have a disability.

The operation of these regulations would continue to be subject to the other provisions, including the exemption provisions, of the FOI Act.

G.   Disclosure of Exempt Information and the Public Interest

The Act allows for the disclosure of information to which the personal information exemption applies, in two sets of circumstances. The first is where, in the opinion of the head of the public body concerned, the public interest that the request should be granted outweighs the public interest that the right to privacy of the individual to whom the information relates should be upheld.[72] This application of the public interest test is discussed in the next paragraph. The second case in which exempt information can be disclosed is where, in the opinion of the head of the public body, the grant of the request would benefit the individual.[73] This provision echoes one of the exceptions to the Canadian personal information exemption which provides that personal information is not exempt where, in the opinion of the head of the institution concerned, disclosure would clearly benefit the individual to whom the information relates.[74] It could apply, for example, where disclosure of personal medical

---

[72] s.28(5)(a).
[73] s.28(5)(b).
[74] Privacy Act (Canada), R.S.C., 1985, s.8(2)(m)(ii).

information was necessary to the treatment of the person concerned and that owing to illness that person was unable to provide the information himself or herself.

In deciding whether the disclosure of personal information would be justified in the public interest, the public body and, on appeal, the Information Commissioner, must attempt to balance the public interest in granting the request against the individual's right to privacy. Consideration of the public interest in the application of personal information exemptions is also a feature of overseas FOI legislation. The Canadian personal information exemption incorporates an express public interest test in that one of the exceptions to the personal information exemption permits disclosure where "the public interest in disclosure clearly outweighs any invasion of privacy that could result from the disclosure".[75] The Australian and U.S. Freedom of Information Acts also require consideration of the public interest in respect of disclosure of personal information. In Australia, the test is in the form of a requirement that disclosure of the requested records amount to an *unreasonable* disclosure of personal information.[76] This has been interpreted as requiring the balancing of the public interest in disclosure against the privacy of individuals.[77] Similarly, the personal privacy exemption in the U.S. applies to disclosures of personal information which would constitute a clearly unwarranted invasion of personal privacy.[78] It has been held that the application of this exemption requires:

> "a balancing of the individual's right of privacy against the preservation of the basic purpose of the Freedom of Information Act 'to open agency action to the light of public scrutiny'".[79]

1. Balancing the public interest in disclosure against the right to privacy

Which of the two interests should be accorded the greater weight is a matter which has been considered by the courts in the various jurisdictions. It is not surprising in view of the use of the words "clearly unwarranted" in the U.S. privacy exemption, that this provision has been interpreted as instructing the court "to tilt the balance in favour of disclosure".[80] In Canada an attempt has been made to deal with the issue of reconciling the interests in governmental disclosure and individual privacy by "weaving the Access to Information Act

---

[75] Privacy Act (Canada), R.S.C., 1985, s.8(2)(m)(i).

[76] Freedom of Information Act 1982 (Cth), s.41(1).

[77] *Re Chandra and Department of Immigration and Ethnic Affairs*, above, n. 7.

[78] Exemption 6.

[79] *Rose v. Department of the Air Force*, 495 F.2d 261 (2d Cir. 1974), 425 U.S. 352 at 372 (1976).

[80] *Getman v. NLRB*, 450 F.2d 670 at 674 (D.C. Cir. 1971); *stay denied*, 404 U.S. 1204 (1971).

and the Privacy Act into a seamless code".[81] In particular, the definition of personal information for the purposes of the personal information exemption in the Access to Information Act is taken from the Privacy Act.[82]

In *Bland v. Canada (National Capital Commission)*[83] the danger of automatic deferral to privacy interests was adverted to in colourful terms by the Canadian Federal Court when it stated:

> "So often in the jurisprudence one sees government institutions refusing to disclose information because its subjects are individuals. Canada is not a nation quantified in terms of automatons, spirits or legal fictions, but in terms of people. In logic, then, of all the information in records under the control of a government institution, the overwhelmingly greater part simply must be about people. That factor does not make their privacy paramount, for if that were the case, 'the public interest in disclosure' would be stillborn."[84]

The court also stated that:

> "under section 2 of the information legislation, 'the public interest in disclosure' exists as a paramount value which is to be suppressed only when and if it clearly does not outweigh any invasion of privacy".[85]

This approach was, however, rejected by the Canadian Supreme Court in *Dagg*. La Forest J., having reviewed the case law relating to the relationship between the Access to Information Act and the Privacy Act, concluded that:

> "Both statutes recognize that, in so far as it is encompassed by the definition of 'personal information' in s.3 of the Privacy Act, privacy is paramount over access."[86]

Consideration of the public interest in the interpretation of s.28(5) would have to take into account the right to privacy in the Irish Constitution, although as previously argued the right to privacy need not override the right of access to personal information.[87]

In terms of the extent of the invasion of privacy necessary to justify a refusal of access to records, it has been established in the U.S. that the invasion of privacy must be tangible and substantial. In one case it was said that "Exemption 6 was directed at threats to privacy interests more palpable than mere possibilities".[88] While the need to establish a genuine risk of invasion of privacy is clear, the Australian Federal Court, whilst acknowledging its use-

---

[81] *Dagg v. Minister of Finance,* above, n. 22, at 397.
[82] s.3.
[83] [1991] 3 F.C. 325; 36 C.P.R. (3d) 289.
[84] *ibid.* at 340–341.
[85] *ibid.* at 340.
[86] Above, n. 22, at 398.
[87] See above, pp. 112–114.
[88] *Rose v. Department of the Air Force,* above, n. 79, at 380 n 19.

fulness, has stopped short of requiring that evidence of specific harm to the individual be demonstrated. In *Colakovski v. Australian Telecommunications Corporation* Lockhart J. said:

> "I do not think it is necessary in order to make out the s.41(1) exclusion that there is some particular unfairness, embarrassment or hardship which would enure to a person by reason of the disclosure. Such matters, if present, would doubtless weigh in favour of exclusion."[89]

In terms of weighing up the benefit to the public interest which disclosure would bring, it appears that there must be some connection with governmental issues and that mere inquisitiveness will not justify a disclosure of personal information. In *Colakovski*, Lockhart J. stated that:

> "if the information disclosed were of no demonstrable relevance to the affairs of government and was likely to do no more than excite or satisfy the curiosity of people about the person whose personal affairs were disclosed, I think disclosure would be unreasonable."[90]

Similarly, in a U.S. case[91] the Supreme Court held that what is to be weighed against the individual's privacy is the preservation of the basic purpose of the FOI Act to open agency action to the light of public scrutiny.

2. Relevance of identity or motive of the applicant

One issue which has arisen in other jurisdictions with respect to the application of the public interest test is whether the identity or motive of the applicant should be taken into account. On the question of identity, it could be argued that the potential invasion of privacy might be less in cases where the person requesting access is related to the individual to whom the information relates. Such relationships could include those between parent and child, wife and husband, or person with a disability and carer. On the other hand, the underlying principle of FOI legislation is that access to information should not be dependent upon the individual establishing any particular interest in obtaining access to it. If, in deciding whether to grant access to information, account is taken of the identity of the applicant, this will arguably offend against that principle.

Another question is whether the motive of the person seeking access should be taken into account. A similar argument to that raised in respect of the question of identity can be advanced in relation to the issue of motive. That is that treating the requester's motive as relevant involves a departure from the basic

---

[89] Above, n. 7, at 123.
[90] *ibid.*
[91] *Rose v. Department of the Air Force*, above, n. 79, at 372.

philosophy of FOI, which is that the right of access applies regardless of any "interest" on the part of the applicant in the records sought.

Against this, however, it can be argued that the public interest in whether to disclose information cannot be determined in a vacuum. In order to decide whether disclosure is in the public interest, it is necessary to look at the circumstances of each case to try to determine where the public interest lies. This will necessarily involve an examination of the motivation of the applicant in seeking access. Indeed, it has been argued in Australia that the taking into account of the applicant's motive is a necessary part of the balancing exercise involved in the application of the reasonableness test. For example, in *Shewcroft and Australian Broadcasting Corporation*[92] Sir William Prentice commented:

> "[I]n deciding whether disclosure of information relating to the personal affairs of (another) person would be 'unreasonable' (s.41(1)); one could envisage the necessity of setting the motivation or need of an applicant against the right to privacy of the person whose 'personal affairs' were cited, in the attempt to weigh the 'reasonableness' or 'unreasonableness' of a requested disclosure. Indeed, the concept of 'unreasonableness' of an action, would seem to involve the requirement of a weighing of factors."[93]

The jurisprudence relating to identity and motive is to a great extent intertwined. The approach of the Australian courts to the issues of identity and motive has broadly been to accept that there is a general public interest in disclosure, but to attach more weight to it where there is some specific reason why disclosure is in the public interest. This approach can be seen, for example, in the decision in *Colakovski*.[94] This case involved an attempt to challenge the use of the personal affairs exemption to refuse access to a document which disclosed the identity of a person who had made nuisance telephone calls to the applicant. As previously noted, the public interest test in the Australian federal personal information exemption is in a form which provides that documents are exempt where their disclosure would involve the unreasonable disclosure of personal information about any person. It was held in *Colakovski* that disclosure was not unreasonable. A factor which was treated as relevant to the question of reasonableness was whether the making of the calls was connected with a burglary of the applicant's house and could therefore provide valuable evidence establishing the commission of a crime. Similarly, in the Victorian case of *Re Lawless and Secretary to Law Department*,[95] the fact that the applicant was seeking access to documents in the hope that they would assist him in overturning a conviction was treated as relevant to the question of reasonableness in the application of the personal affairs exemption.

---

[92] (1985) 7 A.L.N. N307.
[93] *ibid.* at 310–311.
[94] *Colakovski v. Australian Telecommunications Corporation,* above, n. 7.
[95] (1985) 1 V.A.R. 42.

The motive for seeking access to documents has also been treated as relevant in a negative sense by the Victorian Administrative Appeals Tribunal. In *Re Targridge and Road Traffic Authority*[96] and *Re Amusement Machine Operators' Association and Department of Sport and Recreation*[97] the fact that disclosure was sought for purposes of direct mail selling was taken into account by the tribunal in arriving at its decision to uphold the exemption and refuse access to the documents.

The ALRC/ARC review of the FOI Act has recommended that the personal information exemption of the Australian Act be amended to provide that in weighing the public interest in disclosure, an agency may have regard to any special relationship between the applicant and the third party.[98]

In the U.S., on the other hand, the identity and motive of the requester have been treated as irrelevant. In *Department of Justice v. Reporters Committee for Freedom of Press*[99] the U.S. Supreme Court declared, in the closely analogous Exemption 7(C)[100] context, that the privacy versus public interest balance:

"cannot turn on the purpose for which the request for information is made . . . [T]he identity of the requesting party has no bearing on the merits of his or her FOIA [Freedom of Information Act] request."[101]

This finding was affirmed by the Supreme Court in the context of Exemption 6, the personal privacy exemption which said that all FOI Act requesters have an equal and equally qualified right to information and, except in certain cases involving claims of privilege, the identity of the requester is irrelevant to the outcome of the request.[102]

The Irish Act deals with the issue of the requester's motive by expressly requiring that the reason the requester gives for the request and any belief or opinion of the head as to what are the reasons of the requester for the request be disregarded.[103] This does not fully dispose of the issue of whether the requester's identity will be treated as irrelevant. While one way of approaching this question is to permit special relationships to be taken into account in applying the public interest test in the exemption, another approach is to allow

[96] (1988) 2 V.A.R. 604.
[97] (1988) 2 V.A.R. 584.
[98] Australian Law Reform Commission/Administrative Review Council, *op. cit.* above, n. 8, Recommendation 61, para. 10.12.
[99] 489 U.S. 749 (1989).
[100] Exemption 7 provides that the FOI Act does not apply to matters that are "records or information compiled for law enforcement purposes but only to the extent that the production of such law enforcement records or information... (C) could reasonably be expected to constitute an unwarranted invasion of personal privacy."
[101] Above, n. 99, at 771.
[102] *Department of Defense v. FLRA*, 510 U.S. 487 (1994); 114 S. Ct. 1006.
[103] s.8(4).

for an exception to the exemption in respect of such requests. The latter approach has to an extent been incorporated into the FOI Act. While there is no direct provision for such an exception, there is in section 28(6) provision for the making of regulations for the granting of requests for access to personal information of individuals who belong to a class to be specified where the requester concerned is the parent or guardian of the individual. However, this provision does not deal comprehensively with the question whether the identity of the applicant should be a relevant consideration, since it only deals with the position of parents and guardians. It appears, therefore, that there is still some discretion left to the Information Commissioner in deciding whether to treat the identity of the requester as relevant in applying the public interest test.

3. Extent of the proposed dissemination of information

Another issue which has arisen with respect to the application of the public interest test is the extent of the proposed dissemination of the requested information by the requester.

Again, strict adherence to freedom of information principles would seem to suggest that information should be disclosed as though it were to the world at large, and so decisions on whether to disclose information should be made on that basis. Indeed, it would be very difficult to limit the further dissemination of information once it has been disclosed. The disadvantage of this approach is that many applications for access to documents will be turned down, which might be granted if further dissemination of the information could be limited.

The approach to this issue in Australia has not been entirely consistent, although the consensus would appear to favour the treatment of disclosures as being to the world at large. One case in which the limitation of further dissemination of information was treated as significant was *Re Simons and Egg Marketing Board*.[104] Here the Victorian Administrative Appeals Tribunal granted a journalist access to the names and addresses of free-range egg producers in reliance upon the applicant's statement in evidence that the information would not be published and that if a producer refused to allow her to visit the producer's farm, no further contact would be made. However, in *Re Williams and Registrar of the Federal Court of Australia*[105] the federal Administrative Appeals Tribunal clearly favoured the "disclosure to the world at large" approach by taking into account the effect of disclosure to persons other than the applicant. It stated:

---

[104] (1985) 1 V.A.R. 54.
[105] (1985) 8 A.L.D. 219.

> "In considering the test of reasonableness one must not think only of disclosure
> of the documents to this particular applicant . . . One must ask oneself – is it
> reasonable to trumpet to X's friends, employers, rivals associates, family or
> enemies that X is applying for a new job?"[106]

The idea of allowing disclosure of information subject to an undertaking of
confidentiality such as that given in the *Simons* case was rejected by the Australian Law Reform Commission/Administrative Review Council on the basis
that it would be difficult to enforce such conditions and, in any case, enforcement action would come too late. Any damage the conditions were designed
to guard against would already have been done.[107]

H. Consultation with Third Parties

Where the head of a public body decides to disclose personal information on
public interest grounds or on the grounds that the grant of the request would
benefit the individual to whom the information relates, there is an obligation
on the head under section 29 to carry out a process of consultation. This consultation or "reverse FOI mechanism", as it is also known, is aimed at giving
people likely to be affected by FOI disclosures the opportunity to have an
input into the decision whether to release information. As previously discussed,[108] the consultation procedures set out in section 29 require the head of
the public body, before disclosing a record to which the consultation requirements apply, to notify the person to whom the information relates, informing
him or her that the request falls to be granted in the public interest.[109] Any
person who is so notified has the right to make submissions in relation to the
request[110] and the head is obliged to consider such submissions before deciding whether to grant the request.[111] Both the requester and any third party
notified under section 29 have the right to appeal such a decision to the Information Commissioner.[112] Allowance is made in certain circumstances for non-
compliance with the consultation requirements.[113]

---

[106] Above, n. 105, at 224.
[107] Australian Law Reform Commission/Administrative Review Council, *op. cit.* above,
n. 8, para. 10.11.
[108] See above, pp. 241–243.
[109] s.29(2).
[110] s.29(3).
[111] s.29(3)(a).
[112] s.34(1) and 34(15).
[113] s.29(5) and 29(6).

CHAPTER 15

RESEARCH AND NATURAL RESOURCES

RESEARCH AND NATURAL RESOURCES

This exemption is made up of two separate parts. The first is aimed at protecting records relating to current or future research undertaken by or on behalf of a public body, whilst the second is aimed at protecting natural resources. Each will be examined separately.

A. The Research Exemption

1. Introduction

This part of the exemption provides as follows:

> "30.—(1) A head may refuse to grant a request under section 7 if, in the opinion of the head—
>
> (a) the record concerned contains information in relation to research being or to be carried out by or on behalf of a public body and disclosure of the information or its disclosure before the completion of the research would be likely to expose the body, any person who is or will be carrying out the research on behalf of the body or the subject matter of the research to serious disadvantage".

This is a discretionary, harm based exemption. It can be used to withhold access to records where both of the following conditions are met:

(1) the record contains information in relation to research being or to be carried on by or on behalf of a public body; and

(2) disclosure of the information or its disclosure before the completion of the research would be likely to expose the body, any person who is or will be carrying out the research on behalf of the body, or the subject matter of the research to serious disadvantage.

This exemption is subject to a public interest test which provides that the exemption shall not apply to a case in which, in the opinion of the head of the public body concerned, the public interest would on balance be better served by the release of the record.[1]

---

[1] s.30(2).

Similar exemptions are found in the Australian federal FOI Act[2] and in many of the Australian State Acts.[3] The research exemptions in Canada tend to be expressed in terms of protecting the right of public sector employees to priority in the publication of research.[4] While this interest is likely to be protected under the terms of section 30 and its Australian counterparts, their scope is more extensive. In a review of the operation of the Australian federal FOI Act, it was recommended that the research exemption be repealed. The review bodies considered that the exemptions concerning commercially sensitive information and financial and economic interests of the State and public bodies would suffice to ensure that public bodies do not suffer financial disadvantage from premature release of research documents. It also argued that if the only concern is to prevent damage to reputation and career by protecting the researcher's priority of publication, public bodies may be able to use the deferral provisions in the Act to defer access until the research is published.[5]

2. Information in relation to research being or to be carried on by or on behalf of a public body

The first of the two conditions to be satisfied is that the record contains information in relation to research being or to be carried out by or on behalf of a public body. This condition can be further subdivided into three separate requirements. They are that:

(a) the record contains information in relation to research;

(b) the research is being or to be carried out; and

(c) the research is being or to be carried out by or on behalf of a public body.

---

[2] Freedom of Information Act 1982 (Cth), s.43A.

[3] Freedom of Information Act 1982 (Victoria), s.34(4)(b); Freedom of Information Act 1989 (New South Wales), Sched.1, cl.8(1); Freedom of Information Act 1991 (Tasmania), s.32(b); Freedom of Information Act 1991 (South Australia), Sched.1, cl.8; Freedom of Information Act 1992 (Queensland), s.45(3); Freedom of Information Act 1992 (Western Australia), Sched.1, cl.10(5).

[4] See, for example, Access to Information Act (Canada), R.S.C., 1985, s.18(c); Freedom of Information and Protection of Privacy Act (Ontario), R.S.O., 1990, s.18(1)(b); Freedom of Information and Protection of Privacy Act (British Columbia), R.S.B.C., 1996, s.17(2); Freedom of Information and Protection of Privacy Act (Alberta), S.A., 1994, s.24(1)(d); Freedom of Information and Protection of Privacy Act (Manitoba), C.C.S.M, 1998, c.F175, s.28(1)(d).

[5] Australian Law Reform Commission, Report No. 77/Administrative Review Council, Report No. 40, *Open Government: a review of the federal Freedom of Information Act 1982* (Australian Government Publishing Service, Canberra, 1995), para. 11.4.

(a) The record contains information in relation to research

The record must contain information in relation to research. The meaning of "research" was considered by the Queensland Information Commissioner in the context of the equivalent exemption of the Queensland Freedom of Information Act. The applicant sought access to a report recording information relating to worker's compensation insurance. The Information Commissioner quoted two dictionary definitions of research, which he referred to as most closely reflecting the meaning of the word "research" in the context of the exemption. The definitions referred to were:

> "a search or investigation undertaken to discover facts and reach new conclusions by the critical study of a subject or by a course of scientific enquiry"[6]

and

> "diligent and systematic enquiry or investigation into a subject in order to discover facts or principles".[7]

In applying these definitions, the Commissioner concluded that the report in question did not fall within the scope of the exemption, saying:

> "[T]he Report is essentially a record of the business operations and performance of the Board over a number of years. In that sense, it is more akin to the business records or accounts of an organisation than to the results of a research project undertaken to discover facts or principles. I do not consider that s.45(3) was intended to extend to the business accounts, or commonly kept business records, of an organisation."[8]

(b) The research is being or to be carried out

In order to qualify for exemption, the record must relate to research "being or to be carried out". It does not, therefore, apply to records relating to completed research. Difficulties may, however, arise in determining whether a record relates to research which is ongoing, and is therefore likely to be exempt, or whether it concerns completed research. The generation of countless "interim" reports in order to circumvent the Act is unlikely to be tolerated by the Information Commissioner. Where the research is to be carried out in the future, it is likely that evidence will be required of a concrete, rather than a vague, intention of carrying out the research. This would be in keeping with the approach adopted by the Ontarian Information and Privacy Commissioner when, in a case concerning the exemption of records relating to future negotiations

---

[6] *The New Shorter Oxford Dictionary* (Brown ed., Clarendon Press, Oxford, 1993).
[7] *The Macquarie Dictionary* (Herron Publications, West End, Queensland, 1985).
[8] *Re O'Dwyer and Workers' Compensation Board of Queensland* (1995) 3 Q.A.R. 97 at 106.

of public bodies,[9] he issued the following warning against projecting too far into the future:

> "[T]o interpret the phrase 'or to be carried on by or on behalf of an institution of the Government of Ontario' to mean any possible future negotiations including those that have not been presently commenced or even contemplated, is in my view, too wide".[10]

(c) The research is being or is to be carried out by or on behalf of a public body

The research must be "carried out by or on behalf of a public body". This means that it may be carried out by the staff of the public body itself, or it may be carried out on behalf of the public body, for example, by external consultants or contractors.

3. Disclosure of the information would be likely to expose to serious disadvantage

The second of the two conditions which must be met in order for section 31(1)(a) to apply is that "disclosure of the information or its disclosure before the completion of the research would be likely to expose the body, any person who is or will be carrying out the research on behalf of the body or the subject matter of the research to serious disadvantage". This condition can be divided into the following three elements:

(a) Disclosure of the information or its disclosure before the completion of the research must be likely to result in the harm specified.

(b) The harm must be caused either to:
    (i)   the body; or
    (ii) any person who is or will be carrying out research on behalf of the body; or
    (iii) the subject matter of the research.

(c) The disclosure must be likely to expose to serious disadvantage.

(a) Disclosure of the information or its disclosure before the completion of the research must be likely to result in the harm specified

This condition is met where either the disclosure of the information, or its disclosure before the completion of the research, would be likely to result in the harm specified. However, the second of these criteria, namely "disclosure

---

[9]   Freedom of Information and Protection of Privacy Act (Ontario), R.S.O., 1990, s.18(1)(c).
[10] *Re Ministry of Industry, Trade and Technology*, unreported, Information and Privacy Commissioner, Ontario, Order 87, August 24, 1989.

before the completion of the research" appears to be redundant, since "disclosure of information" is broad enough to encompass disclosure of information at any time.

(b) To whom may the harm be caused?

The harm must be caused to:

(i) the body; or

(ii) any person who is or will be carrying out research on behalf of the body; or

(iii) the subject matter of the research.

It is clear that harm to external consultants, as well as to the public body carrying out the research, can be taken into account. In addition, the likelihood of harm occurring to the individuals carrying out research is relevant. Such individuals may be in the employ of a public body carrying out the research, or they may be employed by external bodies carrying out research on behalf of the public body. The harm test can be satisfied not only through the accrual of disadvantage to the body or person carrying out the research, but also through disadvantage to the subject matter of the research. One form of disadvantage which could amount to harm to an individual carrying out research is loss of the right of a researcher to priority of publication of research. This type of disadvantage is expressly guarded against in the Ontarian FOI legislation. The relevant exemption was invoked by the Ontarian Ministry of Natural Resources, in responding to a request for access to records relating to wildlife rehabilitation and the keeping of wild animals in captivity. One of the records sought was a paper written by an employee of the public body, in respect of which the author had sworn an affidavit to the effect that she intended to publish it. The Commissioner, in holding that this record was exempt, declared himself to be persuaded that the employee intended to publish the document in an appropriate scientific form and to be satisfied that the premature release of the record could reasonably be expected to deprive her of priority of publication.[11]

(c) The disclosure must be likely to expose to serious disadvantage

Two matters arise for consideration here: the first relates to the standard of proof necessary to meet the requirements of the harm test; the second concerns the degree of harm which must be established. The standard of proof required is that the disclosure "would be likely" to expose to serious disadvantage. This standard seems to require evidence that the occurrence of the harm

---

[11] *Re Ministry of Natural Resources*, unreported, Information and Privacy Commissioner, Ontario, Order P–811, December 7, 1994.

be more probable than not. In New Zealand, however, the interpretation of the "would be likely to prejudice" standard to mean "more likely than not" was rejected in favour of the lower threshold of "a distinct or significant possibility".[12] The degree of harm provided for in section 30(1)(a) is "serious disadvantage". The standard used in the corresponding provision of the Australian federal Act is the lower one of "disadvantage". The "serious disadvantage" standard, it is submitted, is similar to that of "serious adverse effect"[13] or "significant, adverse effect"[14] found in other exemption provisions in the Irish Act. The closely related Australian "substantial adverse effect" standard has been interpreted in the context of other exemptions in the Australian Act as requiring a degree of gravity[15] and also as requiring that the effect be "serious and significant".[16] Such an interpretation of the "serious disadvantage" would appear justified in the context of section 30(1)(a) also.

B.   The Natural Resources Exemption

This exemption, which is also discretionary, provides as follows:

> "30.—(1) A head may refuse to grant a request under section 7 if, in the opinion of the head—
>
> . . .
>
> (b)   disclosure of information contained in the record could reasonably be expected to prejudice the well-being of a cultural, heritage or natural resource or a species, or the habitat of a species, of flora or fauna."

This exemption is harm based. The proof of harm required is based on the "could reasonably be expected to" standard, which is commonly used in the FOI Act. The standard of proof required to establish that harm "could reasonably be expected" to occur is discussed in detail above at pp. 90–92 above. In short, decisions in Canada and Australia have established that the possibility of the specified harm occurring will not suffice to meet the burden of proof, but neither is it necessary to show evidence of a direct causation between disclosure and harm. Nor does it appear necessary, in either jurisdiction, to show that the occurrence of the harm is more probable than not. In both Canada and Australia, the emphasis is on the reasonableness of the expectation of harm arising out of the disclosure.

---

[12] *Commissioner of Police v. Ombudsman* [1985] 1 N.Z.L.R. 578 at 589, *per* Jeffries J.
[13] s.31(1)(a). See below, p. 308.
[14] s.21(1)(b). See above, p. 160.
[15] *Harris v. Australian Broadcasting Corporation* (1983) 50 A.L.R. 551 at 564.
[16] *Re James and Australian National University* (1984) 6 A.L.D. 687; 2 A.A.R. 327 at 341.

The harm against which the exemption offers protection is prejudice to any of the following:

(1) a cultural resource;

(2) a heritage resource;

(3) a natural resource;

(4) a species of flora or fauna; or

(5) the habitat of a species of flora or fauna.

The exemption is subject to a public interest test which provides that the exemption shall not apply to a case in which, in the opinion of the head of the public body concerned, the public interest would on balance be better served by the release of the record.

Similar exemptions are to be found in state and provincial FOI legislation in Australia[17] and Canada.[18] A similar exemption exists, too, in the Swedish Freedom of Information Act.[19] The exemptions contained in the Canadian, Australian, and Swedish Acts have rarely been invoked and have not been the subject of any case law.

---

[17] Freedom of Information Act 1992 (Queensland), s.42(1)(j); Freedom of Information Act 1991 (Tasmania), s.35A.

[18] Freedom of Information and Protection of Privacy Act (British Columbia), R.S.B.C., 1996, s.18; Freedom of Information and Protection of Privacy Act (Alberta), S.A., 1994, s.27; Freedom of Information and Protection of Privacy Act (Nova Scotia), S.N.S., 1993, s.19; Freedom of Information and Protection of Privacy Act (Manitoba), C.C.S.M., 1998, c.F175, s.31.

[19] Freedom of the Press Act 1994, Chap. 2, article 2(7).

FINANCIAL AND ECONOMIC INTERESTS OF THE STATE AND PUBLIC BODIES

FINANCIAL AND ECONOMIC INTERESTS OF THE STATE AND PUBLIC BODIES

A. Introduction

There are three main aspects to the role of the State and public bodies in the national economy. First, the State acts as a planner of the economy. In fulfilling this role the State may engage in activities aimed at influencing the development of the economy in particular directions. Such activities might include interest rate and currency control. Second, the State has a role in regulating economic activity. Regulation can take the form of licensing or other forms of control of business and financial institutions. Finally, the State may itself act as a player in the economic life, for example, through the involvement of public bodies in commercial activities. Section 31 is concerned with protecting against disclosure records which relate to each of these aspects of the role of the State and public bodies in the economy. It provides as follows:

"31.—(1) A head may refuse to grant a request under section 7 in relation to a record (and, in particular, but without prejudice to the generality otherwise of this subsection, to a record to which subsection (2) applies) if, in the opinion of the head—

(a) access to the record could reasonably be expected to have a serious adverse affect on the financial interests of the State or on the ability of the Government to manage the national economy,

(b) premature disclosure of information contained in the record could reasonably be expected to result in undue disturbance of the ordinary course of business generally, or any particular class of business, in the State and access to the record would involve disclosure of the information that would, in all the circumstances, be premature, or

(c) access to the record could reasonably be expected to result in an unwarranted benefit or loss to a person or class of persons.

(2) This subsection applies to a record relating to—

(a) rates of exchange or the currency of the State,

(b) taxes, revenue duties or other sources of income for the State, a local authority or any other public body,

(c) interest rates,

(d) borrowing by or on behalf of the State or a public body,

(e) the regulation or supervision by or on behalf of the State or a public body of the business of banking or insurance or the lending of money or of other financial business or of institutions or other persons carrying on any of the businesses aforesaid,

(f) dealings in securities or foreign currency,

(g) the regulation or control by or on behalf of the State or a public body of wages, salaries or prices,

(h) proposals in relation to expenditure by or on behalf of the State or a public body including the control, restriction or prohibition of any such expenditure,

(i) property held by or on behalf of the State or a public body and transactions or proposed or contemplated transactions involving such property,

(j) foreign investment in enterprises in the State,

(k) industrial development in the State,

(l) trade between persons in the State and persons outside the State,

(m) trade secrets or financial, commercial, industrial, scientific or technical information belonging to the State or a public body and is of substantial value or is reasonably likely to be of substantial value,

(n) information the disclosure of which could reasonably be expected to affect adversely the competitive position of a public body in relation to activities carried on by it on a commercial basis, or

(o) the economic or financial circumstances of a public body.

(3) Subsection (1) does not apply in relation to a case in which, in the opinion of the head concerned, the public interest would, on balance, be better served by granting than by refusing to grant the request under section 7 concerned."

This exemption, the application of which is discretionary, consists of three paragraphs containing, in all, four separate grounds for refusing access to records. Each element of the exemption is subject to the operation of a harm test. In section 31(1), paragraph (a) incorporates two separate harm based exemptions, while paragraphs (b) and (c) each contains an additional harm based ground for refusing access. The four grounds of exemption are as follows:

(1) Access to the record could reasonably be expected to have a serious adverse effect on the financial interests of the State (section 31(1)(a)).

(2) Access to the record could reasonably be expected to have a serious adverse effect on the ability of the Government to manage the national economy (section 31(1)(a)).

(3) The ground for exemption set out in section 31(1)(b) can be broken down into two cumulative requirements. It must be shown:

(a) that access to the record would involve disclosure of the information that would, in all the circumstances, be premature; and

(b) that premature disclosure of information contained in the record could reasonably be expected to result in undue disturbance of the ordinary course of business generally, or any particular class of business in the State.

(4) Access to the record could reasonably be expected to result in an unwarranted benefit or loss to a person or class of persons (section 31(1)(c)).

Section 31(2) sets out a list of the types of records to which the exemption may apply. It is clear from the text that the list contained in section 31(2) is for illustrative purposes and was not intended to be exhaustive. The exemption can, therefore, be held to apply to records other than those listed in section 31(2). Proof that the record sought falls within the terms of one of the categories listed in section 31(2) will not be sufficient to render the record exempt. One of the limbs of section 31(1) must also be satisfied.

The exemption is subject to a public interest test which is set out in section 31(3). It provides that section 31(1) does not apply where the head of the public body concerned is of the opinion that the public interest, would, on balance, be better served by granting than by refusing to grant the request.

The Australian, Canadian, and New Zealand Acts all include exemptions aimed at protecting against disclosure information relating to the financial and economic interests of government and public bodies.[1] Section 31 bears strongest resemblance to its Australian counterparts.

B. The Harm Test

The standard imposed in the application of the harm tests set out in each of the four separate limbs of this exemption is whether, in the opinion of the head of public body, access to the record "could reasonably be expected" to result in the harm specified.

The standard of proof required to establish that harm "could reasonably be expected" to occur is discussed in detail above at pp. 90–92. In short, deci-

---

[1] Australia: Freedom of Information Act 1982 (Cth), ss.39 and 44; Freedom of Information Act 1982 (Victoria), s.36; Freedom of Information Act 1989 (New South Wales), Sched.1, cl.14; Freedom of Information Act 1991 (South Australia), Sched.1, cl.14; Freedom of Information Act 1991 (Tasmania), s.35; Freedom of Information Act 1992 (Queensland), s.47; Freedom of Information Act 1992 (Western Australia), Sched.1, cl.9.
Canada: Access to Information Act (Canada), R.S.C., 1985, s.18; Right to Information Act (New Brunswick), S.N.B., 1978, s.6(c.1); Freedom of Information Act (Newfoundland), R.S.N., 1990, s.11(c); An Act respecting Access to documents held by public bodies and the Protection of personal information (Quebec), S.Q., 1982, ss.21 and 22; Freedom of Information and Protection of Privacy Act (Manitoba), C.C.S.M., 1998, c.F175, s.28; Freedom of Information and Protection of Privacy Act (Ontario), R.S.O., 1990, s.18(1); Freedom of Information and Protection of Privacy Act (Saskatchewan), S.S., 1990–1991, s.18(1); Freedom of Information and Protection of Privacy Act (British Columbia), R.S.B.C., 1996, s.17; Freedom of Information and Protection of Privacy Act (Nova Scotia), S.N.S., 1993, s.17(1); Freedom of Information and Protection of Privacy Act (Alberta), S.A., 1994, s.24.
New Zealand: Official Information Act 1982, ss.6(d) and 9(2)(d).

sions in Canada and Australia have indicated that establishing the possibility of the specified harm occurring will not suffice to meet the burden of proof, but neither is it necessary to show evidence of a direct causation between disclosure and harm. Nor does it appear necessary, in either jurisdiction, to show that the occurrence of the harm is more probable than not. In both juris-dictions, the emphasis is on the reasonableness of the expectation of harm arising out of the disclosure. Each limb of the exemption will now be exam-ined.

1. **Serious adverse effect on the financial interests of the State: section 31(1)(a)**

The degree of harm required in respect of this limb of the exemption is that of a "serious adverse effect". This standard is somewhat similar to that adopted in the equivalent New Zealand provision (section 6(d)) which requires proof of "serious" damage to the economy and the equivalent Australian federal exemption (section 39), which requires evidence of a "substantial adverse ef-fect" on the financial or property interests of the Commonwealth or of a gov-ernment agency. The "substantial adverse effect" standard has been interpreted, in the context of other exemptions in the Australian Act, as requiring a degree of gravity[2] and also as requiring that the effect be "serious and significant".[3] In the Australian federal case of *Re Connolly and Department of Finance*[4] those interpretations were approved in the context of the section 39. The "sub-stantial adverse effect" standard is also found in the equivalent exemption in the Queensland Act.[5] The Queensland Information Commissioner, in inter-preting this phrase, contrasted it with the "adverse effect" standard found in another of the exemptions[6] in the Queensland Act. The Commissioner stated that the legislature must have intended an "adverse effect" to be one that is "real" or "actual" or "having substance, not illusory". The adjective "substan-tial", the Commissioner concluded, was intended by the legislature to be used in the sense of grave, weighty, significant or serious.[7] Given the fact that the "adverse effect" standard is found in another of the exemptions in the Irish FOI Act,[8] the same distinction between "adverse effect" and "serious adverse effect" could be readily drawn in this jurisdiction.

---

[2] *Harris v. Australian Broadcasting Corporation* (1983) 50 A.L.R. 551 at 564.
[3] *Re James and Australian National University* (1984) 6 A.L.D. 687; 2 A.A.R. 327 at 341.
[4] (1994) 34 A.L.D. 655.
[5] Matter relating to trade secrets, business affairs, and research: Freedom of Information Act 1992 (Queensland), s.49.
[6] *ibid.*, s.45(1)(c).
[7] *Re Cairns Port Authority and Department of Lands; Cairns Shelfco, Third Party* (1994) 1 Q.A.R. 663 at 725.
[8] Security, defence and international relations: s.24.

This element of the exemption is concerned with protecting the financial interests of the State at the macro level. It differs from the equivalent Australian federal provision[9] which exempts from disclosure documents which would have a substantial adverse effect on the financial or property interests of the Commonwealth *or of an agency*. Section 31(1)(a) is not concerned with the effects of disclosure on the financial interests of public bodies but rather with damage to the general financial interests of the State as a whole. Clearly damage to the financial interests of an important public body could have a serious adverse effect on the State as a whole. In the case of a less significant public body, serious damage to its interests would not necessarily amount to "serious adverse effect on the financial interests of the State".

The damage must be caused to the financial interests of the State. The scope of this limb of the exemption is narrower than that of its federal Australian and Queensland counterparts, since the latter also extend to property interests. Harm to the financial interests of the State clearly involves the type of harm which can be quantified in monetary terms. It is primarily concerned with harm arising in the context of the State's direct financial dealings in the areas, for example, of currency matters, interest rates, borrowing, public expenditure, and taxation. Damage to the State's broader interests, such as those in property, industrial development, foreign investment, etc., may also be relevant provided that it results in harm to the financial interests of the State.

Consideration of the scope of the Australian counterparts of this limb of the exemption has been somewhat sparse. In the Australian federal case of *Re Connolly and Department of Finance*[10] the applicant had requested access to records concerning the Australian Government's strategy for disposing of Australia's uranium stockpile. The Administrative Appeals Tribunal (A.A.T.) decided that the documents were exempt, on the grounds that their disclosure would have a substantial adverse effect on the financial or property interests of the Commonwealth. The tribunal based its decision on the fact that the disclosure of the requested documents would reveal the Commonwealth's strategy for selling a very substantial amount of uranium in a thin, sensitive, and confidential market. This would inevitably affect the general spot price of the ore and lower the price which the Commonwealth might reasonably be expected to achieve. The A.A.T. found that it was possible to quantify the meaning of "substantial" by reference to the movements in dollar value of Commonwealth property. There was evidence of a risk of the magnitude of A\$3m and that was held to amount to a substantial adverse effect for the purposes of the exemption.

In the Queensland case of *Re Cairns Port Authority and Department of Lands; Cairns Shelfco, Third Party*[11] the information at issue was valuation

---

[9] Freedom of Information Act 1982 (Cth), s.39.
[10] Above, n. 4.
[11] Above, n. 7.

reports relating to land which was leased to the third party by the applicant. The third party, Cairns Shelfco, had applied for access to the valuations and the applicant, on being consulted by the Department, objected to the disclosure of the valuations *inter alia* on the grounds that their release could reasonably be expected to have a substantial adverse effect on the financial or property interests of the State or an agency. The applicant had claimed that the information was exempt and cited the adverse effects which would result from disclosure, including the fact that it would probably lead to litigation by the third party against the applicant and also that it would put the applicant at a commercial disadvantage in its capacity to negotiate the most favourable terms with respect to the leases. The Queensland Information Commissioner held that neither of these adverse effects could reasonably be expected to result from the disclosure. On the issue of damage to negotiating capacity, the Commissioner pointed out that the situation under consideration was one where a negotiated lease already existed, stating that this was materially different to one in which a landowner is in the course of attempting to negotiate the most favourable terms of a lease with a prospective tenant. A claim for exemption based on a case with facts similar to these would be even less likely to succeed under section 31(1)(a), given the fact that, unlike the corresponding Queensland provision, the harm test in section 31(1)(a) does not expressly cover damage to property interests.

2. Serious adverse effect on the ability of the Government to manage the economy: section 31(1)(a)

This limb of the exemption is aimed at protecting records the disclosure of which could reasonably be expected to have a serious adverse effect on the ability of the Government to manage the economy. The expected effect must be upon the Government's ability to manage the economy, rather than upon the economy itself. There is an equivalent exemption in the Australian[12] and Canadian[13] federal FOI Acts, as well as in state and provincial FOI Acts in Australia[14] and Canada.[15] The scope of this exemption has not, however, been

---

[12] Freedom of Information Act 1982 (Cth), s.44(1).

[13] Access to Information Act (Canada), R.S.C., 1985, s.18(d).

[14] See, for example, Freedom of Information Act 1982 (Victoria), s.36; Freedom of Information Act 1989 (New South Wales), Sched.1, cl.14(a); Freedom of Information Act 1989 (South Australia), Sched.1, cl.14(a); Freedom of Information Act 1991 (Tasmania), s.35(1)(a) and 35(2)(a); Freedom of Information Act 1992 (Queensland), s.47(1); Freedom of Information Act 1992 (Western Australia), Sched.1, cl.9(1).

[15] See, for example, Freedom of Information and Protection of Privacy Act (Ontario), R.S.O., 1990, s.18(1)(d); Freedom of Information and Protection of Privacy Act (British Columbia), R.S.B.C., 1996, s.17(1); Freedom of Information and Protection of Privacy Act (Nova Scotia), S.N.S., 1993, s.17(1); Freedom of Information and Protection of Privacy Act (Alberta), S.A., 1994, s.24(1).

subjected to detailed examination in any of these jurisdictions. In an Ontarian case, the applicant had been denied access to a study relating to a proposed tourism development which had been jointly funded by a government institution and a private company. In ordering that access be granted, the Information and Privacy Commissioner rejected the institution's argument to the effect that forced early release of the study would interfere with the ability of the Government of Ontario, through the institution, to manage the economy. The institution had based this argument on the suggestion that its financing of the study constituted a contribution towards the management of the economy of Ontario.[16]

3. Premature disclosure resulting in undue disturbance of business generally or any particular class of business: section 31(1)(b)

In order to qualify for exemption under this heading, it must be established that:

(1) access to the record would involve disclosure of the information that would, in all the circumstances, be premature; and

(2) premature disclosure of information contained in the record could reasonably be expected to result in undue disturbance of the ordinary course of business generally, or any particular class of business in the State.

In terms of the first requirement, namely that access to the record would involve premature disclosure of information, it is clear that the exemption will not protect from disclosure information relating to schemes or plans which have already been put into effect.

The harm specified must be caused to business generally, or to a particular class of business, and it is not, therefore, concerned with the effect of disclosure on individual business activities.

There is no definition of what constitutes "undue" disturbance. Its meaning will require a qualitative judgment.

4. Unwarranted loss or benefit to a person or class of persons: section 31(1)(c)

The aim of this limb of the exemption is to prevent the use the FOI Act to obtain access to government information, the disclosure of which would enable people to secure for themselves undeserved benefits or would result in unwarranted losses to others such as competitors. "Person" is defined in the Interpretation Act 1937 as "importing a body corporate (whether a corpora-

---

[16] *Re Ministry of Tourism and Recreation*, unreported, Information and Privacy Commissioner, Ontario, Order P–41, March 2, 1989.

tion aggregate or a corporation sole) and an unincorporated body of persons as well as an individual".[17] It will, therefore, include individuals, partnerships, companies, and unincorporated associations. The benefit or loss need not necessarily be commercial or financial in nature.

C. Examples of Information to which the Exemption May Apply

The list of categories of record set out in section 31(2) is provided by way of example only, since it is explicitly stated to be non-exhaustive; nor does falling within the scope of this list automatically render a record exempt. One or other of the injury tests set out in section 31(1)(a), (b), or (c) must be satisfied. The records listed cover:

(1) exchange rates or currency of the State;

(2) taxes or other sources of income for the State or a public body;

(3) interest rates;

(4) public borrowing;

(5) regulation of banking or insurance;

(6) dealings in securities or foreign currency;

(7) regulation of wages, salaries or prices;

(8) public expenditure proposals;

(9) property transactions;

(10) foreign investment in enterprises in the State;

(11) industrial developments in the State;

(12) trade between persons in the State and persons outside the State;

(13) trade secrets or commercial information of substantial value belonging to the State or public bodies;

(14) information the disclosure of which could result in competitive harm; and

(15) economic or financial circumstances of a public body.

The equivalent New Zealand,[18] Australian,[19] and Canadian[20] exemptions also

---

[17] s.11.
[18] Official Information Act 1982, s.6(d).
[19] Freedom of Information Act 1982 (Cth), ss.39 and 44(1).
[20] Access to Information Act (Canada), R.S.C., 1985, s.18.

incorporate lists of classes of records to which the exemption may apply. New Zealand's list consists of six categories of information and is exhaustive of the scope of the exemption. The Canadian and Australian approaches are closer to that adopted in section 31, in that they set out open-ended lists of information to which the exemption may apply. The list in the Canadian federal provision contains six items, and the Australian federal list, seven. The Irish list is more comprehensive than its Australian, Canadian, or New Zealand counterparts. It includes within its scope all of the items listed in the equivalent exemption in each of the other jurisdictions. Matters which appear in the Irish, but not in the Australian, Canadian, or New Zealand lists are industrial developments in the State and economic or financial circumstances of a public body. The last category, in particular, has the potential to be broadly interpreted. It must, however, be borne in mind that such information will only be exempt if its disclosure would result in one of the forms of harm specified in section 31(1).

D. Public Interest Test

The exemption is subject to a public interest test.[21] The test provides that section 31(1) does not apply where, in the opinion of the head of the public body concerned, the public interest would on balance be better served by granting than by refusing to grant the request. The equivalent Australian federal and Queensland exemptions are also subject to a public interest test. The application of the public interest test was considered by the federal A.A.T. in *Re Connolly and Department of Finance*.[22] The applicant had requested access to documents concerning the Government's strategy for the disposal of Australia's uranium stockpile. The tribunal acknowledged the right of the public to know, in general terms, the way in which the Government is carrying out its plan to realise assets that belong to the public. That interest was, however, outweighed by the fact that, in the peculiar circumstances of the uranium industry, the value of the Government's property and that of Australia's uranium producers would be substantially diminished if the requests for access were granted. The taking into account by the tribunal not only of the direct effect on the value of the Government's property, but also of the effect on uranium producers went beyond the terms of the Australian federal exemption, since its scope is limited to consideration of the effects on the government or an agency and does not allow for the taking into account of the effect of disclosure on third parties. In the Queensland case of *Re Cairns Port Authority v. Department of Lands; Cairns, Shelfco Third Party*[23] the public interest was

---

[21] s.31(3).
[22] Above, n. 4.
[23] Above, n. 7.

considered in the context of a request for access to valuation reports relating to land which was leased to Cairns Shelfco by the Port Authority. The Information Commissioner found that the public interest favoured disclosure of the records to the Cairns Shelfco:

> "to enable it to satisfy itself that the valuations had not proceeded on a fundamentally erroneous basis, or if they have, to take any appropriate remedial action which the law permits."[24]

The Commissioner refused to allow that public interest consideration to be outweighed by the fact that disclosure of the documents requested would result in the public body losing money, saying:

> "The fact that any diminution in rent payable by Cairns Shelfco to the CPA [the applicant] would mean that less money was available to the CPA to enable it to carry out its statutory functions, and to reinvest in the development and upgrading of harbour facilities for the benefit of the public, cannot in my opinion, be accepted as a valid public interest consideration favouring non-disclosure, or at least cannot be accepted as one deserving of any substantial weight. The public interest in having funds spent on harbour facilities could not justify those funds being obtained by unfair means, such as levying rent by reference to a valuation which proceeded on a fundamentally erroneous basis."[25]

Therefore, the fact that disclosure may result in financial damage to a public body will not be sufficient to justify the withholding of the record where there are other public interest considerations outweighing that factor.

---

[24] Above, n. 7, at 723.
[25] *ibid.*

CHAPTER 17

ENACTMENTS RELATING TO NON-DISCLOSURE OF RECORDS

ENACTMENTS RELATING TO NON-DISCLOSURE OF RECORDS

A. Introduction

Given the tradition of secrecy in Irish government administration, it is not surprising that a large number of Irish statutes contain restrictions on disclosure of records. The best known of these is the Official Secrets Act 1963, but there are a host of others ranging from the Adoption Acts 1952–1991 to less well-known statutes such as the Turf Development Acts 1946 and 1983, and the Wireless Telegraphy Act 1926. The question faced by the legislature was whether FOI access rights should prevail over these restrictions. On the one hand, it could be argued that the removal of all existing restrictions on disclosure of records could leave important interests unprotected. On the other hand, the retention of existing statutory prohibitions on disclosure of records, by means of an exemption from the FOI Act, for records the subject of such prohibitions, would to a great extent defeat the purposes of the Act. There is also an argument to the effect that the inclusion of a secrecy exemption is superfluous. The other exemption provisions of the FOI Act, it is suggested, should be sufficient in themselves to protect any interests which merit protection and, on that basis, there should be no saver for secrecy provisions in other statutes. That was the approach of the joint Australian Law Reform Commission/Administrative Review Council review on the operation of the Australian federal FOI Act.[1] The review recommended the repeal of section 38 of the Australian FOI Act, which preserves the secrecy provisions of other enactments, saying:

> "the Review considers that the exemption provisions in the FOI Act represent the full extent of information that should not be disclosed to members of the public. Secrecy provisions that prohibit the disclosure of information that would not fall within the exemption provisions are too broad. The Review considers that repealing s38 would promote a more pro-disclosure culture in agencies".[2]

---

[1] Australian Law Reform Commission, Report No. 77/Administrative Review Council, Report No. 40, *Open Government: a review of the federal Freedom of Information Act 1982* (Australian Government Publishing Service, Canberra, 1995).
[2] *ibid.*, para. 11.3.

Nonetheless, overseas FOI legislation generally exempts from the right of access records to which the secrecy provisions of other enactments apply.[3] Legislators in Ireland have approached the question of the relationship between existing restrictions on access to records and the FOI Act by providing for the exemption from FOI access rights of records, the disclosure of which is restricted by other enactments, but specifically excluding from the scope of that exemption a number of legislative restrictions on disclosure which are specifically referred to in the Third Schedule to the Act: the effect is to leave in place existing statutory restrictions on disclosure apart from those listed in the Third Schedule.

The exemption, which is expressed in mandatory terms, provides as follows:

"32.—(1) A head shall refuse to grant a request under section 7 if—
  (a) the disclosure of the record concerned is prohibited by any enactment (other than a provision specified in column (3) of the Third Schedule of an enactment specified in that Schedule), or
  (b) the non-disclosure of the record is authorised by any such enactment in certain circumstances and the case is one in which the head would, pursuant to the enactment, refuse to disclose the record.

(2) A joint committee of both Houses of the Oireachtas shall, if authorised in that behalf by both such Houses (and such a committee so authorised is referred to subsequently in this section as 'the committee')—
  (a) review from time to time the operation of any provisions of any enactment that authorise or require the non-disclosure of a record (other than a provision specified in the said column (3)) for the purpose of ascertaining whether, having regard to the provisions, purposes and spirit of this Act—
     (i) any of those provisions should be amended or repealed, or

---

[3] Australia: Freedom of Information Act 1982 (Cth), s.38; Freedom of Information Act 1982 (Victoria), s.38; Freedom of Information Act 1989 (New South Wales), Sched.1, cl.12; Freedom of Information Act 1991 (South Australia), Sched.1, cl.12; Freedom of Information Act 1991 (Tasmania), s.36; Freedom of Information Act 1992 (Queensland), s.48; Freedom of Information Act 1992 (Western Australia), Sched.1, cl.14.
Canada: Access to Information Act (Canada), R.S.C., 1985, s. 24(1); Right to Information Act (New Brunswick), S.N.B., 1978, s.6(a); Freedom of Information Act (Newfoundland), R.S.N., 1990, s.9(1)(g); An Act respecting Access to documents held by public bodies and the Protection of personal information (Quebec), S.Q., 1982, ss.168–170; Freedom of Information and Protection of Privacy Act (Manitoba), C.C.S.M., 1998, c.F175, s.5(1); Freedom of Information and Protection of Privacy Act (Ontario), R.S.O., 1990, s.67(1) and (2); Freedom of Information and Protection of Privacy Act (Saskatchewan), S.S., 1990–1991, s.23; Freedom of Information and Protection of Privacy Act (British Columbia), R.S.B.C., 1996, s.78; Freedom of Information and Protection of Privacy Act (Alberta), S.A., 1994, s.5.
New Zealand: Official Information Act 1982, s.18(c)(i).
U.S.: Freedom of Information Act 1966, Exemption 3.

   (ii) a reference to any of them should be included in the said column
         (3),
   and
(b) prepare and furnish to each such House a report in writing of the re-
     sults of the review aforesaid and, if it considers it appropriate to do so,
     include in the report recommendations in relation to the amendment,
     repeal or continuance in force of, or the inclusion in the said column
     (3) of a reference to, any of those provisions.

(3) A Minister of the Government shall, in accordance with subsection (6), prepare and furnish to the committee reports in writing—
   (a) specifying, as respects any enactments that confer functions on that
        Minister of the Government or on a public body in relation to which
        functions are vested in that Minister of the Government, any provi-
        sions thereof that authorise or require the non-disclosure of a record,
        and
   (b) specifying whether, in the opinion of that Minister of the Government
        and (where appropriate) any such public body, formed having regard
        to the provisions, purposes and spirit of this Act—
        (i)   any of the provisions referred to in paragraph (a) should be
              amended, repealed or allowed to continue in force, or
        (ii) a reference to any of them should be included in the said column
              (3),
        and outlining the reasons for the opinion.

(4) A Minister of the Government shall cause a copy of a report prepared by him
or her under subsection (3) to be furnished to the Commissioner and to be laid
before each House of the Oireachtas.

(5) The Commissioner may, and shall, if so requested by the committee, furnish
to the committee his or her opinion and conclusions in relation to a report under
subsection (3) or any matter contained in or arising out of such a report or any
matter relating to or arising out of the operation of this section.

(6) The first report under subsection (3) of a Minister of the Government shall
be furnished by him or her in accordance with that subsection not later than 12
months after the commencement of this Act and subsequent such reports of that
Minister of the Government shall be so furnished not later than 30 days after the
fifth anniversary of the day on which the last previous such report by him or her
was so furnished."

The provisions excluded from the scope of the exemption are set out in the
Third Schedule to the Act. These provisions are referred to in the Explanatory
Memorandum to the Bill as "general 'catch-all' secrecy provisions". They
include sections 4, 5, and 9 of the Official Secrets Act 1963, as well as confi-
dentiality provisions in the Industrial Relations Acts 1946–1990, Competition
Act 1991, and Industrial Development Acts 1986–1993. Although they are
referred to as general secrecy provisions, some are quite specific in nature.
For example, the provisions of the Industrial Relations Acts 1946–1990 which

are included in the Third Schedule[4] are aimed at preventing the inclusion in reports of the Labour Court, or of the Labour Relations Commission, or in recommendations of Rights Commissioners of information relating to trade unions or businesses which is not otherwise available. An almost identical provision in the Anti-Discrimination (Pay) Act 1974[5] concerning the inclusion of information relating to trade unions or businesses in recommendations or determinations of Equality Officers is not listed in the Third Schedule, leading one to believe that the compilation of the list of provisions in that Schedule was somewhat haphazard.

Section 32 is subject to a review process, the details of which are set out in section 32(2) to 32(6). The aim of the review process is to subject existing secrecy provisions to scrutiny to see whether they should be repealed, amended or allowed to continue in force. It appears that the broad scope of section 32 is expected to diminish over time as a result of the operation of this review process. It was suggested by the sponsoring Minister, Ms Fitzgerald, that the reason why more provisions were not included in the Third Schedule at the outset was largely a matter of practicality:

> "We had the option of spending a further three years trawling through the secrecy provisions of all other enactments and receiving reports as to whether they should remain, be amended or otherwise. It is proposed instead to charge a committee of the Dáil with carrying out that function, consider the various Acts, receive reports from Government bodies and lay its own report before the House, which will also be placed in the public domain."[6]

B.   Analysis

Apart from the provisions listed in the Third Schedule, existing statutory restrictions on disclosure of records are retained pending their review. The effect of section 32, therefore, is to place the access provisions in the FOI Act in a subordinate position to statutory restrictions on disclosure of records, apart from those listed in the Third Schedule.

This approach is the opposite of that adopted at federal level in Australia and Canada. While the FOI statutes in both those jurisdictions contain secrecy exemptions, the scope of those exemptions is limited to such of those prohibitions as are listed in relevant schedules to the FOI statutes,[7] with the Australian exemption also applying in situations where a restriction on disclosure

---

[4] Industrial Relations Act 1946, s.22; Industrial Relations Act 1969, s.14; Industrial Relations Act 1990, s.25(6).
[5] Anti-Discrimination (Pay) Act 1974, s.8(2).
[6] 149 *Seanad Debates* Col. 1585 (Committee Stage).
[7] Australia: Freedom of Information Act 1982 (Cth), s.38(1); Canada: Access to Information Act (Canada), R.S.C., 1985, s.24(1).

under the FOI Act is expressly applied to the document or information by the provision that contains the prohibition. Interestingly, the Australians originally operated under a regime similar to that adopted under the Irish Act. The Australian Act was amended in 1991 following a recommendation of the Australian Senate Standing Committee on Legal and Constitutional Affairs that the FOI Act should contain an exhaustive list of secrecy provisions which were to prevail over FOI access rights.[8] This recommendation was based on the Committee's view that:

> "[A]ny provision which restricts the application of the FOI Act should be apparent on the face of the FOI Act."[9]

The Canadian and Australian approach is clearly more pro-disclosure than its Irish counterpart, since it requires the identification of those restrictions on disclosure which are to be left in place and prevents provisions falling outside the scope of that list from obstructing the disclosure of records under FOI.

The approach in New Zealand[10] is different to that adopted in Canada or Australia in that it is open-ended. It provides that a request may be refused where the making available of the information requested would be contrary to the provisions of a specified enactment. No list of specified enactments is provided in the Official Information Act. The provision has been taken to mean that a decision-maker is required to point exactly to the provision in question in an Act or regulation which is being used to justify withholding the requested information.[11] The relevant exemption in the U.S. allows the withholding of information where a statute either:

(1) requires that the matters be withheld from the public in such a manner as to leave no discretion on the issue; or

(2) establishes particular criteria for withholding or refers to particular types of matters to be withheld.

Again, no attempt is made to list the provisions of such statutes in the U.S. FOI Act.[12]

---

[8] Senate Standing Committee on Legal and Constitutional Affairs, *Report on the Operation and Administration of the Freedom of Information Legislation* (Australian Government Publishing Service, Canberra, 1987), para. 12.31.

[9] *ibid.*, para. 12.32.

[10] New Zealand: Official Information Act 1982, s.18(c)(i); U.S.: Freedom of Information Act 1966, Exemption 3. This was also the approach in the original version of the Australian exemption, s.38, which was amended in 1991 by the Freedom of Information Amendment Act 1991 (Cth).

[11] Eagles, Taggart, and Liddell, *Freedom of Information in New Zealand* (Oxford University Press, Auckland, 1992), p. 489.

[12] Exemption 3. This was also the approach in the original version of the corresponding Australian exemption, s.38, which was amended in 1991: above, n. 10.

Section 32 applies where disclosure of the requested record is restricted in one or other of the following ways:

(1) the disclosure of the record requested is prohibited by any enactment other than a provision referred to in the Third Schedule; or

(2) the non-disclosure of the requested record is authorised by an enactment referred to in the Third Schedule in certain circumstances and the case is one in which the head of the public body would, pursuant to that enactment, refuse to disclose the record.

In order to qualify for exemption under this provision, it must be shown that:

(1) there is an enactment either:
   (a) prohibiting disclosure, or
   (b) authorising non-disclosure in certain circumstances and the case is one in which the head would, pursuant to the enactment, refuse to disclose the record;
   and

(2) the requested record falls within the category of records prohibited from disclosure or authorised to be withheld by that enactment.

1. Is there an enactment prohibiting disclosure or authorising non-disclosure?

Two matters arise for consideration. The threshold issue is whether the provision being relied upon to justify withholding of the record amounts to an *enactment*. "Enactment" is defined in section 2(1) of the FOI Act as "a statute or instrument made under a power conferred by a statute". Statutory instrument is defined in section 1(1) of the Statutory Instruments Act 1947 as meaning "an order, regulation, rule, scheme or by-law made in exercise of a statutory power".[13] Clearly provisions in Acts, Regulations and Orders will be covered by this definition. Equally clearly, circulars emanating from public bodies will not be covered. Therefore Circular 15/79 on Official Secrecy and Integrity, which sets out obligations of civil servants in relation to official secrecy and integrity, would not qualify as a section 32 enactment,[14] nor will common law rules restricting disclosure of information, such as the law of confidence, fall within the scope of the exemption.

---

[13] See Hogan and Morgan, *Administrative Law in Ireland* (3rd ed., Round Hall Sweet & Maxwell, Dublin, 1998), pp. 33–35 for examples of the various forms of delegated legislation.

[14] April 2, 1979. See Dáil Select Committee on Legislation and Security, *Report on Review of the Official Secrets Act, 1963* (1997), pp. 18–20, for an analysis of the contents of this Circular.

The primary issue to be considered under section 32(1) is whether the enactment relied upon meets either of the disjunctive requirements of that provisions. They are:

(a) that the enactment prohibits disclosure of the record; or

(b) that the enactment authorises non-disclosure of records in certain circumstances and the case is one in which the head would refuse to disclose the record.

(a) Does the enactment prohibit disclosure?

Two main questions arise in respect of the application of this limb of the exemption. The first is whether in order to qualify under section 32(1)(a) it is necessary that the prohibition in question be absolute and exclude any discretionary disclosures. The first part of the equivalent U.S. exemption expressly requires that there be no room for the exercise of discretion, whereas the Australian provision in its original form applied to prohibitions on disclosure whether or not they were subject to qualifications or exceptions. The Irish exemption is silent on the issue. There are, in practice, few absolute prohibitions on disclosure apart from those referred to in the Third Schedule. Most non-disclosure provisions are subject to exceptions. The prohibition on disclosure of information contained in section 16 of the Central Bank Act 1989, for example, is subject to a long list of exceptions. It is unlikely, therefore, that the scope of section 32(1)(a) would be confined to absolute prohibitions.

The other issue arising in respect of section 32(1)(a) is whether prohibitions which are based on the status or identity of the person to whom they are directed, rather than upon the nature of the information itself, come within its scope. In the Australian federal case of *News Corporation Ltd v. National Companies and Securities Commission*[15] enactments restricting or prohibiting disclosure of information were divided into three categories by the Federal Court. Category one was said to include those enactments that define the information to which they apply by intrinsic characteristics, in particular the nature and quality of the information concerned. The second category relied upon the status or capacity of the person in possession of the information, while the third consisted of an intermediate hybrid group. A number of examples of the various categories of provision were given and it was held that the exemption should apply only in respect of enactments in category one. The court said that the secrecy exemption in the Australian federal Act (section 38):

> "should be construed as applying when enactments specify the nature or quality of the information which is not to be disclosed; it has no application if the

---

[15] (1984) 52 A.L.R. 277.

enactment identifies the information merely by reference to the capacity of the person who has received or is in possession of the information."[16]

In another Australian federal case, *Kavvadias v. Commonwealth Ombudsman*,[17] it was claimed that restrictions on disclosure of information in the Australian Ombudsman Act 1976, which included a prohibition on disclosure by an officer of information acquired by reason of his being such an officer, amounted to a prohibition on disclosure within the meaning of the secrecy exemption. This argument was rejected by the Federal Court, which stated:

> "It may be thought adequate for the purposes of the section that the enactment to which it refers should prohibit disclosure of information by reference to it having been received by officers in the course of their duty. Such a prohibition would say nothing directly as to the kind of information in question, which, depending upon the role of the officers, may be of a very wide, almost limitless nature. It seems to us that s38 requires that there be a more direct and explicit reference to the nature of the information itself. Information is the commodity being dealt with in the Act, not the discipline or integrity of officers."[18]

If a similar approach is adopted in this jurisdiction, provisions such as section 44(1) of the Building Societies Act 1989 which prohibits the disclosure by officers or employees of the Central Bank of "any information concerning the business of any building society which may come to his knowledge by virtue of his employment" might be found to lie outside the scope of section 32(1)(a).[19]

(b) Does the enactment authorise non-disclosure of records in certain circumstances and is the case one in which the head would refuse to disclose the record?

The second limb of section 32(1) is made up of two cumulative requirements. They are that:

(i)   the enactment authorises non-disclosure in certain circumstances; and

(ii) the case is one in which the head would, pursuant to the enactment, refuse to disclose the record.

---

[16] Above, n. 15, at 283.
[17] (1984) 52 A.L.R. 728; 1 F.C.R. 80; 6 A.L.D. 47.
[18] *ibid.* at 733.
[19] Other provisions which prohibit disclosure of information primarily by reference to it having been received by officers in the course of their duty include: Gas Act 1976, s.20; Údarás na Gaeltachta Act 1979, s.15; Local Government (Planning and Development) Act 1983, s.13; National Social Service Board Act 1984, s.16; Industrial Development Act 1986, s.43; Combat Poverty Agency Act 1986, s.20; Labour Services Act 1987, s.13; Agriculture (Research, Training and Advice) Act 1988, s.14; Forestry Act 1988, s.33; Bord Glas Act 1990, s.23; National Treasury Management Agency Act 1990, s.14; Pensions Act 1990, s.24; Marine Institute Act 1991, s.15; Radiological Protection Act 1991, s.36(1)(d); Trade and Marketing Promotion Act 1991, s.10; Industrial Development Act 1993, s.5; Irish Medicines Board Act 1995, s.23.

(i) The enactment authorises non-disclosure in certain circumstances

The scope of the second limb of section 32(1) extends beyond provisions which prohibit the disclosure of records to cover enactments which authorise the non-disclosure of records. In order to qualify for exemption under this provision it must be shown that the enactment authorises non-disclosure in "certain circumstances". Thus, it could not apply to very general provisions authorising non-disclosure. This limb of the exemption arguably has a counterpart in Exemption 3(B) of the U.S. FOI Act. That exemption allows the withholding of information where a statute:

> "establishes particular criteria for withholding or refers to particular types of matters to be withheld."

The requirement in the first part of paragraph (B) that an enactment must establish particular criteria for withholding information is somewhat similar to the requirement under section 32(1)(b) that the enactment must authorise disclosure in "certain circumstances". This limb of Exemption 3 has been held not to apply in the absence of statutory guidance on the exercise of the discretion to withhold information. In *CNA Financial Corp. v. Donovan* it was held that the U.S. Trade Secrets Act 1948 which prohibits the unauthorised disclosure of certain commercial and financial information failed to satisfy the first prong of paragraph (B) of Exemption 3 because it "in no way channels the discretion of agency decisionmakers".[20] Thus, it could be argued that in order for section 32(1)(b) to apply, an enactment must contain a degree of guidance on the circumstances in which the discretion to authorise withholding of a record is to be exercised. An example of a discretionary provision which arguably contains the requisite degree of specificity would be section 51 of the Education Bill (No. 2) 1997, which provides:

> "51. Notwithstanding any other enactment, the Minister may refuse access to any information which would enable the compilation of information (that is not otherwise available to the general public) in relation to—
>
> (a) the overall results in any year of students in a particular school in an examination, or
>
> (b) the comparative overall results in any year of students in different schools in an examination."

It is likely that this provision would be held to come within the scope of section 32(1)(b) since it expressly allows for the withholding of information in circumstances where disclosure which would enable the compilation of information relating to examinations, and, therefore, it can be said to authorise non-disclosure "in certain circumstances".

---

[20] *CNA Financial Corp. v. Donovan*, 830 F.2d 1132 at 1137–1143 (D.C. Cir. 1978), *cert. denied*, 485 U.S. 977 (1988) at 1139.

(ii) The case must be one in which the head would, pursuant to the
enactment, refuse to disclose the record

The second requirement of section 32(1)(b) is that the case must be one in
which the head would refuse to disclose the record. Where an enactment allows the head of a public body some discretion in deciding whether to withhold a record, it must be shown that the case is one in which the head of the
public body concerned would choose to exercise his or her discretion to refuse
to disclose the record. It will, therefore, be incumbent upon the head to provide some evidence of his or her approach to disclosure of records of this
nature. The making of such decisions would, however, remain the prerogative
of the head of the public body concerned; it would appear from the text of
section 32(1)(b) that the Information Commissioner does not have the right to
decide whether the case is one in which the head should exercise his or her
discretion in favour of or against disclosure. Instead the role of the Commissioner is to determine whether the case is one in which the head would choose
to exercise his or her discretion to refuse to disclose the record concerned.

2. Does the requested information fall within the category of records prohibited from disclosure or authorised to be withheld by that enactment?

Once it has been established that there is an enactment prohibiting disclosure
or authorising non-disclosure of records in certain circumstances, the question arises whether the requested information falls within the category of information prohibited from disclosure or authorised to be withheld. In some
cases, the answer to this question will be obvious. For example, a request for
access to the index disclosing the original identity of an adopted child clearly
comes within the scope of the prohibition on disclosure of such information
contained in section 22(5) of the Adoption Act 1952. In other situations, however, it may not be clear whether the requested information is covered by the
statutory provision relied upon. In contrast to the corresponding U.S. and New
Zealand exemptions and to the original version of the Australian exemption,
however, there is no express requirement in the Irish Act that the non-disclosure statute *specifically* exempts records from disclosure. The original version
of the Australian exemption was interpreted as requiring that:

> "[t]he enactment must be formulated with such precision that it refers with par-
> ticularity to the information." [21]

Thus, the scope of section 32 might be found to be broader than that of its
overseas counterparts.

---

[21] *News Corporation Ltd v. National Companies and Securities Commission*, above, n. 15,
at 281.

C. Review

Provision is made in section 32 for the review of the operation of provisions authorising or requiring non-disclosure of records.[22] The review, which will be carried out by a joint committee of the Dáil and Seanad, must take place "from time to time". The carrying out of such a review must be authorised by the Dáil and Seanad. Its purpose will be to ascertain, "having regard to the provisions, purposes and spirit" of the Act, whether such provisions should be amended, repealed or included in the Third Schedule to the Act.[23] The results of the review must be reported in writing to each House, as should the committee's recommendations as to amendment, repeal, continuance, or inclusion in the Third Schedule of any of the provisions reviewed, where the committee considers it appropriate to do so.[24] Each Minister of the Government is required to submit a written report to the committee specifying the provisions authorising or requiring non-disclosure of records in enactments which confer functions on the Minister, or on a public body in relation to which functions are vested in the Minister.[25] The report must include the views of the Minister and, where appropriate, of the public body, as to whether "having regard to the provisions, purposes and spirit of the Act" any of the provisions should be amended, repealed, continued in force, or included in the Third Schedule.[26] The report must be furnished to the Information Commissioner and must be laid before each House of the Oireachtas.[27] Provision is also made for the involvement of the Information Commissioner in the review process. The Commissioner has the right to relay to the committee his or her opinions and conclusions relating to the Ministers' reports as well as to any matter relating to or arising out of the operation of section 32.[28] Ministers are obliged to furnish the first report to the committee no later than 12 months after the commencement of the Act.[29] Subsequent reports must be submitted at intervals of five years. The Act does not set out any time limit in respect of the establishment of the necessary committee. It had originally been intended that the Dáil Select Committee on Legislation and Security would deal with this matter. That body had already been charged, pursuant to a commitment in the Programme for Government of the 27th Dáil,[30] with undertaking a review of the Official Secrets Act 1963 on a regular basis, and all other statutory provisions

---

[22] s.32(2).
[23] s.32(3)(b).
[24] s.32(2)(b).
[25] s.32(3)(a).
[26] s.32(3)(b).
[27] s.32(4).
[28] s.32(5).
[29] s.32(6).
[30] *A Government of renewal: A Policy Agreement between Fine Gael, the Labour Party and Democratic Left* (December 1994), para. 57.

which restrict access to information.[31] The Committee completed a review of the Official Secrets Act in January 1997[32] but at the dissolution of the Dáil in May 1997 it had not yet completed the task of reviewing all other statutory provisions which restrict access to information and this work remains unfinished at the time of writing. During the passage of the FOI Bill through the Seanad, the Bill was amended to place responsibility for carrying out the review in the hands of a joint committee of both Houses of the Oireachtas rather than a Dáil committee.[33] Given the requirement that Ministers furnish their first reports within 12 months of the commencement of the Act, it would appear that the committee must be established before the expiry of that period also.

A similar commitment to review secrecy provisions in other enactments was contained in the Canadian Act. The Act required that a parliamentary committee be established or designated to conduct a review of secrecy provisions in other legislation. The committee issued its first report in 1987[34] in which it recommended that the relevant exemption, section 24, together with its corresponding Schedule[35] be repealed, with the only exceptions being made in the case of income tax, census and statistical information. The committee accepted that it was essential that Statistics Canada and Revenue Canada be able to ensure absolute confidentiality, and recommended that those provisions be preserved. At the time of writing, these recommendations have not been put into effect.

---

[31] Orders of Reference of the Select Committee on Legislation and Security, paragraph (1A), adopted March 1, 1995 and cited in: Dáil Select Committee on Legislation and Security, *op. cit.* above, n. 14, Appendix 3, p. A7.

[32] *ibid.*

[33] 150 *Seanad Debates* Col. 104 (Report Stage).

[34] Report of the Standing Committee on Justice and Solicitor General on the Review of the Access to Information Act and the Privacy Act, *Open and Shut: Enhancing the Right to Know and the Right to Privacy* (Queen's Printer for Canada, Ottowa, 1987), Appendix B, p. 117.

[35] Sched. 2.

ACCESS TO AND AMENDMENT OF PERSONAL RECORDS

CHAPTER 18

ACCESS TO AND AMENDMENT OF
PERSONAL RECORDS

A. Access

Individuals have a right of access to records containing their own personal information as part of the general right of access to information granted under section 6 of the Act.

Applicants for access to their own personal records are, to a great extent, treated in the same way as any other applicant. With three exceptions, the exemption and exclusion provisions of the Act are applied to applicants for access to their own files in the same way as they are to any other requester of information under the Act. Two of the exceptions arise in the context of the personal information exemption. The first exception to the rule that individuals seeking access to their own files are treated in the same way as other applicants consists of the non-application of the personal information exemption to requests for access to information relating to the requester.[1] This provision ensures that a person cannot be denied access to his or her own records on the grounds that they contain personal information relating to himself or herself. The second set of circumstances in which applicants for their own records are treated differently to other applicants arises in the context of medical, psychiatric, or social work records. Where a request is made for access to such records and the records relate to the requester, the head of a public body may refuse to grant the request on the grounds that the disclosure of the records might be prejudicial to the physical or mental health or the emotional well-being of the requester.[2] The third exception consists of the non-application of the commercially sensitive information exemption to requests for access to information relating to the requester.[3] This provision prevents public bodies from invoking that exemption to deny a person access to records relating to their own business. Apart from these exceptions, the Act draws no distinction in the application of access rights between those seeking access to their own personal records and other applicants for access to information. Applicants for access to their own personal records may, therefore, be denied such access on the basis of any of the exemptions provided for in the Act.

---

[1] s.28(2)(a).
[2] See above, pp. 284–285.
[3] s.27(2)(c).

Whether applicants for their own personal information should be treated differently to other applicants in the operation of the exemption provisions is a matter of some debate. On the one hand, there are those who argue that all requests should receive equal consideration, since the basis of FOI legislation is that access to records is available as of right and irrespective of the establishment of any interest on the part of the requester in securing such access. It follows that the granting of more favourable treatment to applicants seeking access to their own personal information than to other applicants undermines the basic philosophy of FOI. On the other hand, it is arguably unfair that an applicant's interest in obtaining access to records concerning himself or herself is not taken into account. The fact that a record contains information about an individual should, it is argued, weigh in favour of that record being disclosed to that individual. The second approach was favoured in the joint report of the Australian Law Reform Commission and Administrative Review Council which recommended that the Australian FOI Act be amended to provide that if a document contains personal information of the applicant, that fact is to be taken into account in considering the effect disclosure might have and in determining whether it is in the public interest to grant access to the applicant.[4] This approach is evident also in the attitude of the Supreme Court in *Skeffington v. Rooney*,[5] a case concerning an application for discovery of documents pertaining to a complaint made by the applicant to the Garda Síochána Complaints Board. Keane J. indicated that different public interest considerations arise in cases in which the applicant for discovery is someone other than the complainant.[6]

B.   Amendment

1. Introduction

The Act provides a mechanism for the amendment of records of personal information held by public bodies. Such provisions are common in other jurisdictions. Rights of amendment of personal information are contained in FOI legislation in Australia and New Zealand,[7] whilst the corresponding provisions in the U.S. and Canada[8] are to be found in privacy legislation. The Irish Data Protection Act 1988 provides its own mechanism for the amendment of

---

[4] Australian Law Reform Commission, Report No. 77/Administrative Review Council, Report No. 40, *Open Government: a review of the federal Freedom of Information Act 1982* (Australian Government Publishing Service, Canberra, 1995), para. 4.11.

[5] [1997] 1 I.R. 22.

[6] *ibid.* at 35–36.

[7] Australia: Freedom of Information Act 1982 (Cth), Part V; New Zealand: Official Information Act 1982, s.26.

[8] U.S.: Privacy Act 1974, s.552a(d)(2); Canada: Privacy Act (Canada), R.S.C., 1985, s.19(2).

inaccurate personal data;[9] the two approaches to amendment are compared in Chapter 20.

2. Outline of the amendment provisions

Section 17 of the FOI Act confers on individuals the right to apply to the head of a public body for the amendment of personal information held by that public body, on the grounds that it is incomplete, incorrect or misleading. Once it has been established that the grounds for amendment have been met, amendment of the record is mandatory. Three forms of amendment are provided for. They are:

(1) the alteration of the record to make the information complete, correct or not misleading;

(2) the addition to the record of a statement specifying the respects in which the public body is satisfied that the information is incomplete, incorrect or misleading; and

(3) the deletion of the information.

In the case of a successful application leading to amendment of a record, all reasonable steps must be taken to notify anyone to whom access to the record was given, or any other public body to whom a copy of the record was given in the course of the previous year, of any amendment effected.[10]

Where an application for amendment is unsuccessful, the unsuccessful application or a copy of it must be attached to the record, or if that is not practicable, a notation indicating that the application has been made must be attached, unless the application is considered by the public body to be defamatory or the alterations or additions to which it relates would be unnecessarily voluminous.[11]

Applications for amendment of records must be made in writing, or in such other form as may be determined by the Minister for Finance. The application for amendment must, in so far as is practicable, specify the record in question and the amendment required and it must include information in support of the application.[12] The application must be made by the person to whom the information relates. A decision on an application for amendment must be made within four weeks of receipt of the application. The applicant has a right to appeal a refusal to amend and he or she must be informed of that right.[13]

---

[9] Data Protection Act 1988, s.6.

[10] s.17(5).

[11] s.17(4)(b).

[12] s.17(2).

[13] Internal review: s.14(1)(e); review by Information Commissioner: s.34(1)(b).

3. Personal information

The information in respect of which amendment is sought must be personal information. It must, therefore, fall within the terms of the definition of personal information in section 2(1) of the Act. Personal information is defined as:

> "information about an identifiable individual that—
>
> (a) would, in the ordinary course of events, be known only to the individual or members of the family, or friends, of the individual, or
>
> (b) is held by a public body on the understanding that it would be treated by it as confidential".[14]

4. Personal information held by a public body

The amendment provisions apply in respect of all personal information which is held by a public body.[15] It appears that obtaining access to the information is not a prerequisite of the operation of the section. Thus, amendment could be sought by someone who, although he or she has been denied access to a record, has knowledge of its contents. It will, of course, be more usual for an applicant to have obtained access to a record prior to invoking his or her right to have the record amended. The provisions apply regardless of how such access has been obtained. In particular, the right of amendment of personal information applies whether or not access to the record has been obtained under the FOI Act. It even applies in situations where access to the record has been obtained by unauthorised means.

5. Incomplete, incorrect, or misleading information

Three grounds for amendment of personal information are allowed under the Act. They are that the information is incomplete, that it is incorrect, or that it is misleading. These three grounds for amendment also feature in Australian FOI legislation, along with one additional ground, namely that a record is out of date.[16] The corresponding right in Canada to request correction of personal information applies where the individual believes there is an error or omission

---

[14] The definition of personal information is discussed in greater detail above at pp. 269–280.

[15] The meaning of "held by a public body" is discussed above at p. 56.

[16] Freedom of Information Act 1982 (Cth), s.48(a); Freedom of Information Act 1982 (Victoria), s.39; Freedom of Information Act 1989 (New South Wales), ss.39 and 48; Freedom of Information Act 1991 (South Australia), s.30(c); Freedom of Information Act 1991 (Tasmania), s.37; Freedom of Information Act 1992 (Queensland), s.53; Freedom of Information Act 1992 (Western Australia), s.45(1).

therein.[17] In the U.S. an individual may request amendment of a record on the ground that it is not "accurate, relevant, timely or complete".[18] The right of correction of personal information is available in New Zealand where the information is inaccurate, incomplete or gives a misleading impression.[19] Although, unlike its U.S. and Australian counterparts, the Irish Act does not confer a right to have out-of-date information amended, it could be argued that a record which is out of date would be incorrect or misleading.

Australian case law has provided an exploration of the meaning of the terms "incomplete", "incorrect", and "misleading".

(a) Incomplete

"Incomplete" has been interpreted by the Australian federal Administrative Appeals Tribunal (A.A.T.) as meaning not entire or not unqualified.[20] The A.A.T. held a record to be incomplete where it failed to indicate that there was a difference of medical opinion concerning the diagnosis of the applicant's condition[21] and where a psychological report was not included in a record in circumstances where, upon the suspension of an officer, the provision of such a report was mandatory.[22]

(b) Incorrect

In *Re Leverett and Australian Telecommunications Commission*[23] "incorrect" was interpreted by the A.A.T. to mean "not in conformity with a recognised standard, faulty; not in accordance with fact, erroneous, inaccurate".[24]

(c) Misleading

"Misleading" was interpreted by the A.A.T. in *Re Page and Director-General of Social Security*[25] to mean "leading astray, causing to go wrong, giving the wrong impression".[26] The tribunal also referred in that case to the interpreta-

---

[17] Privacy Act (Canada), R.S.C., 1985, s.12(2); Freedom of Information and Protection of Privacy Act (Ontario), R.S.O., 1990, s.47(2); Freedom of Information and Protection of Privacy Act (British Columbia), R.S.B.C., 1996, s.29; Freedom of Information and Protection of Privacy Act (Alberta), S.A., 1994, s.35; Freedom of Information and Protection of Privacy Act (Manitoba), C.C.S.M., 1998, c.F175, s.39; Freedom of Information and Protection of Privacy Act (Nova Scotia), S.N.S., 1993, s.25.

[18] Privacy Act 1974, s.552a(d)(2).

[19] Official Information Act 1982, s.26.

[20] *Re Page and Director-General of Social Security* (1984) 6 A.L.N. N171.

[21] *Re Resch and Department of Veterans' Affairs* (1986) 9 A.L.D. 380.

[22] *Re Jacobs and Department of Defence* (1988) 15 A.L.D. 645.

[23] (1985) 8 A.L.N. N135.

[24] *ibid.* at N136.

[25] Above, n. 20.

[26] *ibid.* at N173.

tion of the term "misleading" by the U.S. courts to mean "delusive, calculated to lead astray or to lead into error".[27] In the Australian federal case of *Re Sime and Minister for Immigration and Ethnic Affairs*[28] the A.A.T. held that the use of inverted commas surrounding the professional descriptions of the applicants in a departmental report was misleading in the sense of giving a wrong impression, in that it cast doubt on their professional status and integrity.[29]

6. Onus of proof

The Act is silent as to where the onus of proof lies in establishing that a record is incomplete, incorrect and misleading. This contrasts with the corresponding federal Australian provision, where the onus is placed squarely on the public body to establish that its decision was justified or that the A.A.T. should give a decision adverse to the person seeking amendment.[30] It would appear that under the Irish provisions the onus is on the applicant to establish that a record is incomplete, incorrect, or misleading. The difference between the Irish and Australian provisions on this point is not, however, as great as might at first appear, since it has been suggested that under the Australian provisions a public body need only establish that its decision was justified. It need not prove that its record is accurate.[31] The applicant's responsibilities in this matter have been outlined as follows:

> "Unless a claimant, when requested to do so, produces evidence in support of his contention, or the record is, on its face, incomplete, incorrect, out of date or misleading, an agency would be justified in refusing to amend the record".[32]

7. Manner of amendment

Once it has been established that a record is incomplete, incorrect, or misleading, the head of the public body concerned is required to amend it. Three forms of amendment are provided for. They are:

(a) alteration of the record so as to make the information complete or correct or not misleading;

(b) the addition to the record of a statement specifying the respects in which

---

[27] *Diamond Drill Contracting Co. v. International Diamond Drill Contracting Co.*, 106 Wash. 72 at 79.

[28] (1995) 21 A.A.R. 369.

[29] *ibid.* at 375.

[30] Freedom of Information Act 1982 (Cth), s.61.

[31] Senate Standing Committee on Legal and Constitutional Affairs, *Report on the Operation and Administration of the Freedom of Information Legislation* (Australian Government Publishing Service, Canberra, 1987), para. 15.55.

[32] FOI Memorandum No. 28, para. 25 (September 13, 1982) quoted *ibid.*

the public body is satisfied that the information is incomplete, incorrect or misleading; and

(c) the deletion of the information.

The three forms of amendment will now be considered in greater detail.

(a) Alteration

The main issue arising in the context of alteration of a record is how far the head of a public body must go in carrying out such an alteration. The Act requires that the information be made "complete, correct or not misleading", but does not provide any guidance in achieving those results. Nor is it clear whether, in altering a record, it should be done in such a way as to continue to reveal the original contents of the record. The advantage of such an approach is that it would maintain the historical accuracy of the record. On the other hand, it could be argued that such an approach could prejudice the interests of the applicant by revealing information about him or her which had been found to be incomplete, incorrect or misleading.

The difficulty in determining what the corresponding Australian federal provision (Part V of the Freedom of Information Act 1982) was intended to achieve was described by the Australian Senate Standing Committee on Legal and Constitutional Affairs in the following terms:

> "At its narrowest, amendment under Part V could be limited to simple factual information such as dates of birth, periods of employment, addresses and the like, that have been inaccurately recorded due to clerical error. At its broadest, Part V could be interpreted to permit the Administrative Appeals Tribunal to hear evidence and determine the correctness of any fact, opinion, determination or decision relating to personal affairs recorded in a document of any agency or Minister. The narrow interpretation appears to be too narrow. There is no need for elaborate statutory provision merely to correct clerical errors. Agencies have no interest in refusing to correct these errors. The broadest interpretation of Part V, however, is clearly too broad. Chaos would result if Part V could be used to re-litigate before the Tribunal disputes resolved by other tribunals, courts, boards of inquiry etc. The problem is to define in workable fashion an appropriate role for Part V between the two extremes."[33]

Two particular matters have given rise to debate overseas. The first is whether opinions, as opposed to facts, should be subject to amendment. The second is whether the right of amendment should apply to alter a determination which has been made by another person or body.

---

[33] Above, n. 31, paras 15.9–15.10.

(i) Fact/Opinion

Records of personal information held by public bodies can consist of facts or opinions or a mixture of both. Those who are the subject of the opinions expressed may wish to dispute their accuracy. This might occur, for example, in the case of an evaluation of the subject's performance in his or her job. The question is what role amendment rights should play in resolving a dispute concerning the accuracy of such an evaluation. Those advocating a broad approach to amendment rights would argue that the right of amendment should allow for the *de novo* review of the performance evaluation. In such a scenario, the body resolving the amendment dispute would hear evidence on the employee's performance and would arrive at its own conclusion as to the standard of that performance, amending the record to reflect that conclusion. A narrow approach, on the other hand, would limit the scope of amendment rights to an assessment of whether the evaluation as recorded is correct in terms of representing accurately the views of the person carrying out the evaluation. A compromise approach might be to determine whether the record accurately records the unbiased view of a competent and appropriately qualified evaluator.

Different approaches to the question of whether opinions can be subject to amendment have emerged in the various jurisdictions. The amendment of opinions has been accepted as legitimate under the U.S. Privacy Act. In *R.R. v. Department of the Army*[34] the U.S. District Court (District of Colombia) held that:

> "It would defy common sense to suggest that only factually erroneous assertions should be deleted or revised, while opinions based solely on these assertions must remain unaltered in the individual's official file. An agency may not refuse a request to revise or expunge prior professional judgments once all the facts underlying such judgments have thoroughly discredited."[35]

It has, on the other hand, consistently been held by Canadian provincial Information Commissioners that a public body cannot correct an opinion in its records, but can only annotate it.[36] In Australia, a less restrictive approach has been adopted. In *Re Resch and Department of Veterans' Affairs*[37] it was held that:

> "There can be no doubt . . . that statements of fact concerning a person constitute 'information' relating to that person. However, 'information' relating to a

---

[34] 482 F. Supp. 770 (D.D.C. 1980).

[35] *ibid.* at 773.

[36] *Re the Workers Compensation Board*, unreported, Information and Privacy Commissioner, British Columbia, Order No. 124–1996, September 12, 1996. This decision is supported by *Re Ontario Hydro*, Information and Privacy Commissioner, Ontario, Order P–186, July 11, 1990, and the Quebec decision cited therein: *M.C. Centre Hospitalier Regional de l'Outaouais* (1984–1986) 1 C.A.I. 120.

[37] Above, n. 21.

person is not necessarily limited to matters of fact, capable of objective proof, such as date and place of birth, marital status, children, educational achievements, personal history, work history, medical history and the like. It would encompass, as well, matters of opinion communicated or recorded in respect of the person – matters such as an evaluation of personal characteristics, educational performance, work performance, medical diagnoses or prognoses and the like."[38]

In *Re Leverett and Australian Telecommunications Commission* it was held that a professional opinion could be found to be incomplete, incorrect, or misleading on the basis of the total inadequacy of underlying factual information, the existence of bias or ill-will, incompetence or the lack of balance or necessary experience in the person forming the opinion, or the existence of a trivial factual substratum.[39]

Some limitations have, however, been placed on the circumstances in which opinions will be deemed to be incorrect. In *Resch* the tribunal said that the medical opinions the subject of the dispute could not be shown to be incorrect merely by the production of medical opinions to the contrary, and went on to hold that there was no evidence to suggest that the opinions in dispute were not genuinely held.

In the Victorian case of *Stephens v. Victoria Police*[40] the Victorian Administrative Appeals Tribunal distilled from the U.S. decision *R.R. v. Department of Army*[41] the following four circumstances in which an opinion might be found to be incorrect. They were where:

(1) the facts underlying such opinion have been thoroughly discredited or have been demonstrated to be totally inadequate;

(2) the person forming such opinion was tainted by bias or ill-will, incompetence, or lack of balance or necessary experience;

(3) the factual substratum underlying the opinion is so trivial as to render the opinion formed dangerous to rely upon and likely to result in error; or

(4) the facts upon which the opinion was based were misapprehended.

A number of these factors were incorporated into the Australian federal FOI Act in 1991 when that Act was amended to qualify the right to amendment.[42] The amended FOI Act provides that the A.A.T., when considering the application of the right to amend an opinion, must not make a decision in favour of amendment unless:

---

[38] Above, n. 21, at 385.
[39] Above, n. 23.
[40] (1988) 2 V.A.R. 236.
[41] Above, n. 33.
[42] Freedom of Information Amendment Act 1991 (Cth).

(a) the opinion was based on a mistake of fact; or

(b) the author of the opinion was biased, unqualified to form the opinion or acted improperly in conducting the factual inquiries that led to the formation of the opinion.[43]

(ii) Alteration of determination

The A.A.T. has consistently refused to amend records where amendment would, in effect, amount to an overruling of a determination of another person or tribunal. In *Resch,* Hall D.P. stated:

> "there is, in my view, a distinction between a statement of opinion and a determination duly made by an administrative authority such as the Commission charged with responsibility of administering a pensions scheme for veterans. In discharging its statutory duty to 'determine . . . all matters relevant to the determination of the claim', the Commission may be called upon to decide between conflicting medical opinions. A determination duly made by the Commission in relation to a claim for a pension under the Act, however, is not just another expression of opinion."[44]

The tribunal made it clear that the only basis for a challenge to such a determination would be where the determination had been recorded inaccurately.

(b) Addition of a statement

The head of a public body can amend a record by adding to it a statement specifying the respects in which the body is satisfied that the information is incomplete, inaccurate, or misleading. It will not suffice for the public body to merely record that the information contained in the record is disputed; it must identify in what way the information is incomplete, inaccurate, or misleading. The fact that this form of amendment does not involve an alteration of the original record might be viewed as advantageous in terms of maintaining the historical accuracy of the record. It might also be necessary in view of the physical condition of the record.

On the other hand, the use of this method of amending records might be unattractive to applicants for amendment. The fact that the original record is left intact might be felt to prejudice the applicant, despite the addition of a statement explaining that it is incomplete, inaccurate, or misleading.

(c) Deletion

The third form of amendment provided for under section 17 is the deletion from the record of information which is incomplete, inaccurate, or misleading. It is not clear whether the deletion of entire records is contemplated by

---

[43] s.55(6).
[44] *Re Resch and Department of Veterans' Affairs,* above, n. 21, at 389.

this provision. If all of the information contained in a record is either incomplete, inaccurate, or misleading, that would seem to mandate the deletion of that entire record. The use of deletion of information as a means of amending records can be questioned on the grounds that it can be viewed as an attempt to rewrite history. On the other hand, it can be argued that leaving inaccurate material in a record would be unjust even if it is accompanied by a statement acknowledging the inaccuracy of the record. Prior to the amendment of the Australian FOI Act in 1991 it was not clear whether deletion of information was permissible as a form of amendment. The amendment introduced in 1991 had the effect of severely restricting the use of deletion as a form of amendment. It provides that:

> "[t]o the extent that is practicable to do so, the agency or Minister must, when making an amendment . . . ensure that the record of information is amended in a way that does not obliterate the text of the record as it existed prior to the amendment."[45]

In the U.S. it has been accepted that the Privacy Act contemplates the "expungement of inaccuracies" and not merely redress by supplement.[46] However, there are restrictions on the deletion of information in that jurisdiction also. In *Hobson v. Wilson*[47] it was held that the courts will only order expungement of government records where it is necessary to vindicate rights secured by the Constitution or by statute, while in *Fendler v. U.S. Bureau of Prisons*[48] it was held that the expungement of information in a pre-sentence report is not necessary where the information does not pose a real and immediate threat to the parolee.

(d) Alteration, addition of a statement, or deletion

It is not clear from the text of the Act whether the head of the public body concerned is free to choose between the three forms of amendment. The question arises whether it might be open to the head of a public body who has received a request for deletion of information to respond by deciding instead to alter the record concerned. The answer to this question depends on the extent to which the remedy, *i.e.* the form of amendment requested, is viewed as part of the application for amendment. If the remedy is treated as an integral part of the application, then the head must respond by either granting or refusing the application along with the suggested remedy. If, on the other hand, the application and the remedy are seen as separate, then it would be open to the head to make a decision as to whether amendment is justified and then to

---

[45] Freedom of Information Act (Cth), s.50(3).
[46] *R.R. v. Department of the Army,* above, n. 34, at 774.
[47] 737 F.2d 1 at 65 (D.C. Cir. 1984).
[48] 846 F.2d 550 at 554 (9th Cir. 1988).

arrive at his or her own conclusion as to the remedy to be applied, *i.e.* alteration, addition of a statement, or deletion.

Under section 17(2)(a) the Act requires that those applying for amendment must specify in their application the amendment required. Thus, the applicant is required not only to identify the information in dispute, but also to specify the type of amendment sought. This could, for example, consist of an application for the removal of material from a record or of an application for alteration of a misleading statement in the record. It should, therefore, be clear from the application what form of amendment is being requested. On that basis, it would appear that the specification of the amendment as required by section 17(2)(a) forms an integral part of the application. If this is the case, then the head would not be entitled to respond to a request for amendment of a record in a manner other than that requested by the applicant. If the head were to, nonetheless, insist on doing so, it could be viewed as a refusal of the request.

On the other hand, it can be argued that the requirement to specify the amendment was inserted merely for administrative purposes in order to ensure that the disputed information is fully identified and so it does not form an integral part of the application for amendment. If this view is accepted, a head of a public body, on concluding that a record is incomplete, incorrect or misleading, is entitled to decide which form of amendment is most appropriate.

The significance of this distinction lies in the fact that appeals concerning the amendment rights lie only in respect of a refusal to amend. Therefore, it is important to determine whether a decision on the part of the head to effect an amendment other than that specified in the application amounts to a refusal or a grant of the application for amendment. If it is viewed as a granting of the application for amendment, then no right of appeal will be available to the applicant. If, on the other hand, it is seen as a refusal of the application, then the applicant will be able to appeal against the decision.

The better approach would be to view a decision not to grant a request for amendment in the form specified by the requester as a refusal to amend. This interpretation would be in keeping with the broad approach to appeal rights in the Act.

8. Notation

In the case of an unsuccessful application for amendment of a record, the public body is obliged to attach to the record the unsuccessful application for amendment or a copy thereof. If this is not practicable, a notation indicating that the application has been made must be attached to the record. The right to attach a notation indicating that a record is disputed is available in Australia, New Zealand, Canada, and the U.S.[49] The notation provisions differ from the

---

[49] Australia: Freedom of Information Act 1982 (Cth), s.51(2); New Zealand: Official In-

mechanism for the addition to a record of a statement in the case of a success-ful application for amendment of a record. Implementation of the latter provi-sion entails a determination on the part of the head that the record is incomplete, incorrect or misleading, as well as a finding as to the way in which the record offends. In the case of the notation provisions, their only effect is to draw attention to the fact that the applicant has disputed the accuracy of the record. It would appear that there is nothing to stop the body from adding its own further notation indicating, for example, that the application for amendment was unsuccessful.

The notation requirements are subject to two exceptions. Notation is not required where the head of the public body concerned is of the opinion that the application is defamatory or that the alterations or additions to the record would be unnecessarily voluminous. These exceptions appear to apply in the case of both the attachment to the record of the unsuccessful application for amendment, or a copy thereof, and to the attachment to the record of a nota-tion indicating that an application for amendment has been made. It is, how-ever, difficult to envisage circumstances in which the attachment to a record of a notation indicating that an application has been made could be viewed as defamatory or unnecessarily voluminous. Such issues are more likely to arise in the context of the attachment to a record of the application for amendment itself. The onus will be upon the head of the public body to determine whether the application contains defamatory material. Interestingly, the immunity from legal proceedings provided for in respect of the disclosure or publication of information by public bodies under the Act does not apply to acts done in pursuance of section 17.[50] Therefore, the head of the public body, in either acceding to or refusing an application for amendment, will have to ensure that anything added to a record is not defamatory,[51] in breach of the law of confi-dence, contrary to copyright law, or in any way susceptible to legal action.

9. Appeals

Internal review of a refusal to amend a record under section 17 is provided for in section 14(1)(e). There is provision for a further appeal to be taken to the Information Commissioner in section 34(1)(b). Such appeals may only be ini-tiated by the applicant, not by the public body. Appeals may, in turn, be brought to the High Court on a point of law by either party.

---

formation Act 1982, s.26(1)(b); Canada: Privacy Act (Canada), R.S.C., 1985, s.12(2)(b); U.S.: Privacy Act 1974, s.552a(d)(3).
[50] s.45. See below, pp. 368–371.
[51] Qualified privilege will, however, be likely to attach to the amendment of a record by the addition to it of defamatory material.

REVIEW AND ENFORCEMENT

REVIEW AND ENFORCEMENT

A. Models of Review

Given the tradition of governmental secrecy in Ireland, the natural tendency of those working in government is towards restricting the dissemination of official information. A law which establishes a right of access to official information must, therefore, have in place a system for reviewing the decisions of those who control access to official information. Different approaches to review of FOI decisions have been adopted in various jurisdictions. Most jurisdictions provide opportunities for both internal and external review of decisions. A system of internal review is useful in terms of offering a speedy and inexpensive method of resolving disputes.[1] Other perceived advantages of internal review are that they result in more information being released, reduce the number of complaints going to external review, and improve the management culture of public agencies.[2] In order to establish the impartiality of the review process, however, the institution of an external review system is essential. Three main models of external review have emerged in FOI legislation in the common law world.

The first relies on the courts to enforce the law. This is the method of review relied upon in the U.S. and (as a second tier of review) in Canada. Review of FOI decisions by the courts is, mainly for reasons of expense, delay, and formality, not a desirable option. In addition, the courts are by nature generalist bodies and do not have detailed knowledge of specialised areas of law like FOI law. Another problem is that the courts are unsuited to adopting an overall supervisory role in enforcing legislation; they are instead confined to reacting to individual cases as they arise.

Another model uses a tribunal to review decisions. In Australia, for example, primary responsibility for disposition of federal FOI appeals lies in the hands of the Administrative Appeals Tribunal (A.A.T.). Tribunals have a number of advantages over courts in terms of reviewing FOI decisions. They are generally fast, inexpensive, and relatively informal. They are also in a position to engage in a greater degree of specialisation than are the courts, the

---

[1] Cranston, *Legal Foundations of the Welfare State* (Weidenfeld and Nicolson, London, 1985), p. 257.
[2] Baxter, *Freedom of Information – Resolving Disputes: A Report arising from a Government Research Fellowship* (Department of the Environment, 1995), p. 73.

extent of such specialisation depending on whether they are charged with making decisions relating to other legislation also. Where reliance is placed on a tribunal as the principal agent of external review, however, overall monitoring of the operation of the legislation is generally absent. The importance of such a function was recognised in a recent review of the Australian FOI Act where the following passage from a lecture by Mr Justice Michael Kirby, now a member of the Australian High Court, was quoted with approval:

> "It is vital that someone or some agency . . . should be closely monitoring the experience under the FOI Act . . . Otherwise, the preventative value of legislation of this character would be lost, in a concentration of effort on simply responding to individual claims. We should aggregate experience and draw lessons from it. For example, a persistently recalcitrant government agency . . . continuously reversed on appeal, should have its attitude drawn to political and public attention so that they can be corrected, to bring even the most obdurate official into line with the new policy."[3]

The third model involves the carrying out of FOI reviews by an Ombudsman or Information Commissioner. There are some variations within this model. First, decisions on review may be taken either by a specialist Ombudsman/Information Commissioner or by an Ombudsman whose FOI review functions constitute part of his or her wider role of reviewing administrative action. Secondly, decisions of Ombudsmen or Information Commissioners may or may not be binding. Where the Ombudsman/Information Commissioner's decisions are not binding, provision can be made for bringing matters further in the event of non-compliance. The Canadian federal Act, for example, confers on the Information Commissioner the right to apply to the Federal Court for review of a refusal to disclose a record, provided the consent of the requester has been obtained.[4]

In Canada, at federal level, the first level of review is in the hands of a specialist Information Commissioner who does not have the power to make legally binding decisions. The office of Ombudsman in New Zealand, which had originally been established to deal with complaints of maladministration, was given the responsibility of reviewing FOI decisions following the passing of the Official Information Act in 1982. The New Zealand Ombudsman is, in theory, restricted to recommending disclosure of information; however, such recommendations become binding if they are not vetoed within 20 days.[5] In some of the Australian and Canadian state and provincial statutes, specialist

---

[3] Kirby, "Information and Freedom", The Housden Lecture, Melbourne, September 6, 1983, p. 11, cited in Australian Law Reform Commission, Report No. 77/Administrative Review Council, Report No. 40, *Open Government: a review of the federal Freedom of Information Act 1982* (Australian Government Publishing Service, Canberra, 1995), para. 6.2.
[4] Access to Information Act (Canada), R.S.C., 1985, s.42.
[5] Official Information Act 1982, s.32.

Information Commissioners with power to make binding decisions on access have been provided for.[6]

The strength of the specialist Ombudsman/Information Commissioner model lies in the fact that, unlike a general purpose Ombudsman, or the courts, he or she is dealing with only one area of law, thus making it possible for the holder of the office to become expert on the detail of the legislation and, more importantly, on the aims and objectives of the legislation. The Ombudsman/ Information Commissioner can also take on the important task of monitoring the operation and effectiveness of the legislation overall, for example, to see whether it is having the desired impact on the day-to-day operations of public bodies. Such a task would be beyond the scope of the courts or a tribunal. However, a weakness of the Ombudsman/Information Commissioner model can be that his or her decisions are sometimes not legally enforceable. Courts and tribunals, on the other hand, make decisions which are legally enforceable. Even where the Ombudsman or Information Commissioner's decisions are legally binding, problems can arise in terms of approach, in particular where the same individual is exercising the enforceable FOI jurisdiction along with a general purpose Ombudsman's jurisdiction. Attention was drawn by one commentator to the differences between the traditional role of the Ombudsman and that of an Ombudsman/Information Commissioner exercising an FOI jurisdiction in the following terms:

> "[F]reedom of information disputes are always disputes over law: every case raises issues of statutory interpretation and application. They are a different diet from the traditional 'maladministration' fare of the office which is capable of resolution in almost every case by thorough investigation, discussion, persuasion and, often, negotiation and compromise."[7]

The system of review adopted under the FOI Act 1997 is one which involves the use of internal review followed by the hearing of appeals by an Information Commissioner. The Act provides for the appointment of the Ombudsman as Information Commissioner; the current holder of that office also holds the office of Ombudsman. Unlike some of his overseas counterparts and in contrast to his authority as Ombudsman,[8] the Irish Information Commissioner has the power to issue legally binding decisions. In addition to internal review and review by the Information Commissioner, provision is also made for an appeal to the High Court on a point of law. The making of an application for judicial review of a decision made under the FOI Act is, of course, also a possibility, although the existence of an alternative remedy could debar the

---

[6] Canada: Quebec, Ontario, British Columbia, Alberta; Australia: Queensland, Western Australia.

[7] Eagles, Taggart, and Liddell, *Freedom of Information in New Zealand* (Oxford University Press, 1992), p. 546.

[8] Section 6(3) of the Ombudsman Act 1980 gives the Ombudsman the power to recommend certain courses of action following the completion of his or her investigation.

application for judicial review.[9] The Irish Information Commissioner is also vested with powers to monitor the operation of the FOI Act. These will be described below, following discussion of the review mechanisms.

B.   Internal Review

Where the head of the public body made the original decision, the internal review stage will be bypassed. Therefore, internal review is only applicable where the original decision regarding access was made by a delegate of the head of a public body. In such a situation the use of the internal review mechanism will be a condition precedent to the making of an appeal to the Information Commissioner.

1. Decisions subject to internal review

Internal review is only available is respect of certain specified decisions. Section 14 sets out those decisions. They are:

(a) Refusal to grant a request for access under section 7

This covers such refusals of access as those based on the fact that: the record is exempt (Part III);[10] the record is excluded from the scope of the Act (section 46);[11] and that the request is being refused on administrative grounds (section 10).[12] It would also appear to cover a refusal on the grounds that the record was not held by a public body as required by section 6(1),[13] as well as a refusal on the grounds that the record was created prior to the commencement of the Act and does not come within the exceptions to that rule as set out in section 6(5).[14]

(b) Deferral of access

Only one ground for deferral of access to a record can be subjected to internal review, namely where such deferral concerns a document being prepared for

---

[9] There are two lines of authority in this area. The first, which derives from the decision of the Supreme Court in *The State (Abenglen Properties Ltd.) v. Corporation of Dublin* [1984] I.R. 384, appears to lean in favour of an "exhaustion of remedies" requirement, while the second, based on another Supreme Court decision, *P. & F. Sharpe Limited v. Dublin City and County Manager* [1989] I.R. 701, appears to take the opposite approach. See Hogan and Morgan, *Administrative Law in Ireland* (3rd ed., Round Hall Sweet & Maxwell, Dublin, 1998), pp. 734–739.

[10] See Chaps 6 to 17.

[11] See above, pp. 56–60.

[12] See above, pp. 69–70.

[13] See above, p. 56.

[14] See above, pp. 60–63.

the Houses of the Oireachtas (section 11(1)(a)).[15] In the other two circumstances in which deferral of access is provided for, review is dealt with directly by the Information Commissioner.[16]

The reason for this differential treatment is, in the case of section 11(1)(b), that to provide for the channelling of appeals against the use of such powers of deferral direct to the Information Commissioner will help to ensure that they would only be used in exceptional circumstances. In the case of section 11(1)(c), internal review is excluded on the basis of the short time limit involved.

(c) Form of access

Internal review is available in respect of the granting of access to a record in a form other than that specified in the request, *e.g.* where the applicant has requested a copy of a record, but has instead been granted a right to inspect it (section 12).[17]

(d) Granting of access to part of a record

The granting of access to only a part of a record is subject to internal review (section 13).[18] Internal review does not, however, appear to be available in the analogous situation outlined in section 6(10), which allows for the granting of access to part of a record of a government contractor where the remainder of the record contains other matters unrelated to the services provided under the contract.

(e) Refusal to amend

A refusal to amend a record relating to personal information may be the subject of an application for internal review (section 17).[19]

(f) Refusal of reasons for administrative decisions

Internal review may be invoked in respect of a refusal to give reasons for an administrative decision as required under section 18, or a complaint relating to the contents of such a statement of reasons.[20]

(g) Fees

The charging of a fee or deposit in respect of access may be the subject of an application for internal review (section 47).[21]

---

[15] See above, p. 72.
[16] See below, p. 350.
[17] See above, pp. 73–75.
[18] See above, pp. 75–76.
[19] See above, pp. 332–343.
[20] See above, pp. 45–49.
[21] See above, pp. 76–78.

2. Decisions not reviewable internally

Matters which cannot be dealt with by means of internal review include review of a decision concerning the operation of third party consultation requirements.[22] The reasoning behind this exclusion was that the fulfilment of the consultation obligations are time-consuming and therefore, in the case of a dispute concerning the operation of third party consultation requirements, it would be more expedient to allow for review to be carried out by the Information Commissioner rather than requiring the parties to go through the internal review process. Internal review is also precluded in respect of the extension, under section 9, of the time allowed to a public body to consider a request. Such a decision can be appealed to the Information Commissioner. Again the basis for excluding internal review in such circumstances is the issue of delay. Finally, internal review is not available in the case of a deferral of access based on two of the grounds provided for under section 11.[23]

The circumstances in which internal review is available are all expressed in terms of "decisions". It appears, therefore, that any response of a public body falling short of a decision will not be subject to such review. However, the Act ensures that a requester will not be left in limbo as a result of the failure of a public body to arrive at a decision. If no decision is forthcoming within the time period specified in section 8, a decision refusing access will be deemed to have been made.[24]

3. Time limits for applications

Applications for internal review must be submitted within four weeks of the original decision being notified to the applicant but there is provision for extension of this period where, in the opinion of the head, there are reasonable grounds for so doing.[25]

4. Formalities

The applicant for internal review must apply to the head of the public body in

---

[22] See above, pp. 241–243.
[23] Those grounds are:
   (1) deferral on the grounds that the record contains: factual information, performance reports relating to public bodies, or reports of technical experts, where the giving of access before a particular day would be against the public interest (section 11(1)(b) – see above, p. 72); and
   (2) deferral on the grounds that the records are of such interest to the public generally that their contents will be revealed to the Houses of the Oireachtas or otherwise published within a week (section 11(1)(c) – see above, p. 72).
[24] s.41(1).
[25] s.14(7).

writing, or in such other form as may be determined by the Minister for Finance.[26] No such determination has been made by the Minister as yet.

5. Who makes the decision

Section 14(2) provides for the carrying out of internal review by the head of the public body concerned. The decision on internal review need not necessarily be taken by the head of the public body, since the carrying out of the internal review function is one of the functions which can be delegated to a member of the staff of the public body concerned.[27] However, section 14(3) provides that the rank of the person undertaking the review must be higher than that of the original decision-maker.

6. Time limit for completion

The Act stipulates that internal review of a decision shall be completed within three weeks of receipt of the request for review and a notice of the decision taken must be issued within the same period.[28] If no decision on the internal review is forthcoming within the time limit specified, a decision affirming the decision which is the subject of the review will be deemed to have been made.[29]

7. Conduct of the internal review

The Act does not make any reference to the manner in which the internal review is to be conducted. The manner of its operation will therefore be at the discretion of the person carrying out the review. He or she will, however, be bound to adhere to the rules of constitutional justice.[30] The section is also silent as to where the burden of proof will lie.

8. Powers on appeal

Following the carrying out of a review, it is open to the person who has carried out the review "as he or she considers appropriate" to choose one of three courses of action provided for in section 14. These are to affirm the decision, to vary it, or to annul it and substitute "such decision in relation to the matter as he or she considers proper".[31] A decision made on internal review shall, in

---

[26] s.14(2).
[27] s.4(1).
[28] s.14(4).
[29] s.41(2).
[30] See Hogan and Morgan, *op. cit.* above, n. 9, Chaps 10 and 11.
[31] s.14(2)(b).

so far as it is inconsistent with the original decision, have effect in lieu thereof and shall be binding on the parties.[32] While a fresh decision is clearly required of the head on internal review, that decision need not differ from the original one. In the Australian case of *Re Birnbauer and Department of Industry, Technology and Resources*[33] it was held that internal review must amount to "a truly objective reconsideration of the matter".[34]

9. Reasons for the decision

Notice of the decision arrived at on internal review must specify the reasons for that decision.[35] In addition, the provision of the Act under which the request is refused must be specified, and findings on material issues relevant to the decision as well as details of any public interest considerations taken into account in making the decision must be revealed.[36] These additional requirements do not apply in situations where disclosure of the existence or non-existence of the record would be contrary to the public interest or would be damaging to certain specified interests. Nor do they apply where refusal of access was based on the voluminous nature of the request.[37]

10. Implementation of the decision

On the making of a decision on internal review to grant a request for access to a record, the same arrangements apply in respect of the provision of access as are provided for in respect of access requests granted *ab initio*.[38]

C.   Review by the Information Commissioner

1. The Office of the Information Commissioner

The principal means of review of decision provided for under the FOI Act is that of review by the Information Commissioner. The review function of the Information Commissioner will be examined here. The Information Commissioner also has an overall monitoring role in relation to the disclosure of official information in Ireland, the details of which are discussed below.[39]

---

[32] s.14(10).
[33] *[Nos 1, 2, and 3]* (1986) 1 V.A.R. 279.
[34] *ibid.* at 294.
[35] s.8(2)(d). The giving of reasons for the initial decision is provided for under s.8(2)(d).
[36] s.8(2)(d).
[37] s.14(5)(c).
[38] s.14(9).
[39] See below, pp. 367–368.

The office of Information Commissioner is to a great extent modelled on that of the Ombudsman. The same method of appointment is used in respect of both offices, namely their appointment by the President upon a resolution recommending such appointment passed by both Houses of the Oireachtas.[40] The Second Schedule of the Act, which sets out the terms under which the office of Information Commissioner is to be held,[41] is in similar terms to the equivalent provisions in the Ombudsman Act 1980.[42] In both cases the appointment is for a period of six years with eligibility for reappointment for a second or subsequent term. The holder of both offices is required to vacate it on attaining the age of 67 years. Like the Ombudsman, the Information Commissioner is required to be independent in the performance of the functions of the office.[43] This independence is underpinned by the fact that all staff of the Commissioner are civil servants of the State, rather than of the government.[44] Although they constitute separate offices, the Act allows for the appointment of the Ombudsman as Information Commissioner; the current Information Commissioner, Mr Kevin Murphy, is also the Ombudsman. There is, however, one major difference between the two offices. Unlike the Ombudsman, who can only recommend a course of action,[45] the Information Commissioner makes legally binding decisions.[46]

2. Constitutional position

The provisions relating to review by the Information Commissioner must be examined in the light of Articles 34.1 and 37.1 of the Constitution. Article 34.1 underpins the separation of powers by making it clear that the administration of justice is to be the sole prerogative of the judiciary. It provides that:

> "Justice shall be administered in courts established by law by judges appointed in the manner provided by this Constitution, and, save in such special and limited cases as may be prescribed by law, shall be administered in public."

Article 37.1 allows for a relaxation, in certain circumstances, of the requirement that judicial power be exercised only by judges. It provides that:

> "Nothing in this Constitution shall operate to invalidate the exercise of limited

---

[40] Freedom of Information Act, s.33(3); Ombudsman Act 1980, s.2(2).
[41] The Second Schedule deals with issues such as resignation, retirement, and removal from office of the Commissioner, disqualification of certain persons from holding the office of Commissioner, staffing of the Office of the Information Commissioner, and delegation of functions by the Commissioner.
[42] Ombudsman Act 1980, s.2.
[43] Freedom of Information Act 1997, s.33(2); Ombudsman Act 1980, s.4(1).
[44] Second Schedule, para. 7(2); Ombudsman Act 1980, s.10(2). See Hogan and Morgan, *op. cit.* above, n. 9, pp. 79–81.
[45] Ombudsman Act 1980, s.6(3).
[46] s.34(14).

functions and powers of a judicial nature, in matters other than criminal matters, by any person or body of persons duly authorised by law to exercise such functions and powers, notwithstanding that such person or such body of persons is not a judge or a court appointed or established as such under this Constitution."

In determining the constitutionality of the conduct of reviews by the Information Commissioner under the FOI Act two issues arise: first, does the exercise of this function amount to the administration of justice within the meaning of Article 34.1?; if so, does the conduct of such reviews fall within the exception in Article 37.1, on the grounds that it amounts to the exercise of a limited judicial function?

Case law in this area is rather disparate, but Morgan has gleaned the following characteristics of the judicial function from the decided cases.[47] They are:

(1) a dispute as to legal rights (civil) or violations of the law (criminal) which is settled by applying pre-existing law and/or ascertaining facts;

(2) a final and conclusive determination;

(3) trappings of a court – compulsory attendance of parties, witnesses, etc.;

(4) the making of an order characteristic of a court; and

(5) the right to give effect to such order, if necessary, by calling on the executive power of the State.

The conduct of a review by the Information Commissioner could be characterised as a dispute as to legal rights as required by the first of the listed criteria, on the ground that the Act expressly confers a right of access to records held by public bodies.[48] In disposing of a review, the Commissioner is required to affirm, vary, or annul the decision "in accordance with this Act".[49] Therefore, it can be argued that the Commissioner is required to apply preexisting law to the matter in dispute. These factors would seem to point towards the fulfilment of the first of the criteria governing the exercise of a judicial function. Factors pointing to the opposite conclusion, however, include the fact the Commissioner is empowered to endeavour to effect a settlement between the parties.[50] As a result, disputes can be dealt with without

---

[47] Morgan, *The Separation of Powers in the Irish Constitution* (Round Hall Sweet & Maxwell, Dublin, 1997), pp. 52–53. This list was formulated from definitions set out in the following cases: *Lynham v. Butler (No. 2)* [1933] I.R. 74; *The State (Shanahan) v. Attorney General* [1964] I.R. 239; and *McDonald v. Bord na gCon (No. 2)* [1965] I.R. 217.
[48] s.6(1).
[49] s.34(2)(b).
[50] s.34(7).

recourse to the parties' legal rights. Another factor which supports the denial of existence of a judicial function is the heavy reliance on public interest tests in the exemption provisions. The Commissioner, in exercising his or her powers of review, will frequently be called upon to determine whether the public interest favours the disclosure or non-disclosure of the records. In so doing, the Commissioner will, to a great extent, be engaged in the exercise of his or her discretion, rather than the determination of a dispute by the application of pre-existing legal standards.

Questions also surround the applicability of the other characteristics of the judicial function to the exercise of the Commissioner's review function. While the Act provides that the decision of the Commissioner is binding,[51] no mechanism for its enforcement is set out in the Act itself, and so it is not clear whether it can be characterised as final and conclusive. While the Commissioner enjoys some of the trappings of a court, for example, the power to summon witnesses, there is no right to take evidence on oath. Nor is it clear that the Commissioner's decision is an order which is characteristic of a court or that the Commissioner has the right to give effect to his or her decision. One commentator has suggested that a lack of finality in decision-making might be provided for on purpose, in order to ensure that there can be no suggestion that a decision-maker is exercising a judicial function.[52] Thus the lack of clarity concerning the enforceability of the Information Commissioner's decisions might have been designed specifically to overcome the dangers posed by Article 34.1.

To summarise, it would appear that the Commissioner would be unlikely to be found to be exercising a judicial function. Even if the opposite conclusion were to be arrived at, the judicial function being exercised be the Commissioner would be likely to fall into the category of limited judicial functions, the exercise of which are sanctioned by Article 37.1.

Kingsmill Moore J., in *Re Solicitors Act,*[53] put forward the following test for determining whether the exercise of powers or functions were "limited":

> "The test as to whether a power is or is not 'limited' in the opinion of the Court, lies in the effect of the assigned power when exercised. If the exercise of the assigned powers and functions is calculated ordinarily to affect in the most profound and far-reaching way the lives, liberties, fortunes or reputations of those against whom they are exercised they cannot properly be described as 'limited'."[54]

Applying that test in the context of the exercise by the Law Society's Disciplinary Committee of the power to strike the appellants off the role of solicitors, the court found that the powers thus exercised were not limited.

---

[51] s.34(14)(b).
[52] Morgan, *op. cit.* above, n. 47, p. 78.
[53] [1960] I.R. 239.
[54] *ibid.* at 264.

While there will undoubtedly be many FOI disputes, the resolution of which could not be said to profoundly affect lives, liberties, fortunes, or reputations, the exercise by the Commissioner of his or her powers to review decisions under the FOI Act can have a profound effect on the lives of the parties to such disputes. Such far-reaching effects are most likely to arise in the case of applications concerning information which directly relates to individuals. For example, the outcome of a review by the Commissioner of a refusal of access to personal information, or a refusal to amend a record held by a public body which contains personal information relating to an individual, could have enormous impact on the individual concerned. Such a profound impact might also be discerned in the case of a dispute concerning an objection to disclosure of information by a third party, or in the case of a dispute with respect to the adequacy of reasons proffered for an administrative decision. In such situations, it could be argued that the Commissioner would not be engaged in the exercise of limited functions.

On the other hand, the context in which the Information Commissioner exercises his or her power to review decisions can be characterised as one in which the matter at issue (the right of access to records) is not substantive, but rather procedural or subsidiary in nature, and it could be viewed on this ground as limited.

Overall, it is unlikely that the exercise by the Commissioner of his or her powers to review decisions under the FOI Act would be found unconstitutional. Apart from the reasons put forward above, there is some evidence of a shift away from the strict application of Article 34.1 in recent years. As Morgan suggests:

> "the results of these cases . . . signal a mood-swing. . . away from a stringent application of the separation of the judicial function."[55]

3. Decisions subject to review by the Information Commissioner

The Information Commissioner is charged with reviewing a number of different kinds of decisions.[56] The formulation of section 34 is rather complex. In essence, section 34(1)(a) and (c)[57] confer on the Commissioner the power to hear appeals against decisions taken at the internal review stage of the review

---

[55] Morgan, *op. cit.* above, n. 47, p. 103.
[56] s.34(1).
[57] It appears that the legislators intended to exclude from the possibility of appeal to the Information Commissioner the imposition of an access charge of £10 or less, hence the provision in section 34(1)(c) for appeals against charges exceeding £10. The means used to exclude appeals against charges of £10 or less from the right of appeal to the Commissioner is the exclusion from section 34(1)(a) of "decisions referred to in paragraph (c)". This does not, however, have the desired effect. Instead it allows for the hearing of appeals against charges of £10 or less under section 34(1)(a) and for the hearing of appeals against charges exceeding £10 under section 34(1)(c).

process, while section 34(1)(b), (d), (e), and (f) give the Commissioner the power to review decisions which did not qualify for internal review.[58]

The full list of decisions subject to review by the Commissioner is as follows:

(a) Section 34(1)(a)

A decision made on internal review under section 14.

(b) Section 34(1)(b)

A range of decisions which were taken by the head of a public body in the first instance, and were not, therefore, subject to internal review. These are: a decision to refuse access to records; a decision to defer access on certain grounds;[59] a decision to grant access in a form other than that requested;[60] a decision to grant access to only part of a record;[61] a refusal to amend personal records;[62] a refusal to give reasons for an administrative decision as required under section 18; and a complaint relating to the contents of such a statement of reasons.[63]

(c) Section 34(1)(c)

A decision made on internal review to charge an access fee or deposit exceeding £10.

(d) Section 34(1)(d)

A decision to extend the four-week time limit allowed for the consideration by public bodies of access requests.

(e) Section 34(1)(e)

A deferral of access to records where the deferral was based on grounds set out in section 11(1)(b) and 11(1)(c). Those grounds are: that the record contains factual information, performance reports relating to public bodies, or reports of technical experts and the giving of access before a particular day would be against the public interest (section 11(1)(b)); and that the records are

---

[58] Internal review of the decisions referred to in paragraphs (d), (e), and (f) is not provided for in section 14, while paragraph (b) refers to situations in which the initial decision was made by the head of a public body and on that basis internal review was not available.

[59] s.11(1)(a).

[60] s.12.

[61] s.13.

[62] s.17.

[63] s.18.

of such interest to the public that their contents will be revealed to the Houses of the Oireachtas or otherwise published within a week (section 11(1)(c)).

(f) Section 34(1)(f)

A decision which is to be granted subject to the operation of third party consultation requirements.

4. Decisions not subject to review by the Information Commissioner

There are three main exclusions from the Information Commissioner's jurisdiction to review decisions under the Freedom of Information Act. Two of these exclusions are expressly provided for in section 34. The first is a decision made by the Information Commissioner in respect of a record held by the Commissioner.[64] Such a decision shall instead be reviewed by the High Court. The second exclusion provided for under section 34 is review of decisions in respect of which internal review is available,[65] to the extent of requiring internal review as a precondition for review to the Information Commissioner. The third matter which is not subject to review by the Information Commissioner is the issuing of a conclusive certificate or a decision to refuse access to a record which is subject to such a certificate.[66] The High Court has sole jurisdiction in respect of these matters.[67]

5. Refusal or discontinuance of review

The Commissioner can, at his or her own discretion, refuse to carry out a review or may discontinue a review if he or she becomes of the opinion that the application is frivolous or vexatious,[68] or that the application relates to a decision which is not subject to review by the Information Commissioner[69] or where the matter to which the application relates is, has been, or will be, the subject of another review by the Information Commissioner.[70] The applicant, the public body concerned, and any relevant third party must be informed as soon as may be of any decision not to review or to discontinue a review, and the reasons therefor.[71]

---

[64] s.34(1)(i). Where the same person holds both the office of Information Commissioner and Ombudsman, this exclusion shall also apply to decisions made by the Ombudsman in respect of records held by the Ombudsman.
[65] s.34(1)(ii).
[66] s.25(3)(b).
[67] s.42(2).
[68] s.34(9)(a)(i).
[69] s.34(9)(a)(ii). It is curious that a discretion is conferred on the Commissioner to decide to refuse to carry out or to discontinue a review in such circumstances.
[70] s.34(1)(a)(iii).
[71] s.34(10).

6. Who may apply for review

An application for review may be made by a "relevant person". A "relevant person" is defined to mean:

(1) a person who has requested access to a record;

(2) a third party to whom the consultation requirements set out in section 29 apply;

(3) a person who has applied to have a record containing personal information amended under section 17; or

(4) a person who has applied under section 18 to be given reasons for an administrative decision affecting him or her.[72]

Review by the Information Commissioner is not available to public bodies.

7. Formalities

Applications for review must be made in writing or in such other form as may be determined by the Minister for Finance.[73] No such determination has yet been made by the Minister. The reference to "such other form as may be determined" is designed to allow for the submission of applications for review in electronic form, for example, by e-mail. A person who makes an application for review is not required to pay any fee. With two exceptions, applications for review must be submitted within six months of the making of the decision appealed against. The exceptions are applications for review of a decision to extend the time for the consideration by a public body of an access request[74] and applications for review of decisions relating to the operation of the third party consultation requirements.[75] In both cases, the time limit for making applications for review is two weeks after notification of the original decision. The six-month time limit may be extended at the discretion of the Information Commissioner where he or she "is of the opinion that there are reasonable grounds for extending that period".[76]

8. Production of documents

The Commissioner has wide powers in terms of requiring access to information relating to a review. Where, for example, the Commissioner is not satisfied as to the adequacy of the reasons given by the public body for refusing access to records, he or she has the power to direct the head of a public body to

---

[72] s.34(15).
[73] s.34(2).
[74] s.34(4)(a).
[75] s.34(4)(a).
[76] s.34(4)(b).

provide further information in respect of such a refusal.[77] The Commissioner has the power in such circumstances to direct the head to furnish to the requester and to the Commissioner a statement containing any further information in relation to the refusal of access that is in the power or control of the head. This requirement must be complied with no later than three weeks after receipt of the Commissioner's direction.[78] This provision constitutes a response to a classic problem relating to FOI review, *i.e.* that lack of knowledge of the contents of a record hinders the requester in determining whether there are grounds for an appeal. In the U.S. that difficulty was acknowledged in the leading decision of the U.S. Court of Appeals for the District of Colombia Circuit, *Vaughn v. Rosen (I)*,[79] where Wilkey J. said that the:

> "lack of knowledge by the party seeking disclosure seriously distorts the traditional adversary nature of our legal system's form of dispute resolution. Ordinarily, the facts relevant to a dispute are more or less equally available to adverse parties. In a case arising under the FOIA this is not true, we have noted, and hence the typical process of dispute resolution is impossible."[80]

In order to deal with this problem, the court in *Vaughn* devised a set of procedures which have come to be known as the *Vaughn* procedures. These require the government to provide the FOI plaintiff and the court with a itemised "index" of the withheld records that describes each document or withheld portion and gives a detailed justification of the agency's grounds for withholding, correlating each exemption claimed with the record or portion to which it is asserted it applies. These procedures have been adopted by virtually all of the Circuits and the obtaining of a *Vaughn* index has become an essential step in U.S. FOI litigation. It would arguably be open to the Commissioner under section 35 to require the production of a *Vaughn*-type index for the purposes of a review.

The Commissioner has the power to require the furnishing of information or records by any person where the Commissioner is of the opinion that the aforesaid material is relevant to the purposes of a review under section 34 or an investigation under section 36.[81] He or she may also require such a person to attend before him or her for such a purpose.[82] This means that the Commissioner has the right to obtain access to the information in dispute as well as to accompanying files. He or she also has the power to enter any premises occupied by a public body to carry out a number of operations.[83] These operations are:

---

[77] s.35(1).
[78] s.35(2).
[79] 484 F.2d 820 (D.C. Cir. 1973).
[80] *ibid.* at 824.
[81] s.37(1)(a).
[82] s.37(1)(a).
[83] s.37(2).

(1) to obtain from any person found on the premises such information as the Commissioner may reasonably require for the purposes of a review or investigation;

(2) to require a person found on the premises to make available any record in his or her power or control that in the opinion of the Commissioner is relevant to the review; and

(3) to examine and take copies of records made available to the Commissioner or found on the premises.

The Act ensures that persons who are required to supply information or records to the Commissioner cannot hide behind any legal restrictions on the disclosure of information, such as those found in the law of defamation, copyright law, or breach of confidence. Section 37(3) provides that "no enactment or rule of law prohibiting or restricting the disclosure or communication of information shall preclude a person from furnishing to the commissioner such information or record, as aforesaid". This provision is, however, subject to the stipulation that persons who are required to provide information or records to the Information Commissioner are entitled to the same immunities and privileges as a witness in court.[84]

9. Friendly settlement

The Commissioner is permitted to attempt to effect a settlement between the parties at any time during a review.[85] The Commissioner may, for the purpose of endeavouring to effect a settlement between the parties, suspend and, if appropriate, discontinue the review. It is not clear whether the Commissioner's power to suspend or discontinue the review requires the consent of both parties. The powers of suspension and discontinuance may only be exercised by the Commissioner for the purpose of endeavouring to effect a settlement of the dispute; on that basis, it would appear that the consent of both parties to such suspension or discontinuance is a prerequisite, since a settlement cannot be effected without the agreement of both parties. In addition, the power to suspend the review allows for such suspension "for such period as may be agreed with the parties concerned" and for that reason also would appear to be subject to consent of the parties.

10. Conduct of reviews

The role of the Commissioner is to carry out a *de novo* review. Procedure for the conduct of reviews shall be "such as the Commissioner considers ap-

---

[84] s.37(4).
[85] s.34(7).

propriate in all the circumstances of the case".[86] The Act further states that, without prejudice to the foregoing requirement, procedure for the conduct of reviews shall be "as informal as is consistent with the due performance of the functions of the Commissioner".[87]

Before commencing a review, the Information Commissioner must notify the head of the public body concerned, the applicant for review, and any other person who, in the opinion of the Commissioner, should be notified. The head must inform the Commissioner of any third party who would have been notified, had the head of the public body intended to disclose the record.[88] One of the few formal requirements relating to the conduct of a review centres on the right of the head of the public body involved in the dispute, the applicant for review, and any other person whom the Commissioner has notified of the review, to make submissions to the Commissioner in relation to any matters relevant to the review.[89] The Commissioner is obliged to take those submissions into account for the purposes of the review.[90] There appears to be no barrier to the raising in these submissions of new grounds for exemption beyond those already cited by the public body in refusing access to the records. The rules of constitutional justice would, however, require that the applicant be informed of any such new grounds for exemption and that he or she be given the opportunity to argue against the application of such exemption provisions to the records in dispute.

There is no provision in the Act for the taking of evidence on oath. The Act does, however, provide by section 37(7) that it is an offence to refuse to comply with the requirement to supply information or records, or to hinder or obstruct the Commissioner in the performance of his or her duties. Those found guilty are liable on summary conviction to a maximum fine of £1,500 or to imprisonment for a maximum term of six months or to both. Persons who refuse to answer the Commissioner's questions[91] or who answer them untruthfully are be subject to prosecution under that provision.

There is no express right to an oral hearing. Instead, the Act gives the Commissioner the power to determine the form in which submissions should be made. He or she can require such submissions to be made orally, in writing, or in "such other form as may be determined".[92] Subject to what is said in the next paragraph, as the Act makes no reference to the conduct of reviews in public, this matter will also be at the discretion of the Commissioner.[93] No provision is made in the Act for representation of the parties.

---

[86] s.37(6).
[87] s.37(6).
[88] s.34(6).
[89] s.34(8).
[90] s.34(8).
[91] Assuming the privilege against self-incrimination does not apply.
[92] s.34(8).
[93] Regard should also be had to the requirements of Article 6 of the European Convention

Clearly the Commissioner does not have to comply with the rules of evidence in conducting a review. However, since he or she is acting in a quasi-judicial manner, the Commissioner must adhere to the rules of constitutional justice.[94] As Henchy J. stated in *Kiely v. Minister for Social Welfare*:[95]

> "Tribunals exercising quasi-judicial functions are frequently allowed to act informally – to receive unsworn evidence, to act on hearsay, to depart from the rules of evidence, to ignore courtroom procedures, and the like – but they may not act in such a way as to imperil a fair hearing or a fair result."[96]

Thus it will ultimately be up to the courts to decide, for example, whether oral hearings should be held. The requirements of constitutional justice might also oblige the Commissioner to allow for the cross-examination of witnesses[97] or to allow for representation of the parties.[98] The Commissioner has the power to refer any question of law arising in a review to the High Court. He or she can postpone the making of a decision on review pending the determination of the question by the High Court.[99]

11. Onus of proof

The Act places the burden of proof firmly on the body or person opposing disclosure. Section 34(12)(b) provides that a decision to refuse to grant a request shall be presumed not to have been justified unless the head of the public body concerned shows to the satisfaction of the Information Commissioner that the decision was justified. Where the review concerns an objection against disclosure on the part of a third party, the decision to grant access will be presumed to have been justified unless the third party shows to the satisfaction of the Commissioner that it was not so justified.[100]

12. Time limit for completion of review

The Act attempts to encourage the expeditious handling of applications for review by the Office of the Information Commissioner by requiring that deci-

---

on Human Rights. See *Barry v. Medical Council and Fitness to Practise Committee of the Medical Council*, unreported, High Court, 1996 No. 369JR, Costello J., February 11, 1997; unreported, Supreme Court, December 16, 1997; (1998) 4(1) *Medico-Legal Journal of Ireland* 41.
[94] See Hogan and Morgan, *op. cit.* above, n. 9, Chaps 10 and 11.
[95] [1977] I.R. 267 at 276, S.C.
[96] *ibid.* at 281.
[97] *ibid.*; *Re Haughey* [1971] I.R. 217.
[98] *McGrath and O'Ruairc v. Trustees of Maynooth College* [1979] I.L.R.M. 166; *Flanagan v. University College Dublin* [1988] I.R. 724.
[99] s.42(5).
[100] s.34(12)(a).

sions on review be made "as soon as may be".[101] More specifically, the Act establishes time limits for the completion of reviews. In the case of applications for review made during the first three years of operation of the Act, decisions shall be made, "in so far as practicable", not later than four months after receipt of the application.[102] That time limit is shortened to three months once the Act has been in operation for over three years.[103]

13. Reasons for decision

The applicant, the public body concerned, and any relevant third party must be informed of the Commissioner's decision on review and the reasons therefor.[104] Such notification must be given "as soon as may be" and, in so far as practicable, within the time limit for the making of a decision by the Commissioner on review.[105] In order to ensure compliance with this provision, the Information Commissioner is required to specify in his or her annual report the number of cases in which the time limit for giving of notice and reasons for a decision was not adhered to.[106]

14. Powers on appeal

Three options are open to the Commissioner in disposing of a matter following review. They are to affirm, vary, or annul the decision.[107] In annulling a decision the Commissioner may, "if appropriate, make such decision in relation to the matter concerned as he or she considers proper".[108] The Act further provides that a decision on review shall, in so far as it is inconsistent with the decision which has been reviewed, have effect in lieu thereof.[109] These provisions effectively give the Commissioner the power to substitute his or her own decision for that which has been varied or annulled.

15. Implementation of decisions

The Commissioner is required to specify the period within which effect must be given to his or her decision on review.[110] In fixing the time period, the Commissioner is required to have regard to the desirability of giving effect to

---

[101] s.34(3).
[102] s.34(3)(a).
[103] s.34(3)(b).
[104] s.34(10).
[105] s.34(11).
[106] s.34(11)(b).
[107] s.34(2)(b).
[108] s.34(2)(b)(ii).
[109] s.34(14)(a).
[110] s.34(13).

such a decision as soon as may be after notification of the outcome of the review,[111] whilst allowing for the expiration of the time limit for the bringing of an appeal to the High Court.[112]

16. Costs

There is no provision for the awarding of the costs in respect of the holding of the review. Witness expenses and compensation for loss of time according to a rate determined by the Minister can be paid at the discretion of the Commissioner.[113]

17. Enforcement of decisions

Decisions made by the Commissioner on review are stated to be "binding on the parties concerned".[114] This can be contrasted with section 6(3) of the Ombudsman Act 1980 which merely gives the Ombudsman the power to recommend certain courses of action following the completion of his or her investigation. The Freedom of Information Act does not, however, specify the manner in which such decisions may be enforced against a recalcitrant public body. Failure to comply with a decision of the Commissioner on review could be viewed as hindering or obstructing the Commissioner in the performance of his or her duties and would therefore be an offence under section 37(7). It would also appear to be open to the Commissioner to apply by way of judicial review for an order of mandamus requiring the public body to comply with the Commissioner's decision.[115] This remedy has been described as "the most appropriate remedy where the enforcement of a statutory duty is sought".[116] The FOI Act, by providing that the Information Commissioner's decision is binding, clearly establishes a statutory duty on the part of public bodies to comply with that decision. Mandamus has also been held to lie against a Minister[117] so that where the head of a public body is a Minister, he or she may be required to comply with the Commissioner's decision by way of such an order.

18. Publication of decisions

Apart from requiring that the Commissioner's findings be transmitted to the parties to the review, the Act in a separate provision gives the Commissioner

---

[111] s.34(13).
[112] s.44.
[113] s.37(5).
[114] s.34(14)(b).
[115] See generally, Hogan and Morgan, *op. cit.* above, n. 9, Chap. 13.
[116] *ibid.*, p. 700.
[117] *State (King) v. Minister for Justice* [1984] I.R. 169.

the power to prepare and publish commentaries on the practical application and operation of the provisions, or any particular provisions of the Act, including commentaries based on the experience of holders of the office of Commissioner in relation to reviews and decisions following reviews.[118] The Act also gives the Commissioner the power, "if he or she considers it appropriate in the public interest, or in the interests of any person", to prepare and publish a report in relation to any review carried out under the Act, or any matter relating to or arising in the course of such a review.[119] These provisions clearly imbue the Commissioner with the power, though not, oddly, any duty, to issue reports of the cases he or she has decided under the Act.

D. Appeal to High Court

The hearing of appeals under the Act by the High Court may arise in three separate instances. First, there is provision in the Act for the taking of an appeal to the High Court on a point of law from a decision of the Commissioner.[120] An appeal on a point of law would appear to encompass an appeal against the Commissioner's determination on the public interest.[121]

Secondly, an appeal can be made to the High Court on a point of law in respect of the issue of a ministerial certificate or in respect of a refusal of access to a record the subject of such a certificate or a decision on internal review to refuse access to a record the subject of such a certificate.[122] Both of these rights of appeal are available to the parties to the review and to any other person affected by the impugned decision. They may, therefore, be exercised by the applicant, the public body which is a party to the review, or a third party affected by the Commissioner's decision.[123] The third situation in which an appeal can be made to the High Court arises in the case of decisions made in respect of records held by the office of the Information Commissioner.[124] The inclusion of this provision was necessitated by the fact that the Commissioner is precluded from reviewing decisions relating to access to records of his or her own office. Appeals relating to such records must therefore be dealt with directly by the High Court.[125]

---

[118] s.39.

[119] s.40(2).

[120] s.42(1).

[121] This was acknowledged by the sponsoring Minister of State: 477 *Dáil Debates* Col. 772 (Report Stage).

[122] s.42(2).

[123] s.42(1).

[124] s.42(3). This provision also applies to records held by the office of the Ombudsman where the Ombudsman holds the office of Commissioner.

[125] s.34(1)(i).

The Commissioner also has the power to refer any question of law arising in a review under section 34 to the High Court.[126]

Section 42(8) stipulates that a decision of the High Court on appeal or reference shall be final and conclusive. This provision appears to preclude the bringing of an appeal to the Supreme Court.[127]

In the case of an unsuccessful appeal to the High Court, the court has the power to order that some or all of the appellant's costs be paid by the public body, in circumstances where it considers that the point of law raised for consideration on the appeal was of exceptional public importance.[128]

E. Monitoring Functions of the Information Commissioner

The role of the Commissioner in enforcing the Act goes beyond reviewing decisions relating to access to records. It extends to monitoring the operation of the Act generally. The Commissioner is obliged to "keep the operation of the Act under review".[129] Certain powers are conferred on the Commissioner to facilitate this role. In particular, the Commissioner has the right, at any time, to carry out two types of investigation. The first comprises an investigation into the practices and procedures adopted by public bodies for the purposes of compliance with the Act.[130] The Commissioner is obliged to carry out such an investigation in respect of each of the public bodies within three years of the commencement of the Act.[131] The Commissioner also has the power to carry out an investigation into "the practices and procedures adopted by public bodies for the purpose of enabling a person to exercise the rights conferred by the Act and facilitating such exercise".[132] The Commissioner has the power to prepare a report of his or her findings or conclusions resulting from the carrying out of such investigations, as well as on any matter relating to or arising from the performance of such investigatory functions.[133] Copies of such reports may, if the Commissioner considers it appropriate to do so, be provided to the Minister for Finance and to the public bodies concerned. Such reports must be appended to the Commissioner's annual report.[134]

The Commissioner is required to make an annual report on the activities of

---

[126] s.42(5).
[127] See Hogan and Whyte, *Kelly: The Irish Constitution* (3rd ed., Butterworths, 1994), pp. 503–510.
[128] s.42(6).
[129] s.36(1).
[130] s.36(1).
[131] s.36(2).
[132] s.36(3).
[133] s.36(4).
[134] s.36(5).

his or her office to the Houses of the Oireachtas.[135] Any report furnished to the Commissioner by a Minister under section 25(11)[136] must be appended to the annual report as must any report prepared under section 36. The Commissioner may also, in the public interest, or in the interest of a person or public body, publish reports relating to any investigation, review, or other function carried out by him or her or in respect of any matter arising in respect of an investigation, review, or performance of his or her functions.[137]

Finally, the Act places an obligation on the Commissioner to foster and encourage the publication by public bodies of information of relevance or interest to the general public in relation to their activities and functions generally.[138] The publication of such information is stated to be in addition to the requirements as to publication of information imposed upon public bodies by sections 15 and 16 of the Act.

F.   Immunity from Legal Proceedings

The Official Secrets Act 1963 was, in the past, one of the most important barriers to the disclosure of official information by civil servants. The Act specifically provides for immunity from prosecution for those who are authorised to communicate official information by the terms of the FOI Act. In addition, the Act provides for immunity from a range of legal proceedings for acts required or authorised by the FOI Act.

1. Immunity from prosecution under the Official Secrets Act

Section 4(1) is the core provision of the Official Secrets Act 1963. It provides as follows:

> "A person shall not communicate any official information to any other person unless he is duly authorised to do so or does so in the course of and in accordance with his duties as the holder of a public office or when it is his duty in the interest of the State to communicate it."

This provision allows for the communication of official information in three circumstances only:

(1) where a person is duly authorised to do so;

(2) where he or she does so in the course of and in accordance with his or her duties as the holder of a public office; or

---

[135] s.40.
[136] This provision requires Ministers to prepare a report relating to their use of the ministerial certificate mechanism. See above, p. 119.
[137] s.40(2).
[138] s.38.

(3) when it is his or her duty in the interests of the State to communicate the information.

Section 48(1) of the FOI Act places the disclosure of information under the FOI Act into the first of these categories. It provides that a person who is or who reasonably believes he or she is authorised by the FOI Act to communicate official information to another person shall be deemed for the purposes of section 4 of the Official Secrets Act to be "duly authorised" to communicate that information.

The Official Secrets Act contains two other provisions which are relevant to the disclosure of official information. Section 5 which, like section 4, applies to official information in general, makes it an offence for a party to a contract with a Minister or a State Authority to communicate to any third party any information relating to the contract and expressed therein to be confidential. Section 9 applies to a much more limited category of information than is covered by sections 4 and 5, namely information which, if communicated, might prejudice the safety or preservation of the State. Section 9 provides that a person shall not, in any manner prejudicial to the safety or preservation of the State, obtain, record, communicate to any other person, publish, or have in his possession or under his control any information relating to such matters as Defence Forces equipment, munitions of war, Garda Síochána or Defence Forces operations, measures relating to the defence or fortification of any place on behalf of the State, and "any other matter whatsoever, information as to which would or might be prejudicial to the safety or preservation of the State".

Section 48(2) of the FOI Act establishes as a defence to a prosecution under section 5 or 9 that the act to which the charge of the offence relates is authorised, or is reasonably believed by the person charged to be authorised, by the FOI Act. This is not likely to be significant in practice.

2. Immunity from other legal proceedings

Further protection against legal action is found in section 45. This provision grants immunity from civil or criminal proceedings to three groups of people. The first consists of the State, a public body, a head, director, member of staff of a public body, and to a person providing a service for a public body under a contract for services with the body. The second group to which immunity is provided consists of those who have supplied records to public bodies, while the third group protected is the Information Commissioner and members of his or her staff. Immunity is granted to the first group in respect of:

(1) a grant or grant in part of an access request;

(2) the furnishing to a person of a statement of reasons for an administrative decision under section 18; and

(3) the publication of a document specified in section 15 or 16 under which public bodies are required to publish information about their operations, rules, etc. No immunity will, however, lie with respect to the breach of a duty imposed by section 16.

Immunity will apply to such acts only to the extent that they were required or authorised by and complied with the provisions of the FOI Act, or were reasonably believed by the head concerned to have been so required or authorised and to comply with the provisions of the FOI Act.

No immunity is provided for in respect of the amendment of a record in pursuance of the rights conferred by section 17. The contents of a record may be changed as a consequence of the making of an application under section 17 even though the application for amendment is itself refused. This is because section 17(4) obliges the head of a public body, in the case of a refusal to amend a record under section 17, to attach to the record either the application for amendment or, if that is not practicable, a notation indicating that the application has been made. It is possible that an application for amendment could contain material the publication of which would be defamatory, or in breach of copyright or the law of confidence. While section 17(4) provides that the right to have an application for amendment attached to a record does not apply where, in the opinion of the head of the public body concerned, the application is defamatory, the head is not entitled to refuse to comply with section 17(4) on the grounds of breach of other laws such as those relating to copyright or confidentiality. Further, while the head may refuse to attach an application on the grounds that it is defamatory, the onus will be upon the head to determine whether the application is defamatory and if he or she judges an application to be non-defamatory, and this ultimately turns out to be wrong, it appears that he or she will enjoy no immunity from legal action.

Immunity is extended to those who supply records to public bodies in two sets of circumstances. In the first place, immunity is granted to the author of a record with respect to the granting of access to that record. The need for such immunity could arise where a record held by a public body which has been composed by a private individual contains defamatory material. The author would be immune from legal proceedings with respect to the disclosure of this record under FOI. Immunity is granted also to any other person with respect to any publication involved in, or resulting from, the granting of access to a record. Such immunity would provide protection in a situation where a record which is defamatory in nature is supplied to a public body by someone other than its author.[139]

The Commissioner and his or her staff are protected against criminal or civil proceedings in respect of anything said or done in good faith by the Com-

---

[139] s.45(2)(b).

missioner or a staff member in the course of the performance or purported performance of a function of the Commissioner or staff member.[140]

---

[140] s.45(4).

OTHER LEGAL PROVISIONS GOVERNING ACCESS TO OFFICIAL INFORMATION

OTHER LEGAL PROVISIONS GOVERNING ACCESS TO OFFICIAL INFORMATION

A.   Introduction

While the Freedom of Information Act is clearly the most significant statutory provision governing access to official information in Ireland, it by no means comprises a comprehensive code for the provision of such access. Other important statutory provisions conferring rights of access to government information include: the Data Protection Act 1988; the National Archives Act 1986; and the Access to Information on the Environment Regulations 1998.[1] It is essential to the understanding of the FOI Act that the relationships between it and other statutory provisions governing access to information be properly explored. Such an exploration is important in determining the extent to which there is potential for conflict or overlap to arise between the FOI Act and other access provisions. Practical questions which must be addressed in this context, include whether the exercise of the right of access conferred by the FOI Act can be restricted by the operation of other statutory schemes governing access to official information. Another question which will undoubtedly arise in practice is whether an applicant for access or amendment will be able to choose between the various statutory provisions conferring access and amendment rights. It is not always clear from the text of the FOI Act how it was intended that the various statutory provisions should interact with the FOI regime. The aim of this chapter is, therefore, to attempt to clarify the relationships between the FOI Act and the Data Protection Act 1988, the National Archives Act 1986, and the Access to Information on the Environment Regulations 1998, and to compare the FOI access provisions with each of those alternative access regimes.

B.   Relationship of the Freedom of Information Act with the Data Protection Act

The aim of FOI legislation is to open up access to government information. Much of the information held by government departments and public bodies relates to individuals. The Data Protection Act ("DP Act"), which was passed

---

[1] S.I. No. 125 of 1998.

in 1988, and which applies to both the private and public sectors, has the aim of protecting the privacy of personal information relating to individuals.[2]

The two main areas of concern to emerge from an examination of the relationship between the FOI Act and the DP Act are:

(1) the potential for conflict between the right of access to government information under FOI, and the restrictions on the disclosure of third party personal data under the DP Act; and

(2) the possibility of overlap between the right of access to, and amendment of, one's own personal information under the FOI Act, and the access and amendment rights under the DP Act.

The first of these potential difficulties arises from the fact the DP Act places restrictions on the disclosure of personal information. The exercise, under the FOI Act, of the right of access to information may result in the disclosure of personal information relating to individuals. The possibility that conflict might arise between the exercise of the right of access to government information under the FOI Act and the restrictions on the disclosure of personal data imposed by the DP Act was adverted to in the Seanad debate on the FOI Bill when one member stated that: "If one examines the sections of the [FOI] Bill, one will find that it negates the DP Act."[3]

The other problem which may result from the interaction of the two Acts is that of overlap. There is potential for overlap in terms of access to and amendment of an individual's personal records. As part of its role in protecting the privacy of personal information, the DP Act confers on individuals a right of access to their own personal information, as well as the right to have that information corrected in the event that it is incorrectly recorded. The provision of a means of obtaining access to personal information and of ensuring that it is accurate is an integral part of the right to privacy. The FOI Act, in providing a general right of access to government records, confers on individuals the right to access their own records in the hands of government bodies. The FOI Act provides, in addition, a mechanism for the amendment of such records of personal information where they are found to be incomplete, incorrect or misleading. There is clearly a possibility of overlap between the right of access to and amendment of one's own personal information under the FOI Act, and the access and amendment rights under the DP Act.

There are, however, some limits on the extent of the conflict or overlap between the two Acts. The first is that the DP Act only applies to "data", which is defined in the Act as "information in a form in which it can be

---

[2] See Clark, *Data Protection Law in Ireland* (The Round Hall Press, Dublin, 1990); Kelleher and Murray, *Information Technology Law* (Butterworths, Dublin, 1997), Chaps 19–23; Annual Reports of the Data Protection Commissioner.

[3] 149 *Seanad Debates* Col. 1286 (Second Stage), *per* Senator Lanigan.

processed". This has been taken to mean that the Act does not apply to manual files.[4] The FOI Act, on the other hand, applies to "records", a term which has been defined broadly to include both manual and automated material.[5] In addition, conflict or overlap can only arise in respect of data held by certain bodies, since the FOI Act, unlike the DP Act, does not extend to the holders of personal information generally. Its application is instead limited to specified public sector bodies.[6]

1. Relationship between right of access to government information under FOI and restrictions on disclosure of third party personal data in the DP Act

The DP Act, which applies to personal data only, limits the disclosure of such data. The FOI Act itself restricts the right of access to government information in order to protect privacy of individuals. One issue which must be addressed is whether the restrictions provided for in the FOI Act are as comprehensive as the protection conferred on privacy of personal data by the DP Act. In particular, the question arises whether "personal data" relating to third parties, as defined in the DP Act, could be subject to release under the FOI Act. Personal data could become liable to disclosure under the FOI Act in two circumstances. First, where the disclosure of the data does not fall within the scope of any of the FOI exemption provisions; or second, where although the record which is sought to be disclosed is covered by one of the exemptions, the release of the requested record is nonetheless deemed to be in the public interest.

(a) The FOI exemptions and disclosure of personal data

Personal data relating to third parties could become liable to disclosure under the FOI Act where the disclosure of the data falls outside the scope of the FOI exemption provisions. While all of the FOI exemptions can be invoked in denying access to third party personal data, the exemption most likely to be applicable is the personal information exemption. It cannot be assumed that this exemption, as drafted, will necessarily protect all third party personal data

---

[4] See Clark, *op. cit.* above, n. 2, p. 30. See, for comparison, Directive 95/46 on the Protection of Individuals in relation to the processing of personal data [1995] O.J. L281/31, which applies both to the processing of personal data by automatic means and to "the processing otherwise than by automatic means of personal data which form part of a filing system or are intended to form part of a filing system" (Article 3). This Directive must be transposed into national law by October 24, 1998. A consultation paper on the transposition of the Directive into Irish law was issued in November 1997: Department of Justice, Equality and Law Reform, *Directive on the protection of individuals with regard to the processing of personal data and on the free movement of such data: Consultation Paper on Transposition into Irish Law* (1997): see http://www.irlgov.ie/justice.

[5] s.2(1).

[6] The public bodies to which the FOI Act applies are listed in the First Schedule to the Act.

from disclosure. Such data could, for example, become liable to disclosure under the FOI Act, where the definition of personal information in that Act is found to be narrower in its scope than the definition of personal data in the DP Act. In such a case, information which qualifies as personal data under the terms of the DP Act will not be protected from disclosure by the personal information exemption in the FOI Act. The definitions of "personal data" and "personal information" in the respective Acts may be compared to determine whether such a situation could arise. Personal data is defined in the DP Act as:

> "data relating to a living individual who can be identified from the data or from the data in conjunction with other information in the possession of the data controller".[7]

This definition can be contrasted with the definition of personal information in the FOI Act. It provides that personal data means:

> "information about an identifiable individual that—
>
> (a) would, in the ordinary course of events, be known only to the individual or members of the family, or friends, of the individual, or
>
> (b) is held by a public body on the understanding that it would be treated by it as confidential".[8]

The FOI Act definition requires not only that the information be about an identifiable individual, but also that it meet one or other of the two further criteria set out in paragraphs (a) and (b) of the definition. Because of the need to fulfil one of these additional criteria, the FOI Act definition of personal information is narrower than its counterpart in the DP Act.[9] Therefore, while all personal information under the FOI Act might amount to personal data under the DP Act, not all personal data qualifies as personal information. This means that some information which falls within the broad definition of personal data in the DP Act might not be exempt as personal information for the purposes of the narrower FOI Act exemption. Such information could, therefore, become subject to disclosure under the FOI Act.

(b) Disclosure in the public interest

The second situation in which personal data could become subject to disclosure under the FOI Act is where its disclosure is found to be in the public interest. Public interest tests, which are a feature of many of the FOI exemp-

---

[7] Data Protection Act 1988, s.1(1).

[8] s.2(1). The definition goes on to list 12 examples of "personal information" and three exceptions from the definition. See above, pp. 269–279.

[9] On the other hand, the FOI Act definition includes personal information relating to deceased persons, whereas the Data Protection Act confines its protection to the living.

tion provisions,[10] allow for the disclosure of records which would otherwise be exempt, where such disclosure is found to be in the public interest. In the case of the personal information exemption, for example, the head of a public body can decide to disclose personal information to which the exemption applies where in his or her opinion such disclosure would, on balance, be in the public interest.[11] Such personal information could include personal data as defined in the DP Act. There are similar public interest tests in place in respect of a number of the other exemptions, including the confidentiality and commercial information exemptions.

(c) Disclosure of "personal data" under the FOI Act

There is, however, one FOI exemption which could place a blanket prohibition on the disclosure under the FOI Act of "personal data" as defined in the DP Act. This is the exemption with respect to enactments relating to non-disclosure of records (section 32). That exemption, which is not subject to a public interest test, requires the head of a public body to refuse to grant a request for access to information in two situations. The first of these is relevant to the relationship between the DP Act and the FOI Act. It applies in cases where disclosure is prohibited by any enactment, apart from those provisions listed in the Third Schedule to the Act.[12] The DP Act is not listed in the Third Schedule. If the restrictions on disclosure of personal data in the DP Act are interpreted as a prohibition on disclosure for the purposes of section 32 of the FOI Act, the head of a public body would be required to refuse to grant a request for access to such data.

The main restriction on disclosure of personal data is found in section 2(1)(c) of the DP Act. It provides that data:

"(ii) shall not be used or disclosed in any manner incompatible with that purpose or those purposes".

The purposes alluded to refer back to section 2(1)(c)(i) of the Act, which is known as the purpose principle. It provides that data "shall be kept only for one or more specified and lawful purposes".

Thus, disclosure of personal data is prohibited by the DP Act where it is incompatible with the specified and lawful purpose for which the data is kept. It appears, given the use of the conjunctive "and" between "specified" and "lawful", that both these terms must be satisfied if a disclosure is to be compatible with the purpose for which the data is kept. Addressing the issue of the lawfulness of the purpose first, it is unlikely that the lawfulness of the purpose of disclosure under FOI could be called into question. The lawfulness of such

---

[10] See above, pp. 93–115.
[11] s.28(5).
[12] s.32(1)(a).

disclosure is supported by the fact that the FOI Act provides a right of access to records held by public bodies[13] and also by the fact that the Act confers immunity from legal proceedings in respect of disclosures of information under the Act.[14] The term "specified" is not defined in the Act. Clark, in his book on the DP Act, suggests that the only ways in which the purpose may be specified is if it is either specified to the source of the personal data, or it is specified in the register which the Data Protection Commissioner is obliged to establish and maintain under section 16(2) of the DP Act.[15] On that basis, it could be argued that disclosure under FOI legislation would be incompatible with the purpose specified, unless the individual was told, at the time of collection, that disclosure under FOI was one of the purposes for which the data was being collected or such disclosure was listed as one of the purposes of collection of the data in the data controller's entry in the register.

While this provision clearly restricts the disclosure of personal data, it is not certain that it amounts to a prohibition of disclosure for the purposes of section 32. This is because the restrictions on disclosure of personal data contained in the DP Act are subject to a number of exceptions. In particular, section 8(e) of the DP Act excepts disclosures "required by or under any enactment or by a rule of law or order of a court". It could be argued, on the basis of the right of access to records expressly provided for in section 6 of the FOI Act, that disclosure of information under the FOI Act amounts to "disclosure required by or under any enactment". On that analysis, disclosure of personal data under the FOI Act would not amount to a breach of the DP Act.

As can be seen from the foregoing discussion, the interaction between section 32 of the FOI Act and the exception in section 8 of the DP Act is complex and largely circular. Each Act effectively contains a saver provision for other statutory provisions in that, while section 32 of the FOI Act provides for an exemption from the right of access in the case of records, the disclosure of which is prohibited by other statutes, section 8(e) of the DP Act provides for an exception to the prohibition on disclosure of personal data in the case of disclosures required by other enactments. In practical terms, the effect of a finding that the restrictions on disclosure contained in section 2(1)(c)(ii) of the DP Act amount to a prohibition of disclosure within the meaning of section 32 of the FOI Act would be to prevent the use of the FOI Act in obtaining access to automated personal data. If the alternative conclusion is arrived at, namely that disclosure of personal data under the FOI Act amounts to a disclosure "required by or under any enactment" within the meaning of section 8(e) of the DP Act, then the DP Act cannot be used to restrict the disclosure of personal data under the FOI Act. The effect would be to allow the right of

---

[13] s.6(1).

[14] s.45.

[15] As Clark acknowledges, not all data controllers are subject to registration requirements: *op. cit.* above, n. 2, p. 51.

access to information under the FOI Act to "trump" the restrictions on access set out in the DP Act.

Arguments can be advanced in support of both positions. Support for the view that the DP Act should prevail over the FOI Act can be obtained from the constitutional right to privacy[16] and from Ireland's international legal obligations in the area of data protection. The latter arise out of Ireland's membership of the European Union,[17] as well as the incorporation into domestic law, of the Council of Europe Convention for the Protection of Individuals with regard to Automatic Processing of Personal Data.[18]

On the other hand, it could be argued, in view of the central role of the right of access to information in the scheme of the FOI Act, as enunciated, for example, in the long title to the Act, that the FOI Act should prevail over the DP Act. Support for this approach can be gained from the fact that the constitutional right to privacy is not absolute; nor do Ireland's international obligations preclude disclosure of personal data in all cases. Precedent for allowing for the overriding of the DP Act in the interests of the provision of access to information can be found in the Health (Provision of Information) Act 1997, which provides that, notwithstanding the DP Act, information relating to persons who may be invited to participate in a cancer screening programme may be disclosed to the National Cancer Registry Board or the Minister for Health, a health board, hospital, or other body engaged in a cancer screening programme.[19]

The difficulty of reconciling FOI legislation, on the one hand, with data protection/privacy legislation, on the other, has arisen in other jurisdictions. The Australian Law Reform Commission and Administrative Review Council in their joint review of the operation of the Australian federal FOI Act stated:

> "When an FOI request includes a documents that contains the personal information of someone other than the applicant, the unavoidable tension between the right of access provided by the FOI Act and the need to protect personal privacy becomes apparent. Resolving this tension can be difficult."[20]

The Canadian Supreme Court, in considering the relationship between the corresponding Canadian Acts[21] in *Dagg v. Minister of Finance*, said:

---

[16] See above, pp. 111–113.

[17] See in particular: Directive 95/46 on the Protection of Individuals in relation to the processing of personal data, above, n. 4.

[18] The Convention was incorporated into domestic law by the Data Protection Act 1988.

[19] s.1(2).

[20] Australian Law Reform Commission, Report No. 77/Administrative Review Council, Report No. 40, *Open Government: A Review of the Freedom of Information Act 1982* (Australian Government Publishing Service, Canberra, 1995), para.10.2.

[21] Access to Information Act (Canada), R.S.C., 1985; Privacy Act (Canada), R.S.C., 1985.

"This appeal involves a clash between two competing legislative policies - access to information and privacy. For obvious reasons, the appellant and respondent have opposing views as to which of these policies should prevail in this case. It should also come as no surprise that the litigants have markedly different conceptions of the statutes that embody those policies. Recognising the conflicting nature of governmental disclosure and individual privacy, Parliament attempted to mediate this discord by weaving the Access to Information Act and the Privacy Act into a seamless code. In my opinion, it has done so successfully and elegantly. While the two statutes do not efface the contradiction between the competing interests – no legislation possibly could – they do set out a coherent and principled mechanism for determining which value should be paramount in a given case."[22]

There has, unfortunately, been no attempt on the part of the Irish legislature to weave the relevant Irish legislative provision into a "seamless code". The FOI Act contains only one reference to the DP Act and that does not address the fundamental issue of whether the right of access in the FOI Act should prevail over the protection of personal data under the DP Act,[23] nor is there guidance one way or the other in the preparatory materials associated with the FOI Bill. It will be up to the Information Commissioner, and ultimately the High Court, to attempt to reconcile these statutes.

2. Access to and amendment of personal data

(a) Access to personal data

Rights of access to personal information are provided for in both the FOI Act and the DP Act. A right of access to personal data is provided for in section 4 of the DP Act. That section entitles an individual, on making an application in writing, to be informed by a data controller as to whether personal data kept by the data controller includes personal data relating to him or her. It also confers on the individual a right to be supplied with a copy of the information constituting any such data.[24] There are a number of restrictions on the right of access to personal data under the DP Act. The FOI Act also provides a right of access to personal information as part of the general right of access to government information conferred by that Act.

Two questions arise with respect to the relationship between the access rights in both Acts: the first is whether it is open to an applicant for access to personal information to apply under either or both access regimes; the second question is whether the access rights conferred under both Acts are consistent with one another. The issue of consistency is important irrespective of whether a person is entitled to use both sets of access provisions. If the making of

---

[22] (1997) 148 D.L.R. (4th) 385 at 397–398.
[23] s.46(3).
[24] s.4(1)(a)(ii).

applications for access under both sets of provisions is precluded by the legislation, consistency will be important in ensuring that an applicant will not be disadvantaged by being required to use one access route as opposed to the other. On the other hand, if it is open to applicants to submit applications for access under either set of provisions, consistency will be important in discouraging the confusion and waste of resources which could result from the use of both pieces of legislation sequentially, in the event of the applicant being dissatisfied with the outcome of the first application, or indeed, simultaneously.

(i) The interaction of access rights in the two Acts

Section 46(2) of the FOI Act excludes records from the application of the Act which are available for inspection, purchase, or removal by members of the public. The Act goes on, in section 46(3), to provide that a record shall not come within the scope of that exclusion by reason only of the fact that it contains information constituting personal data to which the DP Act applies.[25] Thus, it is clear that the right of access to personal data in the DP Act is preserved notwithstanding the introduction of the FOI Act. Similarly, there is nothing in the DP Act to prevent the use of other means of accessing personal data. Thus, it appears to be open to an individual seeking access to personal information to use either Act. If he or she is dissatisfied with the outcome of the application, there is nothing to prevent the applicant initiating an application for access under the other set of provisions.

(ii) Consistency between the FOI and Data Protection access rights

(A) The scope of the right of access
(I) Bodies subject to access rights While the FOI Act applies only in respect of records held by "public bodies", the DP Act applies to personal information kept by any data controller.

(II) The type of record covered As previously noted, the right of access conferred by the DP Act applies to data which is defined in a way which excludes manual files.[26] The FOI Act, on the other hand, applies to both manual and electronic records.[27]

(III) To whom does the right of access apply? An important difference in the scope of these rights is that access rights under the DP Act are exercisable

---

[25] Section 46(3) of the FOI Act contains the only reference in that Act to the DP Act. However, its effect is limited and its existence does not affect the more fundamental issues considered above at pp. 374–380.

[26] Directive 95/46 on the Protection of Individuals in relation to the processing of personal data, above, n. 4.

[27] See above, pp. 63–65.

only by individuals, while under the FOI Act the right of access applies to "every person" which includes a legal person.

(IV) Retrospection The right of access to personal data under the DP Act applies to all data kept by a data controller. There is no limit with respect to the age of the data. The FOI Act confers a right of access to records created after the commencement of the Act.[28] This limitation is, however, subject to two exceptions, one of which is in respect of records which relate to personal information about the person seeking access to the records.[29] Thus, under both Acts, the right of access to personal information applies retrospectively.

(B) Exclusions and exemptions   The two Acts are subject to a number of exclusions and exemptions. Section 1(4) of the DP Act excludes the following categories of personal data from its scope:

> "(a) personal data that in the opinion of the Minister [for Justice, Equality and Law Reform] or the Minister of Defence are, or at any time were, kept for the purpose of safeguarding the security of the State,
> (b) personal data consisting of information that the person keeping the data is required by law to make available to the public, or
> (c) personal data kept by an individual and concerned only with the management of his personal, family or household affairs or kept by an individual only for recreational purposes."

There is also a list of exemptions from the right of access to personal data in the DP Act. That list is set out in section 5 and it covers the following matters: crime and revenue, prisons, financial malpractice, international relations, estimates of liability for claims, legal privilege, statistics and research, and back-up data.[30]

There are additional restrictions in respect of particular categories of personal data. Regulations provide that access to information constituting health data shall not be provided to the data subject where it would be likely to cause serious harm to the physical or mental health of the data subject. Similarly, social work data is not to be supplied to a data subject if it would be likely to cause serious harm to the physical or mental health of the data subject or to the emotional condition of the data subject.

Like the DP Act, access rights under the FOI Act are subject to a number of exclusions and exemptions. The exclusions fall into the following categories: records held by courts or tribunals;[31] records concerning certain public

---

[28] s.6(4).
[29] s.6(5)(b). NB. Under s.6(6), this exception does not apply in certain circumstances in the case of the personnel records of public bodies.
[30] See further Clark, *op. cit.* above, n. 2, pp. 70–80.
[31] s.46(1)(a).

office holders;[32] non-official records of Oireachtas members;[33] records relating to official documents of either House of the Oireachtas;[34] records relating to specified activities of the Information Commissioner, the Ombudsman and the Comptroller and Auditor General;[35] records relating to confidential information concerning criminal law enforcement;[36] and records otherwise available.[37]

Access rights under the FOI Act are also subject to a number of *exemptions*. These are in respect of the following matters: meetings of the Government;[38] deliberations of public bodies;[39] functions and negotiations of public bodies;[40] parliamentary, court and certain other matters;[41] law enforcement and public safety;[42] security, defence and international relations;[43] information obtained in confidence;[44] commercially sensitive information;[45] personal information;[46] research and natural resources;[47] financial and economic interests of the State and public bodies;[48] and enactments relating to non-disclosure of records.[49] Applicants for access to their own personal records under the FOI Act are, to a great extent, treated in the same way as any other applicant in terms of the application of the exemptions. The only differences are that, first, the personal information and commercially sensitive information exemptions cannot be invoked to deny an individual access to information relating to themselves,[50] and, second, that a request for access to medical, psychiatric, or social work records relating to the requester may be refused on the grounds that their disclosure might be prejudicial to the physical or mental health or the emotional well-being of the requester.[51] The provisions of the

---

[32] s.46(1)(b) and s.46(1)(d).
[33] s.46(1)(e).
[34] s.46(1)(e).
[35] s.46(1)(c).
[36] s.46(1)(f).
[37] s.46(2). Note that s.46(3) of the FOI Act provides that a record will not be regarded as falling into the category of "records otherwise available" by reason only of the fact that it contains information constituting personal data to which the Data Protection Act applies.
[38] s.19, see Chap. 6.
[39] s.20, see Chap. 7.
[40] s.21, see Chap. 8.
[41] s.22, see Chap. 9.
[42] s.23, see Chap. 10.
[43] s.24, see Chap. 11.
[44] s.26, see Chap. 12.
[45] s.27, see Chap. 13.
[46] s.28, see Chap. 14.
[47] s.30, see Chap. 15.
[48] s.31, see Chap. 16.
[49] s.32, see Chap. 17.
[50] s.28(2)(a) and s.27(2)(c). See above, pp. 281 and 260 respectively.
[51] s.28(3).

two Acts modifying access to health and social work records are examined separately below.[52]

It is clear that the FOI Act is subject to a far greater number of exclusions and exemptions than is the DP Act. This could lead to the conclusion that applicants for access to personal information would be better off applying for access under the latter Act. However, not all of the FOI exemptions or exclusions are relevant to applications for access to personal information. In particular, the exemptions relating to meetings of the government, deliberations of public bodies, functions, and negotiations of public bodies, parliamentary, court and certain other matters, and financial and economic interests of the State and public bodies are unlikely to be applicable in respect of applications for access to an individual's own personal information. Most of the exclusions from the FOI Act are irrelevant to applications for access to personal information. It must also be borne in mind that some of the DP Act exemptions might be more relevant to personal data held by the private sector than by the public sector. These include, for example, the exemption relating to estimates of liability for claims.

There are some similarities between the exemptions and exclusions in the two Acts. In particular, the crime, revenue and prisons exemptions in the DP Act cover much the same ground as the law enforcement exemption in the FOI Act. Both exempt civil, as well as criminal, matters and the application of each is subject to an injury test. While the application of the DP Act exemption is mandatory, the use of the FOI Act law enforcement exemption[53] is discretionary.

The areas of international relations and security of the State are also addressed by both Acts. While international relations are the subject of an exemption under both Acts, security of the State is dealt with by way of an exclusion under the DP Act[54] and as an exemption under the FOI Act.[55] The international relations exemption in the DP Act is subject to an injury test, but its application is mandatory. In the case of the FOI Act, the security of the State and international relations exemptions are subject to an injury test and their application is discretionary. While the FOI Act contains an exemption in respect of defence information, there is no separate exemption in respect of such information in the DP Act.

The issue of legal professional privilege is dealt with in similar terms in both Acts. In both Acts the exemption is a class or category type exemption in that it applies regardless of whether any injury might ensue from the provision of access.[56] The application of the exemption is mandatory under both sets of

---

[52] See below, pp. 385–388.
[53] s.23.
[54] s.1(4)(a).
[55] s.24.
[56] Data Protection Act 1988, s.5(1)(g); Freedom of Information Act 1997, s.22(1)(a).

provisions. Both Acts contain exemptions relating to research data. They are, however, expressed in different terms. The DP Act exempts from the access right personal data kept only for the purpose of carrying out research, if the data is not disclosed for any other purpose and the results are not made available in a form that identifies any of the data subjects.[57] The FOI Act exemption, the use of which is discretionary, is subject to an injury test and to a public interest test.[58]

The most important difference existing between the two sets of exemptions and exclusions relates to information obtained in confidence. Certain information obtained in confidence is excluded from the scope of the FOI Act, while other information obtained in confidence is exempt from the right of access to records provided for in that Act. The information which is excluded is that which could reveal the identity of a person who has supplied information relating to the enforcement of the criminal law.[59] The exemption relating to information obtained in confidence covers two categories of information. The first is information given to a public body in confidence and on the understanding that it would be treated by it as confidential, where, in the opinion of the head of the public body, its disclosure would be likely to prejudice the giving to the body of future similar information by the same person or other persons and it is of importance to the body that such further similar information should continue to be given to the body.[60] The second exempts information which, if disclosed, would constitute a breach of a duty of confidence.[61] These provisions concerning confidential information have no counterparts in the DP Act. Thus, an applicant for access to personal information could, on the basis of confidentiality, be refused such access under the FOI Act, but not under the DP Act. The confidentiality exemption in the FOI Act, but not the exclusion, is, however, subject to a public interest test.

In terms of application of the exclusions and exemptions, it appears that there is little to choose between the two Acts. Apart from the additional confidentiality exemption in the FOI Act, there does not appear to be potential for the emergence of major discrepancies in terms of the type of material to which access may be denied under the two Acts.

(C) Comparison of the health/social work access modification provisions in the FOI Act and the DP Act[62]   Section 4(8) of the DP Act enables the Minister for Justice, Equality and Law Reform to modify the right of access

---

[57] s.5(1)(h).
[58] s.30(1)(a).
[59] s.46(1)(f).
[60] s.26(1)(a).
[61] s.26(1)(b).
[62] See also Doran and Cusack, "Access to Medical Records: The Freedom of Information Act 1997" (1997) 3 *Medico-Legal Journal of Ireland* 106. The authors argue that the

conferred on individuals with respect to data relating to themselves in two situations. Such modification of access rights may take place in respect of personal data relating to physical or mental health; or personal data kept for, or obtained in the course of, or while carrying out, social work. Two sets of regulations giving effect to the modifications were introduced in 1989: the Data Protection (Access Modification) (Health) Regulations[63] and the Data Protection (Access Modification) (Social Work) Regulations.[64] The FOI Act also restricts the right of access to records of a medical or psychiatric nature relating to the requester concerned, as well as to records kept for the purposes of, or obtained in the course of the carrying out of, social work in relation to the requester.[65] There are some significant differences in the manner in which access rights are modified under the two Acts.

Each enactment imposes restrictions on the granting of access to health and social work information, where the provision of such access would be damaging to the individual to whom the information relates. The Access Modification (Health) Regulations apply to "health data", which is defined as "personal data relating to physical or mental health", while the FOI Act refers to "records of a medical or psychiatric nature".[66] "Social work data" is defined in the Access Modification (Social Work) Regulations as:

> "personal data kept for, or obtained in the course of, carrying out social work by a Minister of the Government, a local authority, a health board, or a voluntary organisation or other body that carries out social work and is in receipt of moneys provided by such a Minister, authority or board, but excludes any health data within the meaning of the Data Protection (Access Modification) (Health) Regulations 1989 and 'social work' shall be construed accordingly".[67]

The relevant provision of the FOI Act refers to "a record kept for the purposes of, or obtained in the course of the carrying out of, social work in relation to the requester".[68]

The first significant difference between the two regimes is that while the refusal of access to records which, if disclosed, could be damaging to the requester is discretionary under the FOI Act, it is mandatory under the Access Modification Regulations. There is also a difference in the degree of potential

---

approach of the FOI Act is wholly inappropriate in dealing with the specific requirements of medical records and suggest the adoption of an approach similar to that taken in the U.K. Medical Records Act 1990.

[63] S.I. No. 82 of 1989.

[64] S.I. No. 83 of 1989.

[65] s.28(3) and (4).

[66] The FOI Act only applies to public bodies and so medical records in voluntary hospitals or private hospitals are not covered. Health board hospitals are covered and it appears that records of general practitioners operating within the ambit of the General Medical Services Scheme also come within the scope of the Act: see above, p. 52.

[67] reg.2.

[68] s.28(3)(b).

injury to the requester necessary to bring about a refusal of access. Under the Access Modification Regulations, information constituting health or social work data, as the case may be, shall not be supplied to the data subject "if it would be likely to cause serious harm to the physical or mental health (or, in the case of social work data, the physical or mental health or the emotional condition) of the data subject".[69] The FOI Act permits the head of a public body to refuse to grant an access request where, in the opinion of the head, "disclosure of the information concerned to the requester might be prejudicial to his or her physical or mental health".[70] The use of the lower "might prejudice" standard in the FOI Act means that a refusal of access is more likely in the case of an application for access to health or social work information made under that Act, than in the case of an application made under the DP Act.

The effect of a finding that disclosure would be damaging to the applicant differs between the two access regimes. In the case of the Access Modification Regulations, no provision is made for the release of information, which would be damaging in the manner described in the Regulations, if disclosed. The disclosure of such information is, therefore, subject to an absolute prohibition. Under the FOI Act, however, provision is made for the release of records to which access has been denied to "such health professional having expertise in relation to the subject matter of the record as the requester may specify".[71] The implication of such release is that the health professional will then be able to indirectly release the information to the requester. Provision is made in both enactments for the granting of access to an edited version of the health or social work information requested.[72]

Both sets of Access Modification Regulations introduced under the DP Act impose a further general restriction on the disclosure of health or social work data which applies in all cases of disclosure of such information, even where such disclosure would not be damaging to the data subject. In the case of health data held by a data controller who is not a health professional, he or she shall not disclose or withhold such data from an individual to which it relates before consulting with "the appropriate health professional".[73] Where

---

[69] Data Protection (Access Modification) (Health) Regulations 1989, reg.4(1); Data Protection (Access Modification) (Social Work) Regulations 1989, reg.4(1).

[70] s.28(3)(b).

[71] s.28(4)(a).

[72] FOI Act, s.13; Data Protection (Access Modification) (Health) Regulations 1989, reg.4(2); Data Protection (Access Modification) (Social Work) Regulations 1989, reg.4(2).

[73] The "appropriate health professional" is defined in reg.5(2) to mean:

"(a) the person who is the registered medical practitioner, within the meaning of the Medical Practitioners Act, 1978 (No. 4 of 1978) or registered dentist within the meaning of the Dentists Act, 1985 (No. 9 of 1985), currently or most recently responsible for the clinical care of the data subject in connection with the matters to which the information, the subject of the request, relates,

(b) where there is more than one such person, the person who is the most suitable to advise on those matters,

social work data includes information supplied to a data controller by a third party (who is not an employee or agent of the data controller) while carrying out social work, the data controller cannot disclose such information to the data subject without first consulting that third party. No additional restrictions of this type are found in the FOI Act. Unless the disclosure of the record concerned would be prejudicial to the physical or mental health, well-being or emotional condition of the requester, there are no limitations on the disclosure of records of a medical or psychiatric or social work nature relating to the requester.

Decisions on requests under the FOI Act are made by the head of the public body concerned. In the case of a health board, the head is the Chief Executive Officer of the Health Board, who will not usually be a health professional. There, is, however, scope for the delegation of the C.E.O.'s powers under the Act to a member of the staff of the health board, who might be a health professional.[74] The main difference between the two regimes is that decisions on the provision of access to medical or social work records are made following consultation with health professionals in the case of the Access Modification (Health) Regulations (if the data controller is not a health professional), and following consultation with third-party suppliers of social work data in the case of the Access Modification (Social Work) Regulations, while under the FOI Act such decisions are made by the head of public body, who is unlikely to be a health professional and who is not obliged to consult with any health professionals prior to making his or her decision.[75] From the requester's point of view it may be more advantageous to seek access under the FOI Act in order to have an unfettered right of access to health or social work information, the disclosure of which might not be prejudicial to him or her.

(D) Time limits   While the DP Act provides for a time limit for compliance with access requests of 40 days from the satisfaction by the applicant of the procedural requirements laid down in section 4,[76] decisions under the FOI Act on requests for access to records must, in general, be given no later than four weeks after the day on which the request is received.[77]

(E) Charges   The DP Act allows for the charging of a fee in respect of access to personal information. That fee may not exceed either the amount prescribed by regulation or an amount regarded by the Commissioner as reasonable,

---

(c) where there is no person available falling within either subparagraph (a) or (b) of this paragraph, a health professional who has the necessary experience and qualifications to advise on these matters."

[74] s.4(1).
[75] Doran and Cusack, *op. cit.* above, n. 62, at 107, believe that this is "an ill-advised alteration of the role of the doctor in the decision regarding patient access to medical records".
[76] s.4(1).
[77] s.8(1).

having regard to the estimated cost of compilation. A figure of £5 is set by the Regulations.[78] In the case of the FOI Act, access charges are generally made up of two components: a fee for search and retrieval and a fee for a copy of a record.[79] Special arrangements exist in respect of requests for access to personal information. The Act provides that the search and retrieval fee shall not be charged in respect of such requests unless the request relates to a significant number of records. The Act also provides for waiver of the copying fee where it would not be reasonable to charge such a fee, having regard to the means of the requester and the nature of the record requested.

(F) Appeals Complaints relating to refusals to allow access to personal data under the DP Act may be made to the Data Protection Commissioner. The Commissioner has the power to investigate a refusal of a subject's access request[80] and he or she may issue an enforcement notice requiring that such access be given.[81] The data controller may appeal to the Circuit Court against the requirement specified in the enforcement notice within 21 days of the service of the notice.[82] Where no such appeal is brought or where the terms of the notice are confirmed by the court on appeal, the data controller will be subject to prosecution under section 10(9). That provision makes it an offence to fail or refuse, without reasonable excuse, to comply with a requirement specified in an enforcement notice. Under the FOI Act, appeals against a refusal of the head of a public body to grant access to records may be brought internally[83] in the first instance[84] and, if the applicant is not satisfied with the outcome of the internal review process, he or she can make an appeal to the Information Commissioner[85] and ultimately to the High Court on a point of law.[86] The decision of the Information Commissioner on appeal is binding on the public body concerned.[87] It would appear that the decisions of both the Data Protection Commissioner and the Information Commissioner are subject to judicial review.[88]

The system of appeal provided for under the FOI Act is clearly to be preferred to that available under the DP Act. First, it allows for the bringing of internal appeals. That method of appeal, which is not available under the DP

---

[78] Data Protection (Fees) Regulations, 1988 (S.I. No. 347 of 1988).
[79] See above, pp. 76–78.
[80] s.10(1).
[81] s.10(2).
[82] s.26(1)(a).
[83] s.14.
[84] Assuming the original access decision was not made by the head of the public body concerned.
[85] s.34.
[86] s.42.
[87] s.34(14)(b).
[88] See above, pp. 347–348.

Act, has the advantage of being speedy and cost effective. Secondly, and more importantly, the system of appeal provided for under the FOI Act is to be preferred because it gives the applicant himself or herself the right to decide how far to bring the appeal. Under the DP Act it is up to the Data Protection Commissioner to decide whether to issue an enforcement notice. Should he or she decide not to take that route, the matter cannot progress any further.

(G) Comparative evaluation   Overall, in comparing the access provisions of the two Acts, it is clear that while there is little to choose between them in terms of exclusions and exemptions, the greater emphasis which is placed on the use of injury tests and public interest tests in the FOI exemptions seems to render that Act more favourable to the provision of access. The FOI Act is also to be preferred in terms of its time limits and its appeals mechanism. In cases where access rights are exercisable under both Acts it appears, therefore, that the applicant should prefer the FOI Act. Where he or she is unsuccessful, there appears to be no barrier to the making of a subsequent application under the DP Act.

(b) Amendment of personal data

Section 6 of the DP Act provides a right of rectification or erasure of personal data, while section 17 of the FOI Act provides for the amendment of records relating to personal information. Again the issue of overlap between the two sets of provisions arises. Neither Act constitutes a barrier to the use of the amendment provisions provided for in the other. The possibility of overlap between the rights of amendment of personal information provided for under the FOI Act and the provisions for rectification and erasure of personal data under the DP Act is limited, given the differences in the scope of the two Acts. While, on the one hand, the FOI Act has a broader application than the DP Act in that it covers both manual and automated data, there are, on the other hand, a number of ways in which the scope of the amendment rights conferred by the FOI Act is limited by comparison with those available under the DP Act. First, while the FOI Act applies to public bodies only, the DP Act allows for the amendment of personal data held by both public and private sectors. Second, the definition of personal information in the FOI Act is arguably narrower than that of personal data in the DP Act; as a result, personal data in respect of which an application for correction could be made under the latter Act might not qualify as personal information for the purpose of the exercise of the amendment rights provided for under the FOI Act.

A comparison of the amendment rights can be made in respect of the following matters: scope of the right; remedies; time limits; fees; and appeals.

(i) Scope of the right

The right of rectification and erasure under the DP Act applies in respect of data in relation to which there has been a contravention of section 2(1) of the DP Act. Section 2(1) is a broadly framed provision. It provides protection to personal data in respect of its collection, storage, processing, use, disclosure and security. Since the right of rectification and erasure applies in the case of a contravention of any of the terms of section 2(1), its scope is, therefore, broader than that of the amendment rights contained in section 17 of the FOI Act. For example, section 6 of the DP Act confers a right of rectification or erasure where personal data has, in contravention of section 2(1)(a), been unfairly obtained. It also applies in situations where, contrary to section 2(1)(c)(ii), personal data kept for a certain purpose is used or disclosed in a manner incompatible with that purpose. These are matters which are not within the purview of the amendment rights in the FOI Act. There are, however, some areas of overlap between the right of rectification and erasure of the DP Act and the amendment provisions of the FOI Act. Section 2(1)(b) of the DP Act requires a data controller, defined as a person who "controls the contents and use of personal data",[89] to ensure that data is accurate and, where necessary, kept up-to-date. "Inaccurate" is defined to mean "incorrect or misleading as to any matter of fact".[90] Section 2(1)(c)(iii) provides further that data shall be adequate, relevant, and not excessive in relation to the purpose for which it is kept. The first ground for amendment in the FOI Act, namely that information is incomplete, corresponds roughly to the requirement under section 2(1)(c)(iii) of the DP Act that data be adequate. The second ground for amendment provided for under the FOI Act, that the information is incorrect, is similar to the requirement in section 2(1)(b) of the DP Act that data be accurate. The third ground for amendment covered in the FOI Act, namely that information is misleading, is also expressly included within the terms of the DP Act's requirement that data be accurate. There is, however, one important difference between the grounds for amendment of records provided for under the FOI and DP Acts respectively. The DP Act provides for the correction of inaccurate data but only to the extent that they are incorrect or misleading *as to any matter of fact*. The DP Act does not allow a challenge to be made to the accuracy of a statement of opinion. The FOI Act, on the other hand, is not expressly limited to the amendment of matters of fact but appears to cover incorrect or misleading opinions also.[91] It has, however, been suggested that since statements of opinion can involve statements of fact, the correction rights contained in the DP Act may also extend to statements of opinion.[92] An example might be a statement of opinion contained in an employee's performance evaluation report to the effect that, given the employee's poor record of attendance, the person making the evaluation is of the opinion that they are unreliable. If

---

[89] Data Protection Act 1988, s.1(1).
[90] *ibid.*, s.1(2).
[91] See above, pp. 338–340.
[92] Clark, *op. cit.* above, n. 2, p. 49.

the poor attendance record was found to have been incorrectly attributed to the employee in question, then the facts upon which the opinion was based would be untrue, and consequently the opinion itself would be subject to correction.

(ii) Remedies

The remedies available in respect of breaches of section 2(1) of the DP Act are set out in section 6(1) of that Act. Section 6(1) entitles an individual to the rectification or, where appropriate, the erasure of such data. However, in the case of a contravention of section 2(1)(b) (inaccurate and out of date data), the data controller will be deemed to have complied with his or her obligations under section 6 where he or she supplements the data with a statement relating to the matters dealt with by the data, provided the individual has assented to the terms of the statement. These three remedies of rectification, erasure, and supplementation of data are analogous to the three remedies provided for in respect of the FOI amendment rights, namely alteration of a record,[93] the addition of a statement to the record,[94] and deletion of information from a record.[95] It appears that in the case of inaccurate data or data which is out of date, the primary remedy under the DP Act is that of the addition to the data of a statement.[96] Unlike its counterpart in the FOI Act, there is no requirement that the statement explain the respects in which the data is inaccurate. The DP Act does, however, require that the individual to whom the information relates has assented to the terms of the statement.[97] It is only in cases where agreement cannot be reached on the terms of such a statement that the other two remedies come into play. In the case of data which is found to be inadequate under the DP Act,[98] the only remedies available are those of rectification or erasure. The FOI Act, on the other hand, does not distinguish between the various grounds for amendment in the allocation of remedies.

Where an application for amendment of a record of personal information under the FOI Act is unsuccessful, the application or a copy of it must be attached to the record or, if that is not practicable, a notation must be attached indicating that the application has been made, unless the application is considered by the public body to be defamatory or the alterations or additions to which it relates would be unnecessarily voluminous.[99] There is no such obligation in the DP Act. If an application for rectification or erasure is refused, the data controller is under no obligation to annotate the record.

---

[93] s.17(1)(i).
[94] s.17(1)(ii).
[95] s.17(1)(iii).
[96] s.6(1).
[97] s.6(1)(a).
[98] s.2(1)(c)(iii).
[99] s.17(4).

In the case of a successful application for rectification or erasure under the DP Act, the Data Controller is obliged, if compliance with the request under section 6 materially modifies the data concerned, to notify any party to whom the data were disclosed during the 12 months preceding the submission of the request.[100] These provisions are similar to those applying under the FOI Act in respect of successful applications for amendments of personal records. Section 17(5) of the FOI Act requires the head of the public body concerned to take all reasonable steps to notify anyone to whom access to the record was given, or any other public body to whom a copy of the record was given, during the course of the year preceding the date on which the amendment was effected.

(iii) Time limits

In terms of time limits, the FOI Act provides for a shorter time limit for the making of a decision on amendment (four weeks) than is provided for under the DP Act (40 days). However, whilst the DP Act requires the data controller to comply with the request for rectification or erasure within 40 days of receiving it, no time limit for compliance is provided for in the FOI Act.

(iv) Charges

There is no provision for the charging of fees in respect of the exercise of correction rights under either Act.

(v) Appeals

There is provision in the FOI Act for the making of appeals against a refusal by the head of a public body to amend a record of personal information. An appeal can be made internally[101] in the first instance and, if the applicant is not satisfied with the outcome of the internal review process, he or she can make an appeal to the Information Commissioner[102] and ultimately to the High Court on a point of law.[103] The Commissioner may, pursuant to the power conferred upon him or her by section 10 of the DP Act to investigate contraventions of the Act, deal with complaints that a data controller has failed to comply with a request to rectify or erase allegedly inaccurate data, or to make the supplementary statement referred to in section 6(1). Where the Commissioner is of the opinion that the data controller has contravened a provision of the Act, he or she may issue an enforcement notice.[104] The notice sets out the steps which must be taken by the data controller within a specified time limit

---

[100] s.6(2)(b).
[101] s.14.
[102] s.34.
[103] s.42.
[104] s.10.

in order to comply with the Act. The enforcement notice might, for example, require the data controller to rectify or erase any of the data concerned or insert a supplementary statement approved by the Data Protection Commissioner. The data controller may appeal to the Circuit Court against the requirement specified in the enforcement notice within 21 days of the service of the notice.[105] Again, as has been pointed out in the discussion of the enforcement of access rights provided under the DP Act, the issuing of an enforcement notice is entirely at the discretion of the Data Protection Commissioner and so the DP Act appeals mechanism has the disadvantage of being less direct than its FOI counterpart.

(vi) Comparative evaluation

In cases where overlap occurs and where, as a consequence, the aggrieved individual has open to him or her the possibility of applying for amendment of information under either Act, the exercise of the right of amendment conferred by the FOI Act appears to be preferable to that provided for in the DP Act. In particular, the FOI Act provides for a greater range of remedies and provides for the annotation of records where correction has been refused. It also has a shorter time limit for the making of a decision on application for amendment and a superior appeals mechanism. There is nothing in either Act to prevent the use of both sets of amendment provisions sequentially or even at the same time.

C.   Relationship of the FOI Act with the Archives Act

The FOI Act and the National Archives Act ("the Archives Act") both deal with the provision of access to government records. The FOI Act provides a legal right of access to government records.[106] That right, as we have seen, is subject to a number of exclusions and exemptions.[107] The National Archives Act, which was passed in 1986, establishes the National Archives[108] and sets out arrangements for preserving the archival resources of the State. It establishes a right of inspection of archives in the custody of the National Archives.[109] This right is also subject to exceptions.[110]

---

[105] s.26(1)(a).
[106] s.6(1).
[107] See above, pp. 56–60 and Chaps 6–17.
[108] s.3.
[109] s.10(1).
[110] s.8.

1. The interaction of the two Acts

Section 46(2) of the FOI Act eliminates the possibility of overlap in the exercise of the rights provided under the FOI Act and the Archives Act. That provision excludes records from the scope of the FOI Act which are available for inspection by members of the public.[111] Since the right of access provided for under the Archives Act is expressed in terms of the making available of records for the inspection of the public,[112] it clearly comes within the purview of that exclusion. Thus, in the case of records to which the right of inspection in the Archives Act applies, the rights conferred by the Archives Act must be utilised and the use of the FOI Act to access such records is not an option.

2. Comparison of the Archives Act and the FOI Act

(a) Scope of the right

(i) Bodies subject to the access rights

The Archives Act provides a right of access to "archives".[113] Archives are defined to include:

(a) records and documents held in the Public Record Office and the State Paper Office at the commencement of the Archives Act;

(b) departmental records transferred to and accepted for preservation by the National Archives under the Archives Act;

(c) other records acquired by the National Archives from public service organisations, institutions, or private individuals; and

(d) all public records held at the commencement of the Archives Act elsewhere than in the Public Record Office, under an Act repealed by the Archives Act.[114]

The most important of these categories, in terms of comparing the scope of the FOI and Archives Acts, are the second and third.

(A) Departmental records The Archives Act requires, subject to certain exceptions, that departmental records which are more than 30 years old be transferred to the National Archives.[115] Departmental records means records:

> "made or received, and held in the course of its business, by a Department of

---

[111] s.46(2)(a).
[112] s.10(1).
[113] s.10(1).
[114] s.2(1).
[115] s.8(1).

State . . . or any body which is a committee, commission, or tribunal of enquiry appointed from time to time by the Government, a member of the Government or the Attorney General".[116]

"Department of State" is defined to include references to a court and to a scheduled body.[117] A list of scheduled bodies is appended to the Act. These include many of the bodies covered by the FOI Act, as well as many other bodies not yet coming within the scope of the FOI Act such as the Garda Síochána, the Employment Appeals Tribunal, the Labour Court, the Rent Tribunal, the Criminal Injuries Compensation Tribunal, the Censorship of Films Appeal Board, and the Censorship of Publications Appeals Board. Bodies which are covered by the FOI Act, but not the Archives Act, include An Bord Pleanála, the Employment Equality Agency, and some newer bodies established after the passing of the Archives Act such as the Office of the Ombudsman, Environmental Protection Agency, the Irish Sports Council, the Heritage Council, and the Social Welfare Appeals Office. There is, in addition, scope for the extension of the FOI Act to cover a wide range of bodies which are defined in paragraph 1(5) of the First Schedule to the FOI Act.

(B) Other records acquired from public service organisations, institutions, or private individuals Public service organisations are defined in section 1(1) to mean a local authority, health board or a body established by or under statute and financed wholly or partly by grants or loans made by a member of the Government or by the issue of shares taken up by a member of the Government. While records acquired from such bodies and from institutions and private individuals all qualify as "archives" for the purpose of the right of inspection provided for under the Archives Act, the transfer of such records to the National Archives is not required by the Archives Act.

Under section 65 of the Local Government Act 1994, it is a function of a local authority to make arrangements for the proper management, custody, care, and conservation of local archives. The Minister for the Environment may, after consultation with the Director of the National Archives, give advice or directions to local authorities in relation to, *inter alia*, the availability of local archives for public inspection and the circumstances in which local archives, or particular classes of local archives, may be withheld from public inspection. In 1996 a report on the implementation of section 65 was prepared by the Steering Group on Local Authority Records and Archives,[118] in which it was recommended that given the generally poor condition of local authority archives, measures should be taken as soon as possible to secure their future. The work, it was recommended, should be carried out by local authorities in

---

[116] s.2(2).
[117] s.1(2)(b).
[118] Department of the Environment, *Report of the Steering Group on Local Authority Records and Archives* (1996).

two phases: first, the commencement of the task of properly retaining, managing, preserving, and restoring their archives; and, second, the putting in place of arrangements for public access to archives.[119] The Department of the Environment also issued Guidelines relating to the operation of section 65.[120] It appears, however, that the implementation of the Steering Group's recommendations are at an early stage, and that arrangements for public access to local authority archives are not yet in place. There is no statutory basis for the management and inspection of health board archives.

The scope of the FOI Act is broader than the Archives Act in term of its application to local authorities and health boards. Such bodies become subject to the FOI Act by October 21, 1998.[121] The Archives Act, on the other hand, provides a right of inspection with respect to local authority and health board records acquired by the National Archives, but it places no obligation on those bodies to transfer records to the National Archives.

In the case of records acquired from other public service bodies and from institutions and individuals, all of which qualify as "archives" for the purposes of the right to inspection, the scope of the Archives Act is potentially broader than that of the FOI Act, since the latter does not apply to private individuals or institutions and its extension to bodies established by or under statute must await the introduction of the necessary regulations.[122] However, as in the case of health boards and local authorities, such bodies are under no obligation to transfer their records to the National Archives.

(ii) The type of records covered

"Departmental records" are defined in the Archives Act as:

> "books, maps, plans, drawings, papers, files, photographs, films, microfilms and other micrographic records, sound recordings, pictorial records, magnetic tapes, magnetic discs, optical or video discs, other machine-readable records, [and] other documentary or processed material".[123]

As noted above, the archives in respect of which the right of inspection accrue also include records or documents acquired from public service organisations, institutions, and private individuals. The Act offers no definition of "record" or "document" in this context.

The definition of "departmental record" covers much the same ground as its counterpart in the FOI Act. The FOI Act definition of record may have

---

[119] Department of the Environment, *op. cit.* above, n. 118, p. 7.
[120] Department of the Environment, *Guidelines for Local Authorities Archives Services* (1996).
[121] s.1(3).
[122] First Sched., para. 1(5).
[123] s.2(2).

greater flexibility since it includes "any other form . . . or thing in which information is held or stored manually, mechanically or electronically".[124]

(iii) The form in which access is provided

The Archives Act requires only that records be made available for inspection.[125] There is no requirement that the applicant be provided with a copy of a record.[126] The FOI Act provides for a range of forms in which access may be provided.[127] They include the provision of a copy of the record,[128] as well as "a reasonable opportunity to inspect the record".[129] The applicant can specify the form or manner of access required and access must be given in that form unless the head of the public body concerned is satisfied that certain circumstances apply.[130] These include, for example, that the giving of access in the manner requested would be physically detrimental to the record, but also where the giving of access in a different form would be "significantly more efficient".[131] Therefore, while the FOI Act is superior to the Archives Act in that the latter merely provides a right to inspect a record, the right to a copy of a record under the FOI Act can be circumvented.

(iv) To whom does the right of access apply?

The Archives Act confers the right to inspect archival records on the public.[132] This right arguably applies to representatives of companies as well as to individuals. Similarly, the FOI Act provides a right of access to every "person".[133] The definition of "person" in the Interpretation Act 1937 includes legal persons.[134] Thus, the right of access under both Acts appears to be exercisable by either individuals or legal persons.

(iv) Retrospection

The Archives Act provides a right of access to archives which includes departmental records which are at least 30 years old.[135] The FOI Act generally

---

[124] s.2(1).
[125] s.10(1).
[126] It would appear that, in practice, copies of records are provided where this is practicable.
[127] s.12.
[128] s.12(1)(a).
[129] s.12(1)(d).
[130] s.12(2).
[131] s.12(2)(a).
[132] s.10(1).
[133] s.6.
[134] s.11.
[135] The right to inspect archives other than departmental records is not subject to any limitation as to age of the record in question.

applies only to records created after the commencement of that Act. There are, however, two exceptions to that rule: the first is where granting of access to prior records is necessary to the understanding of records created after the commencement of the FOI Act;[136] the second is where the records sought relate to personal information of the applicant.[137] There is, therefore, a considerable "access gap" between the two sets of provisions. That gap will, of course, become progressively narrower, the longer the FOI Act is in existence. On April 21, 1998, it began to affect all those records created between that date and 1968. It will take until 2028 for the gap to be eliminated completely.

(b) Exceptions

The right to inspect archives conferred by the Archives Act is subject to exceptions. These exceptions apply only in the case of departmental records. They consist of:

(1) exceptions to the definition of "departmental record";

(2) exceptions to the obligation to transfer "departmental records" to the National Archives; and

(3) exceptions to the right to inspect archives in the custody of the National Archives.

Excluded from the scope of the definition of departmental records are title deeds relating to properties owned by the State and any part of the permanent collection of a library, museum or gallery.[138]

Certain departmental records are excluded from the obligation to transfer departmental records which are more than 30 years old to the National Archives. These include records which are certified by an authorised officer[139] of a Department as being in regular use in that Department, or as being required in connection with the administration of the Department, in circumstances where their transfer to the National Archives would seriously interfere with the administration of that Department.[140] Also excluded are records which are specified by the Director of the National Archives or by an officer of the National Archives designated for this purpose, as not warranting transfer to the National Archives for preservation.[141]

Section 10(1) sets out exceptions to the right to inspect archives in the

---

[136] s.6(5)(a).

[137] s.6(5)(b).

[138] s.2(2).

[139] Regulation 3(1) of the National Archives Act 1986, Regulations, 1988 (S.I. No. 385 of 1988) defines "authorised officer" for the purposes of ss.7(4), 8(2), 8(4), 8(6), and 10(5) of the Act to mean an officer of not less than Principal or equivalent grade.

[140] s.8(2).

[141] s.8(3).

custody of the National Archives. In the first place, there is no right to inspect archives which were formerly departmental records (other than court or testamentary documents) and are less than 30 years old. In the second place, archives which were formerly departmental records and in respect of which a certificate has been granted under section 8(4) are excluded from the right of inspection. Section 8(4) of the Act gives an authorised officer of a department the power, with the consent of an authorised officer of the Department of the Taoiseach, to certify in relation to particular records or particular classes of records which are more than 30 years old that making them available for inspection by the public would damage certain interests. The three circumstances in which a certificate of this kind can be issued arise where making the records available for inspection by the public:

(1) would be contrary to the public interest;[142]

(2) would or might constitute a breach of statutory duty, or a breach of good faith on the ground that they contain information supplied in confidence;[143] or

(3) would or might cause distress or danger to living persons on the ground that they contain information about individuals, or would or might be likely to lead to an action for damages for defamation.[144]

The second and third of these grounds relate to matters in respect of which there are exemptions under the FOI Act also. The second ground appears to encompass the FOI exemptions relating to information obtained in confidence (section 26) and possibly also that of enactments relating to non-disclosure of records (section 32). The third ground deals with records in respect of which the personal information exemption (section 28) would be likely to be invoked in the FOI Act. One important difference between the exemptions contained in the FOI Act and the certification procedure provided for under section 8 of the Archives Act is that, in the case of section 26 and section 28 of the FOI Act, the application of the exemptions is subject to a public interest test. There is no provision for the overriding of the certification process in the Archives Act in the public interest. Indeed, the only reference to the public interest in the Archives Act is to be found in the first ground for certification. This provision envisages the refusal of access to records which are more than 30 years old on the grounds that their release would be contrary to the public interest.[145] Thus, the role of the public interest in the Archives Act is to support efforts to restrict access to government records. No guidance is provided as to the circumstances in which this exemption should be applied, and its

---

[142] s.8(4)(a).
[143] s.8(4)(b).
[144] s.8(4)(c).
[145] s.8(4)(a).

open-ended nature means that it could be used by an official to justify the withholding of records on an infinite variety of grounds. No statistics are published in respect of the use of the certification provisions contained in the Archives Act.[146]

Section 8(11) of the Archives Act gives the Taoiseach the power to prescribe classes of records in respect of which a certificate may be issued under the terms of section 8(2)[147] or section 8(4). This power has been exercised in the National Archives Act, 1986 (Prescription of Classes of Records) Order, 1997.[148] It prescribes certain classes of record for the purposes of section 8(2) or 8(4), regardless of which department, scheduled body, or court they emanate from. Other classes of records are prescribed where they emanate from particular departments, scheduled bodies or courts. The former category includes records relating to matters such as personnel, pensions and wages and salaries paid to individual civil servants. Classes of records which are prescribed with respect to particular departments include records relating to allegations of social welfare fraud, which are prescribed with respect to the Department of Social Welfare. The FOI Act also contains some class type exemptions.[149]

(c) Time limits

Records in the custody of the National Archives are either available for inspection or they are not. There is no provision for the making of an application to access archival records and hence, the issue of time limits for responding to access requests is irrelevant in the context of the Archives Act. What is important is how soon records are in fact transferred to the National Archives after they have passed the 30-year mark. It appears, owing to problems of resources, that not all records of government departments have been transferred to the National Archives. The position with respect to records of scheduled bodies and the courts would appear to be even more serious.[150]

---

[146] Even if such statistics were published, they could give rise to difficulties of interpretation, since most certificates apply in respect of multiple files.

[147] Section 8(2) provides for the exclusion of records from the scope of the Act which are certified by an authorised officer of the department as being in regular use in that department or as being required in connection with the administration of the department, in circumstances where their transfer to the National Archives would seriously interfere with the administration of that department.

[148] S.I. No. 281 of 1997.

[149] See above, pp. 84–85.

[150] National Archives Advisory Council, *A Future for Our Past; Strategic Plan for the National Archives 1996-2001* (1996). According to this report, which was published in 1996, 14 departments had completed the transfer of their pre-1961 records, while the remaining two were in the process of finalising their transfer. In the case of scheduled bodies, only eight had completed the transfer of their pre-1961 records, with at least 30 still holding large backlogs of records due for transfer. The report stated that the Na-

(d) Charges

There is no provision in the Archives Act for the charging of fees to inspect records in the possession of the National Archives. Charges are, however, imposed with respect to the copying of archival materials. The provision of access to records under the FOI Act is, with certain exceptions, subject to a charge.[151]

(e) Appeals

Two safeguards exist to prevent unjustified withholding of records under the Archives Act. In the first place, the Taoiseach has the power to direct that records be made available for public inspection which are more than 30 years old and which have been retained in a department or, if transferred to the National Archives, continue to be withheld.[152] In addition, a record can only be certified under section 8(4) of the Archives Act with the consent of an authorised officer of the Department of the Taoiseach. There is, however, no independent system for appealing against a decision not to make records over the age of 30 years available for inspection in the National Archives. This contrasts with the approach in the FOI Act where an internal appeals system is in place as well as an independent external appeals mechanism.[153]

(f) Comparative evaluation

Even though there is not any possibility of overlap in the exercise of the access rights provided under the two Acts, a comparison of the rights conferred by the two Acts is useful in gauging the extent to which they reveal a coherent approach to access to government records. It is· generally accepted that the older records are, the less likely they are to be sensitive, and the less need there is to withhold them from disclosure. It might, therefore, have been expected that legislative provisions regarding access to public records under the Archives Act would be more liberal than those found in the FOI Act. However, the opposite appears to be the case. In comparing the provisions of the Archives and FOI Acts, it becomes clear that the access regime provided for under the former allows for the exercise of a far greater degree of discretion on the part of officials in making decisions as to whether to make records

---

tional Archives held most of the older records of the Supreme, High and Circuit Courts, but some offices of the High Court had never transferred records and of the 40 or so District Court Offices, only a handful had transferred any records: see p. 6.

[151] See above, pp. 76–78.

[152] s.11. This provision has been used only once. The Taoiseach ordered the disclosure of 13 Cabinet documents which had been withheld on the grounds that their disclosure was precluded by the decision in *Attorney General v. Hamilton (No. 1)* [1993] 2 I.R. 250. See Shanahan, "Reynolds orders release of Cabinet papers", *Irish Times*, January 1, 1993.

[153] See Chap. 19.

available. This is especially evident when one compares the detail of the FOI exemptions with the open-ended nature of section 8(4) of the Archives Act. The absence from the scheme of the Archives Act of an independent system for reviewing decisions made under that Act exacerbates the problem with respect to excessive reliance on the discretion of officials in decision-making.[154] That is not to say that the legislative provisions contained in the Archives Act are necessarily being applied in a restrictive manner. The absence of published statistics on the utilisation of the exceptions provided for under the Archives Act makes it impossible to assess the practical operation of this Act.

3. Records management

One of the main concerns of the Archives Act is to facilitate the preservation of departmental records. The Act bestows on the Director of the National Archives a number of functions in this regard. They include the inspection and examination of arrangements for the preservation of departmental records and, with the consent or at the request of the appropriate member of the Government, the examination of departmental records,[155] and the giving of advice to a member of the Government and to any public service organisation on the management, preservation, and reproduction of records under their control.[156] Another important function of the Director[157] is to authorise disposal of departmental records where he or she is satisfied that the records do not warrant preservation by the National Archives. Section 19(3) of the Archives Act gives the Minister for Finance the power, following consultation with the Director of the National Archives, to make regulations "for the proper management and preservation of Departmental records in the custody or care of a Department of State". Such regulations have not, however, been introduced. Good record-keeping is also essential to the exercise by the public of their rights under the FOI Act. Section 15(5) of the FOI Act provides that the Minister shall ensure that appropriate measures are taken by public bodies in relation to training of staff, organisational arrangements, and such matters as the Minister considers appropriate for the purpose of facilitating compliance by public bodies with the Act, and that the Minister may make regulations for the management and maintenance of records held by public bodies. The Minister is obliged to consult with the Information Commissioner and the Director of the National Archives prior to making such regulations. The conferral on the Min-

---

[154] *cf.* s.43 of the Australian federal Archives Act 1983, which provides for review by the Administrative Appeals Tribunal of decisions relating to access to archival material.

[155] s.4(1)(d).

[156] s.4(1)(e).

[157] This function can be delegated by the Director to another officer of the National Archives: s.7(2).

ister of the power to make such regulations confirms the legislative basis for
the introduction of binding standards relating to the management of public
records, which was first set out in section 19(3) of the Archives Act.

D. Relationship with the Access to Information on the Environment Regulations

1. Background

The introduction of a right of access to information on the environment[158] was
mandated by the Directive on Freedom of Access to Information on the Environment, which was adopted in 1990.[159] The Directive required that, with
effect from December 31, 1992 and subject to certain exceptions, information
relating to the environment held by a public authority should be made available, on request, to any person without that person having to prove an interest.
The Directive was implemented in Ireland primarily by the Access to Information on the Environment Regulations[160] of May 20, 1993, which were introduced pursuant to sections 6 and 110 of the Environmental Protection
Agency Act 1992. Guidance Notes, which had no legal status but which offered an explanation of the Regulations, were published by the Department of
the Environment along with the Regulations.[161] A review of the operation of
the Regulations was undertaken after one year.[162] The main issues raised by
the review included dissatisfaction with the definition of "public authority" in
the Regulations, the breadth of the discretionary grounds for refusing access,
the length of the time limit for the provision of access, and the lack of a review
procedure. Arising from that review, new Regulations were introduced in 1996
to replace the earlier 1993 Regulations.[163] The 1996 Regulations were replaced

---

[158] See generally: Wates, "Chapter 7: Ireland" in *Access to Environmental Information in
Europe: The Implementation and Implications of Directive 90/313/EEC* (Hallo ed.,
Kluwer, 1996); Meehan, "Access to Information on the Environment Under Irish and
EC Law" (1994) 12 *Irish Law Times* 85 and 114; Mullany, "Implementation of the EC
Directive on Freedom of Access to Information in Ireland and other Member States"
(1994) 12 *Irish Law Times* 138; Earthwatch, *Access to Environmental Information: A
report on the Implementation of EC Directive 90/313/EEC in Ireland* (2nd ed.,
Earthwatch, Bantry, 1994); Meehan, "Freedom of Access to Information on the Environment: Recent Developments and Official Responses" (1998) 16 *Irish Law Times* 55;
Ryall, "Access to Information on the Environment" (1998) 5(2) I.P.E.L.J. 48.
[159] Council Directive 90/313: [1990] O.J. L158/56.
[160] S.I. No. 133 of 1993.
[161] Department of the Environment, *Access to Information on the Environment: Guidance
Notes* (1993).
[162] Department of the Environment, *Review of the implementation of Council Directive 90/
313 of 7 June 1990 on freedom of access to information on the environment* (1997).
[163] Access to Information on the Environment Regulations, 1996 (S.I. No. 185 of 1996).

by the Access to Information on the Environment Regulations, 1998[164] ("the 1998 Regulations"). The 1998 Regulations reproduce the 1996 Regulations almost verbatim. They provide a right of access to information relating to the environment held by public authorities. That right is subject to exclusions and exemptions. Time limits for responding to requests are set out in the 1998 Regulations and there is provision for the charging of access fees. No appeal system is provided for under the Regulations. In practice, the Ombudsman deals with appeals in cases where the public body concerned falls within his or her remit. The remedy of judicial review is, of course, also available to a person whose request for access to information is refused.

The implementation of Directive 90/313/EEC is supported also by separate statutory rights of access to environmental information which exist in the areas of planning and development, pollution control, major accident hazards, and waste management. Considerable improvements to statutory rights of access to such information were made with the introduction in the mid-1990s of new legislative provisions. The Local Government (Planning and Development) (No. 2) Regulations 1995,[165] for example, provides that files on appeals received by An Bord Pleanála on or after April 10, 1995, can be inspected by members of the public for a period of five years after appeals are determined by the Board. These Regulations reversed the previous position, whereby An Bord Pleanála refused to allow access to Inspectors' reports on the grounds that they represented information held in connection with, or for the purposes of, a judicial function.[166] The Environmental Protection Agency (Licensing) (Amendment) (No. 2) Regulations, 1995[167] provide for the making available of all Environmental Protection Agency reports for the purposes of proposed determinations or decisions on applications for integrated pollution control licences. Similarly, 1997 Regulations introduced under the Waste Management Act 1996 provide for the granting of public access to information concerning the licensing of waste disposal activities.[168]

Both Directive 90/313/EEC and the FOI Act provide a right of access to information, thus giving rise to the possibility of overlap between them. Two main issues arise. The first concerns the interaction between the access rights under the two sets of provisions and, in particular, whether it will be open to an applicant to apply for access to information relating to the environment under both the Directive and the FOI Act.

The second question concerns the extent to which the two sets of provisions which provide a right of access to information relating to the environment are consistent with one another. The issue of consistency is important,

---

[164] S.I. No. 125 of 1998.
[165] S.I. No. 75 of 1995.
[166] Department of the Environment, *op. cit.* above, n. 162, p. 4.
[167] S.I. No. 76 of 1995.
[168] Waste Management (Licensing Regulations) 1997 (S.I. No. 133 of 1997).

whether or not a person is entitled to use both sets of access provisions. If the making of applications for access under both sets of provisions is precluded by the legislation, consistency will be important in ensuring that an applicant will not be disadvantaged by being required to use one access regime, as distinct from the other. On the other hand, if it is open to applicants to submit applications for access under either set of provisions, consistency will be important in discouraging the confusion and waste of resources which could result from the use of both pieces of legislation sequentially, in the event of the applicant being dissatisfied with the outcome of the first application, or, indeed, their use simultaneously.

2. The interaction of access rights in the FOI Act, the Directive, and 1998 Regulations

The focus of this discussion will be on comparing the rights of access conferred by the 1998 Regulations with those provided for under the FOI Act. Directive 90/313/EEC is, however, likely to satisfy the conditions for direct effect under Community law,[169] which means that the rights set out in the Directive are conferred directly on individuals and may be invoked before national courts.

The FOI Act contains no express reference to the relationship between that Act and the Directive or the 1998 Regulations. The FOI Act does, however, contain a provision which arguably excludes information from the scope of that Act to which the Directive or 1998 Regulations applies. That provision is section 46(2), which provides:

> "[T]his Act does not apply to—
>
> (a) a record that is available for inspection by members of the public whether upon payment or free of charge, or
> (b) a record a copy of which is available for purchase or removal free of charge by members of the public,
>
> whether by virtue of an enactment (other than this Act) or otherwise."

In a 1997 review of the implementation of Directive 90/313/EEC prepared by the Department of the Environment for the Commission of the European Union, the department put forward the view that the effect of section 46(2) is to exclude from the scope of the FOI Act information to which the Access to Information on the Environment Regulations applies:

> "One of the provision [sic] of this legislation [the FOI Act] is that information which is available under other legislative provisions will *not* be subject to the

---

[169] See Case 26/62 *Van Gend en Loos v. Nederlandse Belastingenadministratie* [1963] E.C.R. 1; Case 41/74 *Van Duyn v. Home Office* [1974] E.C.R. 1337; Case C–236/92 *Comitato di Coordinamento per la Difesa della Cava* [1994] E.C.R. I–483.

Freedom of Information Act. Consequently, environmental information which is available under the Access to Information on the Environment Regulations, 1996, will not be covered by the Freedom of Information legislation."[170]

One practical implication of the exclusion from the scope of the FOI Act of information relating to the environment would be that a public body, on receiving a request for access to information under the FOI Act, would have to satisfy itself that the information sought did not constitute information relating to the environment as defined in the 1998 Regulations, since such information would be outside the scope of the FOI Act.

The interpretation of section 46(2) as excluding from the scope of the FOI Act information to which the 1998 Regulations applies, however, is open to question. It is not clear that information in respect of which an application for access can be made under the 1998 Regulations amounts to either "a record that is available for inspection by members of the public" or a record "a copy of which is available for purchase or removal, free of charge by members of the public". Section 46(2) appears to have been designed to exclude information from the scope of the FOI Act which is "available" automatically or in a passive sense. The Explanatory Memorandum to the Bill refers to section 46(2) as being concerned with information which is "publicly available". The exclusion of records otherwise available is a feature of many overseas FOI Acts.[171] Such information could, for example, include information which is available for inspection in public offices, such as the electoral register or planning applications. The right of access to information relating to the environment provided under Directive 90/313/EEC and the 1998 Regulations must, in contrast, be exercised in an active way in order to lead to the making available of information. Regulation 6(1) of the 1998 Regulations states that:

> "A public authority shall . . . subject only to the conditions and exceptions provided for in these Regulations, make available any information relating to the environment to which these Regulations apply *to any person who requests it*."[172]

Similarly, Directive 90/313/EEC requires that Member States shall ensure that public authorities are required to make available information to any natural or legal person *at his request*.[173]

Regulation 6(2) of the 1998 Regulations sets out certain formal requirements relating to the making of requests for access under the Regulations. Requests must be in writing, they must state the name and address of the person making the request, and they must be as specific as possible about the information being sought.

---

[170] Department of the Environment, *op. cit.* above, n. 162. Emphasis in original.
[171] Australia: Freedom of Information Act 1982 (Cth), s.12; Canada: Access to Information Act (Canada), R.S.C., 1985, s.68.
[172] Emphasis added.
[173] Art.3(1).

It is clear that under the 1998 Regulations information relating to the environment is not automatically made available. It will only be made available in response to a request where it has been established that the information requested is information relating to the environment within the meaning of the 1998 Regulations and in circumstances where none of the various exclusions or exemptions provided for under the Regulations are applicable. The release of information under the 1998 Regulations is, therefore, far from automatic and, on that basis, it is submitted that such information could not be said to be "available" in the sense of either limb of the exclusion in section 46(2).

The evidence appears to weigh against the department's interpretation of the FOI Act and to favour an interpretation which allows for the utilisation of the FOI Act to seek access to information to which the 1998 Regulations applies. It is worth considering whether the opposite proposition might be true, *i.e.* that the use of the 1998 Regulations to obtain access to information which comes within the scope of the FOI Act is precluded by the terms of the Regulations. The 1998 Regulations apply to:

> "information relating to the environment other than –
>
> . . .
>
> (b) subject to sub-article (2),[174] information which, under any statutory provision apart from these Regulations, is *required to be made available*, whether for inspection or otherwise, *to persons generally*."[175]

If the provision of access to information in response to a FOI request is viewed as a requirement that the information be made available to persons generally, then the 1998 Regulations could not be used to gain access to information coming within the terms of the FOI Act. It is not clear, however, that such an interpretation is warranted. The provision of access to information in response to an FOI request cannot be viewed as the making available of the information to persons generally. FOI requests are responded to by the provision of access to information to the requester, not its publication to the population at large.

It appears, therefore, that persons seeking access to information relating to the environment are entitled to use either, or indeed both, sets of provisions. In particular, it appears that where an applicant has been unsuccessful in obtaining access to information under one piece of legislation, he or she is entitled to initiate an application under the other.

---

[174] reg.5. Sub-regulation (2) lists a number of legislative measures providing for specific rights of access to information on the environment. Its effect is to allow for the exercise of the rights conferred by the 1998 Regulations to obtain access to information covered by the named legislative provisions. The FOI Act is not amongst the listed legislative measures. See Ryall, *op. cit.* above, n. 158.
[175] Emphasis added.

3. Consistency between the FOI Act and the 1998 Regulations

The FOI Act and the1998 Regulations can be examined to determine the extent to which the right of access to information relating to the environment is dealt with consistently in both pieces of legislation.

(a) Scope of the right of access

(i) Bodies subject to access rights

The 1998 Regulations apply to information relating to the environment which is held by "public authorities". No definitive list of public authorities is contained in the 1998 Regulations. Instead, public authorities are defined in regulation 4(2)(a) and (b).[176] In article 4(2)(a), public authorities are defined in a manner which, as well as requiring that the authority in question falls into one of the categories listed in the text of the regulations, also requires that they meet two further criteria.

The additional criteria which must be met in order for a body to qualify as a public authority within the meaning of the 1998 Regulations are, first, that the authority has "public administration functions and responsibilities" and, second, that it possesses information relating to the environment.

The categories of public authorities listed in regulation 4(2)(a) are: (i) a Minister of the Government; (ii) the Commissioners of Public Works in Ireland; (iii) a local authority for the purposes of the Local Government Act 1941; (iv) a harbour authority within the meaning of the Harbours Act 1946; (v) a health board established under the Health Act 1970; (vi) a board or other body established by or under statute; (vii) a company in which all the shares are held by, or on behalf of, or by directors appointed by, a Minister of the Government; or (viii) a company in which all the shares are held by a board, company, or other body referred to in paragraph (vi) or (vii) of this definition.

The requirement that the authority have public administration functions and responsibilities seems to preclude the application of the 1998 Regulations to bodies whose functions and responsibilities are purely commercial in nature. It has even been argued by a government research body that it was not covered by the forerunner to the 1998 Regulations on the grounds that it did not have public administration functions.[177]

Some doubt exists as to whether An Bord Pleanála is covered by the 1998 Regulations.[178] These doubts centre on the board's argument that it is a quasi-

---

[176] This definition is taken from the definition of "public authority" in s.3 of the Environmental Protection Agency Act 1992.

[177] This argument was put forward by EOLAS, the Irish Science and Technology Agency (now part of Forbairt): Earthwatch, *Access to Environmental Information: A report on the Implementation of EC Directive 90/313/EEC in Ireland* (2nd ed., Earthwatch, Bantry, 1994), p. 4 n 3.

[178] This argument was raised in respect of the 1996 Regulations, which were identical to

judicial, rather than an administrative body. Bodies acting in a judicial or leg-islative capacity were exempted under the Directive.[179] The 1998 Regulations deal with this exemption by reference to the information, rather than to the body involved. It excludes from the scope of the 1998 Regulations informa-tion "held in connection with or for the purposes of any judicial or legislative function".[180] The position of An Bord Pleanála will, therefore, be considered in the section dealing with the exclusions from the scope of the 1998 Regula-tions.

Regulation 4(2)(b) extends the definition of public authority for the pur-poses of the Regulations to include "any person or body, other than a public authority as defined in paragraph (a), which is under the control of such a public authority and has public responsibilities for the environment and pos-sesses information relating to the environment". This part of the definition is aimed at including contractors to public authorities within the scope of the 1998 Regulations, *e.g.* private waste management contractors.

The FOI Act applies to public bodies. These are listed in the First Sched-ule to the Act. Three main categories of body are referred to in the First Sched-ule. The first consists of those bodies which are covered by the Act from the date of its commencement. These are the departments of State and a range of agencies of central government, all of which are named in the Schedule. The second category consists of local authorities and health boards, which will become subject to the Act on or before October 21, 1998. Finally, there is a list of public bodies which can be made subject to the Act by regulation. The bodies to which the application of the Act can be thus extended are: the Garda Síochána, statutory bodies, bodies established under the Companies Acts 1963–1990 in pursuance of powers conferred by statute where such bodies are financed wholly or partly out of the public purse, any other bodies fi-nanced wholly or partly out of the public purse, a company in which a major-ity of the shares are held by or on behalf of a Government Minister, any body, organisation or group appointed by the Government or a Minster, any other body, organisation or group on which functions concerning the general public have been conferred by statute (but only to the extent of such public func-tions), and a subsidiary of any of the preceding categories of bodies.[181] There is provision also for the application of the Act to records in the possession of independent contractors of public bodies where the records relate to the serv-ice being carried out by the contractor for the public body. In such a situation, the record is deemed to be held by the public body.[182]

---

the 1998 Regulations in terms of defining public authorities: Wates, *op. cit.* above, n. 158, p. 122.
[179] Council Directive 90/313 on Freedom of Access to Information on the Environment, Article 2(6).
[180] reg.5(1).
[181] First Sched., para. 1(5).
[182] s.6(9).

The scope of application of the two sets of provisions can be compared. Assuming the additional criteria relating to public administration functions and possession of information relating to the environment in the Regulations are met, it is clear that there is some overlap. For example, the Commissioners of Public Works, health boards, and local authorities are covered by both sets of provisions. While the FOI Act applies to the departments of State, the 1998 Regulations apply to Ministers of the Government. The Regulations were, however, interpreted in the Guidance Notes issued by the Department of the Environment as applying to government departments exercising explicit regulatory or management functions relating to the environment.[183] The Environmental Protection Agency, which is included in the list of public bodies in the First Schedule to the FOI Act, also appears to come within the scope of the 1998 Regulations, on the basis that it is a body established under statute which has public administration functions and possesses information relating to the environment. An Bord Pleanála is also included in the list of public bodies in the First Schedule to the FOI Act. As noted above, the application of the 1998 Regulations to this body is in dispute.[184]

The scope of application of the 1998 Regulations is, as things stand, wider than that of the FOI Act. The 1998 Regulations apply, for example, to the harbour authorities and to all bodies established by or under statute, as well as to companies in which the shares are held by or on behalf of a Government Minister. Bodies which have been accepted in the Guidance Notes issued by the Department of the Environment as coming within the remit of the 1998 Regulations include the National Authority for Occupational Safety and Health,[185] the National Radiological Protection Institute, the Marine Institute, and regional and central fisheries boards.[186] None of these bodies come within the scope of the FOI Act. The FOI Act has, however, the potential to apply to a broader range of bodies possessing information relating to the environment than the 1998 Regulations. First, there is no requirement under the FOI Act that the bodies in question have public administration functions and responsibilities and, second, there is scope for the extension of the FOI Act by regulation. Regulations can, for example, be introduced under the First Schedule, paragraph 1(5)(f) to extend the application of the Act to:

"any other body, organisation or group on which functions in relation to the general public or a class of the general public stand conferred by any enactment".

Thus, private bodies on which statutory functions have been conferred can become subject to the FOI Act.

---

[183] Department of the Environment, *op. cit.* above, n. 161, p. 4.
[184] Above, n. 178.
[185] This body has been renamed the Health and Safety Authority.
[186] Department of the Environment, *op. cit.* above, n. 161, p. 4.

To summarise, it is clear that there is already some overlap between the two sets of provisions. The bodies which have seen the greatest level of activity in terms of utilisation of the access rights conferred by the 1998 Regulations are the local authorities,[187] which from October 1998 are also covered by the FOI Act. The level of overlap is likely to increase as the scope of the FOI legislation is extended.

(ii) The type of information covered

The 1998 Regulations, in contrast to the FOI Act, apply to information rather than to records. "Information relating to the environment" is defined in the Environmental Protection Agency Act 1992 in section 110 for the purposes of that Act[188] as:

> "any available information in written, visual, aural or data base form on the state of water, atmosphere, soil, fauna, flora, land and natural sites and on actions (including those which give rise to nuisances such as noise) or measures adversely affecting, or likely to so affect, these and on actions or measures designed to protect these, including administrative measures and environmental management programmes".[189]

It is not clear whether this definition could be held to extend to verbal information. Verbal information might be held to qualify as aural information on the basis that it can be heard. It is unlikely that the definition could apply to information of which a person has knowledge. Whether or not the definition extends to verbal information or information of which a person has knowledge is, in any case, somewhat academic, since it would be difficult to prove the existence of such knowledge.

The FOI Act definition of record covers a broad spectrum of forms in which information may be recorded. "Record" is defined to include any memorandum, book, plan, map, drawing, diagram, pictorial or graphic work or other document, any photograph, film or recording (whether of sound or images or both), any form in which data (within the meaning of the Data Protection Act 1988) are held, any other form (including machine-readable form) or thing in

---

[187] A survey carried out by the Department of the Environment in February 1997 showed that local authorities accounted for 85 per cent of all requests under the Regulations: Department of the Environment, *op. cit.* above, n. 162, p. 6.

[188] The predecessor to the 1998 Regulations, the Access to Information on the Environment Regulations, 1996 (S.I. No. 185 of 1996), were made under the Environmental Protection Agency Act 1992 and so the definition of environmental information contained in that Act was used for the purposes of the 1996 Regulations. The 1998 Regulations were made pursuant to s.3 of the European Communities Act 1972 and there is therefore some doubt as to whether the definition set out in the Environmental Protection Agency Act applies to the 1998 Regulations. See Ryall, *op. cit.* above, n. 158, at 48 n 4.

[189] This definition reproduces the definition of information relating to the environment in Directive 90/313/EEC (Art.2(a)) almost verbatim.

which information is held or stored manually, mechanically, or electronically and anything that is a part or a copy, in any form, of any of the foregoing or is a combination of two or more of the foregoing.

The reference to "written, visual, aural or data base" forms referred to in the definition of information for the purposes of the 1998 Regulations seems to cover most of those forms.

The definition of information relating to the environment was examined by the Ombudsman in a case in which an environmental group applied to a local authority for access to information consisting of the daily monitoring results on the water supply of a small town. The results were prepared by the local authority's curator at the local water treatment plant. One of the main arguments put forward by the local authority was that the information requested referred to the state of treated water, while the Regulations were intended to relate to water in its untreated or natural state. That argument was rejected by the Ombudsman who, without elaborating, stated that the information contained in the curator's daily report sheets was information relating to the environment within the meaning of the definition pertaining to the Regulations.[190]

(iii) The form in which access is provided

It is not clear whether the Directive and the 1998 Regulations confer a right to a copy of a record or whether the right of access is confined to a right to inspect information. The form in which access is to be provided is not made explicit in either the Directive or the 1998 Regulations. The public authority is merely required, under regulation 6(1), to make information "available". Public authorities have, however, been advised by a circular letter from the Department of the Environment that the presumption of public access to information requires barriers to access to be kept to a minimum and that requests for copies of documents should be facilitated in so far as is possible.[191] Under the FOI Act access to a record must be given in the form requested save in certain circumstances.[192] One of the exceptions provided for is where the giving of access in another form or manner would be "significantly more efficient".[193] Thus, the right of access to a copy of a record is not automatic under either the FOI Act or the 1998 Regulations.

(iv) To whom does the right of access apply?

The right of access to information relating to the environment under the 1998 Regulations and the right of access to records under the FOI Act both apply to

---

[190] *Annual Report of the Ombudsman* (1994), p. 50.
[191] Circular Letter EPS 2/95 of May 8, 1995 referred to in Department of the Environment, *op. cit.* above, n. 162, p. 10.
[192] s.12(2).
[193] s.12(2)(a).

"any person". The Directive requires that information be made available "to any natural or legal person". On the basis of the definition of "person" in the Interpretation Act 1937,[194] the exercise of the rights conferred by the 1998 Regulations and the FOI Act rights is not limited to individuals, but extends to legal persons; nor is the exercise of either set of access rights confined to Irish citizens or residents.

(v) Retrospection

The Directive provides that information relating to the environment held by a public body be made available with effect from December 31, 1992.[195] The FOI Act, on the other hand, confers a right of access to records created after the commencement of the Act on April 21, 1998.[196] This limitation is, however, subject to two exceptions. One exception is in respect of records which relate to personal information about the person seeking access to the records[197] and the other concerns records created before the commencement of the Act, access to which "is necessary or expedient in order to understand records created after such commencement".[198]

(b) Exclusions and exemptions

(i) Exclusions

Two categories of information are excluded from the scope of the 1998 Regulations. These are set out in regulation 4(4). The first concerns information held in connection with or for the purposes of any judicial or legislative function, while the second covers information which is required to be made available, whether for inspection or otherwise, to persons generally under any statutory provision.

(A) Judicial or legislative function   The 1998 Regulations do not apply to "information held in connection with or for the purposes of any judicial or legislative function".[199] The Guidance Notes issued by the Department of the Environment give the following interpretation of legislative and judicial functions. Legislative function is said to be "likely to be construed as including both the preparation of legislative proposals for the Oireachtas, e.g. by Government Departments and the Attorney General's Office, and the preparation and making of secondary legislation, e.g. Regulations, Orders, Bye-laws, by

---

[194] s.11.
[195] Council Directive 90/313 on Freedom of Access to Information on the Environment, Article 9(1): [1990] O.J. L158/56.
[196] s.6(4).
[197] s.6(5)(b).
[198] s.6(5)(a).
[199] reg.5(1)(a).

Ministers and other responsible authorities".[200] This exclusion might be found to overlap with the FOI exemptions relating to deliberations of public bodies (section 20) and parliamentary matters (section 22(1)(c)). The former is subject to a public interest test, while the latter is not.

Judicial function is described in the 1993 Guidance Notes as being:

> "likely to be construed as including processes of determination by Ministers and other public authorities which are open to the hearing of submissions from different parties and in relation to which the Irish courts have already decided that the authority concerned is required to act in a judicial manner".[201]

The Irish courts have considered the nature of the judicial function in a number of decisions and the following indicators of the judicial function have been gleaned by Morgan from the case law.[202] They are:

(1) a dispute as to legal rights (civil) or violations of the law (criminal) which is settled by applying pre-existing law and/or ascertaining facts;

(2) a final and conclusive determination;

(3) trappings of a court – compulsory attendance of parties, witnesses, etc.

(4) the making of an order characteristic of a court;

(5) the right to give effect to such order, if necessary, by calling in the executive power of the State.

Prior to the introduction of the 1998 Regulations, An Bord Pleanála had argued that it was exempt from the scope of the Directive in its appellate functions on the basis that it is a body "acting in a judicial or legislative capacity". The Department of the Environment has indicated that in its view An Bord Pleanála acts as an administrative tribunal and, therefore, comes within the terms of the Directive. The courts have not yet had the opportunity of deciding this issue.

The FOI Act excludes records held by courts and tribunals with two exceptions. These are in respect of records which were not created by the court or tribunal and the disclosure of which was not prohibited by the court or tribunal, and records relating to the general administration of the court or tribunal. The exclusion in the 1998 Regulations seems to go further than this in that it excludes all records held in connection with or for the purposes of any judicial function.

---

[200] Department of the Environment, *op. cit.* above, n. 161, p. 3.
[201] *ibid.*
[202] From Morgan, *The Separation of Powers in the Irish Constitution* (Round Hall Sweet & Maxwell, Dublin, 1997), pp. 52–53. This list was formulated from definitions set out in the following cases: *Lynham v. Butler (No. 2)* [1933] I.R. 74; The *State (Shanahan) v. Attorney General* [1964] I.R. 239; and *McDonald v. Bord na gCon (No.2)* [1965] I.R. 217.

(B) Information otherwise available   The second exclusion concerns information which is required to be made available whether for inspection or otherwise to persons generally under any statutory provision.[203] No such exclusion is provide for in Directive 90/313/EEC and it has been referred to as "the major loophole in Ireland's transposition of the Directive".[204] The aim of this exclusion is to ensure that the 1998 Regulations do not apply in circumstances where arrangements for access are already provided for under other legislation.[205] This exclusion applies, even if the other statutory provision merely confers a right to inspect information as opposed to a right to obtain a copy thereof. The exclusion is framed in terms broadly similar to the corresponding exclusion in the FOI Act, with the main difference being that the 1998 Regulations' exclusion applies only in respect of information "available under" other statutory provisions, while the FOI Act exclusion applies to information available "by virtue of an enactment or otherwise".[206] Therefore records would be excluded from the FOI Act if they were available through any means, such as under statute, pursuant to an administrative scheme, or on a voluntary basis, while the exclusion in the 1998 Regulations applies only in respect of information available under statutory provisions.

(ii) Exemptions

The 1998 Regulations provide for both mandatory and discretionary exemptions, while Directive 90/313/EEC provides for discretionary exemptions only. The mandatory exemptions are in respect of personal information relating to individuals, material supplied to the public authority by a third party and information which, if disclosed, would be damaging to the environment. The personal information exemption provides that a public authority shall not make available information which relates to "personal information held in relation to an individual who has not given consent to the disclosure of the information".[207] The Guidance Notes issued by the Department of the Environment suggest that, in most cases, an opportunity should be given to an individual to give consent to the release of information before a request for access to such information is refused.[208]

---

[203] reg.5(1)(b).

[204] Wates, *op. cit.* above, n. 158, p. 124.

[205] Regulation 5(2) removes from this exclusion certain specified access provisions, namely: s. 5 of the Local Government (Planning and Development) Act 1992 and any regulations made thereunder; ss.10 and 31 of the Air Pollution Act 1987 and any regulations made thereunder; and ss.6 and 87 of the Environmental Protection Agency Act 1992 and any regulations made thereunder. Thus the rights conferred by the 1998 Regulations can be exercised with respect to information covered by these provisions.

[206] s.46(2).

[207] reg.7.

[208] Department of the Environment, *op. cit.* above, n. 161, p. 6.

The personal information exemption contained in the 1998 Regulations is much broader than its counterpart in the FOI Act because it only allows for the disclosure of personal information where the individual concerned has consented to such disclosure. The FOI Act allows for the disclosure of personal information in a number of circumstances. These include, for example, where the disclosure of the information is necessary in order to avoid a serious and imminent danger to the life or health of an individual.[209] The FOI personal information exemption, unlike its counterpart in the 1998 Regulations, is also subject to a public interest test.[210]

Under the 1998 Regulations, material supplied to the public authority by a third party is exempt where that third party was not, or is not, capable of being put under a legal obligation to supply the material.[211] This exemption is designed to protect information supplied voluntarily to a public authority. There is no obvious counterpart to this exemption in the FOI Act. The nearest corresponding exemption is probably the confidentiality exemption.[212] That exemption only applies in respect of information given in confidence and there are a number of other limitations on its application. It is also subject to a public interest test.

The 1998 Regulations provide for the mandatory exemption of information which, if disclosed, would make it more likely that the environment to which such information relates would be damaged.[213] Its closest counterpart in the FOI Act is section 30(1)(b), which allows for the exemption of records where disclosure of information contained in the record could reasonably be expected to prejudice the wellbeing of a cultural, heritage, or natural resource or a species, or the habitat of a species of flora or fauna.

Three discretionary exemptions are provided for in the 1998 Regulations. They are in respect of:

(1) international relations, national defence or public security;[214]

(2) matters which are *sub judice*, or which are under inquiry (including disciplinary inquiries), or which are the subject of preliminary investigation proceedings;[215] or

(3) commercial or industrial confidentiality, or intellectual property, or where the information relates to internal communications of the public authority or to material which is still in the course of completion.[216]

---

[209] s.28(2)(e).
[210] s.28(5).
[211] reg.7.
[212] s.26.
[213] reg.7.
[214] reg.8(1)(a).
[215] reg.8(1)(b).
[216] reg.8(1)(c).

The 1998 Regulations contain an additional discretionary ground for refusal of a request for access to information relating to the environment: a public authority may refuse to accede to such a request where the request is "manifestly unreasonable having regard to the volume or range of information sought".[217] Each of these four discretionary exemptions can be compared with the corresponding FOI Act provisions.

(A) International relations, national defence, or public security   The 1998 Regulations allow for the exemption of information where it "affects" international relations, national defence, or public security. The FOI Act also contains a security, defence, and international relations exemption but it only applies where access to the record requested could reasonably be expected to "affect adversely" those interests. The requirement that disclosure "affect adversely" is stronger than the requirement that it "affect", in which case the scope for exemption under the 1998 Regulations is greater.

(B) Matters which are *sub judice*, or which are under inquiry (including disciplinary inquiries), or which are the subject of preliminary investigation proceedings   The scope of this exemption extends in Directive 90/313/EEC and in the 1993 Regulations to matters which are *or have been* under inquiry. The 1998 Regulations apply only to those maters which are currently *sub judice* or under inquiry.[218] The *sub judice* rule has been defined as the prohibition of publication of material which has a tendency to interfere with the due administration of justice in particular proceedings.[219] Breach of the *sub judice* rule can only arise in the context of a specific case and litigation must be proceeding or be known to be imminent.[220] Matters which are under inquiry also appear to require the existence of a specific inquiry, while "preliminary investigation proceedings" appear to be limited to situations where a formal investigation has been commenced. Examples given in the Guidance Notes issued by the Department of the Environment of the types of information likely to be exempted under this provision are: information in connection with intended prosecution of offences by the D.P.P. or by local or public authorities, information affecting enforcement proceedings, material arising from public or disciplinary inquiries; and information relating to preliminary or other proceedings instituted by the E.C. Commission.[221] In each of these cases, however, it appears to be necessary that there be evidence of the existence of a

---

[217] reg.8.
[218] reg.8.
[219] *Attorney General for New South Wales v. John Fairfax & Sons Ltd* [1980] 1 N.S.W.L.R. 362; *Desmond v. Glackin (No. 1)* [1993] 3 I.R. 1.
[220] *Attorney-General v. Times Newspapers Ltd* [1974] A.C. 273, *per* Diplock J.; [1973] 3 All E.R. 54; [1973] 3 W.L.R. 298.
[221] Department of the Environment, *op. cit.* above, n. 161, p. 6.

specific and imminent inquiry. The issue of matters which are *sub judice* is subsumed in the contempt of court exemption in the FOI Act.[222] Matters under inquiry or the subject of preliminary investigation proceedings could fall within section 20 (Deliberations of public bodies), or section 23 (Law enforcement). However, these exemptions are not absolute. The latter is subject to an injury test (*i.e.* access to the record must prejudice or impair the interest being protected), while the former is subject to a public interest test.

(C) Commercial or industrial confidentiality, or intellectual property, or where the information relates to internal communications of the public authority or to material which is still in the course of completion
(1) Commercial or industrial confidentiality, or intellectual property The Guidance Notes issued by the Department of the Environment suggest that this exemption should only come into play where a public authority is satisfied that "real and substantial commercial or industrial interests are threatened".[223] The Guidance Notes go on to say that:

> "the fact that the release of information e.g. relating to a pollution incident, might damage the reputation of a company is not adequate reason for withholding this information. Equally, it would be very difficult on these grounds to refuse to supply information on the composition of emissions, including volumes."[224]

The application of this exemption was examined in a case which was appealed to the Ombudsman. A local authority had received a request for access to data on effluent discharges from an industrial plant. The authority had sought the views of the company involved and, in the light of its response to the effect that release of the information would seriously conflict with the confidentiality associated with the company's industrial, technological and commercial know-how, the local authority decided that it would not be correct to release the information. In reviewing this decision, the Ombudsman stated that, in exercising its discretion to refuse to make available information where it affects commercial or industrial confidentiality, a local authority should first assess all available evidence. It is not sufficient for the local authority merely to quote the reasons for objecting to the release of the information given by the company which had supplied the information.[225]

The corresponding exemptions in the FOI Act are those relating to information obtained in confidence (section 26) and commercially sensitive information (section 27). Both of these exemptions are subject to public interest tests.

---

[222] s.22(1)(b).
[223] Department of the Environment, *op. cit.* above, n. 161, p. 7.
[224] *ibid.*
[225] *Annual Report of the Ombudsman* (1995), pp. 21–22.

The 1998 Regulations, unlike Directive 90/313/EEC and the 1993 Regulations, do not exempt information on the basis that it affects the confidentiality of proceedings of public authorities.

(II) Internal communications of the public authority The Guidance Notes suggest that this exemption would take in such information as internal minutes, reports or other communications between officials or different public authorities, or between officials and Ministers, letters to and from members of the public and public representatives.[226] The Ombudsman has considered a claim that the daily report sheets relating to water quality which were prepared by a local authority's curator at the local water treatment plant was an internal communication. The daily report sheets consisted of factual information on the quantities of chemicals added to quantities of water together with comments written by the curator. The local authority concerned argued that the primary purposes of recording information on the daily report sheets was to alert the engineer to any problems that might arise, for management control use, and chemical stock control purposes. The authority argued further that the reports were prepared by junior staff and, as such, were internal communications. These were to be distinguished from reports prepared by relatively senior local authority personnel which would normally be based on factual information and would indicate the corporate view on the matter under discussion in the report, concluding that "if it does not reflect the corporate view, then it remains an internal communication".[227] The Ombudsman concluded that, with the exception of the comments column, the daily report sheets were not internal communications. Interestingly, the Ombudsman went on to say that even if the daily report sheets were "internal communications", it was:

> "not reasonable for the Local Authority to exercise its discretion to refuse to make the sheets available to the environmental group as the reasons advanced by the Local Authority in support of this position . . . were not valid reasons under the Regulations".[228]

This seems to indicate that the Ombudsman is prepared to incorporate a reasonableness test into the 1998 Regulations; indeed, the incorporation of such a test is expressly referred to by the Ombudsman in his Annual Report for 1994.[229] The Ombudsman arrived at this position notwithstanding the absence of any public interest test in Directive 90/313 or in the 1998 Regulations.

---

[226] Department of the Environment, *op. cit.* above, n. 161, p. 7.
[227] *Annual Report of the Ombudsman* (1994), p. 49.
[228] *ibid.*, p. 50.
[229] In his Annual Report, *ibid.*, p. 27, the Ombudsman says:
"In relation to the discretionary exceptions in the Regulations, it is not sufficient for a public authority to quote one or more of these – they must also demonstrate that, in refusing to release the information, they have exercised their discretion reasonably. Although not specifically provided for in either the Directive or the Regulations, I

The corresponding exemptions in the FOI Act are those relating to deliberations of public bodies (section 20) and functions and negotiations of public bodies (section 21). Each of these exemptions is subject to a public interest test. In addition, the latter incorporates an injury test while the former expressly excludes from its scope "factual (including statistical information) and analyses thereof".[230] Thus, information such as the comments on the daily report sheets to which access was denied under the 1998 Regulations might not have been exempt from disclosure under section 21.

(III) Material still in the course of completion Public authorities often gather information as a step in the carrying out of an investigation. They may seek to withhold such raw data on the basis that it is material still in the course of completion. It has been reported, for example, that access to the findings of the fire authorities in relation to an accident at a chemical plant was refused by a local authority on the basis that the overall investigation of which the findings formed part was not complete.[231] The danger with an exemption of this type is that it is open to abuse. There is no requirement that the material must be due for completion within a certain time limit. The FOI Act does not contain any exemption which directly corresponds with this exemption. The FOI exemption relating to financial and economic interests of the State and public bodies (section 31) provides for the exemption of records which, if disclosed prematurely, could harm certain interests. This exemption is, again, subject to a public interest test. The Act also allows for the deferral of access to records in certain limited circumstances.[232] There are safeguards in place to ensure that such deferral may not be of indefinite duration.

(D) Manifestly unreasonable requests A request for access to information relating to the environment may be refused on the basis that the request is "manifestly unreasonable having regard to the volume or range of information sought".[233] This wording was introduced in 1996 to replace the original provision, which allowed for refusals where the request "is manifestly unreasonable or is formulated in too general a manner".[234] The latter had been regarded

---

will, in addition, apply a 'harm test' to the information which is the subject of the request. This test, which is particularly appropriate to the discretionary as opposed to the mandatory exemptions in the Regulations, is designed to test the reasonableness of the public authority's refusal to release the information requested. This test takes the form that if the release of information is not expressly excluded by the Regulations, what harm, if any, would it do to release it."

[230] s.20(2)(b).
[231] Earthwatch, *op. cit.* above, n. 158, pp. 13–14.
[232] s.11.
[233] reg.8.
[234] Access to Information on the Environment Regulations, 1993 (S.I. No. 133 of 1993), reg.6(2).

as being too vague. There is a corresponding, but more precisely worded provision in the FOI Act.[235] It allows for the refusal of a FOI request where, in the opinion of the head of a public body, "granting the request would, by reason of the number or nature of the records concerned or the nature of the information concerned, require the retrieval and examination of such number of records or an examination of such kind of the records concerned as to cause a substantial and unreasonable interference with or disruption of the other work or the procedures of the public body concerned".[236] This provision has the advantage over the "manifestly unreasonable" exemption in the 1998 Regulations of detailing the type of interference with a public authority's work which would justify a refusal of access. The FOI provision goes on to require a public body, before refusing a request on this ground, to first assist or offer to assist the applicant to amend the request so that it does not offend in the manner described.[237] No such safeguard is provided for in the 1998 Regulations. Public authorities were, however, asked by a Department of the Environment Circular[238] to give all reasonable assistance to persons seeking information to allow the formulation of requests to be consistent with the requirements of the 1996 Regulations.

(iii) Time limits

Public authorities are required, under the terms of the 1998 Regulations, to respond as soon as possible to a request for information.[239] A response is required not later than one month from the date on which the request is received. This response time was reduced from the response time of two months provided for under the 1993 Regulations.[240] The 1998 Regulations do not specify the type of response required within the one-month period. In particular, they do not require that the request be either granted or refused. It has been suggested that an obstructive public authority might simply wait until the time limit has elapsed before referring the person requesting the information to a different public authority, or disputing the validity of the request on technical grounds.[241] The one-month time limit can be extended to two months where a public authority is unable to meet the one-month limit because of the nature or extent of the request.[242] Where the extended time limit is availed of, the authority is required to give the applicant notice in writing stating why it is unable to respond to the request within the one-month time limit and specifying

---

[235] s.10(1)(c).
[236] s.10(1)(c).
[237] s.10(2).
[238] Circular Letter EPS 3/96.
[239] reg.10(1).
[240] Above, n. 234, reg.8(1).
[241] Earthwatch, *op. cit.* above, n. 158, p. 8.
[242] reg.10(2).

the date, not later than two months from the date on which the request was received, before which the response shall be made.[243] Under the FOI Act, decisions on requests for access to records must, in general, be given no later than four weeks after the day on which the request is received.[244] The decision must be either to grant the request, to refuse it, or to grant it in part. There is provision for extension of time limits for a period not exceeding four weeks where meeting the original time limit is not reasonably possible in view of the large quantity of records requested or in view of the number of related requests received by the body in respect of which decisions have not yet been made.[245] Where the time limit for making a decision has been extended, the applicant must be informed of the period of the extension and the reasons for it.

(iv) Charges

The 1998 Regulations allow for charges to be levied in respect of the making available of information. There is a proviso to the effect that a charge shall not exceed an amount which is reasonable having regard to the cost of making the information available.[246] The Guidance Notes issued by the Department of the Environment stated that charges should not be imposed in respect of information that might have been freely provided in the past. It also suggested that charges could be based on the costs connected with such activities as searching, retrieving, compiling, or copying the information.[247] There is no provision for the waiver of charges.

The FOI Act contains much more detailed provisions relating to charges.[248] The Act allows for charges to be levied in respect of the cost of search and retrieval of records, as well as the cost of reproducing records. The search and retrieval charge will be based on an hourly rate to be prescribed by regulation. The number of hours in respect of which the charge will be levied will be based on the time that was spent or ought to have been spent in carrying out the search and retrieval efficiently. There is provision for the setting of a maximum fee by regulation in respect of the cost of reproducing records, but not in respect of search and retrieval charges. In the case of records containing personal information, there will be no charge for search and retrieval unless the request relates "to a significant number of records". There is also provision for the waiver of reproduction charges in the case of records containing personal information where it would not be reasonable to include such costs in the calculation of fees, having regard to the means of the requester and the

---

[243] reg.10(2).
[244] s.8(1).
[245] s.9(1).
[246] reg.11.
[247] Department of the Environment, *op. cit.* above, n. 161, p. 7.
[248] See above, pp. 76–78.

nature of the record concerned. Further provision for waiver or reduction of fees of both kinds is provided for where, in the opinion of the head of the public body concerned, the information contained in the record would be of particular importance to the understanding of an issue of national importance.

(v) Appeals

Article 4 of the Directive provides that:

> "A person who considers that his request for information has been unreasonably refused or ignored, or has been inadequately answered by a public authority, may seek a judicial or administrative review of the decision in accordance with the relevant national legal system."

No system of appeals is, however, provided for in the 1998 Regulations. The Guidance Notes issued by the Department of the Environment recommend the implementation of an internal review procedure.[249] It is open to applicants for access to information to seek judicial review of a public authority's decision to refuse access to information relating to the environment. Given the cost involved in embarking upon such a course of action and the fact that legal aid does not seem to be available to support such cases, it is unlikely to be availed of except in extreme cases. The alternative method of obtaining review of a refusal of access to information is to make a complaint to the Ombudsman. Such a course will, however, be available only in respect of bodies which come within the jurisdiction of the Ombudsman Act 1980.[250] One key agency not coming within the Ombudsman's jurisdiction is the Environmental Protection Agency. Even where a body does come within the Ombudsman's remit, the Ombudsman has no power to order release of a record; he or she can only make non-binding recommendations.[251] The lack of a comprehensive appeals system has been identified as a major cause of concern.[252] A commitment has been made to address this problem by "drawing on the arrangements for an appeals mechanism which have emerged under the general Freedom of Information legislation", but no details have been provided.[253]

Appeals against a refusal by the head of a public body to grant access to records under the FOI Act may be brought internally, in the first instance,[254] and, if the applicant is not satisfied with the outcome of the internal review process, he or she can make an appeal to the Information Commissioner[255]

---

[249] Department of the Environment, *op. cit.* above, n. 161, p. 5.
[250] The Ombudsman's remit is confined to the actions of public bodies set out in the First Schedule to the Ombudsman Act 1980.
[251] Ombudsman Act 1980, s.6(3).
[252] See, for example, Department of the Environment, *op. cit.* above, n. 162, p. 11.
[253] *ibid.*
[254] s.14.
[255] s.34.

and ultimately to the High Court on a point of law.[256] The decision of the Information Commissioner on appeal is binding on the public body concerned.[257] The appeals system provided under the FOI Act is clearly stronger than that available in respect of the 1996 Regulations.

(vi) Comparative evaluation

The right of access provided for under the FOI Act is superior to that available under the 1998 Regulations in a number of respects. In particular, the scope for exempting and excluding information from the right of access is much greater in the case of the 1998 Regulations than the FOI Act. Apart from the use of more detailed and narrower definitions of exempt material in the FOI Act, the application of the FOI exemptions is limited by the operation of the injury and public interest tests which are contained in a number of those exemptions. In addition, the system for appealing decisions made under the 1998 Regulations has been accepted, at an official level, as being inferior to the FOI appeals mechanism.[258] The FOI Act also has advantages over the 1998 Regulations in terms of time limits for responding to access requests and the potential for waiver of charges. Clearly, an applicant seeking access to information relating to the environment would be better served by making his or her application under the FOI Act, if that avenue were open to him or her.

---

[256] s.42.
[257] s.34(14).
[258] Department of the Environment, *op. cit.* above, n. 162, p. 11.

INDEX

access, right of, 29, 51–81
applications, 65–67
Archives Act provisions,
    comparisons with, 394–404.
    See also Archives Act
bodies covered, 51–55
    limitation to specified functions,
      53
    listed bodies, 51
    "public bodies", 30, 51
charges, 76–78; *see also* Charges
    and fees
constitutional rights and, 109–113
Data Protection Act restrictions
    and, 375–380
decisions on access. *See* Decisions
    on access
definition of "record", 63–65
drafts and informal notes, 64
electronic records, 64–65
environmental information, to,
    404–425. *See also*
    Environmental information
excluded records, 30, 56–60; *see*
    also Excluded records
exempt records, 30–31, 83–119.
    See also Exemptions
freedom of expression and,
    109–111
grant of access. *See* Grant
    of access
health/social work modification
    provisions
    comparisons between Data
      Protection and FOI Acts,
      385–388
independent contractors employed
    by public bodies, records of,
    52
interest of applicant, 51, 68

access, right of—*contd.*
modification of provisions,
    allowance for, 54–55
personal information. *See* Personal
    information; Personal
    information exemption
personnel records, 62
persons by whom rights
    exercisable, 55–56
refusal of access. *See* Refusal of
    access
requests for access, 65–67
retrospective effect, 30, 60–63,
    382, 398–399
    extension by regulation, 62–63
review of decisions. *See* Review of
    FOI decisions
right to communicate and, 111,
    113
right to privacy and, 111–113
scope of FOI Act, 29–30, 51–65
    extension by regulation, 52–53
    limits to, 29–30
time limits for decisions, 67–68
time limits for provision of access,
    73
transfer of requests, 66–67
types of records covered, 56
Access to Information on the
    Environment Regulations
    1998, 404–405. *See also*
    Environmental information
bodies subject to access rights,
    409–412
    categories of public authorities
      listed, 409
    public administration functions,
      requirement of, 409
    "public authorities", 409, 410
charges, 423

Freedom of Information Law in Ireland

personal information exemption
  (section 28)—*contd.*
  deceased persons, personal
    information of, 285–286
  definition of "personal
    information," 268–269,
    269–279
    categories of information, 270,
      272–273, 273–276
    criteria, 270–271
    employment information,
      274–275
    excluded categories of
      information, 269,
      276–279
    financial information, 274
    identifiable individual,
      information relating to,
      271
    identifying numbers or symbols,
      275
    interpretation of listed
      categories, 274–276
    legal persons or groups,
      271–272
    mutual understanding as to
      confidentiality, 272–273
    names of individuals, 275–276
    subject of the information,
      271–272
  exceptions to exemption, 266,
    280–284
    consent to disclosure, 282
    individual informed of possible
      disclosure, 283
    information concerning the
      requester, 281
    information publicly available,
      282–283
    necessity to avoid danger to life
      or health, 283–284
  excluded categories of information,
    269, 276–279
  health/social work access
    modification provisions, 266,
    269, 284–285
  Data Protection Act provisions,
    comparison with, 385–388

personal information exemption
  (section 28)—*contd.*
  joint personal information, 281
  parents or guardians, requests by,
    286–287
  presumption in favour of
    exemption, 267
  public interest test, 86, 266–267,
    269, 287–294, 377
    consultation with third parties,
      87, 294
    extent of proposed
      dissemination of
      information, 293–294
    identity or motive of applicant,
      relevance of, 290–293
    right to privacy and, 288–290
  right to privacy and, 265, 288–290
  scope, 267. *See also* definition of
    "personal information"
    (*above*)
  terms of exemption, 265–267
  third party personal information,
    disclosure of, 375–376
personnel records, 62
photocopies, charges for, 77
policy-making, 146
  deliberations of public bodies. *See*
    Deliberative processes
    exemption
political embarrassment, 96
Portugal, 5
precedents
  publication requirements, 42
President of Ireland
  records relating to
    exclusion from scope of FOI
      Act 1997, 57
prices, regulation of, 312
privacy, right to, 108, 379
  marital privacy, 112
  nature of, 112–113
  personal information exemption
    and, 265
    public interest test, 288–290
  provenance of, 112
  public interest tests and, 111–113,
    288–290